T0223106

Lecture Notes in Artificial Intelligence 1297

Subseries of Lecture Notes in Computer Science
Edited by J. G. Carbonell and J. Siekmann

Lecture Notes in Computer Science

Edited by G. Goos, J. Hartmanis and J. van Leeuwen

Springer
Berlin
Heidelberg
New York
Barcelona
Budapest
Hong Kong
London
Milan
Paris
Santa Clara
Singapore
Tokyo

Nada Lavrač   Sašo Džeroski (Eds.)

Inductive
Logic Programming

7th International Workshop, ILP-97
Prague, Czech Republic
September 17-20, 1997
Proceedings

 Springer

Series Editors

Jaime G. Carbonell, Carnegie Mellon University, Pittsburgh, PA, USA
Jörg Siekmann, University of Saarland, Saarbrücken, Germany

Volume Editors

Nada Lavrač
Sašo Džeroski
J. Stefan Institute
Jamova 39, 1000 Ljubljana, Slovenia
E-mail: Nada.Lavrac@ijs.si
         Saso.Dzeroski@ijs.si

Cataloging-in-Publication Data applied for

Die Deutsche Bibliothek - CIP-Einheitsaufnahme

Inductive logic programming : 7th international workshop ;
proceedings / ILP-97, Prague, Czech Republic, September 17 - 20,
1997. Nada Lavrač ; Sašo Džeroski (ed.). - Berlin ; Heidelberg ; New
York ; Barcelona ; Budapest ; Hong Kong ; London ; Milan ; Paris ;
Santa Clara ; Singapore ; Tokyo : Springer, 1997
  (Lecture notes in computer science ; Vol. 1297 : Lecture notes in
  artificial intelligence)
  ISBN 3-540-63514-9

CR Subject Classification (1991): I.2, D.1.6

ISBN 3-540-63514-9 Springer-Verlag Berlin Heidelberg New York

© Springer-Verlag Berlin Heidelberg 1997
Printed in Germany

Typesetting: Camera ready by author
SPIN 10546341   06/3142 – 5 4 3 2 1 0   Printed on acid-free paper

Foreword

The Seventh International Workshop on Inductive Logic Programming, ILP-97, held in Prague, Czech Republic, 17–20 September 1997, continues a tradition of International ILP Workshops that started in 1991. ILP-97 was the main scientific event of the ILP Week in Prague, including a Summer School on Inductive Logic Programming and Knowledge Discovery in Databases, 15–17 September 1997, and a meeting on Representation Issues in Reasoning and Learning of the European Network of Excellence in Computational Logic (Compulog Net) area Computational Logic and Machine Learning, on 20 September 1997.

The scientific program of ILP-97 consisted of three invited lectures, by Usama Fayyad, Jean-François Puget, and Georg Gottlob, and 26 papers presented at plenary sessions, describing theoretical, empirical, and applied research in ILP. In the proceedings, the invited lectures and nine selected papers are published as long papers, and the remaining 17 papers as short papers. Each of the 34 submitted papers was reviewed by two referees.

The ILP Week in Prague was organized by the Czech Technical University, Faculty of Electrical Engineering. Our gratitude goes to the local chair Olga Štěpánková, the chair of the Compulog Net area meeting Peter Flach, the members of the Organizing Committee, the ProTyS Congress Agency and all other individuals who helped in the organization of the workshop. We wish to thank Alfred Hofmann and Anna Kramer of Springer-Verlag for their cooperation in publishing these proceedings. We also wish to thank all the researchers for submitting their papers to ILP-97, and the PC members for their help in the reviewing process. Finally, we would like to acknowledge the sponsors of ILP-97, the Summer School on ILP and KDD, and the Compulog Net area meeting for supporting these scientific events.

Ljubljana,   Nada Lavrač
June 1997   Sašo Džeroski

Program Chairs

Nada Lavrač and Sašo Džeroski
J. Stefan Institute, Ljubljana, Slovenia

Local Chair

Olga Štěpánková
Czech Technical University, Faculty of Electrical Engineering
Prague, Czech Republic

Program Committee

F. Bergadano (Italy)   H. Boström (Sweden)   I. Bratko (Slovenia)
W. Cohen (USA)   L. De Raedt (Belgium)   P.A. Flach (The Netherlands)
S. Matwin (Canada)   S.H. Muggleton (UK)   M. Numao (Japan)
D. Page (UK)   C. Rouveirol (France)   C. Sammut (Australia)
M. Sebag (France)   A. Srinivasan (UK)   S. Wrobel (Germany)

Organization Committee

Dimitar Kazakov, Jiří Lažanský, Lenka Lhotská, and Tomáš Vlček

Organizational Support

The ProTyS Ltd. Congress Agency, Prague

Sponsors of ILP-97

- ML Net, European Network of Excellence in Machine Learning
- Compulog Net, European Network of Excellence in Computational Logic
- Czech Technical University, Faculty of Electrical Engineering, Prague
- J. Stefan Institute, Ljubljana

Sponsors of the Summer School and Area Meeting

- ESPRIT IV Project 20237 Inductive Logic Programming 2
- Compulog Net, European Network of Excellence in Computational Logic

Table of Contents

Part I

Invited Papers

Knowledge Discovery in Databases: An Overview

Usama Fayyad

Microsoft Research

One Microsoft Way, Redmond, WA 98052-6399, USA
Fayyad@microsoft.com
http://wwww.research.microsoft.com/dtg/fayyad

Abstract. Data Mining and knowledge Discovery in Databases (KDD) promise to play an important role in the way people interact with databases, especially decision support databases where analysis and exploration operations are essential. Inductive logic programming can potentially play some key roles in KDD. This is an extended abstract for an invited talk in the conference. In the talk, we define the basic notions in data mining and KDD, define the goals, present motivation, and give a high-level definition of the KDD Process and how it relates to Data Mining. We then focus on data mining methods. Basic coverage of a sampling of methods will be provided to illustrate the methods and how they are used. We cover a case study of a successful application in science data analysis: the classification of cataloging of a major astronomy sky survey covering 2 billion objects in the northern sky. The system can outperform human as well as classical computational analysis tools in astronomy on the task of recognizing faint stars and galaxies. We also cover the problem of scaling a clustering problem to a large catalog database of billions of objects. We conclude with a listing of research challenges and we outline area where ILP could play some important roles in KDD.

1 Introduction

Data Mining and Knowledge Discovery in Databases (KDD) are rapidly evolving areas of research that are at the intersection of several disciplines, including statistics, databases, pattern recognition/AI, visualization, and high-performance and parallel computing. In this paper, *which is intended to be strictly a companion reference to the invited talk, and not a presentation of new technical contributions*, we outline the basic notions in this area and show how data mining techniques can play an important role in helping humans analyse large databases.

We do not cover application case studies in this paper. Applications are covered in [8], and in the special issue of *Communications of the ACM* [4] (see http://www.research.microsoft.com/datamine/CM-contents.htm). A new technical journal, *Data Mining anf Knowledge Discovery*, dedicated to this area has been recently launched. See http://www.research.microsoft.com/datamine for more details.

2   From Transactions to Warehouses to KDD

With the widespread use of databases and the explosive growth in their sizes, individuals and organizations are faced with the problem of making use of this data. Traditionally, "use" of data has been limited to querying a reliable store via some well-circumscribed application or canned report-generating entity. While this mode of interaction is satisfactory for a wide-class of well-defined processes, it was not designed to support data exploration and ad hoc querying of the data. Now that capturing data and storing it has become easy and inexpensive, certain questions begin to naturally arise: Will this data help my business gain an advantage? How can we use historical data to build models of underlying processes that generated such data? Can we predict the behaviour of such processes? How can we "understand" the data? These questions become particularly important in the presence of massive data sets since they represent a large body of information that is presumed to be valuable, yet is far from accessible. The currently available interfaces between humans and machines do not support navigation, exploration, summarization, or modelling of large databases.

As transaction processing technologies were developed and became the mainstay of many business processes, great advances in addressing problems of reliable and accurate data capture were achieved. While transactional systems provided a solution to the problem of logging and book-keeping, there was little emphasis on supporting summarization, aggregation, and ad hoc querying over off-line stores of transactional data. A recent wave of activity in the database field has been concerned with turning transactional data into a more traditional relational database that can be queried for summaries and aggregates of transactions. Data warehousing also includes the integration of multiple sources of data along with handling the host of problems associated with such an endeavour. These problems include: dealing with multiple data formats, multiple database management systems (DBMS), distributed datbases, unifying data representation, data cleaning, and providing a unified logical view of an underlying collection of nonhomogeneous databases.

On-line Transactions   Data
Processing (OLTP)   Warehousing

Fig. 1. The Evolution of the View of a Database System

A data warehouse represents a large collection of data which in principle can provide views of the data that are not practical for individual transactional sources. For example, a supermarket chain may want to compare sales trends across regions at the level of products, broken down by weeks, and by class of store within a region. Such views are often precomputed and stored in special-purpose data stores that provide a multi-dimensional front-end to the underlying relational database and are sometimes called multi-dimensional databases.

Data warehousing is the first step in transforming a database system from a system whose primary purpose is reliable storage to one whose primary use is decision support. A closely related area is called On-Line Analytical Processing (OLAP) named after principles first advocated by Codd [3].

The current emphasis of OLAP systems is on supporting query-driven exploration of the data warehouse. Part of this entails precomputing aggregates along data "dimensions" in the multi-dimensional data store. Because the number of possible aggregates is exponentional in the number of "dimensions", much of the work in OLAP systems is concerned with deciding which aggregates to precompute and how to derive other aggregates (or estimate them reliably) from the precomputed projections. Figure 2 illustrates one such example for data representing summaries of financial transactions in branches of a nationwide bank. The attributes (dimensions) have an associated hierarchy which defines how quantities are to be aggregated (rolled-up) as one moves to higher levels in the hierarchy.

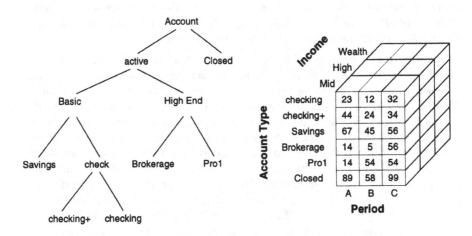

Fig. 2. An Example Multi-diemnsional view of relational data.

Note that the multidimensional store may not necessarily be materialized as in principle it could be derived dynamically from the underlying relational database. For efficiency purposes, some OLAP systems employ "lazy" strategies in precomputing summaries and incrementally build up a cache of aggregates.

2.1 Why Data Mining?

Unlike OLAP, data mining techniques allow for the possibility of computer-driven exploration of the data. This opens up the possibility for a new way of interacting with databases: specifying queries at a much more abstract level than SQL permits. It also facilitates data exploration for problems that, due to high-dimensionality, would otherwise be very difficult to explore by humans, regardless of difficulty of use of, or efficiency issues with, SQL.

A problem that has not received much attention in database research is the *query formulation problem*: how can we provide access to data when the user does not know how to describe the goal in terms of a specific query? Examples of this situation are fairly common in decision support situations. For example, in a business setting, say a credit card or telecommunications company would like to query its database of usage data for records representing fraudulent cases. In a science data analysis context, a scientist dealing with a large body of data would like to request a catalog of events of interest appearing in the data. Such patterns, while recognizable by human analysts on a case by case basis are typically very difficult to describe in a SQL query or even as a computer program in a stored procedure. A more natural means of interacting with the database is to state the query by example. In this case, the analyst would label a training set of examples of cases of one class versus another and let the data mining system build a model for distinguishing one class from another. The system can then apply the extracted classifier to search the full database for events of interest. This is typically more feasible because examples are usually easily available, and humans find it natural to interact at the level of cases.

Another major problem which data mining could help alleviate is the fact that humans find it particularly difficult to visualize and understand a large data set. Data can grow along two dimensions: the number of fields (also called dimensions or attributes) and the number of cases. Human analysis and visualization abilities do not scale to high-dimensions and massive volumes of data. A standard approach to dealing with high-dimensional data is to project it down to a very low-dimensional space and attempt to build models in this simplified subspace. As the number of dimensions grow, the number of choice combinations for dimensionality reduction explode. Furthermore, a projection to lower dimensions could easily transform an otherwise solvable discrimination problem into one that is impossible to solve. If the analyst is trying to explore models, then it becomes infeasible to go through the various ways of projecting the dimensions or selecting the right subsamples (reduction along columns and rows). An effective means to visualize data would be to employ data mining algorithms to perform the appropriate reductions. For example, a clustering algorithm could pick out a distinguished subset of the data embedded in a high-dimensional space and proceed to select a few dimensions to distinguish it from the rest of the data or from other clusters. Hence a much more effective visualization mode could be established: one that may enable an analyst to find patterns or models which may otherwise remain hidden in the high-dimensional space.

Another factor that is turning data mining into a necessity is that the rates of growth of data sets exceeds by far any rates that traditional "manual" analysis techniques could cope with. Hence, if one is to utilize the data in a timely manner, it would not be possible to achieve this goal in the traditional data analysis regime. Effectively this means that most of the data would remain unused. Such a scenario is not realistic in any competitive environment where those who do utilize data resources better will gain a distinct advantage. This sort of pressure is present in a wide variety of organizations, spanning the spectrum from business, to science, to government. It is leading to serious reconsideration of data collection and analysis strategies that are nowadays causing a build up of huge "write-only" data stores to accumulate.

3 KDD and Data Mining

The term *data mining* is often used as a synonym for the process of extracting useful information from databases. In this paper, as in [9], we draw a distinction between the latter, which we call KDD, and "data mining". The term *data mining* has been mostly used by statisticians, data analysts, and the management information systems (MIS) communities. It has also gained popularity in the database field. The earliest uses of the term come from statistics and the usage in most cases was associated with negative connotations of blind exploration of data without a priori hypotheses to verify. However, notable exceptions can be found. For example, as early as 1978, [16] used the term in a positive sense in a demonstration of how generalized linear regression can be used to solve problems that are very difficult for humans and for traditional statistical techniques of that time to solve. The term KDD was coined at the first KDD workshop in 1989 [18] to emphasize that "knowledge" is the end product of a data-driven discovery.

In our view KDD refers to the overall *process* of discovering useful knowledge from data while *data mining* refers to a particular *step* in this process. Data mining is the application of specific algorithms for extracting patterns from data. The additional steps in the KDD process, such as data preparation, data selection, data cleaning, incorporating appropriate prior knowledge, and proper interpretation of the results of mining, are essential to ensure that useful knowledge is derived from the data. Blind application of data mining methods (rightly criticized as "data dredging" in the statistical literature) can be a dangerous activity easily leading to discovery of meaningless patterns. We give an overview of the KDD process in Figure 3. Note that in the KDD process, one typically iterates many times over previous steps and the process is fairly messy with plenty of experimentation. For example, one may select, sample, clean, and reduce data only to discover after mining that one or several of the previous steps need to be redone. We have ommitted arrows illustrating these potential iterations to keep the figure simple.

3.1 Basic Definitions

We adopt the definitions of KDD and Data mining provided in [9] as

Knowledge Discovery in Databases: is the *non-trivial process of identifying valid, novel, potentially useful, and ultimately understandable patterns in data.*

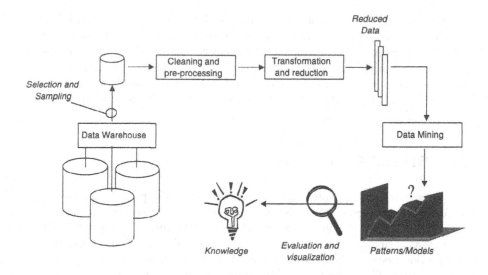

characterized in a very simplified sense. A pattern can be considered as *knowledge* if it exceeds some interestingness threshold. This is by no means an attempt to define "knowledge" in the philosophical or even the popular view. It is purely user-oriented, domain-specific, and determined by whatever functions and thresholds the user chooses.

Data Mining: is a step in the KDD process consisting of applying computational techniques that, under acceptable computational efficiency limitations, produce a particular enumeration of patterns (or models) over the data [9].

Note that the space of patterns is often infinite, and the enumeration of patterns involves some form of search in this space. Practical computational constraints place severe limits on the subspace that can be explored by a data mining algorithm.

The data mining component of the KDD process is concerned with the algorithmic means by which patterns are extracted and enumerated from data. The overall KDD process (Figure 3) includes the *evaluation* and possible *interpretation* of the "mined" patterns to determine which patterns may be considered new "knowledge."

4 Data Mining Methods: An Overview

Data mining techniques can be divided into five classes of methods. These methods are listed below. While much of these techniques have been historically defined to work over memory-resident data (typically read from flat files), some of these techniques are beginning to be scaled to operate on databases. Examples in classification (Section 4.1) include decision trees [17] and in summarization (Section 4.3) association rules [1].

4.1 Predictive Modeling

The goal is to predict some field(s) in a database based on other fields. If the field being predicted is a numeric (continuous) variable (such as a pysical measurement of e.g. *height*) then the prediction problem is a *regression* problem. If the field is categorical then it is a *classification* problem. There is a wide variety of techniques for classification and regression. The problem in general is cast as determining the most likely value of the variable being predicted given the other fields (inputs), the training data (in which the target variable is given for each observation), and a set of assumptions representing one's prior knowledge of the problem.

Linear regression combined with non-linear transformation on inputs could be used to solve a wide range of problems. Transformation of the input space is typically the difficult problem requiring knowledge of the problem and quite a bit of "art". In classification problems this type of transformation is often referred to as "feature extraction".

In classification the basic goal is to predict the most likely state of a categorical variable (the class). This is fundamentally a density estimation problem.

If one can estimate the probability that the class $C = c$, given the other fields $X = x$ for some feature vector x, then one could derive this probabilty from the joint density on C and X. However, this joint density is rarely known and very difficult to estimate. Hence one has to resort to various techniques for estimating. These techniques include:

1. Density estimation, e.g. kernel density estimators [5] or graphical representations of the joint density [13].
2. Metric-space based methods: define a distance measure on data points and guess the class value based on proximity to data points in the training set. For example, the K-nearest-neighbour method [5].
3. Projection into decision regions: divide the attribute space into decision regions and associate a prediction with each. For example linear discriminant analysis finds linear separators, while decision tree or rule-based classifiers make a piecewise constant approximation of the decision surface. Neural nets find non-linear decision surfaces.

4.2 Clustering

Also known as segmentation, clustering does not specify fields to be predicted but targets separating the data items into subsets that are similar to each other. Since unlike classification we do not know the number of desired "clusters", clustering algorithms typically employ a two-stage search: An outer loop over possible cluster numbers and an inner loop to fit the best possible clustering for a given number of clusters. Given the number K of clusters, clustering methods can be divided into three classes:

1. Metric-distance based methods: a distance measure is defined and the objective becomes finding the best K-way partition such as cases in each block of the partition are closer to each other (or centroid) than to cases in other clusters.
2. Model-based methods: a model is hypothesized for each of the clusters and the idea is to find the best fit of that model to each cluster. If M_k is the model hypothesized for cluster k, then one way to score the fit of a model to a cluster is via the likelihood:

$$\text{Prob}(M_k|D) = \text{Prob}(D|M_k)\frac{\text{Prob}(M_k)}{\text{Prob}(D)}$$

The prior probability of the data D, $\text{Prob}(D)$ is a constant and hence can be ignored for comparison purposes, while $\text{Prob}(M_k)$ is the prior assigned to a model. In maximum likelihood techniques, all models are assumed equally likely and hence this term is ignored. A problem with ignoring this term is that more complex models are always preferred and this leads to overfitting the data.
3. Partition-based methods: basically enumerate various partitions and then score them by some criterion. The above two techniques can be viewed as special cases of this class. Many techniques in the AI literature fall under this category and utilize ad hoc scoring functions.

4.3 Data Summarization

Sometimes the goal is to simply extract compact patterns that describe subsets of the data. There are two classes of methods which represent taking horizontal (cases) or vertical (fields) slices of the data. In the former, one would like to produce summaries of subsets: e.g. producing sufficient statistics, or logical conditions that hold for subsets. In the latter case, one would like to predict relations between fields. This class of methods is distinguished from the above in that rather than predicting a specified field (e.g. classification) or grouping cases together (e.g. clustering) the goal is to find relations between fields. One common method is called association rules [1]. Associations are rules that state that certain combinations of values occur with other combinations of values with a certain frequency and certainty. A common application of this is market basket analysis were one would like to summarize which products are bought with what other products.

4.4 Dependency Modeling

Insight into data is often gained by deriving some causal structure within the data. Models of causality can be probabilistic (as in deriving some statement about the probability distribution governing the data) or they can be deterministic as in deriving functional dependencies between fields in the data [18]. Density estimation methods in general fall under this category, so do methods for explicit causal modeling (e.g. [10] and [13]).

4.5 Change and Deviation Detection

These methods account for sequence information, be it time-series or some other ordering (e.g. protein sequencing in genome mapping). The distinguishing feature of this class of methods is that ordering of observations is important and must be accounted for.

5 Research Challenges

Successful KDD applications continue to appear, driven mainly by a glut in databases that have clearly grown to surpass raw human processing abilities. For examples of success stories in applications in industry see [2] and in science analysis see [7]. More detailed case studies are found in [8]. Driving the healthy growth of this field are strong forces (both economic and social) that are a product of the data overload phenomenon. I view the need to deliver workable solutions to pressing problems as a very healthy pressure on the KDD field. Not only will it ensure our healthy growth as a new engineering discipline, but it will provide our efforts with a healthy dose of reality checks; insuring that any theory or model that emerges will find its immediate real-world test environment.

The fundamental problems are still as difficult as they have been for the past few centuries as people considered difficulties of data analysis and how to mechanize it. The challenges facing advances in this field are formidable. Some of these challenges include:

1. Develop mining algorithms for classification, clustering, dependency analysis, and change and deviation detection that scale to large databases. There is a tradeoff between performance and accuracy as one surrenders to the fact that data resides primarily on disk or on a server and cannot fit in main memory.

2. Develop schemes for encoding "metadata" (information about the content and meaning of data) over data tables so that mining algorithms can operate meaningfully on a database and so that the KDD system can effectively ask for more information from the user.

3. While operating in a very large sample size environment is a blessing against overfitting problems, data mining systems need to guard against fitting models to data by chance. This problem becomes significant as a program explores a huge search space over many models for a given data set.

4. Develop effective means for data sampling, data reduction, and dimensionality reduction that operate on a mixture of categorical and numeric data fields. While large sample sizes allow us to handle higher dimensions, our understanding of high dimensional spaces and estimation within them is still fairly primitive. The curse of dimensionality is still with us.

5. Develop schemes capable of mining over nonhomogenous data sets (including mixtures of multimedia, video, and text modalities) and deal with sparse relations that are only defined over parts of the data.

6. Develop new mining and search algorithms capable of extracting more complex relationships between fields and able to account for structure over the fields (e.g. hierarchies, sparse relations); i.e. go beyond the flat file or single table assumption.

7. Develop data mining methods that account for prior knowledge of data and exploit such knowledge in reducing search, that can account for costs and benefits, and that are robust against uncertainty and missing data problems. Bayesian methods and decision analysis provide the basic foundational framework.

8. Enhance database management systems to support new primitives for the efficient extraction of necessary sufficient statistics as well as more efficient sampling schemes. This includes providing SQL support for new primitives that may be needed (e.g. [12]).

9. Scale methods to parallel databases with hundreds of tables, thousands of fields, and terabytes of data. Issues of query optimization in these settings are fundamental.

10. Account for and model comprehensibility of extracted models; allow proper tradeoffs between complexity and understandability of models for purposes of visualization and reporting; enable interactive exploration where the analyst can easily provide hints to help the mining algorithm with its search.

11. Develop theory and techniques to model growth and change in data. Large databases, because they grow over a long time, do not typically grow as if

sampled from a static joint probability density. The question of how does the data grow? needs to be better understood (see articles by P. Huber, by Fayyad & Smyth, and by others in [14]) and tools for coping with it need to be developed.

12. Incorporate basic data mining methods with "any-time" analysis that can quantify and track the trade-off between accuracy and available resources, and optimize algorithms accordingly.

6 ILP and KDD: Prospects and Challenges

ILP techniques address the problem of inferring models from data. Hence, they fit the definition of data mining methods. However, unlike standard statistical classification or clustering methods, ILP methods allow for the possibility of describing much richer structure in data. For example, One can learn a *descriptive* theory that describes the data or a logic program that serves as a *generative* model. For an excellent paper on how KDD and ILP fit together, the reader is referred to [6].

We summarize some aspects of ILP that makes its potential role in KDD exceedingly important:

Representation of data: extends to include relations between items (training points) and allows for exploring data sets that are not limited to a single table of attribute value pairs or feature vectors. Representing general relations as attribute-value pairs results in blowing up data sizes on disk and in memory representations.

Representation of Models: The expressive power of the model language is capable of representing much more complex model than the traditional propositional models used in decision trees and rules. In fact, the models can be as complex as full logic programs.

Feature Extraction: ILP methods can explore many techniques for feature extraction prior to model learning. This includes using prior knowledge (domain theory) to dynamically derive features as well as deriving new features by making explicit implicit hidden facts via deriving logic programs to compute these.

Convenient representation of prior knowledge: a big challenge in KDD is the use of prior knowledge to guide discovery and mining. ILP provides a very natural mechanism for expressing (deterministic) background knowledge and its use during discovery.

Relational Databases: there is a natural fit between the standard representation used in relational databases (and the query language SQL) and ILP representations and techniques. This allows for an easy way to define the interface between database and learning algorithm. In addition, it enables the algorithm to "browse" the tables of a database system as a natural part of its search. This alleviates the need of adding intermediate data representations between the database schema and the learning algorithm.

Support for deductive databases: Deductive databases [20] are able to aid in exploring a database and in executing more complex queries. There is a strong match between logic programming and the typical deductive database representation (several use Prolog in fact). This makes it convenient to allow the domain-specific knowledge encoded in the deductive database to be accessible by the learning program.

Understandability: the patterns derived via ILP are already symbolically expressed and hence should not be too difficult to understand by humans in many cases.

Post processors for derived patterns: If basic patterns are easier to derive via optimized traditional statistical pattern recognition techniques, then ILP can be used to enhance the derived models by using ILP techniques as a second stage. Hence the low-level interface to data can be via more traditional Data mining algorithms, while the second stage involves reasoning about the derived models and building more complex models. Hence traditional data mining techniques ould serve as "data reduction" tools to reduce size of input to more expensive (search-intensive) ILP techniques

Data access costs dominate: When dealing with large databases, the dominant cost is by far the data access cost. Thus "in-memory" operations of search and inference may not necessarily dominate the search time.

6.1 Limitations and Challenges for ILP in KDD

While the data representation scheme in ILP is well-matched to that of relational databases, the patterns of access required by ILP operations may not necessarily be efficient. A major challenge is to study the access patterns of ILP techniques and optimize the data scans so the information necessary to drive a multitude of steps in the inductive search process are derived in as few scans of the data as possible. ILP algorithms, because they assume data is memory resident perform many expensive joins over multiple relations without considering the true costs of such joins. This might require a rethinking of the basic design of some ILP methods.

The other major limitation and challenge for ILP is the need for a mechanism to represent uncertainty and probabilistic models. Many desired models in data mining applications are by their very nature probabilistic and not deterministic. Such models include characterization of probability density functions or explicit representation of uncertainty over derived models, missing values, and accounting for noise in the data. Without an integration with probabilistic techniques, it will be difficult to allow ILP methods to fulfill their potential promise in data mining.

7 Concluding Remarks

KDD holds the promise of an enabling technology that could unlock the knowledge lying dormant in huge databases. Perhaps the most exciting aspect is the possibility of the birth of a new research area properly mixing statistics, databases, automated data analysis and reduction, and other related areas. The mix could produce a new breed of algorithms, tuned to working on large databases and scalable both in data set size and in parallelism.

In this paper, we provided an overview of this area, defined the basic terms, and covered some sample case studies of applications in science data analysis. We also outlined prospects and challenges for the role of ILP in KDD. We concluded by listing future challenges for data mining and KDD. While KDD will draw on the substantial body of knowledge built up in its constituent fields, it is our hope that a new science will inevitably emerge as these challenges are addressed, and that suitable mixtures of ideas from each of the disciplines constituting the KDD field will greatly enhance our ability to exploit massive and ever-changing data sets.

7.1   Resources on the Web

To learn more about this area, there are several websites. We outline main ones here from which others are easily reachable:

- *Data Mining and Knowledge Discovery*, An International Journal:
  http://www.research.microsoft.com/datamine
- Special issue of the *Communications of the ACM* [4]:
  http://www.research.microsoft.com/datamine
- Knowledge Discovery Mine: moderated discussion list, archival of other resources, tools, and news items: http://www.kdnuggets.com
- International conferences on Knowledge Discovery and Data Mining, all reachable from the third conference: KDD-97, web site:
  http://www-aig.jpl.nasa.gov/kdd97

References

1. Agrawal, R., Mannila, H., Srikant, R., Toivonen, H., and Verkamo, I. "Fast Discovery of Association Rules", in *Advances in knowledge Discovery and Data Mining*, pp. 307–328, U. Fayyad, G. Piatetsky-Shapiro, P. Smyth, and R. Uthurusamy (Eds.), MIT Press, 1996.
2. R. Brachman, T. Khabaza, W. Kloesgen, G. Piatetsky-Shapiro, and E. Simoudis, Industrial Applications of Data Mining and Knowledge Discovery, *Communications of ACM*, vol. 39, no. 11. 1996.
3. E.F. Codd (1993). "Providing OLAP (On-line Analytical Processing) to User-Analysts: An IT Mandate". E.F. Codd and Associates.
4. *Communications of The ACM*, special issue on Data Mining, vol. 39, no. 11.
5. R.O. Duda and P.E. Hart *Pattern Classification and Scene Analysis*. New York: John Wiley and Sons, 1973.
6. S. Džeroski. "Inductive Logic Programming and Knowledge Discovery in Databases", in In *Advances in Knowledge Discovery and Data Mining*, Fayyad et al (Eds.), pp. 117 – 152, MIT Press, 1996.

7. U. Fayyad, D. Haussler, and P. Stolorz, "Mining Science Data", *Communications of ACM*, vol. 39, no. 11. 1996.

8. U. Fayyad, G. Piatetsky-Shapiro, P. Smyth, and R. Uthurusamy (Eds.) *Advances in Knowledge Discovery and Data Mining*, MIT Press, 1996.

9. U. Fayyad, G. Piatetsky-Shapiro, and P. Smyth. "From Data Mining to Knowledge Discovery: An Overview." In *Advances in Knowledge Discovery and Data Mining*, Fayyad et al (Eds.) MIT Press, 1996.

10. Glymour, C., Scheines, R., Spirtes, P. Kelly, K. *Discovering Causal Structure*. New York, NY: Academic Press, 1987.

11. C. Glymour, D. Madigan, D. Pregibon, and P. Smyth. "Statistical Themes and Lessons for Data Mining", *Data Mining and Knowledge Discovery*, vol. 1, no. 1, 1997.

12. J. Gray, S. Chaudhuri, A. Bosworth, A. Layman, D. Reichart, M. Venkatrao, F. Pellow, and H. Pirahesh, "Data Cube: A Relational Aggregation Operator Generalizing Group-by, Cross-Tab, and Sub Totals", *Data Mining and Knowledge Discovery*, vol. 1, no. 1, 1997.

13. D. Heckerman, "Bayesian Networks for Data Mining", *Data Mining and Knowledge Discovery*, vol. 1, no. 1, 1997.

14. J. Kettenring and D. Pregibon (Eds.) *Statistics and Massive Data Sets, Report to the Committee on Applied and Theoretical Statistics*, National Research Council, Washington, D.C. 1996.

15. Kaufman, L. and Rousseeuw, P. J. 1990. Finding Groups in Data: An Introduction to Cluster Analysis, New York: Wiley.

16. Leamer, Edward, E. *Specification searches: ad hoc inference with nonexperimental data*, Wiley, 1978

17. M. Mehta, R. Agrawal, and J. Rissanen, "SLIQ: a fast scalable classifier for data mining", *Proceedings of EDBT-96*, Springer Verlag, 1996.

18. G. Piatetsky-Shapiro and W. Frawley (Eds). *Knowledge Discovery in Databases*, MIT Press 1991.

19. A. Silberschatz and A. Tuzhilin, 1995. On Subjective Measures of Interestingness in Knowledge Discovery. In *Proceedings of KDD-95: First International Conference on Knowledge Discovery and Data Mining*, pp. 275-281, Menlo Park, CA: AAAI Press.

20. J. Ullman. *Principles of Database and Knowledge Base Systems*, vol. 1, Rockville, MA: Computer Science Press, 1988

On the Complexity of Some Inductive Logic Programming Problems [*]

Georg Gottlob, Nicola Leone, Francesco Scarcello

Institut für Informationssysteme
Technische Universität Wien
Paniglgasse 16, A-1040 Wien, Austria;
Internet: gottlob@dbai.tuwien.ac.at

Abstract. The bounded ILP-consistency problem for function-free Horn clauses is described as follows. Given a set E^+ and E^- of function-free ground Horn clauses and an integer k polynomial in $E^+ \cup E^-$, does there exist a function-free Horn clause C with no more than k literals such that C subsumes each element in E^+ and C does not subsume any element in E^-. It is shown that this problem is Σ_2^P complete. We derive some related results on the complexity of ILP and discuss the usefulness of such complexity results.

1 Introduction

The complexity analysis of reasoning problems in various areas such as non-monotonic reasoning (NMR), logic programming (LP), machine learning (ML), and inductive logic programming (ILP) has attracted much attention and interest in the last years. It was shown that several important reasoning problems are not only intractable, i.e. **NP** hard, but reside at higher levels of the polynomial hierarchy. In particular, it turned out that a large number of problems in NMR and LP reside at the *second level of the polynomial hierarchy* and are complete for either Σ_2^P or the dual class Π_2^P.

In the present paper we deal with the *bounded ILP-consistency problem for function-free Horn clauses*, described as follows. Given a set E^+ and E^- of function-free ground Horn clauses and an integer k polynomial in $E^+ \cup E^-$, does there exist a clause C having at most k literals such that C subsumes each element in E^+ and C does not subsume any element in E^-? We show that this problem is Σ_2^P complete. We also derive some results on the complexity of related ILP problems.

A proof that a given reasoning problem A is complete for a particular complexity class in the polynomial hierarchy, say, Σ_2^P, provides us with a deep qualitative understanding of the problem. For example, we can "extract" the following benefits from such a proof or result:

[*] This work has been supported by *FWF (Austrian Science Funds)* under the project P11580-MAT "A Query System for Disjunctive Deductive Databases" and by the *ISI-CNR, Istituto per la Sistemistica e l'Informatica (Italian National Research Council)*, under grant n.224.07.5.

- The proof allows us to recognise the sources of complexity in the problem and thus provides a systematic way of finding tractable subcases (by eliminating all these sources). For example, if a problem is **NP**-complete, then it contains basically one source of intractability, related to a choice to be made among exponentially many candidates. If a problem is Σ_2^P-complete then there are usually two intermingled sources of complexity. One is, as in **NP**, a choice problem, and the other one is a checking problem (checking whether the choice was a good choice) which is co-**NP** hard and depends on this choice. In order to prove a problem A Σ_2^P hard, we usually reduce a well-known other Σ_2^P hard problem B to A. Assuming that the sources of complexity of B are identified, the sources of complexity of A become clear via the translation.

- The complexity result enables us to classify the problem and helps identifying other problems in the same complexity class to which the problem is polynomially translatable. For these other problems practical solution algorithms may already exist which we can take profit of. For example, in this paper we show that a relevant ILP problem, the *bounded Horn clause consistency problem* is complete for the complexity class Σ_2^P. On the other hand, it was shown that the relevant decision problems in disjunctive logic programming (DLP) and in Reiter's default logic [28] are also Σ_2^P complete [16, 9, 11]. It follows that our ILP problem can be polynomially translated into equivalent DLP or default logic problems and solved by sophisticated existing software packages for DLP or default logic [8, 10, 3]. In such a way one can profit from the highly efficient data management and search pruning techniques implemented in these systems. Note that such translations can be given for the bounded Horn clause ILP problem as well, i.e., for the *search* problem of *finding* a Horn clause C with no more than k literals that subsumes E^+ and does not subsume any clause in E^-. We are currently investigating and experimenting implementations of ILP problems on top of the DLP system described in [10].

- The complexity result enables us to establish negative translation results as well. For example, there are several forms of nondisjunctive logic programming i.e., LP with negation in rule bodies, but without disjunction in rule heads. The strongest form of nondisjunctive logic programming for which practical interpreters were constructed is Logic Programming under the *stable model semantics* [13]. It was shown that this form of logic programming is **NP** complete [21]. Therefore, unless the Polynomial Hierarchy collapses, it is not the case that the bounded Horn clause ILP-consistency problem can be polynomially translated to a nondisjunctive logic programming problem. Of course also such "negative" results are very useful. They prevent researchers or programmers to waste their precious time attempting to effectively solve a problem using techniques, programming languages, or formalisms that are not enough powerful.

- The theory of molecular computing envisages the possibility of nonelectronic devices based on natural phenomena that overcome classical intractability by exploiting massive parallelism. In [1], DNA strings are used as elementary processing units. **NP** hard problems can be solved in polynomial time if a sufficient (exponential) number of DNA strings with certain properties is provided and if certain elementary operations are assumed to be feasible. A basic model of DNA computing [1] was formally defined and studied in [20]. The complexity of this method and of some relevant extensions is studied in [31]. In [31] it was recently proved that the basic model of DNA computing of [20], can be used to solve precisely the problems in the complexity class $\Delta_2^P = \mathbf{P^{NP}}$ in polynomial time, while a second, slightly more powerful model, is able to solve precisely all problems in the class $\Delta_3^P = \mathbf{P}^{\Sigma_2^P}$ in polynomial time. Thus, once we have shown that a problem is in Σ_2^P, it is solvable in polynomial time by a DNA computer. Note that due to such results on DNA computers, the exact location of a problem in the Polynomial Hierarchy becomes yet more interesting. In fact, a **PSPACE** complete problem would most likely not be solvable in polynomial time by the above quoted models of DNA computers, while a Σ_2^P complete problem can be solved in polynomial time by the second, but probably not by the first model. On the other hand, any **NP** complete problem is solvable by DNA computers of either type. The future will show which type of DNA computers can be realized in practice, and whether such computers will exist at all.

In summary, the complexity analysis of a problem gives us much more than merely a quantitative statement about its tractability or intractability in the worst case. Rather, locating a problem at the right level in the polynomial hierarchy gives us a deep *qualitative* knowledge about this problem which – in many cases – can be exploited for applications.

2 Preliminaries and Previous Results

2.1 Complexity Theory

We assume that the reader has some background on the concept of **NP**-completeness [12, 17]. Upon the class **NP**, the polynomial hierarchy (PH) has been defined as a subrecursive analog to the Kleene arithmetical hierarchy. For any complexity class C, let $\mathbf{NP}^C$ denote the decision problems solvable in polynomial time by some nondeterministic oracle Turing machine with an oracle for any problem in C. The classes Δ_k^P, Σ_k^P, and Π_k^P of PH are defined as follows:

$$\Delta_0^P = \Sigma_0^P = \Pi_0^P = \mathbf{P}$$

and for all $k \geq 0$,

$$\Delta_{k+1}^P = \mathbf{P}^{\Sigma_k^P}, \quad \Sigma_{k+1}^P = \mathbf{NP}^{\Sigma_k^P}, \quad \Pi_{k+1}^P = \mathrm{co}\Sigma_{k+1}^P.$$

In particular, $\mathbf{NP} = \Sigma_1^P$, co-$\mathbf{NP} = \Pi_1^P$, $\Sigma_2^P = \mathbf{NP^{NP}}$, and $\Pi_2^P = \mathrm{co}\text{-}\mathbf{NP^{NP}}$. The classical **NP**-complete problem is to decide if a collection

$C = \{L_{i,1} \vee \cdots \vee L_{i,n_i} : 1 \leq i \leq m\}$ of propositional clauses is simultaneously satisfiable (SAT). This problem is still **NP**-complete if each clause $L_{i,1} \vee \cdots \vee L_{i,n_i}$ in C contains only positive literals or only negative literals (MSAT) [12]. The most prominent Σ_2^P-complete problem is to decide the validity of a formula from $QBF_{2,\exists}$, the set of quantified Boolean formulae of form $\exists x_1 \cdots \exists x_n \forall y_1 \cdots \forall y_m E$, where $E = E(x_1, \ldots, x_n, y_1, \ldots, y_m)$ is a propositional formula built from atoms $x_1, \ldots, x_n, y_1, \ldots, y_m$.

2.2 Inductive Logic Programming

The computational complexity of learning concepts from examples or from particular kind of queries to an hypothetical teacher, has been deeply investigated in many papers from different research areas (see, for instance, [14, 32, 19, 18, 6, 4, 5, 7]), ranging from computational learning theory to artificial intelligence.

In this paper we focus on some complexity problems arising in inductive logic programming (ILP) [22, 23, 24]. This relatively new field is concerned with the induction of concepts expressed in clausal form (typically first order Horn clauses) from examples and background knowledge. Compared with previous frameworks, ILP should result more expressive, because first order theories are allowed instead of only propositional formulae. Furthermore, the introduction of background knowledge can be useful for a simpler modeling of some learning tasks.

We next describe formally the problems addressed by ILP. Our formalization is similar to the presentation in [18].

Let $\mathcal{L}$ denote the language of first order logic. An *ILP setting* is a tuple $S = \langle \mathcal{L}_B, \mathcal{L}_H, \vdash, L_E \rangle$, where:

- $\mathcal{L}_B \cup \mathcal{L}_H \cup \mathcal{L}_E \subseteq \mathcal{L}$, and
- $\vdash$ is a correct provability relation for the language $\mathcal{L}$.

The *ILP-learning* problem for an ILP setting S is:

Given $\langle B, EX^+, EX^- \rangle$, with $B \in \mathcal{L}_B$ (background Knowledge), $EX^+ \in \mathcal{L}_E$ (positive examples), and $EX^- \in \mathcal{L}_E$ (negative examples), find an hypothesis $H \in \mathcal{L}_H$ such that: (i) $H \wedge B \vdash ex \ \forall ex \in EX^+$, (ii) $H \wedge B \nvdash ex \ \forall ex \in EX^-$, and (iii) $B \wedge H \nvdash \square$ (i.e., H is consistent with B).

The *ILP-consistency* problem for an ILP setting S is the problem of deciding whether a solution for the *ILP-learning* problem does exist or not.

It is worth noting that solving the ILP problem is not sufficient in general for a correct learning of the unknown concept from which the given examples are taken. To be sure that our hypothesis H coincides with the unknown concept (or it is at least a good approximation) we need some learnability model which provides sufficient conditions for a correct identification of the concept.

One of the most important and well studied approach is Valiant's Probably-Approximately-Correct (PAC) learning. PAC learning is a probabilistic distribution free approach to learning. There exists a fixed but unknown probability distribution D according to which examples are drawn and against which the quality of approximation is evaluated.

Following [18], we next define when an ILP setting is PAC learnable.

Definition 1. An ILP setting $S = \langle \mathcal{L}_B, \mathcal{L}_H, \vdash, L_E \rangle$ is (polynomially) PAC learnable, if and only if there exists an algorithm PLEARN and a polynomial function $m(\frac{1}{\epsilon}, \frac{1}{\delta}, n_e, n_c, n_b)$, so that for every $n_e > 0$, every $n_b > 0$, every background knowledge $B \in \mathcal{L}_B$ of size n_b or less, every concept $C \in \mathcal{L}_H$ with size n_c or less, every $\epsilon : 0 < \epsilon < 1$, every $\delta : 0 < \delta < 1$, and every probability distribution D, for any set of examples $E = E^+ \cup E^-$ of C, drawn from $\mathcal{L}_E$ according to D and containing at least $m(\frac{1}{\epsilon}, \frac{1}{\delta}, n_e, n_c, n_b)$ examples

1. PLEARN, on input E, B, ϵ, and δ outputs a hypothesis $H \in \mathcal{L}_H$ such that

$$P(D(Cover(H) \ \Delta \ Cover(C)) > \epsilon) < \delta,$$

   where $Cover(X) = \{e \in \mathcal{L}_E \mid X, B \vdash e\}$ and Δ denotes the simmetric set difference;
2. PLEARN runs in time polynomial in $\frac{1}{\epsilon}, \frac{1}{\delta}, n_e, n_c, n_b$, and the number of examples, and
3. for all $e \in \mathcal{L}_E$, the truth of the statement $e \in Cover(H)$ can be tested in polynomial time.

The polynomial function $m(\frac{1}{\epsilon}, \frac{1}{\delta}, n_e, n_c, n_b)$ is called the sample complexity of the algorithm PLEARN.

A very frequently used provability relation is ϑ-subsumption [29, 27]:

Definition 2. A clause C ϑ-*subsumes* a clause E ($C \vdash_\vartheta E$), iff there exist a substitution ϑ such that $C\vartheta \subseteq E$. If S is a set of clauses, then $C \vdash_\vartheta S$ if C subsumes all clauses in S.

2.3 Complexity Results in ILP

In a recent interesting paper [18], Kietz and Džeroski proved that a restricted class of function free clauses (i.e. clauses without function symbols, including constants), namely k-discriminative non recursive ij-determinate predicate definitions, are PAC learnable.

They also considered whether it is possible to remove some syntactical restriction without loosing the polynomial-time learnability. The answer was negative, since the consistency problem for $\mathcal{L}_H = \{i2\text{-determinate Horn clauses}\}$ turned out to be PSPACE-hard, if i is variable.

Furthermore, a weaker restriction on the way variables in a clause can be linked has been analysed.

Definition 3 [18]. A Horn clause is linked if all of its literals are linked. A literal is linked if at least one of its terms is linked. A term is linked with a linking-chain of length 0 if it occurs in the head of the clause. A term in a literal is linked with a linking-chain of length $d+1$, if another term in the same literal is linked with a linking-chain of length d. The depth of a term is the minimal length of its linking-chains. A linked Horn clause which has maximal depth of terms i and maximal arity of literals j, is called i,j-nondeterminate.

In [18] it was also shown that the consistency problem for the ILP setting

$$\langle \emptyset, 1,2\text{-nondeterminate function-free Horn clauses}, \vdash_\vartheta, \text{ground Horn clauses} \rangle$$

is **NP**-hard. As a consequence, such a setting is not PAC-learnable as long as the widely assumed **RP** $\neq$ **NP** conjecture is true.

Other important results are contained in the work [6] by Cohen and Page, that give an overview of the most useful techniques for deriving either positive or negative results in the PAC-learning and learning from equivalence queries frameworks.

In the latter learning model, the learner receives information about the unknown concept by asking *equivalence queries*. An equivalence query is a concept in the hypothesis language which is sent to an oracle that replies "equivalent" if the given concept is equivalent to the unknown concept, or it returns a counterexample. If an ILP setting S is learnable from equivalence queries, then S is also PAC-learnable.

As it was pointed out [6, 26], a non-learnability result for a setting S based on a consistency-hardness result does not entail the non-learnability of some setting more expressive than S.

A stronger result can be obtained by an evaluation hardness argument, i.e. by showing that there exists a concept in the language whose evaluation is not feasible in polynomial time. *Evaluation*, in this context means deciding whether an example is or is not implied (via the respective $\vdash_\vartheta$ relation) by a hypothesis. Indeed, if a setting is PAC-learnable, then it should always be possible to find an hypothesis which is consistent with the given examples and evaluable in polynomial time [30].

Along these lines, Cohen and Page [6] proved that the ILP setting $S_{k,A} = \langle$ground facts of bounded arity$A$, k-linked Horn clauses, $\models$, ground facts$\rangle$, for any fixed $k \geq 1$ and any fixed $A \geq 3$ is not PAC-learnable, and neither is any setting at least as expressive as $S_{k,A}$.

They also found some positive results. For instance, it turns out that a setting strictly more expressive than the one based on ij-determinate non recursive clauses (as hypothesis language) is PAC-learnable.

3 The Bounded Horn Clause ILP-Consistency Problem

The ILP-consistency problem can be very hard or even undecidable even for very simple logic programming settings.

However, one is not always interested in finding *arbitrarily large* solutions. Rather, it makes sense to impose an upper bound on the size of the desired solutions. It makes further sense to require that this bound be polynomially related to the size of the supplied example and counterexample sets.

Definition 3.1 *The* bounded ILP-learning *problem for an ILP setting S is:*

> *Given* $\langle B, EX^+, EX^- \rangle$ *and an integer* k, *with* k *polynomially bounded in the size of* $\langle B, EX^+, EX^- \rangle$, $B \in \mathcal{L}_B$, $EX^+ \in \mathcal{L}_E$, $EX^- \in \mathcal{L}_E$, *find an hypothesis* $H \in \mathcal{L}_H$ *with at most* k *literals, such that: (i)* $H \wedge B \vdash ex$ $\forall ex \in EX^+$, *and (ii)* $H \wedge B \not\vdash ex$ $\forall ex \in EX^-$, *and (iii)* $B \wedge H \not\vdash \square$ *(i.e.,* H *is consistent with* B*).*

The bounded ILP-consistency *problem for an ILP setting S is accordingly defined.*

The NP-completeness of the ϑ-subsumption checking is a well-known result [12, 2]. Nevertheless, we state a lemma about the complexity of the complementary problem, whose proof will be useful for a better understanding of the theorem below.

Observe that, if ϑ-subsumption is adopted as the provability relation of the ILP setting, then Condition (iii) of the definition of the ILP learning problem (both in general and bounded version) is not relevant, as ϑ-subsumption guarantees consistency. Therefore, in the sequel of the paper, we will not consider this condition for ILP settings based on ϑ-subsumption.

Lemma 4 (Baxter [2]). *Given a function-free Horn clause* C *and a ground Horn clause* P, *deciding whether* $C \not\vdash_\vartheta P$ *is co-**NP**-complete.*

PROOF. *Membership in co-**NP**.* We decide whether $C \vdash_\vartheta P$ (the complementary problem of $C \not\vdash_\vartheta P$) in **NP** as follows. Guess a substitution ϑ for C, check that $C\vartheta \subseteq P$. Since the size of a substitution for C is polynomial in the size of C, and the containment check can be done in polynomial time, the problem lies in **NP**. As a consequence, deciding whether $C \not\vdash_\vartheta P$ is in co-**NP**.

*co-**NP**-Hardness.* We transform the (co-**NP**-hard) problem of deciding whether a QBF $\Psi = \forall Z E$ is in $QBF_{1,\forall}$, where E is in 3DNF, into deciding whether a horn clause C does not subsume a ground Horn clause P.

Let $Z = \{z_1, \ldots, z_n\}$, and $E = E_1 \vee \cdots \vee E_t$.

To clarify the transformation, we will use QBF $\Psi = \forall z_1, z_2, z_3, z_4 E$, where $E = (z_1 \wedge \neg z_2 \wedge z_3) \vee (\neg z_1 \wedge z_2 \wedge z_4)$, as a running example.

Let z_1^i, z_2^i, z_3^i denote the (positive) boolean variables of E_i. A falsifying scheme for E_i is a triple $f = \langle b_1, b_2, b_3 \rangle$ of boolean values such that assigning b_k to z_k^i ($1 \leq i \leq 3$) makes E_i false. We denote by $fs(E_i)$ the set of the falsifying schemes for E_i.

For instance, in our running example, $\langle 0, 0, 0 \rangle$, $\langle 0, 1, 0 \rangle$, and $\langle 1, 1, 1 \rangle$ are some falsifying schemes for $E_1 = z_1 \wedge \neg z_2 \wedge z_3$. Falsifying schemes represent the boolean assignments to the variables of E_i that do not satisfy E_i; therefore, every conjunct E_i has exactly 7 falsifying schemes.

Consider the following ground Horn clause $P(E)$:

$$P(E) = \leftarrow \bigwedge_{1 \leq i \leq t} \bigwedge_{f \in fs(E_i)} p_i(f).$$

For the running example, we will build the following ground horn formula including all the falsifying schemes for the two conjuncts:

$$\begin{aligned}
P(E) = \ &\leftarrow p_1(0,1,1) \wedge p_1(0,0,1) \wedge p_1(0,1,0) \wedge p_1(1,1,0) \wedge \\
&p_1(1,1,1) \wedge p_1(0,0,0) \wedge p_1(1,0,0) \wedge \\
&p_2(1,0,1) \wedge p_2(1,0,0) \wedge p_2(1,1,1) \wedge p_2(1,1,0) \wedge \\
&p_2(0,0,1) \wedge p_2(0,0,0) \wedge p_2(0,1,0)
\end{aligned}$$

Moreover, let $C(E)$ be the following Horn clause:

$$C(E) = \leftarrow \bigwedge_{1 \leq i \leq t} p_i(Z_1^i, Z_2^i, Z_3^i).$$

In our example, we get

$$C(E) = \leftarrow p_1(Z_1, Z_2, Z_3) \wedge p_2(Z_1, Z_2, Z_4).$$

The following equivalence holds:

$$C(E) \not\vdash_\vartheta P(E) \iff \Psi \in \mathrm{QBF}_{1,\vee}$$

Indeed, the substitutions that can prove the subsumption $C(E) \vdash_\vartheta P(E)$ map necessarily the Z_j variables to $\{0,1\}$ and therefore correspond to boolean truth assignment to the variables z_j $(1 \leq j \leq n)$ of Ψ. In particular, given a substitution ϑ, $C(E)\vartheta \subseteq P(E)$ holds if and only if ϑ represents a truth assignment that falsifies E. Therefore, there exists no truth assignment falsifying E (i.e., $\Psi \in \mathrm{QBF}_{1,\vee}$) if and only if there exists no substitution ϑ such that $C(E)\vartheta \subseteq P(E)$ (i.e., $C(E) \not\vdash_\vartheta P(E)$).

For instance, we can easily recognise that the formula Ψ of the running example is not valid. Indeed, let ϑ be the following substitution for the variables in $C(E)$: $\{Z_1 = 1, Z_2 = 1, Z_3 = 0, Z_4 = 0\}$. Then, $C(E)\vartheta \subseteq P(E)$, since both $p_1(1,1,0)$ and $p_2(1,1,0)$ belong to $P(E)$. Hence, $C(E) \vdash_\vartheta P(E)$. $\square$

Let S_{HC} be the setting $\langle \emptyset, \text{function-free Horn clauses}, \vdash_\vartheta, \text{ground Horn clauses} \rangle$. Then, the following theorem holds.

Theorem 5. *The bounded ILP-consistency problem for S_{HC} is Σ_2^P-complete.*

PROOF. *Membership in Σ_2^P.* Let a set EX^+ of positive examples, EX^- of negative examples and an integer k be given. From the definition of S_{HC}, EX^+ and EX^- are ground Horn clauses. If the set of positive examples EX^+ is empty, then the problem is trivial, as the clause $\leftarrow q$, where q is a predicate which does not appear in EX^- is a solution.

Assume now that EX^+ is not empty and let $Pred(EX^+)$ be the set of predicates (symbols) appearing in EX^+. Then, every possible witness of the consistency, that is, every clause C that subsumes the positive examples (and does not subsume the negative ones), will contain *only* predicates from $Pred(EX^+)$. Therefore, we can decide the bounded ILP consistency problem at hand as follows. Guess a clause C with a number of atoms less than or equal to k whose predicates are taken from $Pred(EX^+)$, and check the following: (i) for each clause P in EX^+, verify that $C \vdash_\vartheta P$; (ii) for each clause P' in EX^-, verify that $C \nvdash_\vartheta P'$.

The size of C is polynomial in the input, as k is polynomially bounded, and each predicate in C is present in the input. Moreover, from Lemma 4, checking whether $C \nvdash_\vartheta P'$ can be done in co-**NP** (and checking that $C \vdash_\vartheta P$ can be done in **NP**). Therefore, by a polynomial number of calls to an **NP** oracle, we are able to check that the guessed clause C is indeed a solution. The bounded ILP-consistency problem for $\mathcal{S}_{HC}$ is hence in Σ_2^P.

Σ_2^P-*Hardness.* We transform deciding that a QBF $\Phi = \exists X \forall Y E$ is in QBF$_{2,\exists}$, where E is a 3DNF, into deciding whether there exists a function-free Horn clause C, with at most k literals, such that $C \vdash_\vartheta EX^+$ and $C \nvdash_\vartheta ex \quad \forall ex \in EX^-$, where k, EX^+ and EX^- are given in input.

Without loss of generality, we assume that Φ does not contain useless variables or redundant or trivially unsatisfiable conjuncts. More precisely, we assume that (i) the same boolean variable does not occur twice in the same conjunct of E; (ii) each boolean variable in X appears at least in one conjunct of E; (iii) there exists no conjunct of E containing only Y-variables not appearing in any other conjunct of E; and (iv) each conjunct E_i contains exactly 3 boolean variables.

To clarify the transformation, we will use QBF

$$\Phi_0 = \exists x_1, x_2 \forall y_1, y_2 (x_1 \wedge \neg x_2 \wedge y_1) \vee (\neg x_1 \wedge x_2 \wedge y_2)$$

as a running example.

We next specify k, EX^+ and EX^-. Let $X = \{x_1, \ldots, x_m\}$, $Y = \{y_1, \ldots, y_n\}$, $E = E_1 \vee \cdots \vee E_t$, and let z_1^i, z_2^i, z_3^i denote the (positive) boolean variables of a conjunct E_i. Moreover, let $0, 1, c, ch, cx_1, \cdots, cx_m, cy_1, \cdots, cy_n, cx_1', \cdots, cx_m'$, be distinct constants.

For the QBF Φ, we fix $k = t + m$, that is we look for function-free Horn clauses having at most k atoms, where k is the number of conjunct in Φ plus the number of X variables (i.e., the number of the variables existentially quantified).

We have only one positive example, which we call *master example*:

$$ex1^+ = \ \leftarrow \bigwedge_{1 \le i \le t} p_i(const(z_1^i), const(z_2^i), const(z_3^i))$$
$$\bigwedge_{1 \le j \le m} val_j(cx_j, cx_j') \bigwedge_{1 \le j \le m} val_j(cx_j', cx_j)$$

where

$$const(z) = \begin{cases} cx_k & \text{if } z \text{ is a } X \text{ variable } x_k \\ cy_k & \text{if } z \text{ is a } Y \text{ variable } y_k \end{cases}$$

For the sample QBF Φ_0, the *master example* $ex1^+(\Phi_0)$ is the following (ground Horn) clause:

$$\leftarrow p_1(cx_1, cx_2, cy_1) \wedge p_2(cx_1, cx_2, cy_2) \wedge$$
$$val_1(cx_1, cx_1') \wedge val_2(cx_2, cx_2') \wedge val_1(cx_1', cx_1) \wedge val_2(cx_2', cx_2)$$

We next define the negative examples. We call *enforcing examples*, the following negative examples:

(n1) For each predicate p_i $(1 \leq i \leq t)$, $ex1^-_{p_i}$ is the clause obtained from $ex1^+$ by replacing the (only) atom with predicate p_i by $p_i(c, c, c)$.

(n2) For each predicate val_j $(1 \leq i \leq m)$, $ex1^-_{val_j}$ is the clause obtained from $ex1^+$ by replacing both the atoms with predicate val_j by $val_j(c, c)$ (i.e., $val_j(ch, cx_j) \wedge val_j(ch, cx_j')$ is replaced by $val_j(c, c)$).

We denote the set of *enforcing examples* by $EX1^-$.

For the running example, the enforcing example $ex1^-_{p_1}$ and $ex1^-_{val_1}$ are the following ground horn clauses:

$$\leftarrow p_1(c, c, c) \wedge p_2(cx_1, cx_2, cy_2) \wedge$$
$$val_1(cx_1, cx_1') \wedge val_2(cx_2, cx_2') \wedge val_1(cx_1', cx_1) \wedge val_2(cx_2', cx_2)$$

$$\leftarrow p_1(cx_1, cx_2, cy_1) \wedge p_2(cx_1, cx_2, cy_2) \wedge$$
$$val_1(c, c) \wedge val_2(cx_2, cx_2') \wedge val_2(cx_2', cx_2)$$

Finally, we define the negative example ex_2^-, which we call *checking example*:

$$ex_2^- = P(E) \bigwedge_{1 \leq j \leq m} val_j(1, 0)$$

where $P(E)$ is the ground clause specified in the proof of Lemma 4.

In the running example, ex_2^- is the following ground Horn clause:

$$\leftarrow p_1(0, 1, 1) \wedge p_1(0, 0, 1) \wedge p_1(0, 1, 0) \wedge p_1(1, 1, 0) \wedge$$
$$p_1(1, 1, 1) \wedge p_1(0, 0, 0) \wedge p_1(1, 0, 0) \wedge$$
$$p_2(1, 0, 1) \wedge p_2(1, 0, 0) \wedge p_2(1, 1, 1) \wedge p_2(1, 1, 0) \wedge$$
$$p_2(0, 0, 1) \wedge p_2(0, 0, 0) \wedge p_2(0, 1, 0) \wedge$$
$$val_1(1, 0) \wedge val_2(1, 0)$$

We claim that the QBF Φ is valid if and only if there exists a function-free Horn clause C, with at most k literals, such that C subsumes $ex1^+$ and C does not subsume any example in $EX1^- \cup \{ex2^-\}$.

Only if part. Assume Φ is valid. Then, there exists an assignment T to the boolean variable belonging to the set X such that, for every assignment to the variable in the set Y, the 3DNF formula E is satisfied.

Now, consider the following function free Horn clause:

$$C: \quad \leftarrow \bigwedge_{1 \leq i \leq t} p_i(Z_1^i, Z_2^i, Z_3^i)$$
$$\bigwedge_{1 \leq j \leq m} val_j(X_j', X_j'')$$

where we have

(i) Z_j^i is the (X or Y) variable corresponding to the boolean variable appearing in the j-th position of the conjunct E_i (e.g., for $E_i = x_1 \wedge \neg x_2 \wedge y_1$, we have $p_i(X_1, X_2, Y_1)$);

(ii) if $T(x_j) = true$, then X_j' is the variable X_j and X_j'' is a new variable (independent from all other variables); otherwise ($T(x_j) = false$), X_j'' is the variable X_j and X_j' is a new variable.

C subsumes the master example and cannot subsume any of the enforcing examples. Furthermore, if the val_j atoms in C can be mapped into all the val_j ground atoms in the checking example, then each X variable X_j must be bound to value 1 if $T(x_j) = true$ and to value 0 if $T(x_j) = false$. Indeed, in the checking example, we have $val_j(1, 0)$ (for each $j \in \{1, \ldots, m\}$). Then if variable X_j appears in the first place of the atom with predicate val_j (i.e., $val_j(X_j, X_j'') \in C$), it should be set to value 1; otherwise (i.e., $val_j(X_j', X_j) \in C$), it is forced to unify with constant 0.

Therefore, the assignment to the X variables is encoded in the clause C by means of the positions of each variable in the corresponding val_j atom. When we check the validity of E by verifying whether $C \vdash_{\vartheta} ex2^-$, the values of X variables are all fixed according to the assignment T. Hence, following Lemma 4, C cannot subsume the checking example, or it should exist an assignment to the Y variables which falsifies the formula E.

If part. Suppose there exists a function free Horn clause C with at most k literals which subsumes the master example and does neither subsume any enforcing example nor the checking example. We prove that, in such a case, Φ is valid.

Fact a). Since $C \vdash_{\vartheta} ex1^+$, we know all predicates in C are among those used in the master example $ex1^+$.

Fact b). In the master example we have a different constant for each variable we want to be distinct. In particular, we have a different constant for each boolean variable appearing in the formula E. Thus, each variable in C corresponds to only one boolean variable appearing in the formula E. Furthermore, the two variables appearing in a val_j atom are distinct.

Fact c). From the enforcing examples, we know at least one atom for each predicate used in the master example must belong to C. Indeed, assume there is no atom in C with a predicate p_i. Then, C should subsume the enforcing example $ex1_{p_i}^-$, by applying the same substition used to subsume the master example. The same clearly holds for the val_j predicates.

Fact d). From fact c), and from the hypothesis C contains at most k literals, we can conclude C contain exactly one atom for each predicate appearing in the master example. In particular, only one atom for each predicate val_j can appear in C.

Let ϑ be a substitution such that $C\vartheta \subseteq ex1^+$ (such a ϑ exists by hypothesis) and let $\bar{\vartheta}$ be the (non ground) substitution which acts as follows on a variable Z appearing in C:

- if $\vartheta(Z) = cx_j$ then $\bar{\vartheta}(Z) = X_j$;
- if $\vartheta(Z) = cx'_j$ then $\bar{\vartheta}(Z) = X'_j$;
- if $\vartheta(Z) = cy_i$ then $\bar{\vartheta}(Z) = Y_i$;

where $1 \leq i \leq n$ and $1 \leq j \leq m$. Let $\bar{C}$ be the function free Horn clause obtained by applying the substitution $\bar{\vartheta}$ to the clause C, i.e. $C\bar{\vartheta} = \bar{C}$. It is easy to verify that $\bar{C} \vdash_\vartheta ex1^+$.

Fact e). $\bar{C} \nvdash_\vartheta ex$ for any negative example ex. Assume this is not true, i.e. there exists a negative example ex and a substitution ϑ^- such that $\bar{C}\vartheta^- \subseteq ex$. Then, by definition of $\bar{C}$, we get $C\bar{\vartheta}\vartheta^- \subseteq ex$, a contradiction.

From facts a), b), c), d), and e), the clause $\bar{C}$ has necessarily the following form:

$$\bar{C}: \quad \leftarrow \bigwedge_{1 \leq i \leq t} p_i(Z_1^i, Z_2^i, Z_3^i)$$
$$\bigwedge_{1 \leq j \leq m} val_j(X'_j, X''_j)$$

where we have

(i) Z_j^i is the (X or Y) variable corresponding to the boolean variable appearing in the j-th position of the conjunct E_i (e.g., for $E_1 = x_1 \wedge \neg x_2 \wedge y_1$, we have $p_1(X_1, X_2, Y_1)$);
(ii) for each predicate val_j, either X'_j or X''_j must be the variable X_j, and the two variable are distinct.

Now, let T be the following truth value assignment for the X boolean variables of the formula Φ: $T(x_j) = true$ if $val_j(X_j, X''_j)$ appears in clause $\bar{C}$ (i.e., if X_j is the first argument of the predicate val_j); $T(x_j) = false$ if $val_j(X'_j, X_j)$ appears in clause $\bar{C}$ (i.e., if X_j is the second argument of the predicate val_j).

For assignment T, there exists no possible truth value assignment to variable in Y such that the 3DNF formula E is not satisfied. Indeed, if such an assignment existed, then $\bar{C}$ would satisfy the (negative) checking example, contradicting the hypothesis C is a solution of the ILP problem. $\square$

It is worthwhile noting that now we have a precise characterisation of the sources of complexity we encounter in solving the above ILP problem: the subsumption test for checking whether a clause subsumes an example, and the choice of the positions of variables in the atoms. In fact, as we will see, even if we exactly know the format of the clause we are looking for, the complexity of the ILP consistency problem is Σ_2^P-complete. We next formalise the concept of format of a hypothesis, and the related ILP problems.

Definition 6. A *template* is a first order formula $\mathcal{T} \in \mathcal{L}_H$. The set of the instances of $\mathcal{T}$ is $\mathcal{I}(\mathcal{T}) = \{C \in \mathcal{L}_H \mid C = \mathcal{T}\vartheta \text{ for some substitution } \vartheta\}$

The *template* ILP-*learning* problem for an ILP setting $\mathcal{S}$ then defined as follows:

Definition 3.2 *Given $\langle B, EX^+, EX^- \rangle$ and a template $\mathcal{T}$, with $B \in \mathcal{L}_B$, $EX^+ \in \mathcal{L}_E$, $EX^- \in \mathcal{L}_E$, find an hypothesis $H \in \mathcal{I}(\mathcal{T})$, such that: (i) $H \wedge B \vdash ex$ $\forall ex \in EX^+$, and (ii) $H \wedge B \nvdash ex$ $\forall ex \in EX^-$.*

The template *ILP*-consistency *problem for an ILP setting S is accordingly defined.*

In the *template* ILP-*consistency* problem for S_{HC}, we know the template or "skeleton" of the solution we are looking for. The only information we do not get from the input is the identity/non-identity of variables in the desired instance of $\mathcal{I}(\mathcal{T})$.

However, the knowledge of the skeleton of the clause, does not reduce the complexity of the consistency problem for the ILP setting S_{HC}. The following theorem is an easy consequence of the proof of Theorem 5.

Theorem 7. *The template ILP-consistency problem for S_{HC} is Σ_2^P-complete.*

4 Further Complexity Results

In this section, we focus on learning one 1,2-nondeterminate function-free Horn clause. First, we point out the complexity of ϑ-subsumption is still NP-complete, even under such a restriction. In fact, we further restrict this setting by allowing only one atom for each predicate in the clause.

Proposition 8. *Given a 1,2-nondeterminate function-free Horn clause C where all the atoms have distinct predicates and a ground Horn clause P, deciding whether $C \vdash_\vartheta P$ is **NP**-complete. Hardness holds even if C and P are definite horn clauses.*

PROOF. Membership in **NP** is immediate, following the same reasoning of Lemma 4. Next we show the problem is **NP**-hard.

We reduce the **NP**-complete problem of deciding whether a graph G is 3-colorable to the problem of deciding whether a 1,2-nondeterminate function-free Horn clause C subsumes a ground Horn clause.

Let $G = (N, E)$ a graph and N and E be the sets of its nodes and edges, respectively. Let $|N| = n$ and $|E| = m$.

Consider the following 1,2-nondeterminate function-free Horn clause C:

$$h(B) \leftarrow \bigwedge_{e_i(x_j, x_k) \in E} pe_i(X_j, X_k) \bigwedge_{1 \le j \le n} b_j(B, X_j)$$

Given an edge $e_i \in E$, define T_i to be the following conjunction:

$$pe_i(1, 2) \wedge pe_i(1, 3) \wedge pe_i(2, 1) \wedge pe_i(2, 3) \wedge pe_i(3, 1) \wedge pe_i(3, 2).$$

Then, P is the following Horn clause:

$$h(b) \leftarrow \bigwedge_{1 \le i \le m} T_i \bigwedge_{1 \le j \le n} b_j(b, 1) \wedge b_j(b, 2) \wedge b_j(b, 3)$$

Now we claim that G is 3-colorable if and only if $C \vdash_\vartheta P$.

Only if part. Assume G is 3-colorable and let Col be a legal coloring for G, i.e. a mapping from the set N of nodes to the set $\{1, 2, 3\}$ of colors such that: (i) each node is colored with some color; and (ii) there exists no edge $e_i(x_j, x_k)$ such that $Col(x_j) = Col(x_k)$. Now, let ϑ be the following substitution for the variables appearing in C:

- $\vartheta(X_j) = Col(x_j)$ for $1 \leq j \leq n$;
- $\vartheta(B) = b$

It is clear that $C\vartheta \subseteq P$, since in each conjunction T_i, all (and only) the legal coloring for the endpoints of the corresponding edge are encoded.

If part. Suppose there exists a substitution ϑ such that $C\vartheta \subseteq P$. Let Col be the following coloring: $Col(x_j) = \vartheta(X_j)$ for $1 \leq j \leq n$. Note that each variable X_j must to be bound to a value in $\{1, 2, 3\}$ in order to subsume one of the atoms of the form $b_j(b, c)$, with $c \in \{1, 2, 3\}$.

Furthermore, if existed an edge $e_i(x_j, x_k)$ such that $Col(x_j) = Col(x_k) = c$, then the corresponding atom $pe_i(c, c)$ should belong to $C\vartheta$. Since, for any c, $pe_i(c, c)$ does not appear in T_i, we get $C\vartheta \not\subseteq P$, a contradiction. $\square$

Let $\mathcal{S}_{1,2HC}$ be the setting $\langle \emptyset, 1,2\text{-nondeterminate function-free Horn clauses}$ *whereallthe* atoms have distinct predicates, $\vdash_\vartheta$, ground Horn clauses$\rangle$.

As a consequence of the above proposition, we know that for the setting $\mathcal{S}_{1,2HC}$, in general, given an hypothesis $H \in \mathcal{L}_H$ and an example $e \in \mathcal{L}_E$, the problem of deciding whether $e \in Cover(H)$ or not, is not feasible in polynomial time (unless $\mathbf{P} = \mathbf{NP}$). This evaluation hardness result, extends our knowledge of ILP settings which are not efficiently learnable. In particular, settings with arity of the predicates limited to 2 can be added to those considered by Cohen and Page in [6], where they showed hardness results for the setting $\mathcal{S}_{k,A}$, for any $A \geq 3$ (see Section 2.3 above).[2]

Moreover, since all the ILP settings at least as expressive as $\mathcal{S}_{1,2HC}$ inherit its evaluation hardness, we also extend a similar result stated in [18] only for the 1,2-nondeterminate function-free Horn clause. Indeed, Kietz and Džeroski showed that the consistency problem for the above setting (without requiring only one atom per predicate) is **NP**-hard.

In fact, we find out that the consistency problem for the setting $\mathcal{S}_{1,2HC}$ is located at the second level of the polynomial hierarchy.

Theorem 9. *The ILP-consistency problem for $\mathcal{S}_{1,2HC}$ is Σ_2^P-complete.*

PROOF. *Membership in Σ_2^P.* Let a set EX^+ of positive examples and EX^- of negative examples be given. Every appropriate clause C that subsumes the positive examples will contain at most $minPred(EX^+)$ predicates, where $minPred(EX^+)$ is the minimal number of predicates of the clauses in EX^+.

---

[2] Note that, in the proof of Proposition 8, C is not self resolving and P is not tautological, then the result holds for provability relation $\models$ too [15].

Therefore, we decide the ILP consistency problem at hand as follows. Guess a clause C with a number of predicates less than or equal to $minPred(EX^+)$ and perform the following checks: (i) for each clause P in EX^+, verify that $C \vdash_\vartheta P$; (ii) for each clause P' in EX^- verify that $C \not\vdash_\vartheta P'$.

From Proposition 8, checking whether $C \vdash_\vartheta P$ can be done in **NP** (and checking that $C \not\vdash_\vartheta P'$ can be done in co-**NP**). Therefore, by a polynomial number of calls to an **NP** oracle we are able to check that the guessed clause C is indeed a solution. The ILP-consistency problem for $S_{1,2HC}$ is hence in Σ_2^P.

Σ_2^P-*Hardness (Sketch).* We transform deciding that a QBF $\Phi = \exists X \forall Y E$ is in $QBF_{2,\exists}$, where E is in 3DNF, into deciding whether there exists a 1,2-nondeterminate function-free Horn clause C such that $C \vdash_\vartheta EX^+$ and $C \not\vdash_\vartheta ex$ $\forall ex \in EX^-$, where EX^+ and EX^- are given sets of ground Horn clauses (positive and negatives examples, respectively).

The proof is very similar to hardness part of the proof of Theorem 5, but we have to modify the p_i predicates in order to limit the arity to 2. In fact the two sources of complexity we have seen before does hold in this case as well. Namely, the evaluation hardness of the given setting (see Proposition 8) and the degree of freedom in the relative position of two variables. Note that, for the latter point, predicates of arity 2 are sufficient to encode the choice of either $val_j(X_j, X_j')$ or $val_j(X_j', X_j)$. $\square$

References

1. L.M. Adleman. Molecular Computation of Solutions to Combinatorial Problems. *Science* 266, pp. 1021–1024, 1994.
2. L. D. Baxter. The NP-completeness of Subsumption. Unpublished manuscript, 1977.
3. P. Cholewinski, V.W. Marek, and M. Truszczynski Default Reasoning System DeReS *Proc. Fifth Intl. Conference on Principles of Knowledge Representation and Reasoning (KR'96)*, Cambridge, MA, Nov.5-8, 1996.
4. W. Cohen. PAC-Learning Recursive Logic Programs: Efficient Algorithms. *Journal of Artificial Intelligence Research*, 2: 501–539, 1995.
5. W. Cohen. PAC-Learning Recursive Logic Programs: Negative Results. *Journal of Artificial Intelligence Research*, 2: 541–573, 1995.
6. W. Cohen and C. D. Page. Polynomial Learnability and Inductive Logic Programming - Methods and Results. *New Generation Computing*, 13(3-4): 369–409, 1995.
7. L. De Raedt and S. Džeroski. First order jk-clausal theories are PAC-learnable. *Artificial Intelligence*, 70: 375–392, 1994.
8. J. Dix and M. Müller. Implementing Semantics of Disjunctive Logic programs Using Fringes and Abstract properties. *Proc. Second Intl. workshop on Logic Programming and Nonmonotonic reasoning (LPNMR-93)*, Lisbon, Portugal, July 1993, pp. 43–59, MIT Press.
9. T. Eiter and G. Gottlob. On the Computational Cost of Disjunctive Logic Programming: Propositional Case. *Annals of Mathematics and Artificial Intelligence*, 15(3/4):289–323, 1995.

10. T. Eiter, N. Leone, C. Mateis, G. Pfeifer, and F. Scarcello. A Deductive System for Nonmonotonic Reasoning. In *Proc. 4th International Conference on Logic Programming and Nonmonotonic Reasoning (LPNMR '97)*, Lecture Notes in AI (LNAI), J. Dix, U. Furbach, and A. Nerode Eds., Springer, Berlin, 1997 (to appear).

11. T. Eiter, G. Gottlob, and H. Mannila. Disjunctive Datalog. *ACM Trans. on Database Syst.*, September 1997. To appear.

12. M. R. Garey and D. S. Johnson. *Computers and Intractability – A guide to the Theory of NP-completeness*. Freman, San Francisco, CA, 1979.

13. M. Gelfond and V. Lifschitz. The Stable Model Semantics for Logic Programming. In *Logic Programming: Proc. Fifth Intl Conference and Symposium*, pp. 1070–1080, Cambridge, Mass., 1988. MIT Press.

14. E. M. Gold. Language Identification in the Limit. *Information and Control*, 10:447–474, 1967.

15. G. Gottlob. Subsumption and Implication. *Information Processing Letters*, 24:109–111, 1987.

16. G. Gottlob. Complexity Results for Nonmonotonic Logics. *J. Logic and Computation*, 2(3):397–425, June 1992.

17. D. S. Johnson. A Catalog of Complexity Classes. In J. van Leeuwen, editor, *Handbook of Theoretical Computer Science*, volume A, chapter 2. Elsevier Science Publishers B.V. (North-Holland), 1990.

18. J.U. Kietz and S. Džeroski. Inductive logic programming and learnability. *SIGART Bulletin* 5(1): 22–32 (Special issue on Inductive Logic Programming), 1994.

19. D. Haussler. Quantifying inductive bias: AI learning algorithms and Valiant's model. *Artificial Intelligence*, 36(2):177–221, 1988.

20. R.J. Lipton. Using DNA to solve NP-complete Problems. *Priceton University*.

21. W. Marek and M. Truszczyński. Autoepistemic Logic. *JACM*, 38(3):588–619, 1991.

22. S. H. Muggleton. Inductive Logic Programming. *New Generation Computing*, 8(4):295–318, 1991.

23. *Inductive Logic Programming*, S. H. Muggleton ed., Academic Press, London, 1992.

24. S. H. Muggleton and L. De Raedt. Inductive Logic Programming: Theory and Methods. *Journal of Logic Programming*, 19,20:629–679, 1994.

25. Muggleton, S., and Page, D., A learnability model for universal representations. In *Proc. Fourth International Workshop on Inductive Logic Programming*, pages 139-160. GMD, Bonn, 1994.

26. C. D. Page and A. M. Frish. Generalization and Learnability: a study of constrained atoms. In *Inductive Logic Programming*, pp.29–61, S. H. Muggleton ed., Academic Press, London, 1992.

27. G. D. Plotkin. A note on Inductive Generalization. In *Machine Intelligence*, pp. 153–163, B. Meltzer and D. Michie eds., American Elsevier, 1970.

28. R. Reiter. A Logic for Default Reasoning. *Artificial Intelligence*, 13:81–132, 1980.

29. J. Robinson. A machine-oriented logic based on the resolution principle. *Journal of the ACM*, 12(1):23–41, 1965.

30. R. E. Schapire. The Strength of Weak Learnability. *Machine Learning*, 5:197–227, 1990.

31. Diana Rooß and Klaus Wagner. On the Power of DNA Computation. *Information and Computation*, 131(2):95–109, 1996.

32. L. G. Valiant. A Theory of the Learnable. *Communications of the ACM*, 27:1134–1142.

Inductive Logic Programming and Constraint Logic Programming (Abstract)

Jean-François Puget

ILOG SA
rue de Verdun 9
BP 85
94253 Gentilly Cedex
France
Email: puget@ilog.fr

The main distinction between ILP and other fields of Machine Learning is the use of Prolog as the basic language for expressing learned hypothesis. Recent work in ILP tried to extend the approach to variants such as indefinite clauses, or non monotonicity. In the meantime, the Logic Programming community has been exploring the use of constraints as programing primitives, yielding better results on combinatorial and numerical applications. We propose to the ILP community to use Constraint Logic Programming languages as target instead of Prolog. We will introduce the basics of CLP, and give some examples of learning constraints.

Part II

Papers

Learning Phonetic Rules in a Speech Recognition System

Zoltán Alexin[1], János Csirik[2], Tibor Gyimóthy[3],
Mark Jelasity[3] and László Tóth[3]

[1] Department of Applied Informatics, József Attila University
Árpád tér 2, H-6720 Szeged, Hungary
Phone: (36) +(62) 454293, Fax: (36) +(62) 312292
e-mail: alexin@inf.u-szeged.hu

[2] Department of Computer Science, József Attila University
Árpád tér 2, H-6720 Szeged, Hungary
Phone: (36) +(62) 454370, Fax: (36) +(62) 312292
e-mail: csirik@inf.u-szeged.hu

[3] Research Group on Artificial Intelligence
Hungarian Academy of Sciences,
Aradi vértanuk tere 1, H-6720 Szeged, Hungary
Phone: (36) +(62) 454139, Fax: (36) +(62) 312508
e-mail: gyimi, jelasity, tothl@inf.u-szeged.hu

Abstract. Current speech recognition systems can be categorized into two broad classes; the knowledge-based approach and the stochastic one. In this paper we present a rule-based method for the recognition of Hungarian vowels. A spectrogram model was used as a front-end module and some acoustic features were extracted (e.g. locations, intensities and shapes of local maxima) from spectrograms by using a genetic algorithm method. On the basis of these features we developed a rule set for the recognition of isolated Hungarian vowels. These rules represented by Prolog clauses were refined by the IMPUT Inductive Logic Programming method. [4]

1 Introduction

Current speech recognition systems can be categorized into two broad classes; the knowledge-based approach and the stochastic one. Those systems belonging to the former use a set of rules for the acoustic-phonetic decoding of speech. Those systems which use stochastic techniques are usually based on Hidden Markov Models or Neural Networks [10]. In each type of system the recognition process starts with a so-called front-end which converts the digitally recorded speech signal into a time-frequency representation. This representation shows how energy as a function of time and frequency is distributed in the signal. The most frequently used representation is the spectrogram, where the speech signal

---

[4] This work was supported by the grants ESPRIT 20237 and PHARE TDQM 9305-02/1022 ("ILP2/HUN").

is sliced up into short segments (called *frames*) and then the absolute values of the Discrete Fourier Transform of these frames are computed.

Systems based on stochastic approaches use one of these representations for recognition by calculating a distribution from the incoming signal and comparing it with the pre-stored (taught) ones of the signals to be recognized. In knowledge-based systems phonetic features [5] are extracted from the spectrogram. These features can be detected by finding acoustic cues or acoustic events in the spectrogram.

The output of the front-end module is a time-feature mapping which shows phonetic features presented at a given moment. The next step in a speech recognition system is to convert these features into a string of phonemes. During this transformation phonotactic rules can be applied e.g. if we have an [s] with *strong* detection followed by a [d] for which the feature *voicedness* is weak, the [d] should be corrected to [t] since phonotactic rules say that [s] can never be followed by a [d].

In this paper we present a rule-based method for the recognition of Hungarian vowels. A spectrogram model was used as a front-end module because it could be easily converted back to speech. We modified the graphical representations of spectrograms and investigated the effect of these modifications on speech signal. The goal of this work was to determine the most significant parts in the spectrograms. After that some acoustic features were extracted (e.g. locations, intensities and shapes of local maxima) from spectrograms by using a genetic algorithm method [6]. On the basis of these features we developed a rule set for the recognition of isolated Hungarian vowels. These rules represented by Prolog clauses were refined by the IMPUT [1] Inductive Logic Programming [9, 12] method. We compared our results with the rules published in the generally accepted Hungarian phonetics handbook [2]. The main advantage of our approach was that we provided a simple learning model for determining speaker-specific recognition rules of Hungarian vowels. We strongly believe that this model can be applied to the recognition of other phonemes as well. The long-term goal of our work being to develop a complete continuous speech recognition system for the Hungarian language. The development of this system is presently being done in cooperation with Morphologic Ltd, a leading commercial company of the Hungarian Language Processing field.

First, in Section 2 the necessary background information on speech recognition is provided. In Section 3 the learning model used is given. Section 4 contains conclusions and future work.

2 Extraction of Acoustic Features

2.1 Characterizing Vowels

In phonetics, the traditional way of characterizing a vowel is to describe its *formants*. In this paper however a slightly different approach will be used for reasons described below.

It is well-known that the spectrum of a (static) vowel is a quasi-periodic signal having a special envelope [13]. The frequency of the periodic component is responsible for the pitch level of the vowel and the envelope carries the information that makes the phoneme-classification of the signal possible. It is generally accepted [13] that (at least in the case of vowels) the site and value of the local maxima of the envelope are sufficient for classification (see Figure 1 for an illustration of the above terms).

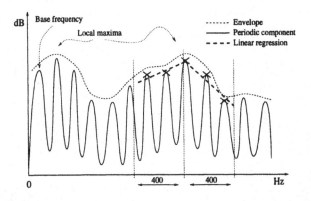

Fig. 1. In this figure some basic terms and method of extracting the steepness features (see Section 2.2) are illustrated.

The first definition of formants can now be given: The frequency values corresponding to the local maxima are called *formants* and the value of a local maximum is the *intensity* of the formant. The usual notation is the following: F0 denotes the base frequency and Fi denotes the ith maximum place (in increasing order).

From a computational point of view the above definition of formants is not quite sufficient. The problem is that in the case of many vowels (especially [u] and [o]) certain formants (usually F1 and F2) get too close to each other forming only one local maximum in the envelope.

2.2 Acoustic Features

Based on the observations of Section 2.1 the local maxima of the envelope were used instead of the formants. A local maxima was described using the following four features: *location*, *intensity*, *left steepness*, *right steepness*.

The site and intensity are rather usual features, the left and right steepnesses supposedly characterizing the shape of the *hill* to be investigated.

All features were extracted from the spectral decomposition of the original wave signals of the sample vowels. Clearly, the envelope had to be determined first. To achieve this goal, an adaptation and specialization of a genetic algorithm based method GAS [6]) was used. GAS is a function-structure discovering algorithm with heuristic features and it is capable of finding multiple local maxima of any given objective function. In our case, the objective function was the spectral decomposition of the signal (as a function of frequency) and thus the local maxima found formed an approximation of the envelope. This process is illustrated in Figure 2.

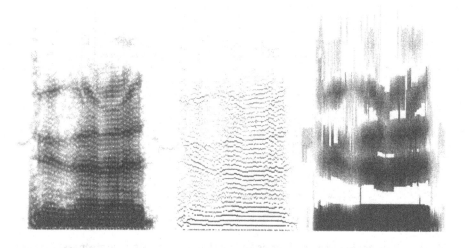

Fig. 2. This figure shows the three stages of signal processing. The first picture shows the original spectrogram of the Hungarian word [tiz3n3ɟ], the second shows the peeks of the periodic component (the approximation of the envelope) and the third picture was generated from the list of 4-tuples (maximum location, value, left and right steepness) of every frame (column).

3 Learning Rules for Hungarian Vowels

3.1 The Learning Task

The learning problem we would like to tackle is a vowel recognition task. We had five samples for each of the following Hungarian vowels: [u], [o], [ɔ], [a] and [ɛ]. Each sample was given by the same male speaker. Samples for one vowel differ in the intonation and pitch level. Though the samples were static vowels (1 sec. approximately) the approach is relevant for single frames as well.

The task was to find recognition rules for each vowel in the form of a Prolog program. First, we tried to apply the recognition rules published in the phonetic handbook [2], but their efficiency proved to be poor for our samples. The main reason of it might have been that these rules were rather theoretical and therefore cannot accommodate with our *specific* samples. Then we made a generalization on this approach in order to get an *overly-general* program for each vowel. After that IMPUT [1] was used to refine these initial programs.

For each vowel we had similar initial programs. These programs were trained by five different learning configurations, then we got five different specialized programs, one for each vowel. (Initial programs differ from each other only in frequencies of formants). For training IMPUT to learn a given vowel we used the samples for that vowel as positive examples and all of the other samples as negative examples. Each learning configuration consisted of 5 positive and 20 negative examples. The result was tested against the same size sample set. The very first experiences are discussed in Section 3.4.

3.2 Prolog Representation of Acoustic Features

In this model we used formants[5] as the most characteristic features for the recognition of vowels. The formants were selected from the spectrogram by a genetic algorithm mentioned in Section 2. One formant for a vowel [ɔ] is listed below:

```
Field           Value          Variance

Size of cluster :      95.169082%
Center (Hz):    131.603923     45.998686
Left angle :    1.488087       0.019766
Right angle :   -1.288563      0.013596
Intensity :     246.050761     5.114175
...
```

In this file five consecutive lines determine one formant. A file may contain up to ten formants. The Size parameter is the length of the formant in percent of the whole length of the speech signal, the Center parameter is the mean frequency of the formant, the Left and Right angles are the slopes of the peak, while the Intensity is the height of the peak (*volume*) in a logarithmic scale.

The Variance values were not used in the learning process excepting the Center (Hz) variance. The floating point values were converted to discrete values — either Prolog atoms, or integer numbers (in the case of angle and frequency values).

Each formant was then represented by a six-tuple. The components of a tuple are: discrete size, integer frequency, discrete frequency fluctuation, integer left angle, integer right angle, discrete intensity in that order.

A vowel can be characterized by a set of formants therefore a sound was represented by a set of six-tuples, where each tuple corresponds to one formant. For example the formants of the vowel [ɔ] given above was described with the next Prolog term: sound([(fulllength, 125, veryveryshort, 85, 110, loud), (fulllength, 2350, veryshort, 75, 110, noise), (fulllength, 3550, wide, 75, 120, noise)]).

3.3 Initial Hypothesis for the Recognition of Vowels

As it was mentioned earlier, the standard recognition rules published in [2] were needed to generalize for the Hungarian vowels, because of its non-satisfactory

---

[5] In Section 2.2 it was mentioned that instead of *formants* local maxima of the envelopes were determined, however, for the sake of simplicity, in the following we refer to these local maxima as formants.

behavior on our samples. It was done in the following way:

The original rules required three neighboring formants (F1, F2, F3) to be present contemporarily in a sample. In our initial program we introduced one new formant F4, and required only any two of these formants be present contemporarily within a sample. The mean frequencies of the formants were left unchanged. The most important part of the initial program for the vowel [ɔ] looks like this:

```
a_vowel(L) :- a_exist_formant_1(L), a_exist_formant_2(L).
a_vowel(L) :- a_exist_formant_1(L), a_exist_formant_3(L).
a_vowel(L) :- a_exist_formant_1(L), a_exist_formant_4(L).
a_vowel(L) :- a_exist_formant_2(L), a_exist_formant_3(L).
a_vowel(L) :- a_exist_formant_2(L), a_exist_formant_4(L).
a_vowel(L) :- a_exist_formant_3(L), a_exist_formant_4(L).

a_exist_formant_1(List) :-
          member((S, Hz, HzW, _, _, Int), List),
          a_accept_size_1(S), a_accept_hertz_1(Hz),
          a_accept_hzwidth_1(HzW), a_accept_int_1(Int).

a_exist_formant_2(List) :-
          member((S, Hz, HzW, _, _, Int), List),
          a_accept_size_2(S), a_accept_hertz_2(Hz),
          a_accept_hzwidth_2(HzW), a_accept_int_2(Int).
...
a_accept_size_1(Size) :- size(Size).
a_accept_hertz_1(Hertz) :- a_formant_1(Hertz).
a_accept_hzwidth_1(HertzW) :- width(HertzW).
a_accept_int_1(Int) :- intensity(Int).

a_accept_size_2(Size) :- size(Size).
a_accept_hertz_2(Hertz) :- a_formant_2(Hertz).
a_accept_hzwidth_2(HertzW) :- width(HertzW).
a_accept_int_2(Int) :- intensity(Int).
...
a_formant_1(Hertz) :- between(Hertz, 500, 750).
a_formant_2(Hertz) :- between(Hertz, 900, 1250).
...
size(fulllength).
size(long).
size(short).
size(veryshort).
size(veryveryshort).
...
```

These initial programs recognized all positive examples for each vowel but covered many negative examples as well. Therefore we had to specialize them.

3.4 The Revision of the Initial Hypothesis

The ILP method IMPUT [1] has been used to refine the above mentioned initial programs. IMPUT is an abductive and interactive ILP tool. It uses unfolding transformation and clause removal to revise a program. In IMPUT an interactive debugger [7] has been built for making easier to find the best place of unfolding. IMPUT requires an *oracle* involved in the learning process, but it gives — in return — more efficient results (smaller and more precise theories).

To evaluate the results it should be noted, that there is no precise distinction between all of the vowels. Some speech data can be recognized both as [ɔ] or [a], other can be recognized both as [o] or [u]. The decision is sometimes subjective.

For the sake of demonstartion let us see the case of the vowel [ɔ]. The initial program covered all the 5 positive and 15 (60%) from negative examples. Doing the consecutive unfolding we got a rather special theory that recognized only 2 negative examples from the training set for [a]. Having the samples closely inspected, it revieled that the discretized sample for [ɔ] and [a] do not differ much. In this special case there were no possible distinction between these samples and the theory. When tested the results with a new set of data, we got that the inferred theory recognized the 5 positive examples and 5 (25%) from the negative examples. The results were almost similar in the case of the other vowels, excep for [o], where we got worse result. Although, the number of the incorrectly recognized negative examples reduced significantly comparing to the initial programs we were not fully satisfied with the resulted ones. One possible solution would be to continue the specialization process by using more training examples. However, a good recognizer must be able to learn a speaker-specific rules from very few examples. Hence, we try to modify the initial recognizer programs by introducing new acoustic features and rules.

4 Conclusion and Future Work

Knowledge-based systems and stochastic systems have been competing since the possible methods of speech recognition were first studied [14, 15]. The usual argument against knowledge-based systems is that they are not flexible enough. Many authors try to cure this drawback by incorporating fuzzy decision logic or neural networks into their systems [4]. In the eighties the expert system approach was very popular [11], but since the way several information sources should be integrated was never fully understood, these systems could not offer any real improvement. Even with these disadvantages, many knowledge-based speech recognizers were reported to outperform the state-of-the-art template matching based systems. Some of these [5] use a very similar phonetic feature set to what we applied. The results of these systems show that this is a possible approach to speech recognition, although there are many problems yet to be solved.

Our approach for vowel recognition should be considered as a first step on a long road. Our goal was to test whether the IMPUT ILP method could be applied for the very difficult and complex problem of speech recognition. It should also be mentioned that the recognition of vowels is the case where the classic pattern-matching models give the best fit. Really serious improvements therefore cannot be expected. Knowledge-based systems were reported to outperform stochastic systems when fine phonetic distinctions are necessary, as in the case of stop consonant identification [8]. Our next task now is to find the important features for these and all the other types of phonemes. Methods to extract these features should also be found in time too. Then the detection of these features and their conversion into phonemes must be described by rules, like those presented in this paper. Finally, this all should be put into the general framework of the speech recognition system. We expect that ILP methods will in many cases be applicable for the refinement of these rules.

References

1. Alexin, Z., Gyimóthy, T., Boström, H.: Integrating Algorithmic Debugging and Unfolding Transformation in an Interactive Learner in Proceedings of the 12th European Conference on Artificial Intelligence ECAI-96 ed. Wolfgang Wahlster, Budapest, Hungary (1996) 403–407 John Wiley & Son's Ltd. (1996)
2. Bolla, Kálmán: Magyar fonetikai atlasz, A szegmentálás hangszerkezet elemei Nemzeti Tankönyvkiadó Rt Budapest (1995) in Hungarian
3. Cooke, M. (eds.): Visual Representations of Speech Signals, Wiley, 1993
4. Fohr, D., Haton, J., Laprie, Y.: Knowledge-Based Techniques in Acoustic-Phonetic Decoding of Speech: Interest and Limitations, International Journal on Pattern Recognition and Artificial Intelligence Vol. 8, No. 1, (1994) 133–153
5. Huebener, K., Carson-Berndsen, J.: Phoneme Recognition Using Acoustic Events, Verbmobil Technical Report No. 15, June 1994
6. Jelasity, M., Dombi, J.: GAS, an Approach on Modeling Species in Genetic Algorithms. Proceedings of the EA'95 (1995)
7. Kókai, G., Alexin, Z., Kocsis, F.: The IDT System and its Application for Learning Prolog Programs. Proc. of the Sixth International Conference on Artificial Intelligence and Information Control Systems of Robots (AIICSR-94) Smolenice Castle Slovakia September 12-16. (1994) 315–320
8. Lamel, L. F.: A knowledge-based system for stop consonant identification based on speech spectrogram reading, Computer Speech and Language (1993) 2, 169–191
9. Lavrač, N., Džeroski, S.: Inductive Logic Programming: Techniques and Applications Ellis Horwood, (1994)
10. Mammachandran, R. P., Mammone, R. J. (eds.): Modern Methods of Speech Processing, Kluwer Academic, 1995
11. Mercier, G. et al.: Recognition of speaker-dependent continuous speech with KEAL, IEE Proceedings Vol. 136, Pt.1, No.2, April (1989)
12. Muggleton, S., De Raedt, L.: Inductive Logic Programming: Theory and methods, Journal of Logic Programming 19 (20) (1994) 629–679
13. Rabiner, L. R., Schafer, R. W.: Digital Processing of Speech Signals Prentice Hall (1978)
14. Waibel, A., Lee, K. (eds.): Readings in Speech Recognition, Morgan Kaufmann (1990)
15. Zue, V. W.: The Use of Speech Knowledge in Automatic Speech Recognition, Proc. IEEE, Vol. 73, No. 11, (1985) 1602–1615

Cautious Induction in Inductive Logic Programming

Simon Anthony and Alan M. Frisch

Department of Computer Science, University of York, York. YO1 5DD. UK.
Email: {simona, frisch}@cs.york.ac.uk

Abstract. Many top-down Inductive Logic Programming systems use a greedy, covering approach to construct hypotheses. This paper presents an alternative, *cautious* approach, known as *cautious induction*. We conjecture that cautious induction can allow better hypotheses to be found, with respect to some hypothesis quality criteria. This conjecture is supported by the presentation of an algorithm called CILS, and with a complexity analysis and empirical comparison of CILS with the Progol system. The results are encouraging and demonstrate the applicability of cautious induction to problems with noisy datasets, and to problems which require large, complex hypotheses to be learnt.

1 Introduction

Within the Inductive Logic Programming (ILP) paradigm [4, 2], many of the *top-down* (or *refinement-based*) systems, such as FOIL [5] and Progol [3], employ a *greedy*, covering approach to the construction of a hypothesis. Informally, from the training sample and background knowledge, the learner searches a space of clauses to find a *single* clause which covers some *subset* of the positive examples, and is "best" with respect to some quality criteria. This is shown conceptually in figure 1, where the +'s represent positive examples from a training sample, and the set labelled c represents the set of positive examples covered by the clause c.

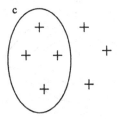

Fig. 1. Clause c covering a subset of the positive examples.

Once found, c is added to the hypothesis and the positive examples it covers are removed from the training sample. This process is then repeated with the remaining examples and background knowledge to find a further clause c', as shown in figure 2. Clause c' is also added to the hypothesis and the positive examples it covers are removed from the training sample. This process continues until the hypothesis covers all the positive examples. Notice that a *repeated search* of the space of clauses is necessary, and that each search is with respect to an increasingly small set of positive examples. Therefore, the selection of a clause is dependent on the clauses already included in the hypothesis. For instance, the selection of c' was based upon its coverage of the positive examples left uncovered by c. In other words, repeatedly selecting the locally "best" clause is assumed to determine the globally "best" hypothesis.

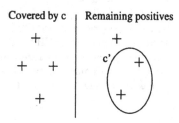

Fig. 2. Clause c' covering a subset of the remaining positive examples.

This assumption will not hold in general. For instance, consider the seven positive examples in the problem depicted above. The space of clauses might contain clauses d and d' which, if hypotheses containing fewer clauses are preferred, together form a "better" hypothesis, covering all the positive examples. This is shown in figure 3.

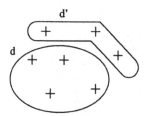

Fig. 3. Two clauses, d and d', covering the seven positive examples.

Cautious Induction is an approach which performs a *single, complete* search through the space of clauses and retains a nonempty set of *candidate* clauses, all of which meet some quality criteria. A subset of these candidate clauses is then selected to form a hypothesis which covers all the positive examples. Informally, the task of searching for the candidate clauses has been separated from the task of choosing which clauses to include in the hypothesis. Accordingly, our conjecture is that cautious induction avoids the dependency on the order of clause selection, and can allow "better" hypotheses, such as the hypothesis $\{d, d'\}$ in the example above, to be found.

This conjecture is supported by the presentation of an algorithm called CILS (Cautious Inductive Learning System) which implements this approach. CILS is validated by a complexity analysis and an empirical comparison against the Progol system. In particular, this comparison highlights the potential of cautious induction for learning complex hypotheses, and also for learning in the presence of noise.

The rest of this paper is organised as follows: the learning setting is defined in section 2. Refinement is introduced in section 3 together with a description of CILS. Section 4 introduces Progol and reports both a theoretical and an empirical comparison against CILS, and we draw some conclusions in section 5.

2 The Learning Setting

Unless otherwise noted, this paper will assume the following learning setting, which we shall refer to as the *normal* setting. The teacher selects a *target concept* and provides the learner with a finite, nonempty *training sample* of *examples*, each of which is correctly labelled[1] as either *positive* or *negative*. From this training sample and any available background knowledge the learner constructs a hypothesis of the concept. Since our representation is that of logic programs, examples are atoms built over a *target predicate* and the background knowledge is a finite set of definite clauses[2]. The hypothesis is represented as a finite set of nonrecursive definite clauses whose heads are built over the target predicate and whose bodies consist of literals built over predicates defined in the background knowledge. It will be useful to introduce the following relationship between a hypothesis and an example, known as *coverage*.

Definition 1 (Coverage) *Let B denote background knowledge, T a training sample and c a clause. An example $e \in T$ is said to be* covered *by c, with respect to B, if $B \cup \{c\} \models e$, and* uncovered *otherwise. Example e is said to be* covered *by a hypothesis H, with respect to B, if H contains at least one clause which covers e, and* uncovered *otherwise.*

In this setting, a hypothesis H must satisfy the following two conditions with respect to the background knowledge and a training sample T:

- *Completeness*: H must cover *every* positive example in T, and
- *Consistency*: H must leave *every* negative example in T uncovered.

---

[1] We shall later relax this assumption to allow noisy data.

[2] Throughout this paper clauses shall be represented as a set of literals.

A hypothesis satisfying these conditions is said to *explain*, or to be *correct* with respect to, that training sample. Additionally, we shall require that each clause within a hypothesis must cover at least one positive example (to avoid redundancy). Since more than one hypothesis may explain a given training sample, we introduce the following two *quality* criteria by which one hypothesis H is to be preferred to another.

- H should be as *accurate* as possible in classifying unseen examples, and
- H should be as *small* as possible, under the assumption that simpler explanations are more likely to be correct.

The question of how these two criteria are to be measured is postponed until section 4.3. We conclude this section with one final notational convention: the cardinality of a set of objects S shall be denoted $|S|$.

3   The Search for Clauses

We now turn to consider the task of finding the clauses which make up a hypothesis. From the outset it will be useful to define the *size* of a clause as the total number of literals in its head and body, and to introduce *subsumption* in order to allow us to talk of the generality and specificity of clauses.

Definition 2 (Subsumption) *Let c and c′ denote two clauses. Clause c subsumes clause c′ iff there exists a substitution θ such that cθ ⊆ c′. We say that c is more general than c′, and, conversely, that c′ is more specific than c.*

3.1   Conventional Refinement

Search by refinement can be viewed as the search of a tree[3] of clauses. Informally, search begins with a set of *initial clauses* and an *evaluation function* is used to select a clause from this set. If this clause satisfies some *goal condition* the search terminates, otherwise the selected clause is removed. Provided the evaluation of the clause meets some quality criteria (verified by a *pruning function*), a *refinement operator* is applied to generate a set of *refinements* (*incremental specialisations*) which are added to the set. An incremental specialisation of a clause c is typically defined to be the addition of a literal, built over a predicate defined in the background knowledge, to the body of c. Each such predicate is often accompanied by a nonempty, finite set of *usage declarations* (sometimes referred to as *mode* declarations) which impose *type* and *mode* restrictions on the literals that are to be added to a clause. More precise definitions of these concepts are provided below.

---

[3] Refinement is often viewed as the search of a graph. By allowing a clause to appear more than once, we simplify our presentation to talk in terms of trees.

Definition 3 (Usage Declarations) *Let c denote a clause and let p denote either the target predicate or a predicate defined in the background knowledge. A usage declaration for p specifies the functional structure that each argument of p must have, and restricts the symbols that may occupy positions within each argument when a literal, built over p, is added to c. Positions that are to be occupied by a variable symbol are given one of the following two modes:*

- Positive – *indicating that this position must contain a variable symbol already present in c, or*
- Negative – *indicating that this position may contain any variable symbol.*

Positions that are to be occupied by a constant are given the mode declaration Hash. *Each of these mode declarations is accompanied by a* type *declaration. A literal is said to* satisfy *a usage declaration, with respect to a clause c, if its functional structure matches that of the declaration, and the positions in its arguments are occupied by appropriate symbols of the correct mode and type.*

Although very similar to the *Mode declarations* used by Progol, usage declarations do not include a *recall*. The recall is described in section 4.1.

Definition 4 (Initial Clauses) *Let p denote the target predicate of a learning problem and U a set of usage declarations for p. The set of initial clauses, denoted IC, is the nonempty set of all bodiless clauses whose heads are built over p and satisfy U (up to variable renaming).*

Definition 5 (Refinement Operator) *Let c denote a clause, U a set of usage declarations and* PRED(B) *the set of predicates defined in the background knowledge B. Furthermore, for a predicate $p \in$ PRED(B), let* LIT$_U(c,p)$ *denote the set of literals built over p that satisfy U with respect to c. A refinement operator ρ is a function from a single clause to a set of clauses, each member of which contains an additional body literal. $\rho(c)$ is therefore defined as:*

$$\rho(c) = \{c \cup \{l\} \mid l \in \text{LIT}_U(c,p) \text{ and } p \in \text{PRED}(B)\}$$

The set of all clauses that can be generated by the repeated application of ρ to a clause from *IC* is known as the *refinement space*. Each clause in this space is known as a *refinement*. Typically a teacher specified *size* parameter is also used, restricting the size of the refinements and ensuring that the refinement space is finite.

Definition 6 (Evaluation Function) *Let T denote a training sample and c a clause. An* evaluation function *returns a real number for c based on a number of attributes of c, typically:*

- *the number of positive and negative examples from T covered by c, and*
- *the size of c.*

Given a set of clauses C, BEST(C) *denotes a clause from within C which maximises the evaluation function.*

The implementation of the evaluation function dictates the strategy adopted by the refinement operator in searching the refinement space. Typically this function is defined to allow an A* strategy to be used.

Definition 7 (Pruning Function) *Let c denote a clause. The boolean function* PRUNE(c) *is true if it is expected that c and all its subsequent refinements do not meet the quality criteria for a hypothesis clause, and false otherwise. This judgement is usually made by deciding if the value of* EVAL(c) *is likely to increase or decrease with further refinement.*

Definition 8 (Goal Condition) *Typically the goal condition of a search by refinement is satisfied when a consistent clause is selected, and that clause can be shown to be the "best" clause in the refinement space, with respect to the quality criteria.*

A top-down learning system is distinguished by its implementation of each of these concepts. These implementations are combined to produce a strategy for searching the refinement space, as shown in the following algorithm.

Algorithm 9 (Search by Refinement) *Let* BEST *denote an evaluation function,* ρ *a refinement operator,* PRUNE *a pruning function, and* IC *the set of initial clauses in some learning problem. The following algorithm searches a refinement space and returns the first clause satisfying the goal condition:*

```
let C = IC
let c = BEST(C)
while c does not meet the goal condition
      let C = C - {c}
      if PRUNE(c) = false then
            let C = C ∪ ρ(c)
      let c = BEST(C)
end while
return c
```
The algorithm will always return a clause since IC *is nonempty by definition.*

3.2 Cautious Refinement in CILS

Recall that in cautious induction a single, complete search of the refinement space is performed, and a *set* of candidate clauses that satisfy the quality criteria are retained. Since we are no longer looking for an individual clause in the refinement space the search terminates when all clauses in the refinement space have been either examined or pruned. Consequently, CILS requires rather different pruning conditions from other learning systems. In deciding whether to prune a clause CILS examines both the coverage and size of the clause, and, in particular, its relationship to the candidate clauses that have already been found. Both of these criteria exploit CILS' evaluation function, which is defined below. The trade-off used between the coverage and size of a clause is similar to that employed by other learning systems such as Progol [3], and provides an effective yet simple way of guiding the search towards clauses of a suitable generality.

Algorithm 10 (CILS' Evaluation Function) *Let c denote a clause,* $P(c)$ *and* $N(c)$ *the number of positive and negative examples from training sample* T *covered by c, and* $SZ(c)$ *the size of c. The evaluation function* EVAL *is given by:*

$$\text{EVAL}(c) = P(c) - (N(c) + SZ(c))$$

Algorithm 11 (CILS' Pruning Function) *Let c denote a clause and* EVAL *denote CILS' evaluation function. Furthermore, let* $P(c)$ *denote the number of positive examples from training sample* T *covered by c,* $SZ(c)$ *the size of c, and size a teacher specified restriction on the size of any clause in the refinement space. The function* PRUNE(c) *is true if any of the following conditions hold for c:*

- $P(c) < SZ(c)$ *in which case* EVAL$(c) < 0$, *and for any subsequent refinement* c' *of c,* EVAL$(c') < 0$,
- $SZ(c) > size$, *or*
- *a "better" candidate clause has already been found. If the selected clause c covers a set* P *of positive examples, then a "better" clause* c' *covers a set* P' *of positives where* $SZ(c) \geq SZ(c')$ *and* $P \subseteq P'$.

Each predicate defined in the background knowledge is accompanied by a finite, nonempty set of usage declarations which, together with a size parameter, form the syntactic bias used by CILS. Where the usage declaration requires one or more constants to appear in a literal, each positive example is used to find potential constants. A new literal is then generated for each distinct alternative. Since CILS examines or prunes every refinement, its search by refinement differs from algorithm 9, and is presented below.

Algorithm 12 (CILS' Search by Refinement) *Let* Can *denote the set of candidate clauses,* C *a set of clauses and* T^+ *the set of positive examples from a training sample* T. *Furthermore, let* BEST *denote CILS' evaluation function,* PRUNE *CILS' pruning conditions,* ρ *CILS' refinement operator and* IC *the set of initial clauses. CILS' search by refinement proceeds as follows:*

```
let  C = IC
let  Can = T⁺
while C ≠ ∅
     let  c = BEST(C)
     let  C = C - {c}
     if PRUNE(c) = false then
          if c is consistent and EVAL(c) ≥ 0 then
               let Can = Can ∪ {c}
          otherwise
               let  C = C ∪ ρ(c)
end while
return Can
```

Each positive example is itself included as a candidate clause since it has an evaluation of 0. This also ensures that a complete hypothesis can always be generated from the set of candidate clauses. Currently a greedy cover-set algorithm is used to construct the hypothesis from the set of candidate clauses. Despite this admittedly greedy aspect of CILS, notice that each candidate clause has been found *independently* of the others.

4 Comparison of CILS with Progol

This section compares, with a complexity and an empirical analysis, CILS against the ILP learner Progol [3]. Progol has been successfully applied to a variety of real-world applications and is regarded by many as the state-of-the-art in ILP systems. To aid our comparison of these algorithms an introduction to Progol is given in the following subsection.

4.1 The Progol Algorithm

Progol adopts a greedy, covering approach to the construction of a hypothesis. To avoid generating clauses which cover no positive examples, Progol bounds each refinement space from below by a most specific clause, $\perp$, constructed from a single positive example[4]. $\perp$ is required to cover the positive example e used in its construction, and, since every refinement must subsume $\perp$, they must all cover e. This is shown in figure 4. Thus Progol uses two algorithms during learning: one to construct $\perp$, and one to search the ensuing refinement space. The following two subsections outline these algorithms in order to give some insight into our evaluation of Progol.

Construction of $\perp$ Since $\perp$ is most specific, it contains all the literals that may appear in any refinement. The target predicate, and each predicate defined in the background knowledge are each accompanied by a usage declaration, and a positive integer known as the *recall*[5]. For recall r, all possible literals that satisfy a usage declaration are each added at most r times to $\perp$, with a bound placed on variable depth to ensure this process terminates.

Search by Refinement An A* search strategy is used to search the refinement space. In particular, since any clause in this space must subsume $\perp$, the literals in the body of such a clause must be a subset of those in the body of $\perp$. However, notice that if a binding between variables in a literal in $\perp$ is *split* when that literal is added to a clause, the resulting refinement will still subsume $\perp$. Progol allows variable bindings to be split in this way, provided that each resulting literal

---

[4] In fact, Progol treats a training sample as a *sequence* of examples, and $\perp$ is constructed from the first example in this sequence.

[5] Given a literal l which satisfies a usage declaration, the recall determines how many solutions of l are found, and each is added as a separate literal to the body of $\perp$.

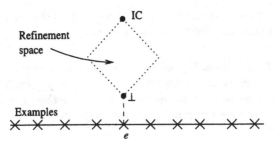

Fig. 4. The refinement space in Progol, bounded from above and below.

satisfies a usage declaration for the predicate over which it is built. Therefore, informally, Progol's refinement operator passes left to right over the literals in the body of $\bot$. For a particular literal l and clause c being refined, the set of refinements of c consists of clauses of the form $c \cup \{l'\}$, where each l' is a copy of l having a different split of the variable bindings in its arguments. In spite of the differences in the refinement operator, Progol's goal condition, evaluation function and pruning conditions are of the form described in section 3.1.

Criticisms of Progol Whilst the use of $\bot$ ensures that each refinement covers at least one positive example, a number of other problems are introduced. We outline two that are of particular interest to us here:

- any constant symbol in a literal in a refinement must be present in the corresponding literal in $\bot$. Thus all constant symbols must be determined from a single positive example.
- if the training sample is noisy, $\bot$ may be constructed from a noisy positive example, possibly adding an unwanted clause to the hypothesis and affecting the remainder of the hypothesis' construction.

4.2 Analysis of Algorithm Complexity

This subsection compares the space complexities of CILS and Progol. The complexity bounds presented are slightly simplified to improve their readability. It will be useful to begin by introducing the concepts of Bell Numbers and *DDBF*-trees.

Bell Numbers and *DDBF*-trees

Definition 13 (Bell Numbers) *The Bell Number $B(m)$ is the number of distinct partitions of m objects. $B(m)$ is defined by the following expression:*

$$B(m) = \begin{cases} 1 & \text{if } m = 0 \\ \sum_{i=0}^{m-1} \binom{m-1}{i} B(i) & \text{otherwise} \end{cases}$$

Bell numbers allow us to determine the cardinality of the set of initial clauses IC, as is demonstrated by the following theorem.

Theorem 14 (The cardinality of IC). *Let p denote a target predicate having at most j positions in its arguments, and let n $(0 \le n \le j)$ denote the number of positions in p that are to contain constant symbols. Furthermore, let T denote a set of n-tuples of possible constant values for the positions in p. The cardinality of IC is given by:*

$$B(j - n).|T|$$

Proof. Consider the $(j - n)$ positions in the arguments of p as a set S, and a variable symbol as a partition of S. Up to variable renaming, there are $B(j - n)$ distinct partitions, by variable symbols, of its $(j - n)$ positions. For each distinct partition there are $|T|$ different n-tuples for the n constants, giving $B(j - n).|T|$ unique literals built over p in IC. □

Recall that the refinement space searched by CILS can be represented as a tree. However, it turns out that the branching factor of this tree varies with its depth since the number of distinct variables in a clause (and hence the number of literals satisfying a usage declaration) increases as more literals are added to that clause. In order to capture this phenomenon, we introduce the concept of a *Depth-Dependent Branching Factor tree* (*DDBF*-tree). Such a tree is shown in figure 5.

Definition 15 (*DDBF*-tree) *A DDBF-tree is a tree whose branching factor at a given node is dependent on the depth of that node.*

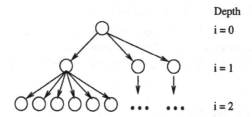

Fig. 5. A *DDBF*-tree with branching factor $3(i + 1)$ at depth i.

For branching factor b_i at depth i, it can be seen that the number of nodes at a given depth n $(n > 0)$ is at most $(b_{n-1})^n$. Hence the total number of nodes in a *DDBF*-tree, up to and including those nodes at depth n, is at most $n.(b_{n-1})^n$.

Space Complexity of CILS CILS' refinement space is a forest of *DDBF*-trees, the cardinality of the forest being precisely the cardinality of the set *IC*. Furthermore the cardinality of CILS' refinement operator when refining a clause of size *s* is the branching factor of the *DDBF*-tree at depth *s*. Therefore the space complexity of CILS is the total number of nodes in each of the *DDBF*-trees. By determining an upper bound on the cardinality of CILS' refinement operator we can determine the space complexity of CILS. The proofs of the following theorem and its corollary are given in appendix A.

Theorem 16 (Complexity of CILS' Refinement Operator). *Let c denote a clause being refined, let* $\text{SZ}(c)$ *denote the size of c and let j denote an upper bound on the number of positions in the arguments of the target predicate and all predicates defined in the background knowledge. Furthermore, let U denote a set of usage declarations and* T^+ *the set of positive examples from training sample T. The cardinality of CILS' refinement operator is upper bounded by:*

$$(\text{SZ}(c).j)^j.\text{B}(j).|T^+|.|U|$$

Corollary 17 (Space Complexity of CILS). *Let s denote a teacher specified restriction on clause size and let j, U and* T^+ *be defined as in theorem 16. The space complexity of CILS is upper bounded by:*

$$(s.j.\text{B}(j).|T^+|.|U|)^{js+1}$$

In the worst case, CILS must search each node in this refinement space. In addition, a subset of the resulting set of candidate clauses must be selected to form the final hypothesis.

Space Complexity of Progol By comparison, we present the following two theorems based on those given by Muggleton [3] for the space complexity of Progol.

Theorem 18 (Space complexity of $\perp$ ([3], theorem 26)). *Let |U| denote the cardinality of the set of usage declarations U, and let r denote an upper bound on the recall associated with these declarations. Furthermore, let i denote a teacher specified upper bound on variable depth in* $\perp$*, and let j denote an upper bound on the number of positions in the arguments of any predicate. The size of* $\perp$ *is upper bounded by:*

$$(r.|U|.j)^{2ij}$$

Theorem 19 (Space complexity of Progol ([3], theorem 39)). *Let s denote a teacher specified restriction on the size of a clause,* $|\perp|$ *denote the size of* $\perp$ *given in theorem 18, and let j denote the upper bound on the number of positions in the arguments of any predicate. The size of the refinement space searched by Progol is upper bounded by:*

$$|\perp|^s.j.s^j$$

Notice that in the worst case, Progol must construct $\perp$ and search the ensuing refinement space once for *each* positive example in the training sample.

Discussion The expression bounding the space complexity of CILS reveals two unfortunate aspects of the algorithm. Firstly, the size of the refinement space grows polynomially in the cardinality of the set of positive examples. This results from the constant selection algorithm used in CILS, which examines each positive example to find constants to include in a refinement. In contrast, Progol uses the recall r of each usage declaration in the construction of $\perp$ to generate r potential tuples of constants. This difference is negligible where the recall is equal to the cardinality of the set of positive examples. Secondly, the refinement space searched by CILS contains some redundancy since a separate tree is searched for each member of IC. Progol avoids this difficulty by using $\perp$ as a lower bound on the refinement space.

Recently, Srinivasan [6] has developed an *induce-max* operator for Progol which constructs and searches a refinement space for *each* positive example in the training sample. A greedy subset-cover algorithm constructs a hypothesis from the clauses found. Although similar to our approach, two important differences remain:

- the problem of constants in $\perp$ as noted in section 4.1, and
- a repeated search of refinement spaces is still performed.

The time required by *induce-max* is the same as that for the worst case of Progol, although notice that one refinement space is *always* constructed for each positive example.

In conclusion, notice that the space complexity of CILS is of a similar order to that of Progol and both are exponential in j and s, and polynomial in $|U|$, $|T^+|$ and r. However, although CILS' refinement space is likely to be larger in general, CILS only constructs one such space. Notice also that the time required by Progol is dependent on the number of refinement spaces constructed and searched. In other words, Progol runs in time proportional to the number of clauses in the hypothesis whilst CILS runs in time independent of this. Hence, CILS is likely to run faster than Progol where the number of clauses in the hypothesis exceeds the proportion by which CILS' refinement space is larger than Progol's.

4.3 Empirical Comparison

The Dataset CILS and Progol were compared using a reduced mutagenesis dataset, made available in the Progol4.1 distribution [1]. The goal of learning is to identify the properties of a compound that make it active as a mutagen [7]. The target predicate is `active/1`, with background knowledge consisting of around 13,000 clauses, the majority of which are atomic. A noisy training sample of 101 positive and 60 negative examples is presented to each learner by the teacher. Until now we have assumed training samples to be free from noise, and so we pause to explain how each algorithm is extended to handle noisy examples.

Handling Noise Progol, unlike CILS, was originally designed to handle noisy data. In Progol, the completeness requirement for clauses is relaxed, with a clause being required to cover no more than a teacher specified positive integer of negative examples. This setting is known as the *noise parameter*. A similar noise parameter was introduced to CILS, allowing a clause to be added to the set of candidate clauses if it covers no more than the specified number of negative examples.

Experimental Procedure and Results A 10-fold cross-validation test was carried out on the data using a variety of settings for the noise and size parameters. The algorithms were compared by considering:

- the average time taken to construct the 10 hypotheses at a particular noise setting. Note that these runtimes are for an SGI Indy workstation. Additionally, note that Progol is written in C whilst CILS is written in Sicstus Prolog (version 3.0).
- the average quality of the 10 hypotheses at a particular noise setting. Quality is measured in terms of the average number of clauses in the 10 hypotheses, together with their average accuracy in predicting the seen negative, and the unseen positive and negative examples.

The results of the experiments with the size parameter set to 2 are tabulated in table 1. Each line represents the average performance of the 10 hypotheses produced at each given level of noise.

Discussion Most significant is the markedly different effects of the noise parameter on the hypotheses produced. Higher levels of noise allow CILS to construct smaller, more general hypotheses covering more positive and negative examples than those of Progol. This behaviour stems from the greedy approach to hypothesis construction used by Progol, in which a number of refinement spaces are searched, each with respect to progressively fewer positive examples. Since clauses found in these latter spaces have fewer positive examples to cover, they must also cover fewer negative examples if they are to satisfy Progol's goal condition. In contrast, the cautious search of a *single* refinement space in CILS allows all clauses to make equal use of the relaxed consistency condition.

Two important differences are apparent in the time taken to construct hypotheses by the two systems. Firstly, CILS' runtime was independent of the setting of the noise parameter whilst Progol's runtime increased as the level of noise decreased. This behaviour was anticipated from the complexity analysis of the previous subsection since the size of the hypothesis is inversely related to the noise setting. Secondly, despite its implementation in Prolog, CILS was significantly faster than Progol at all levels of noise. This results from the refinement spaces searched by CILS and Progol being of a similar size whilst the hypothesis contains a large number of clauses.

			Progol			
			Seen		Unseen	
Noise	Secs	Size	NC(%)	PC(%)	NC(%)	TC(%)
15	169.0	34.4	90.0	61.4	81.7	68.9
10	194.0	37.2	93.0	55.4	80.0	64.6
5	368.8	48.3	98.5	49.5	88.3	64.0
2	406.9	51.5	100.0	49.5	91.7	65.2
1	406.9	51.5	100.0	49.5	91.7	65.2
0	406.9	51.5	100.0	49.5	91.7	65.2

			CILS			
			Seen		Unseen	
Noise	Secs	Size	NC(%)	PC(%)	NC(%)	TC(%)
15	63.5	19.1	59.8	75.2	51.7	66.5
10	58.1	36.6	89.3	58.4	81.7	67.1
5	57.1	37.0	90.1	55.4	85.0	66.5
2	57.1	47.0	95.4	49.5	85.0	62.7
1	57.4	49.1	97.2	49.5	88.3	64.0
0	57.5	51.5	100.0	47.5	93.3	64.6

Table 1. Empirical Comparison of CILS against Progol.

(Notes: Seen and Unseen refer to the examples that were used to construct and test the 10 hypotheses respectively, and Size refers to the average number of *clauses* in these hypotheses. PC, NC and TC indicate the average number of positive, negative and total examples correctly labelled by the 10 hypotheses.)

5 Conclusions

The encouraging comparison of CILS against Progol has demonstrated the potential of cautious induction. In particular this analysis has highlighted its applicability to problems involving:

- noisy datasets, since the search by refinement is not centred on a single, possibly noisy, positive example, and
- large, complex hypotheses, since CILS runs in time independent of the number of clauses in a hypothesis.

We propose to continue this work in several directions. Firstly, we are currently investigating ways in which the redundancy in the refinement operator can be removed. This may be possible through the use of different forms of syntactic bias. Also, we are interested in altering the constant selection algorithm to allow the algorithm's time and space complexity to become independent of the cardinality of the training sample. This is likely to involve statistical sampling of positive examples from which to find the possible constants. Finally, further analysis and experimentation on a wider range of datasets should provide a clearer insight into the benefits of cautious induction over conventional greedy approaches.

References

1. S. Muggleton. Progol 4.1 distribution, release notes and example sets.
2. S. Muggleton. Inductive logic programming. *New Generation Computing*, 8:295–318, 1991.
3. S. Muggleton. Inverse entailment and Progol. *New Generation Computing*, 13:245–286, 1995.
4. S. Muggleton and L. De Raedt. Inductive logic programming – theory and methods. *Journal of Logic Programming*, 19-20:629–679, 1994.
5. J. R. Quinlan. Learning logical definitions from relations. *Machine Learning*, 5:239–266, 1990.
6. A. Srinivasan. P-Progol 2.1 distribution, release notes and example sets.
7. A. Srinivasan, S. Muggleton, M. J. E. Sternberg, and R. D. King. Theories for mutagenicity: A study in first-order and feature-based induction. Technical Report PRG-TR-8-95, Oxford University Computing Laboratory, 1995.

Acknowledgements

We thank David Page and Alistair Willis for their comments and suggestions concerning this work. The first author is funded by an EPSRC studentship, and by a travel award from Data Connection Ltd.

A Proofs of theorem 16 and corollary 17

Proof (Theorem 16). Each of the $sz(c)$ literals in c contains at most j distinct variables and so there are at most $sz(c).j$ variables in c. Each new literal (constructed from a particular usage declaration in U) to be added to c will require at most j existing variables. There are $\binom{sz(c).j}{j}$ ways of choosing j variables from those already in c which is upper bounded by $(sz(c).j)^j$. The new literal will also require at most j new variables and at most j constant symbols. Since there are $|T^+|$ different tuples of constant symbols, there are at most $B(j).|T^+|$ combinations of constants and new variable symbols, from theorem 14. Therefore there are $(sz(c).j)^j.B(j).|T^+|$ literals that satisfy each of $|U|$ usage declarations, giving an upper bound on the cardinality of CILS' refinement operator of:

$$(sz(c).j)^j.B(j).|T^+|.|U|$$

□

Proof (Corollary 17). From the expression for the total number of nodes in a *DDBF*-tree and the result of theorem 16, the space complexity of CILS is upper bounded by:

$$(B(j).|T^+|).s(((s-1).j)^j.B(j).|T^+|.|U|)^s$$

which, when simplified, gives an upper bound on CILS' space complexity of:

$$(s.j.B(j).|T^+|.|U|)^{js+1}$$

$\square$

Generating Numerical Literals During Refinement

Simon Anthony and Alan M. Frisch

Department of Computer Science, University of York, York. YO1 5DD. UK.
Email: {simona, frisch}@cs.york.ac.uk

Abstract. Despite the rapid emergence and success of Inductive Logic Programming, problems still surround number handling—problems directly inherited from the choice of logic programs as the representation language. Our conjecture is that a generalisation of the representation language to Constraint Logic Programs provides an effective solution to this problem. We support this claim with the presentation of an algorithm called NUM, to which a top-down refinement operator can delegate the task of finding numerical literals. NUM can handle equations, in-equations and dis-equations in a uniform way, and, furthermore, provides more generality than competing approaches since numerical literals are not required to cover all the positive examples available.

1 Introduction

Many of the concepts that we might wish to learn involve numbers. However, within the Inductive Logic Programming (ILP) paradigm [6], such numerical reasoning is poorly handled—a problem inherited from the choice of logic programs as the representation language.

Several other researchers have addressed this problem. Within the representation language of conventional logic programs, Muggleton and Page [5] examined the use of higher-order logic within Progol, allowing equations to appear as arguments to higher-order predicates. More recently Srinivasan [8] has built-into Progol a form of lazy evaluation allowing constants in literals to be left unevaluated until refinement. In a positive only learning setting, Karalič's FORS system [3] constructs hypotheses by fitting low error regression lines through disjoint subsets of the training sample. Sebag and Rouveirol [7] have considered extending the representation language to Constraint Logic Programs (CLPs), and examine the generation of constraints to discriminate between features of a single positive and several negative examples. A more detailed examination of several of these existing approaches is provided in Section 4.

This paper addresses the problem within a *top-down* (or *refinement-based*) setting, and advocates the generalisation of the representation language to that of CLP. An algorithm called NUM is presented which generates literals that are built over numerical predicates for addition to clauses. NUM therefore interacts with a refinement operator in the following way. The refinement operator continues to generate literals built over non-numerical predicates as before. However, if a literal is to be built over a numerical predicate, this task is delegated to NUM. NUM returns a set of literals built over this numerical predicate which the refinement operator can use to produce refinements. By design, this interaction should be possible with most existing refinement operators in top-down ILP systems.

The rest of this paper is organised as follows: Section 2 provides an introduction to CLP, and defines the learning setting used throughout the paper. NUM is presented, by example, in Section 3, with Section 4 comparing our approach to existing work on number handling in ILP. We conclude in Section 5, and discuss further extensions and applications of this approach.

2 Background

2.1 The CLP Scheme

The CLP scheme [1] extends conventional logic programming by introducing a set Σ (a *signature*) of *interpreted* predicate and function symbols, whose interpretation is fixed by an associated *Σ-structure $\mathcal{D}$*. $\mathcal{D}$ consists of a set D, known as the computation domain, and an assignment of relations and functions on D to the symbols in Σ which respects the arities of these symbols. Somewhat improperly, we shall consistently refer to uninterpreted predicate symbols as *predicate symbols*, and interpreted predicate symbols as *constraint symbols*.

It will be useful to introduce the following notation and terminology. The existential closure of a logical formula ϕ shall be denoted $\bar{\exists}\phi$ and the universal closure of ϕ shall be denoted $\bar{\forall}\phi$. A *$\mathcal{D}$-model* of a formula is a model of the formula with the same domain as $\mathcal{D}$ and the same interpretation for the symbols in Σ as $\mathcal{D}$. Thus, for formulas μ and ϕ, we write $\mu \models_{\mathcal{D}} \phi$ to denote that ϕ is true in all $\mathcal{D}$-models of μ. The set of definable, uninterpreted predicate symbols shall be denoted Π. An *ordinary atom* has the form $p(t_1, ..., t_j)$, where the $t_1, ..., t_j$ are terms and $p \in \Pi$. Likewise, a *constrained atom* has the form $p(t_1, ..., t_j)$, where the $t_1, ..., t_j$ are terms and $p \in \Sigma$. An *atom* is either an ordinary atom or a constrained atom and a *literal* is an atom or a negated atom. A *CLP-program* is a set of *constrained clauses* of the form $h \leftarrow b_1, ..., b_n$, where h is an ordinary atom and the $b_1, ..., b_n$ are atoms.

The pair $\langle \Sigma, \mathcal{D} \rangle$ is known as a *constraint object* and a constraint symbol is said to *belong* to any constraint object in which it appears in the signature Σ. A constraint object $\mathcal{X}$ represents a particular instance of the CLP scheme, denoted CLP($\mathcal{X}$), and defines a CLP language. In order to implement a CLP language a constraint solver is required that is capable of solving conjunctions of constraints built over the constraint symbols in Σ. For instance, Jaffar et al. have developed and implemented the object $\Re$ in the language CLP($\Re$) [2], which allows constraints over a computation domain of real numbers. This language, and other similar languages which handle numbers, contain a constraint solver capable of solving sets of linear equations.

This paper often refers to a conjunction of constraints, known as a *constraint store*. A constraint store C is said to be *satisfiable* if there exists an assignment of elements of D to the variables in C such that C evaluates to *true*. This assignment is known as a *solution* of the constraint store. A solution of a constraint c *with respect to* a constraint store C is a solution of the conjunction $c \wedge C$. We shall assume the existence of a decision procedure capable of deciding whether a constraint store is satisfiable.

2.2 The Learning Setting

This paper assumes the following learning setting. The teacher selects a *target concept* and provides the learner with a finite, nonempty *training sample* of *examples*, each of which is correctly labelled as either *positive* or *negative*. From this training sample and any available background knowledge, the learner constructs a hypothesis of the concept. Since this paper uses the representation language of $\mathrm{CLP}(\mathcal{X})$, where $\mathcal{X}$ is a constraint object, examples are ordinary atoms built over a *target predicate* and the background knowledge is a finite set of constrained clauses[1]. A hypothesis is a finite set of nonrecursive constrained clauses whose heads are ordinary atoms built over the target predicate and whose bodies consist of literals built over either predicate symbols defined in the background knowledge or constraint symbols belonging to $\mathcal{X}$. It will be useful to introduce the following relationship between a hypothesis and an example, known as *coverage*.

Definition 1 (Coverage) *Let B denote background knowledge, T a training sample, c a constrained clause and $\mathcal{D}$ a Σ-structure. An example $e \in T$ is said to be* covered *by c, with respect to B and $\mathcal{D}$, if $B \cup \{c\} \models_{\mathcal{D}} e$, and* uncovered *otherwise. Example e is said to be* covered *by hypothesis H, with respect to B and $\mathcal{D}$, if H contains at least one clause which covers e, and* uncovered *otherwise.*

In this setting, a hypothesis H must satisfy the following two conditions with respect to the background knowledge and a training sample T:

- *Completeness*: H must cover *every* positive example in T, and
- *Consistency*: H must leave *every* negative example in T uncovered.

A hypothesis satisfying these conditions is said to *explain*, or to be *correct* with respect to that training sample. Additionally, we shall require that each clause within such a hypothesis must cover at least one positive example (to avoid redundancy).

2.3 Top-down Learning

Search by refinement (top-down search) considers more general clauses before more specific clauses. To allow us to talk precisely about the generality and specificity of a clause, we introduce a generality ordering over clauses, known as *subsumption*.

---

[1] Throughout this paper we use the word clause to mean a *definite* clause.

Definition 2 (Subsumption) *Let $c = h \leftarrow C, B$ and $c' = h' \leftarrow C', B'$ be two constrained clauses where B and B' are sets of atoms, and C and C' are conjunctions of constraints. Furthermore, let $\mathcal{D}$ denote a Σ-structure. Clause c subsumes clause c' with respect to $\mathcal{D}$ iff there exists a substitution θ such that $(\{h\} \cup B)\theta \subseteq \{h'\} \cup B'$ and $\models_{\mathcal{D}} \bar{\forall}(C' \rightarrow C\theta)$. We say that c is more general than c', and, conversely, that c' is more specific than c.*

Therefore, and informally, search by refinement begins with some *most general clause* from which a *refinement operator* is used to generate a set of *incremental specialisations* or *refinements*. An incremental specialisation of a clause c is typically defined to be the addition to the body of c of a literal built over a predicate symbol defined in the background knowledge or a constraint belonging to the constraint object $\mathcal{X}$. Each such predicate symbol or constraint symbol is accompanied by a nonempty, finite set of *usage declarations* that restrict the forms of literals that may be added to a clause.

Definition 3 (Usage Declaration) *Let p denote a predicate symbol defined in the background knowledge B or a constraint symbol belonging to the constraint object $\mathcal{X}$. A usage declaration for p is a meta-predicate usage/1 whose single argument is an atom or constraint, built over p, each argument of which contains a usage term. A usage term is a term in which each variable symbol has been replaced with one of the following two mode declarations:*

- Positive *(denoted $+$) – indicating that this position must contain a variable symbol already present in the clause,*
- Negative *(denoted $-$) – indicating that this position may contain any variable symbol,*

and each constant symbol either appears in the usage term, or has been replaced by the mode declaration Hash *(denoted $\#$), indicating that this position must contain a constant symbol. Each of these mode declarations is accompanied by a type declaration[2]. The mode and type declaration for a particular symbol are collectively known as a* symbol declaration. *An* instance *of a usage declaration is a copy of the atom or constraint in its argument, with each symbol declaration replaced by an appropriate variable or constant symbol.*

For instance, the usage declaration for the predicate **add/2**, which returns in its third argument the sum of the first two arguments, might be:

$$usage(add(+int, +int, -int))$$

Definition 4 (Refinement Operator) *Let c denote a constrained clause, U a set of usage declarations, and* ALL$(B, \mathcal{X})$ *the set of all predicate symbols defined in the background knowledge B and constraint symbols belonging to the constraint object $\mathcal{X}$. For some $p \in$* ALL$(B, \mathcal{X})$, *let* LIT$_U(c, p)$ *denote the set of literals built*

---

[2] A variable symbol takes the type of the first argument of the first literal in which it appears in a left to right reading of a clause.

over p that are instances of U with respect to c. A refinement operator ρ is a function from a single clause to a set of clauses, where each member of the set contains an additional body literal:

$$\rho(c) = \{c \vee \neg l \mid l \in \text{LIT}_U(c, p) \text{ and } p \in \text{ALL}(B, \mathcal{X})\}$$

Let mgc be some most general clause. The set of clauses generated by the repeated application of ρ to mgc and its subsequent refinements is known as a refinement space.

3 Generating Numerical Literals with NUM

We shall use the representation language of CLP($\Re$), and define a *numerical literal* to be a literal built over a constraint symbol belonging to the object $\Re$. For the remainder of this paper we shall restrict our attention to the following three forms of numerical literals:

- *Equations* – built over the $=/2$ constraint symbol,
- *In-equations* – built over one of the $</2$, $\leq/2$, $>/2$, $\geq/2$ constraint symbols, and
- *Dis-equations* – built over the $\neq/2$ constraint symbol.

Where no ambiguity can arise, we say that a numerical literal *covers* an example if its addition to the clause being refined produces a clause which covers this example. Finally, we shall assume the existence of a constraint solver capable of solving conjunctions of linear equations, or simplifying conjunctions of linear in-equations and dis-equations.

The principal difficulty in generating numerical literals in hypotheses is determining the values of any constant symbols that are to appear. To avoid committing to a particular constant too early, we place a variable in each hash mode position when instantiating a usage declaration for a numerical literal. We shall refer to the variables occupying hash mode positions as *c-variables* and to literals containing c-variables as *literal schemas* (since the assignment of a value to each c-variable produces a distinct numerical literal). Therefore literal schemas are members of a *meta-language*, also represented in CLP($\Re$), since they describe at least one numerical literal.

To ensure each literal schema covers as many positive and as few negative examples as possible, we impose constraints on the c-variables, and store these constraints in a constraint store. This is known as the *constraining* of a literal schema. Once all the examples have been examined, one solution is found for each literal schema, producing a set of numerical literals. This solution is arbitrary since all solutions of a literal schema will cover the same set of examples. Literal schemas themselves cannot appear in a hypothesis clause since they violate the usage declarations. To illustrate the above discussion, consider the following usage declaration for a linear equation:

$$usage((+real) = (\#real) \times (+real) + (\#real))$$

Literal schemas that are instances of this declaration will initially have a c-variable in place of each of the two hash mode symbol declarations. Thus, when refining a clause $(t(X,Y) \leftarrow)$, the literal schema $Y = C_1 \times X + C_2$ (where C_1 and C_2 denote the two c-variables), amongst others, will be an instance of this declaration. We then constrain this literal schema to cover as many positives and as few negatives as possible. Thus, for instance, if the literal schema above is required to cover the positive example $t(1,2)$, the constraint $2 = C_1 \times 1 + C_2$ is added to the constraint store. Notice that all solutions of this schema, with respect to the constraint store, will now cover $t(1,2)$.

In order to allow the constraining of a literal schema to be handled by our constraint solver, restrictions are imposed over the form that a numerical literal (specified in a usage declaration) may take. Each position in an argument of a numerical literal is required to be a *summation* of usage terms, each of which is of the form $\#real \times t$ or t, where t is any usage term involving only interpreted functions, positive mode symbol declarations and specific constant values. For instance, the following are admissible usage declarations[3]:

$$usage((\#real) \times (+real) \leq (\#real) \times pow((+real), 2))$$
$$usage((+real) \neq (\#real) \times pow((+real), 2) + (+real))$$

For the sake of simplicity, the examples considered in this report are all two dimensional. For consistency, the target predicate of each problem shall be $t/2$, and the most general clause shall be written $(t(X,Y) \leftarrow)$, where X and Y are both of type *real*. As such, a training sample consists of pairs of cartesian coordinates and no background knowledge is provided. In general however, examples may be non-ground atoms describing lines or planes in the cartesian space. Furthermore, NUM can be effectively applied to the refinement of any clause by any refinement operator of the form described by Definition 4.

3.1 Finding Equations

Consider the problem of identifying a linear relationship in the following training sample.

Training Sample: A		Usage Declarations
$t(-2,-2)$	$\neg t(-1,1)$	
$t(-1,6)$	$\neg t(-1,-2)$	
$t(2,0)$	$\neg t(2,4)$	$usage((+real) = (\#real) \times (+real) + (\#real))$
$t(3,-2)$	$\neg t(3,0)$	
$t(4,1)$	$\neg t(4,-1)$	

In refining the clause $(t(X,Y) \leftarrow)$, one of the instances of the usage declaration for $=/2$ will be the literal schema: $Y = C_1 \times X + C_2$. Notice that constraining this literal schema with two positive examples produces two constraints in the

---

[3] pow/2 denotes an interpreted function returning the value of the first argument raised to the power of the second.

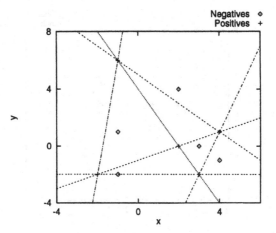

Fig. 1. The possible linear equations from training sample: A.

form of linear equations. The constraint solver can then solve these two equations, which uniquely determines the values of the *c*-variables and produces a numerical literal. Therefore, by drawing subsets of cardinality 2 from the positive examples, all possible linear equations between the positives can be found, and each of these is returned as a numerical literal to the refinement operator. In the general case, for any literal schema containing n *c*-variables, subsets of cardinality n must be drawn from the positive examples. These subsets are known as *generating subsets*. From our example above, the generating subsets produce the equations shown in Figure 1.

Each of these equations is returned, as a numerical literal, to the refinement operator, and refinement continues in the normal way. Therefore, we can expect a learner to produce a complete and consistent hypothesis such as the following:

$$t(X,Y) \leftarrow Y = 0.5 \times X - 1$$
$$t(X,Y) \leftarrow Y = -2 \times X + 4$$

This approach can also be used to find nonlinear relationships. Consider the following training sample and usage declaration[4] from which to find a cubic relationship between the positive examples:

Training Sample: B		Usage Declarations
$t(-2,-5)$	$\neg t(1,-1)$	
$t(-1,1)$	$\neg t(-1,-1)$	$usage((+real)) = pow((+real),3)$
$t(0,1)$	$\neg t(-2,3)$	$-(+real) + (\#real))$
$t(1,1)$	$\neg t(1,3)$	
$t(2,7)$	$\neg t(2,2)$	

---

[4] Notice that we have used the usage declarations to restrict the form of the equation, again to ease our presentation. The same hypothesis can be found if an arbitrary cubic equation is specified.

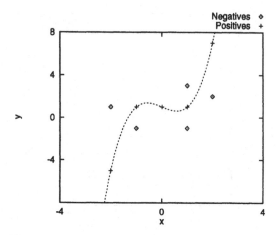

Fig. 2. Finding a nonlinear relationship from training sample: B.

The usage declaration has only one hash mode position and hence singleton generating subsets are drawn from the set of positive examples. However, since each positive example lies on the same line, each numerical literal produced is identical, allowing a learner to produce the following complete and consistent hypothesis, depicted in Figure 2.

$$t(X, Y) \leftarrow Y = pow(X, 3) - X + 1$$

3.2 Finding In-Equations and Dis-Equations

When moving from equations to in-equations and dis-equations, the values of the c-variables cannot be uniquely determined from the generating subset. As such, the constraints on each of the c-variables are initially tightened using the negative examples, attempting to prevent the literal schema from covering them. Then the positive examples that are absent from the generating subset are used to further tighten these constraints, attempting to ensure that the literal schema covers as many other positives as possible. The negatives are used first since each hypothesis clause must eventually be consistent but not necessarily complete.

Again, we shall use a worked example to illustrate the operation of the algorithm. Consider the following problem of generating in-equations to enclose a region of the cartesian space containing the positive examples from the following training sample.

Training Sample: C		Usage Declarations
$t(-1,3)$	$\neg t(-1,4)$	
$t(1, 4.5)$	$\neg t(-1, 2)$	
$t(0, 3.5)$	$\neg t(1, 2)$	$usage((+real) \leq (\#real) \times (+real) + (\#real))$
$t(0.5, 2.5)$	$\neg t(1, 6)$	$usage((+real) \geq pow((+real), 2) + (\#real))$
$t(2, 6)$	$\neg t(2, 4)$	

The usage declarations allow the learner to attempt to bound the region from above using linear in-equations, and from below using quadratic in-equations. Let us consider the constraining of the following instance of the linear in-equation usage declaration:

$$Y \leq C_1 \times X + C_2$$

This literal schema contains two c-variables indicating that pairs of positive examples are to be drawn from the training sample. Let us assume that the pair $\{t(-1,3), t(0, 3.5)\}$ is initially selected. Substituting these examples into this literal schema adds the following constraints to the constraint store.

$$3 \leq C_1 \times (-1) + C_2 \quad \text{and} \quad 3.5 \leq C_1 \times 0 + C_2$$

For each of the negative examples, we substitute the values for X and Y into the *inversion* of the literal schema. The inversion of a literal schema is simply a copy of the schema with the constraint symbol replaced by its inverse. Importantly, this copy involves no renaming of variables. In our example, the inversion of the above literal schema is:

$$Y > C_1 \times X + C_2$$

The constraint resulting from the substitution of a negative example into this literal schema is added to the constraint store *only if* the resulting store is satisfiable. If the constraint cannot be added the resulting numerical literal will cover this negative example. The following table projects the constraints on $C1$ and $C2$ from the constraints in the constraint store, and demonstrates how each is tightened as the negative examples are considered.

Negative	Constraint	Satisfiable	C_1	C_2
$t(-1, 4)$	$4 > C_1 \times (-1) + C_2$	yes	–	$3.75 \leq C_2$
$t(-1, 2)$	$2 > C_1 \times (-1) + C_2$	no	–	$3.75 \leq C_2$
$t(1, 2)$	$2 > C_1 \times 1 + C_2$	no	–	$3.75 \leq C_2$
$t(1, 6)$	$6 > C_1 \times 1 + C_2$	yes	$0.25 \leq C_1$	$3.75 \leq C_2$
$t(2, 4)$	$4 > C_1 \times 2 + C_2$	no	$0.25 \leq C_1$	$3.75 \leq C_2$

Notice that so far the c-variables are both lower bounded, and that the resulting numerical literal will cover three negative examples. The algorithm then considers each of the remaining positive examples in turn, and substitutes each into the literal schema to produce a constraint. These constraints are again added to the constraint store only if the resulting store is satisfiable. If a constraint cannot be added the corresponding positive example will be left uncovered by the resulting numerical literal. The effects of these constraints on C_1 and C_2 are shown in the following table.

Positive	Constraint	Satisfiable	C_1	C_2
$t(1, 4.5)$	$4.5 \leq C_1 \times 1 + C_2$	yes	$0.25 \leq C_1 < 1.5$	$3.75 \leq C_2 < 5$
$t(0.5, 2.5)$	$2.5 \leq C_1 \times 0.5 + C_2$	yes	$0.25 \leq C_1 < 1.5$	$3.75 \leq C_2 < 5$
$t(2, 6)$	$6 \leq C_1 \times 2 + C_2$	yes	$0.\dot{6} \leq C_1 < 1.5$	$4 \leq C_2 < 5$

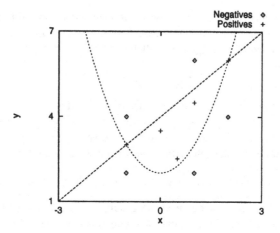

Fig. 3. Hypothesis enclosing the region containing the positives in training sample: C.

Therefore from the choice of the pair $\{t(-1,3), t(0,3.5)\}$, the algorithm produces the literal schema:

$$Y \leq C_1 \times X + C_2 \text{ where } \begin{array}{l} 0.\dot{6} \leq C_1 < 1.5 \\ 4 \leq C_2 < 5 \end{array}$$

Other possible literal schemas are found by examining the other possible generating subsets. One solution of each of these schemas, together with those found for other instances of the linear in-equation usage declaration make up the set of literals returned to the refinement operator. NUM can then be called again to carry out the same process for each instance of the usage declaration for the quadratic in-equation. In particular, this results in the discovery of the following literal schema:

$$Y \geq pow(X, 2) + C_3 \text{ where } 1 \leq C_3 < 2$$

Solutions of this schema cover all the positive examples and the two negatives left uncovered by the linear in-equation schema found above. Since none of the literal schemas introduce new variables, a learning system can be expected to find a complete and consistent hypothesis similar to the one shown below and in Figure 3.

$$t(X, Y) \leftarrow Y \geq pow(X, 2) + 2, Y \leq 1 \times X + 4$$

3.3 Inexact Equations and Approximation Constraints

As described thus far, NUM handles perfect data and finds exact relationships between the positive examples. In order to allow inexact relationships to be found, we introduce the *approximation constraint*.

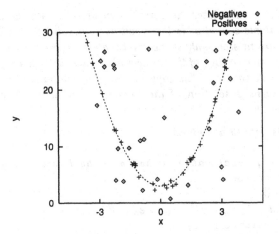

Fig. 4. A training sample for an approximate quadratic equation.

Definition 5 (Approximation Constraint) *The approximation constraint, denoted $\simeq/2$, is defined as an equation which holds, for some X, Y and error term ϵ, if $Y \pm \epsilon = X$. Thus numerical literals built over $\simeq/2$ can be solved, for some teacher specified value ϵ, as:*

$$Y \simeq X \quad \Leftrightarrow \quad (Y - \epsilon \leq X) \wedge (Y + \epsilon \geq X)$$

Consider, for example, finding an inexact quadratic relationship between a set of positive examples. A training sample of 30 positive and 30 negative examples was generated from the following approximate constraint with error $\epsilon = 1$.

$$Y \simeq 2 \times pow(X, 2) + 3$$

This training sample together with the corresponding inexact quadratic equation is shown in Figure 4. From a suitable usage declaration, the following literal schema can be found:

$$Y \simeq C_1 \times pow(X, 2) + C_2 \text{ where } \begin{array}{l} 1.927 \leq C_1 < 2.039 \\ 2.756 \leq C_2 < 3.149 \end{array}$$

3.4 The NUM algorithm

We conclude this section with a more formal presentation of the algorithm and an analysis of its complexity.

Algorithm 6 (The NUM algorithm) *Let u denote a usage declaration for a numerical literal having n hash-mode symbol declarations and let T^+ denote the set of positive and T^- the set of negative examples from a training sample T. Furthermore, let Lits denote a set of literal schemas, and let CONSTRAIN, INVERSE and SOLVE denote the following three functions:*

- CONSTRAIN(l, e) *substitutes the variables in literal l with the corresponding values in example e, and adds the resulting constraint on the c-variables in l to the constraint store only if the resulting constraint store is satisfiable.*
- INVERSE(l) *returns a copy of the numerical literal l, with its constraint symbol replaced with its inverse. This copy involves no renaming of variables.*
- SOLVE(l) *returns a solution of the numerical literal l with respect to the constraint store.*

The algorithm is defined as follows:

```
input a usage declaration u having n hash mode symbol
       declarations
let Lits = ∅
let GenSet = {{e₁, ..., eₙ} | e₁, ..., eₙ ∈ T⁺}
for each instance lit of u
    for each S ∈ GenSet
        let lit' be a copy of lit with all variables renamed
        for each e⁺ ∈ S
            CONSTRAIN(lit', e⁺)
        end for
        let inv = INVERSE(lit')
        for each e⁻ ∈ T⁻
            CONSTRAIN(inv, e⁻)
        end for
        for each e⁺ ∈ (T⁺ − S)
            CONSTRAIN(lit', e⁺)
        end for
        let Lits = Lits ∪ {SOLVE(lit')}
    end for
end for
return Lits
```

Notice that in the case of equations, unique values are found for the c-variables from the generating subset. Such equations can therefore be found by this algorithm within a positive only learning framework. Notice also that this algorithm can be used to find the set of examples covered by the clause being refined following the addition of a numerical literal to its body.

Theorem 7 (Complexity of NUM). *Let u denote the usage declaration for a numerical literal, $|u|$ the number of instances of u, and n the number of hash mode symbol declarations in u. Furthermore, let T^+ denote the number of positive examples in the training sample T. The complexity of the algorithm is upper bounded by:*

$$|u|.|T^+|^n.|T|$$

Proof. Recall that examples are *atomic*, as defined in Section 2.2. Therefore, there are $\binom{|T^+|}{n}$ ways of choosing subsets of cardinality n from a set T^+, which is upper bounded by $|T^+|^n$. Multiplying this by the number of instances of u and the cardinality of the training sample gives the above result and completes the proof. $\Box$

Notice that the complexity of NUM increases polynomially with the size of the training sample. From this observation we are currently investigating if we can predict the number of generating subsets needed to be confident of finding all the required numerical literals from a single usage declaration. Notice also that one generating subset is required for each occurrence of a numerical literal in a hypothesis. Therefore, if the hypothesis contains m numerical literals, each having at most n hash-mode positions in their corresponding usage declarations, then the training sample must contain at least $m \times n$ positive examples in order to find this hypothesis.

4 Comparison to Other Work

Some of the main approaches to number handling in ILP are compared to our approach with respective advantages and differences highlighted.

4.1 Higher-Order Predicates in Progol

Progol [4] is an ILP system which finds hypothesis clauses by searching a refinement space which is bounded from below by a *most specific clause* $\perp$, constructed from a single positive example[5]. Since all clauses in the refinement space must subsume $\perp$, the body of each clause must consist of some subset of the literals in the body of $\perp$. Accordingly, any constant symbols appearing in a literal in a hypothesis clause must be present in the corresponding literal in $\perp$, and hence derived from a single positive example.

Muggleton and Page [5] consider the use of higher-order logic to allow numerical reasoning in Progol. A higher-order predicate, for instance num/1, is defined in the background knowledge with one clause for each possible form of equation. In their work, the authors restrict themselves to the following four forms of equation:

$$Y = C_1 \times X + C_2 \qquad Y = C_1 \times pow(X, C_2)$$
$$Y = pow(C_1, X) \qquad C_1 = pow(X, 2) + pow(Y, 2)$$

The clauses defining num/1 must guess the constant values for these equations from the single positive example used to construct $\perp$. For instance, consider the following clause, similar to that provided by Muggleton and Page, for linear equations:

```
num(Y = M * X + C) :- not(Y==X), M1 is Y / X,
          round(M1, M), C1 is Y - M * X, round(C1, C).
```

---

[5] In fact, Progol views the training sample as a *sequence*, and $\perp$ is constructed from the first example in this sequence.

Clearly, in the general case, this clause is unlikely to find the equation of a line relating a number of positive examples. However, this rather obvious shortcoming is not immediately apparent in the examples presented by Muggleton and Page since:

1. the restricted forms of equations considered by the authors only contain a small number of constants, and
2. the training samples are ordered to ensure that the first positive example would yield suitable values, when rounded, for the constants in the desired equation.

For instance, given this definition of num/1, Progol will be unable to find the simple linear equation $(t(X, Y) \leftarrow Y = 3 \times X + 4)$ from the following positive examples regardless of the order in which they are presented.

$$t(-2, -2) \quad t(-1, 1) \quad t(0, 4) \quad t(1, 7) \quad t(2, 10)$$

Furthermore, this approach cannot handle in-equations and dis-equations since there is no clear way of determining the values of constants, other than by random selection. It is also incapable of handling more general forms of equations, particularly those involving more constants.

4.2 Lazy Evaluation in Progol

In order to overcome Progol's commitment to constants in $\perp$, Srinivasan and Camacho [8] have recently developed what they term *lazy evaluation* of literals. Background knowledge predicate symbols to be lazily evaluated are added as literals to the body of $\perp$ with Skolem constants occupying any positions in which a constant symbol is to appear. These literals shall be called *lazy literals*. During refinement, a lazy literal from $\perp$ is added to a clause only if:

1. constants can be found to replace the Skolem constants (for instance linear and nonlinear regression techniques can be used to find constants for equations), and
2. the resulting clause is both *consistent* and *complete*.

The completeness requirement in the second of these two points highlights a problem with this approach. It is assumed that sufficient non-lazy predicate symbols are available to discriminate positive examples not related by the same lazy literal. Thus, only one lazy literal may appear in any clause. For instance, consider the problem of finding a hypothesis to explain the training sample shown in Figure 5, where the body of $\perp$ contains only the single lazy literal:

$$Y = sk_1 \times X + sk_2$$

The completeness requirement necessitates fitting a line through all the positive examples, producing a very poor fit. For this relationship to be captured more accurately by Srinivasan and Camacho, the background knowledge must contain sufficient non-lazy predicate symbols to identify a feature common to one set of related positive examples and absent from the other.

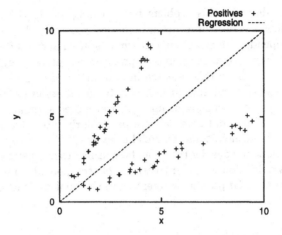

Fig. 5. Fitting a regression line through a set of positive examples.

4.3 Disjunctive Version Spaces

Sebag and Rouveirol [7] have also examined the possibility of using CLP to improve number handling in ILP. They attempt to reformulate the search of the refinement space as a Constraint Satisfaction Problem (CSP), and thus delegate the complexity of this search to existing constraint solvers. In particular, their work focuses on the problem of generalising a single positive example against a number of negative examples. These examples are represented as clauses, with no background knowledge.

A hypothesis (a single clause) must *subsume* the positive example e^+ (since it is a clause) and none of the negatives. This discrimination is achieved by adding to the body of the hypothesis at most one of the following, for each negative example e^-:

1. a literal present in the body of e^+ but not e^-, or
2. a numerical literal containing variables already present in the hypothesis clause.

The latter of these is of interest to us here. Sebag and Rouveirol restrict a numerical literal to be a simple equation or in-equation of the form: $X < c$ or $X - Y < c$ (for some constant c). These forms are built-in, and in contrast to our approach and those involving Progol above, no mechanism exists for the teacher to specify particular forms of numerical literals. As a result, neither nonlinear relationships, nor relationships in more than two dimensions can be found.

5 Conclusions

A continuing problem within ILP has been the poor handling of numbers offered by ILP systems. Using the improved number handling capabilities of the CLP scheme we have addressed this problem by providing an algorithm capable of uniformly handling a variety of forms of numerical reasoning. In particular this algorithm is independent of a particular learning system and has been shown to be more general than several competing approaches to number handling in ILP.

We propose to continue this research in two further directions. The first is to incorporate this algorithm into one, or possibly a variety of existing ILP systems and compare its performance against other proposed approaches to number handling on several large datasets. We are particularly interested in using our approach to analyse economic and financial data.

Secondly, we hope to consider the benefits of using other constraint objects in learning. These would allow a similar treatment of other, possibly non-numerical, computation domains. Of particular interest are the boolean and finite domain constraint objects.

References

1. J. Jaffar and M. J. Maher. Constraint logic programming: A survey. *Journal of Logic Programming*, 19-20:503–583, 1994.
2. J. Jaffar, S. Michaylov, P. Stuckey, and R. H. C. Yap. The CLP($\Re$) language and system. Technical Report RC 16292-72336, IBM Watson Research Centre, 1990.
3. A. Karalič and Ivan Bratko. First order regression. To appear in the journal of Machine Learning, 1997.
4. S. Muggleton. Inverse entailment and Progol. *New Generation Computing*, 13:245–286, 1995.
5. S. Muggleton and C. D. Page. Beyond first-order learning: Inductive logic programming with higher-order logic. Technical Report PRG-TR-13-94, Oxford University Computing Laboratory, 1994.
6. S. Muggleton and L. De Raedt. Inductive logic programming – theory and methods. *Journal of Logic Programming*, 19-20:629–679, 1994.
7. M. Sebag and C. Rouveirol. Constraint inductive logic programming. In *Proceedings of the 5th International Workshop on Inductive Logic Programming*, pages 181–198. Published as a technical report at the Katholieke Universiteit Leuven, 1995.
8. A. Srinivasan and R. Camacho. Experiments in numerical reasoning with inductive logic programming. To appear, 1997.

Acknowledgements We thank David Page, Graeme Moss and Chris Wood for their comments and ideas concerning this work, and Sue Brassington for reading various drafts of this paper. The first author is funded by an EPSRC studentship, and by a travel award from Data Connection Ltd.

Lookahead and Discretization in ILP

Hendrik Blockeel and Luc De Raedt

Katholieke Universiteit Leuven
Department of Computer Science
Celestijnenlaan 200A
3001 Heverlee
e-mail: {Hendrik.Blockeel, Luc.DeRaedt}@cs.kuleuven.ac.be

Abstract. We present and evaluate two methods for improving the performance of ILP systems. One of them is discretization of numerical attributes, based on Fayyad and Irani's text [9], but adapted and extended in such a way that it can cope with some aspects of discretization that only occur in relational learning problems (when indeterminate literals occur). The second technique is lookahead. It is a well-known problem in ILP that a learner cannot always assess the quality of a refinement without knowing which refinements will be enabled afterwards, i.e. without looking ahead in the refinement lattice. We present a simple method for specifying when lookahead is to be used, and what kind of lookahead is interesting. Both the discretization and lookahead techniques are evaluated experimentally. The results show that both techniques improve the quality of the induced theory, while computational costs are acceptable.

1 Introduction

Propositional learning has been studied much more extensively than inductive logic programming (ILP), and at this moment the former field is better understood than the latter. However, ILP shares many techniques, heuristics etc. with propositional learning, and therefore it can often profit from results obtained for propositional learners. Due to several aspects of ILP that do not occur in propositional learning, it is often necessary to adapt these techniques to the specific ILP context.

In this paper, we discuss two such upgrades of propositional learning results to the ILP context. The first is discretization of continuous attributes. Irani and Fayyad [9] have presented a propositional method that divides a continuous domain into several subsets which can then be used as discrete values. We will briefly discuss the method, show that ILP poses some problems with respect to discretization that do not occur in propositional learning, and propose an adaptation of the method.

The second topic we shall discuss, is the use of lookahead. It is a well-known problem with relational learners that most heuristics (e.g. information gain) have problems with assessing the quality of a refinement of a rule, because a single literal that is added by the refinement step may not cause any gain, but may be very important to make the addition of gainful literals possible later on (because it introduces new variables). The advantage of adding a literal may only become clear further down the refinement tree. In general, heuristics that work well for propositional learners do not always perform as well for relational learners.

We propose a lookahead technique to alleviate this problem. By allowing the learner to look more than one level ahead in the refinement lattice, it may be able to assess the quality of a refinement more accurately.

Both the discretization and lookahead methods have been implemented in a novel ILP system called TILDE, and we present experimental results confirming the usefulness of both techniques.

This text is organized as follows. In Section 2, we briefly discuss the ILP setting that is used. In Section 3 we discuss discretization, in Section 4 lookahead. Conclusions are presented in Section 5.

2 The Learning Setting

We essentially use the *learning from interpretations* paradigm for inductive logic programming, introduced by [4], and related to other inductive logic programming settings in [3].

In this paradigm, each example is a Prolog knowledge base (i.e. a set of definite clauses), encoding the specific properties of the example. Furthermore, each example is classified into one of a finite set of possible classes. One may also specify background knowledge B in the form of a Prolog knowledge base.

More formally, the problem specification is :

Given: a set of classes C, a set of classified examples E, and a background theory B,
Find: a hypothesis H (a set of definite clauses in Prolog), such that for all $e \in E$: $H \wedge e \wedge B \models c$, and $H \wedge e \wedge B \not\models c'$ where c is the class of the example e and $c' \in C - \{c\}$.
Our experiments have been done with the ILP system TILDE[1], which represents the induced hypotheses as logical decision trees (these are a first order logic upgrade of the classical decision trees used in propositional concept learning).

Example 1. Suppose a number of machines are under revision. Some have to be sent back to the manufacturer, and others can be kept. The aim is to predict whether a machine needs to be sent back.

Given the following set of examples (each example represents one machine):

Example 1	Example 2	Example 3	Example 4
class(keep)	class(sendback)	class(sendback)	class(keep)
worn(gear)	worn(engine)	worn(control_unit)	worn(chain)
worn(chain)	worn(chain)		

and the following background knowledge:

Background knowledge
replaceable(gear)
replaceable(chain)
not_replaceable(engine)
not_replaceable(control_unit)

the following decision tree (in first order logic) represents a correct classification procedure:

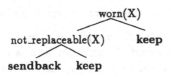

We wish to stress that — although for our experiments we use only TILDE— the techniques, problems and solutions discussed in this paper generally apply to any ILP-learner.

3 Discretization

3.1 Principle

The motivation for discretizing numeric data is twofold and based on the findings in attribute value learning. On the one hand, there is an efficiency concern. On the other hand, by discretizing the data, one may sometimes obtain higher accuracy rates.

Most current ILP systems ([13, 12] generate numbers during the induction process itself, which may cause a lot of overhead: at each refinement step (a lot of) constants need to be generated. TILDE, however, discretizes numeric domains beforehand, which makes the induction process much more efficient. It is known that in a propositional learning context this does not necessarily decrease the quality of the induced hypothesis (it may even increase; see e.g. [2]).

In our approach to discretization, the user can declaratively identify the relevant queries and the variables for which the values are to be discretized. For instance, to_be_discretized(atom(A,B,C,D), [D]) states that the fourth argument of *atom* should be discretized.

The resulting numeric attributes are then discretized using a simple modification of Fayyad and Irani's method. The details of this method can be found in [9] and [7]. In short, the algorithm finds a threshold that partitions a set of examples into two subsets such that the average class entropy of the subsets is as small as possible. This procedure is applied recursively on S_1 and S_2 until some stopping criterion is reached.

With respect to Fayyad and Irani's algorithm, two adaptations were made. Firstly, Fayyad and Irani propose a stopping criterion that is based on the minimal description length principle, but for TILDE we found this method to generate very few thresholds. Therefore TILDE's discretization procedure accepts a maximal number of thresholds as a parameter. This has the additional advantage that one can experiment with different numbers of thresholds.

A second adaptation made to Fayyad and Irani's method specifically concerns non-determinacy. Due to the fact that one example may have multiple or no values for a numeric attribute, we use sum of weights instead of number of examples in the appropriate places of Fayyad and Irani's formulae (in the attribute value case all values have weight 1 as each example has only one value for one attribute). The sum of the weights of all values for one numeric attribute or query in one example always equals one, or zero when no values are given.

Example 2. Consider an example $E_1 = \{p(1), p(2), p(3)\}$, and some threshold $T = 2.5$. In a propositional context T would partition a set of examples S into S_1 (examples that have a value < 2.5) and S_2, the rest. In our context, E_1 has weight $2/3$ in S_1, and $1/3$ in S_2.

Aside from the generation of subintervals, there is the topic of how these intervals should be used. We see several possibilities:

- Using inequalities to compare whether a value is less than a discretization threshold; this corresponds to an *inequality* test in the discrete domain.
- Checking whether a value lies in some interval bounded by two consecutive thresholds. Such an interval test corresponds with an *equality* test in the discretized domain.
- Checking whether a value lies in an interval bounded by non-consecutive thresholds. This corresponds to an *interval* test in the discrete domain.

The three approaches have been used and compared in our experiments.

3.2 Experimental Evaluation

We evaluate the effect of discretization on two datasets: the Musk dataset (available at the UCI repository [11]) and the Diterpene dataset, generously provided to us by Steffen Schulze-Kremer and Sašo Džeroski. Both datasets contain non-determinate numerical data, which makes them fit to test our discretization procedure on. We refer to [5] and [8] for precise descriptions of the datasets.

On the Musk dataset, we have compared the discretization approaches using equality tests, and using inequality tests. On the Diterpene dataset, the interval and inequality approaches were compared with using no discretization at all. In Figure 1, theory accuracies are plotted against the maximal number of thresholds that was given. Figure 2 shows running times on the Diterpene dataset.

Our conclusions are that the way in which discretization results are used (discrete (in)equalities, intervals) significantly influences the accuracy of the induced theory, as well as the efficiency of the induction process. A good choice of the number of thresholds is also important. Accuracy often shows a clear trend of reaching a maximum at some number of thresholds, then slowly decreases. A good combination of thresholds and discretization method may increase both accuracy and efficiency.

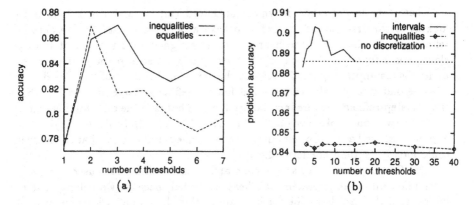

Fig. 1. Influence of number of thresholds on accuracy: (a) Musk dataset, comparing equalities and inequalities; (b) Diterpene dataset, comparing intervals with inequalities and no discretization at all

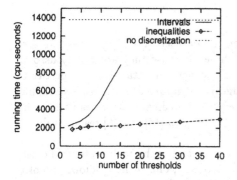

Fig. 2. Comparison of running times for the different approaches (Diterpene dataset)

4 Lookahead

4.1 Principle

An important problem in ILP is that refinement of a clause by adding a literal may result in little immediate improvement, although the literal may introduce new variables that are important for classification. For greedy systems, this may heavily influence the induction process. Although some systems have some provisions to cope with the problem (e.g. FOIL [13] automatically adds determinate literals), it is still an open question how it can best be solved.

A possible technique for coping with the problem, is to make the learner look ahead in the refinement lattice. When a literal is added, the quality of the refinement can better be assessed by looking at the additional refinements that will become available after this one, and looking at how good these are. This technique is computationally expensive, but may lead to significant improvements to the induced theories.

There are several ways in which lookahead can be performed. One is to look at further refinements in order to have a better estimate for the current refinement. In that case, the heuristic value assigned to a refinement c' of a clause c is a function of c' and $\rho(c')$, where ρ is a classical refinement operator under θ-subsumption. ρ itself does not change with this form of lookahead.

A second kind of lookahead is to redefine the refinement operator itself so that the two-step-refinements are incorporated in it. That is, if the original refinement operator (without lookahead) is ρ', then $\rho(c) = \rho'(c) \cup \{\rho'(c')|c' \in \rho'(c)\}$. This approach, as well as the former one, can be extended in the sense that the learner could look more than one level ahead.

The TILDE system follows the second approach. It relies on the user to provide some information about when lookahead is needed, because we believe that in many cases the user has a better idea about this than what a learning system can derive on the basis of e.g. determinacy. The user can provide templates of the form lookahead(C_1, C_2), specifying that whenever a conjunction is added matching C_1, the conjunction C_2 may be added as well.

4.2 Experimental Evaluation

We have tested the effect of lookahead on two datasets: the Mutagenesis dataset and the Mesh dataset. These two were chosen because they are widely used as ILP benchmarks, and because they contain structural data where properties of neighbouring substructures (atoms or edges) are important for classification, but the link to a neighbour itself (bonds, *neighbour* predicate) provides little or no gain (therefore lookahead is important). We refer to [14] and [6] respectively for more information on these datasets.

Both datasets repeatedly were partitioned into 10 subsets. Two tenfold cross-validations were run based on each such partition; one without allowing lookahead, and one with lookahead. In Figure 3, each dot represents one partition; dots above the straight line are those partitions where accuracy with lookahead was higher than without lookahead. For both the Mutagenesis and Mesh datasets, improvements obtained by using lookahead are significant at the 1% level.

TILDE's performance is compared with FOIL's and Progol's on the Mutagenesis dataset in Table 1. It can be seen that, although lookahead is computationally expensive, it is still much cheaper than an exhaustive search (such as Progol performs).

	FOIL	Progol	TILDE, no lookahead	TILDE, lookahead
accuracy	61 %	76 %	74.6 %	77.0 %
time	4950 s	117039 s	23 s	539 s

Table 1. Results on Mutagenesis dataset

We conclude that in both cases the ability to use lookahead improves TILDE's

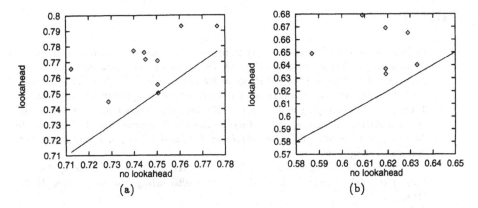

Fig. 3. Comparison of TILDE's performance with and without lookahead, (a) on the Mutagenesis data; (b) on the Mesh data

performance significantly. Computational complexity also increases, but is still acceptable.

5 Conclusions and Related Work

We have presented two methods for improving the performance of ILP-systems: discretization, as an extended version of propositional discretization; and lookahead, which in itself is an feature that can be added to any greedy search technique. We have evaluated these methods experimentally. Conclusions are that both techniques can lead to higher accuracy. Discretization also increases efficiency, but lookahead has a negative effect on this. An interesting observation is that the way in which discretization results are used (inequality tests or interval tests) can have a significant impact on prediction accuracy.

Although our experiments only concern TILDE, the proposed techniques are generally applicable; other ILP systems might profit from them as well.

Our work has of course heavily been influenced by several publications on discretization ([9, 7]) and especially [15]. The idea of using lookahead in ILP has been uttered several times before (e.g. [10]).

Acknowledgements

Hendrik Blockeel is supported by the Flemish Institute for the Promotion of Scientific and Technological Research in Industry (IWT). Luc De Raedt is supported by the Fund for Scientific Research of Flanders. This work is also part of the European Community Esprit project no. 20237, ILP2.

The authors thank Steffen Schulze-Kremer, the Max-Planck Institute for Molecular Genetics, Berlin, and Sašo Džeroski, for providing the Diterpene dataset; and Wim Van Laer and Sašo Džeroski for previous research on discretization for ILP systems.

References

1. H. Blockeel and L. De Raedt. Experiments with top-down induction of logical decision trees. Technical Report CW 247, Dept. of Computer Science, K.U.Leuven, January 1997. Also in Periodic Progress Report ESPRIT Project ILP2, January 1997. http://www.cs.kuleuven.ac.be/publicaties/rapporten/CW1997.html.

2. J. Catlett. On changing continuous attributes into ordered discrete attributes. In Yves Kodratoff, editor, *Proceedings of the 5th European Working Session on Learning*, volume 482 of *Lecture Notes in Artificial Intelligence*, pages 164–178. Springer-Verlag, 1991.

3. L. De Raedt. Induction in logic. In R.S. Michalski and Wnek J., editors, *Proceedings of the 3rd International Workshop on Multistrategy Learning*, pages 29–38, 1996.

4. L. De Raedt and S. Džeroski. First order jk-clausal theories are PAC-learnable. *Artificial Intelligence*, 70:375–392, 1994.

5. T. G. Dietterich, R. H. Lathrop, and T. Lozano-Pérez. Solving the multiple-instance problem with axis-parallel rectangles. *Artificial Intelligence*, 89(1-2):31–71, 1997.

6. B. Dolšak and S. Muggleton. The application of Inductive Logic Programming to finite element mesh design. In S. Muggleton, editor, *Inductive logic programming*, pages 453–472. Academic Press, 1992.

7. J. Dougherty, R. Kohavi, and M. Sahami. Supervised and unsupervised discretization of continuous features. In A. Prieditis and S. Russell, editors, *Proc. Twelfth International Conference on Machine Learning*. Morgan Kaufmann, 1995.

8. S. Džeroski, S. Schulze-Kremer, K. R. Heidtke, K. Siems, and D. Wettschereck. Applying ILP to diterpene structure elucidation from 13C NMR spectra. In *Proceedings of the 6th International Workshop on Inductive Logic Programming*, pages 14–27, August 1996.

9. U.M. Fayyad and K.B. Irani. Multi-interval discretization of continuous-valued attributes for classification learning. In *Proceedings of the 13th International Joint Conference on Artificial Intelligence*, pages 1022–1027, San Mateo, CA, 1993. Morgan Kaufmann.

10. N. Lavrač and S. Džeroski. *Inductive Logic Programming: Techniques and Applications*. Ellis Horwood, 1994.

11. C.J. Merz and P.M. Murphy. UCI repository of machine learning databases [http://www.ics.uci.edu/~mlearn/mlrepository.html], 1996. Irvine, CA: University of California, Department of Information and Computer Science.

12. S. Muggleton. Inverse entailment and progol. *New Generation Computing*, 13, 1995.

13. J.R. Quinlan. FOIL: A midterm report. In P. Brazdil, editor, *Proceedings of the 6th European Conference on Machine Learning*, Lecture Notes in Artificial Intelligence. Springer-Verlag, 1993.

14. A. Srinivasan, S.H. Muggleton, and R.D. King. Comparing the use of background knowledge by inductive logic programming systems. In L. De Raedt, editor, *Proceedings of the 5th International Workshop on Inductive Logic Programming*, 1995.

15. W. Van Laer, S. Džeroski, and L. De Raedt. Multi-class problems and discretization in ICL (extended abstract). In *Proceedings of the MLnet Familiarization Workshop on Data Mining with Inductive Logic Programming (ILP for KDD)*, 1996.

Data Mining via ILP: The Application of Progol to a Database of Enantioseparations

Christopher H.Bryant[1]

School of Computing and Mathematics, University of Huddersfield, HD1 3DH, UK. **

Abstract. As far as this author is aware, this is the first paper to describe the application of Progol to enantioseparations. A scheme is proposed for data mining a relational database of published enantioseparations using Progol. The application of the scheme is described and a preliminary assessment of the usefulness of the resulting generalisations is made using their accuracy, size, ease of interpretation and chemical justification.

1 Introduction

This paper describes a scheme for performing data mining on a chemical database and makes a preliminary assessment of the results of applying the scheme. The scheme utilises Progol, a domain independent ILP tool which is available in the public domain. As far as this author is aware, this is the first paper to describe the application of Progol to enantioseparations.

An enantioseparation [11] is the separation of two enantiomers. In order to perform an enantioseparation a chiral selector must be used which has a preference for one of the enantiomers in the pair as a consequence of its stereochemistry. This is usually achieved by selecting a suitable Chiral Stationary Phase (CSP).

The main areas to which ILP has been applied previously [1] are scientific discovery, knowledge acquisition and programming assistants. Applications of ILP to scientific discovery and knowledge acquisition include drug design, protein folding, diterpene structure elucidation from ^{13}C NMR spectra [7], diagnosis of faults in the power supply of satellites and rheumatology diagnosis. Work conducted as part of the project described in this paper applied Golem to enantioseparations [4].

2 Drug Separation Data

The research described in this paper used data that was taken from a recent study [6] that investigated the ability of seven CSP chiral selectors to separate enantiomeric drugs. The training data set [2] contains data on 197 separations involving 50 drugs whose structures vary widely.

** c.h.bryant@hud.ac.uk   Tel: +44-1484-473047   Fax: +44-1484-421106
URL: http://www.hud.ac.uk/schools/comp+maths/private/chb/top.html

The data was downloaded from a relational database of enantioseparations which uses attributes to represent chemical structural features of enantiomers. (For a description of the design of the database see [2].) Names of attributes in the database represent occurrences of chemical features and the values of these attributes represent the distances of the chemical features from the chiral centre in terms of the number of connecting bonds. There are three attributes for each chemical feature represented in the database. These represent the first, second and third occurrence of a feature. (Full details of the representation of chemicals in the database are given in both [3] and [2].)

3 The Induction Scheme

This section describes a scheme for the induction of the generalisations needed for recommending a suitable CSP chiral selector for a given enantiomer pair.

3.1 Why Progol was Selected

A non-interactive, non-incremental ILP tool was sought. The use of an interactive ILP tool was precluded because there was no suitable expert available to act as an oracle. The use of an incremental tool was unnecessary because all of the data was available prior to induction.

The three most widely field tested tools of this type are FOIL [10], Golem [9] and Progol [8]. Golem and Progol were preferred to FOIL because they have been applied successfully to chemical domains previously. Progol[3] was used rather than Golem because it does not suffer from some of the limitations of Golem such as the prohibition of non-ground unit clauses in the input files and the restriction to including only determinate clauses.

3.2 Knowledge Representation

One of the aims of the scheme is to induce generalisations that will suggest which CSP chiral selector should be used to separate a given enantiomer pair. To represent such generalisations using first order logic it is necessary to use a predicate that maps enantiomer pairs to CSP chiral selectors. Hence the predicate separates_on(E, C), where E=enantiomer pair and C=CSP chiral selector, is used to represent the separations in the data. The separates_on literals are divided into two groups, positives and negatives, which reflect whether the separation they represent is successful.

The bias of Progol gives rise to a choice of four options for representing the relationships between the data on enantioseparations and the data on chemical features of enantiomers. In each option D = distance from the chiral centre.

1. **has_feature(F, E, D)** F = chemical feature (including the occurrence).

---

[3] Version C4.1 of Progol was used in this project.

2. **has_feature(F, O, E, D)** Here F = chemical feature and O = occurrence of a chemical feature.
3. **<chemical_feature>(E, D)**
4. **<chemical_feature>(O, E, D)**

The second and fourth options require the names of the chemical feature attributes to be split into their constituent feature and occurrence parts. The third and fourth options require a predicate for each of the chemical feature attributes.

The induction scheme described in this paper uses the second choice for reasons explained in Sect. 3.3. It is interesting to compare Progol with Golem in this respect. Golem only allows the third predicate because Golem is restricted to inducing determinate literals.

(Obviously the language bias of Progol would allow many other predicates that represent the chemical features of enantiomers, not least because it accepts non-ground unit clauses.[4] However, since the approach taken in this project is to develop rules from data stored in the database, the only predicates considered are those for which instantiations can be generated by downloading and reformatting data from the database.)

3.3 Generalising Distances, Occurrences and Features

Enabling Progol to Generalise Distances. Providing Progol with just those predicates selected in Sect. 3.2 is not sufficient to enable it to make useful generalisations about the domain because, without additional background predicates, Progol is not able to make generalisations about the distance at which the chemical features of an enantiomer pair must occur in order that the pair be separated by a given CSP chiral selector. Without additional background predicates Progol will only induce clauses that reason about the presence of chemical features at particular distances or at no particular distance. This author believes that for a machine induction tool to be of use for enantioseparations it must be able to generalise distance values in a more flexible manner than this. This section describes the component of the scheme that allows Progol to make such generalisations. The generalisations are expressed as clauses of the form shown below where gd is a constant representing a merge of distance values.

separates_on(E, C):- has_feature(F, O, E, gd).

An example of this form of clause is:–

separates_on(E, dnbpg):– has_feature(bg6, third_closest, E, one_or_two).

where bg6 represents a six-membered aromatic ring and dnbpg represents the chiral selector (R)-N-(3,5-dinitrobenzoyl)-phenylglycine.

---

[4] The separate issue of using non-ground unit clauses to represent background chemical knowledge is discussed later in this paper.

If the background knowledge includes a series of clauses of the form shown below, where the constant gd is a generalisation of another constant sd, and the modes[5] shown below[6] are declared then Progol is able to generalise distances.

has_feature(F, O, E, gd):- has_feature(F, O, E, sd).
:–modeh(1,separates_on(+enantiomer_pair,#csp))?
:–modeb(500,has_feature(#feature,#occurrence,+enantiomer_pair,#distance))?

Enabling Progol to Generalise Occurrences. The previous section described the component of the scheme that enables Progol to make useful generalisations about the distance of chemical features from the chiral centre. In the absence of any clauses in the background knowledge for generalising occurrences and given the modes declared, Progol was restricted to inducing clauses that reason about the presence of *particular occurrences of* chemical features. This author believes that in some cases it may not matter whether a chemical feature is the closest, second closest or third closest occurrence of that feature, as long as the feature is present at a particular distance or within a range of distance values. If a machine induction tool is to be able to induce clauses from the database that reflect this then it must be capable of generalising the data on both the occurrences and the distances. Progol can be given this capability by declaring that the term occurrence can be either – or #. Of course, this assumes that there is a term representing the occurrence data. Thus this component of the scheme requires that either the second or fourth choice predicate for representing features (described in Sect. 3.2) is used to represent the relationships between the data on enantioseparations and the data on chemical features of enantiomers. When the predicate has_feature(F, O,E, D) is used the mode declarations listed in Sect. 3.3 are supplemented by the one shown below. This enables Progol to reason about particular occurrences of chemical features or any occurrence of chemical features.

:–modeb(500,has_feature(#feature,–occurrence,+enantiomer_pair,#distance))?

Enabling Progol to Generalise Features. Chemists often reason in terms of chemical features that are more general than those that are represented in the database. For example, reasoning about features such as aromatic rings or carbonyl groups is common place in chemistry but these features are not represented in the database. Enabling a machine induction tool to generalise the data

---

[5] modeh/2 and modeb/2 describe the 'forms' of literals that are allowed in the head and body respectively of a hypothesised clause. The first term, referred to as the recall number, specifies an upper bound on the number of successful calls to a predicate. The second term declares the mode and type of each term of the predicate. Types may be unary predicates defined in the background knowledge. Modes are either input (+), output (-) or constant (#).

[6] The value required for the recall number was determined empirically by increasing the verbosity of Progol.

in the database on the chemical features would give it the potential to generate more concise clause-sets and to make discoveries that would not be possible otherwise.

Many of the chemical features represented in the database have more general chemical features in common and some of these, in turn, have yet more general features in common. The relationships between these features can be represented in first-order predicate logic using the two clauses shown below and ground instantiations of the isa predicate. (Note that is_a and isa are two different predicates.) It must be emphasized for those readers not familiar with the domain that these ground unit clauses represent concepts that are omnipresent in chemistry.

is_a(A, B):– isa(A, B).   is_a(A, C):– isa(A, B), is_a(B, C).

This requires that the features are represented by a term; thus this component of the scheme requires that the first or second choice of predicate for representing features (see Sect. 3.2) is used. Since the component of the scheme for generalising occurrence data requires that the second or fourth choice of predicate is used, the scheme uses the second choice, namely has_feature(F, O, E, D).

4   Results of Applying the Scheme to the Data Set

Progol induced clauses for five of the seven CSP chiral selectors. The clauses are all short: they have either one or two literals in their body. This makes it easy to interpret them and to understand why particular separations are covered by particular clauses.

Consider the clauses for (R)-N-1-(α-naphthyl)ethylaminocarbonyl-(S)indoline-2-carboxylic acid which are shown in Fig. 2 together with their English translation. Clause a covers eleven of the 21 successful separations on the CSP chiral selector mentioned. When the clause is considered in conjunction with the structures of the enantiomers covered by the clause it becomes apparent that the clause represents the fact that the enantiomers fit the structural template shown in Fig. 1.

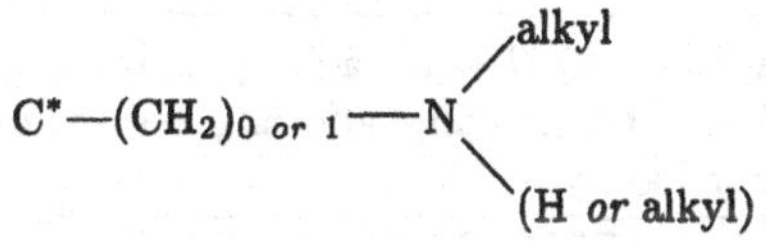

$$C^*-(CH_2)_{0 \; or \; 1}-N \Big\langle {\mathrm{alkyl} \atop \mathrm{(H \; or \; alkyl)}}$$

Fig. 1. Structural template of enantiomers from which clause a was induced.

Clause b covers five more of the successful separations on the selector and clause c another two. Again it is clear why the separations are covered by the clauses. The structural features referred to in the clauses are easily discerned on the structure diagrams: both clauses refer to ring features and the structure diagrams of the enantiomers covered by these clauses show graphical depictions of rings. Together the three clauses for (R)-N-1-(α-naphthyl)ethylaminocarbonyl-(S)indoline-2-carboxylic acid cover 18 of the 21 successful separations on this selector in the data set. Each one excludes all the failed separations on the selector.

---

a) separates_on(A, '(R)-N-1-(alpha-naphthyl)ethylaminocarbonyl-
                    (S)indoline-2-carboxylic_acid') :–
        has_feature(alkyl, B, A, two_or_three),
        has_feature(amine, closest, A, one_or_two).

Enantiomers will separate on (R)-N-1-(α-naphthyl)ethylaminocarbonyl-(S) indoline-2-carboxylic acid if they have:–
1. an alkyl chain two or three bonds away from the chiral centre.
2. at least one amine group and the closest such group to the chiral centre is one or two bonds away.

---

b) separates_on(A, '(R)-N-1-(alpha-naphthyl)ethylaminocarbonyl-
                    (S)indoline-2-carboxylic_acid') :–
        has_feature(bg6, second_closest, A, more_than_three),
        has_feature(ring, closest, A, zero_or_one).

Enantiomers will separate on (R)-N-1-(α-naphthyl)ethylaminocarbonyl-(S) indoline-2-carboxylic acid if they have:–
1. at least two six-membered aromatic rings and the second closest of these to the chiral centre is more than three bonds away.
2. at least one ring and the closest ring to the chiral centre is either at the centre or one bond away from the chiral centre.

---

c) separates_on(A,'(R)-N-1-(alpha-naphthyl)ethylaminocarbonyl
                    -(S)indoline–2-carboxylic_acid') :–
        has_feature(rg5, closest, A, one).

Enantiomers will separate on (R)-N-1-(α-naphthyl)indoline-2-carboxylic acid if they have at least one five-membered aliphatic ring and the closest such ring to the chiral centre is one bond away.

Fig. 2. Clauses induced by Progol from the data on attempted separations on (R)-N-1-(α-naphthyl)ethylaminocarbonyl-(S)indoline-2-carboxylic acid.

It is impossible to justify the clauses by referring to the paper from which the data was taken because the paper does not attempt to rationalise the separations that it reports. However a booklet [5] produced by a company which supplies the CSP chiral selectors does provide some justification for the clauses.

Table 1. Numbers of separations and accuracies.

CSP chiral selector	Number of Separations		Failed[a]	Accuracy(%)	
	Successful			Training	Test[b]
	In the data set	Covered by clauses			
c	21	18	19	93	65
d	19	16	21	93	58
e	4	4	14	100	78
f	3	2	16	95	84[h]
g	2	2	15	100	88[h]

[a] The number of failed separations in the data set is equal to the number of failed separations excluded by the clauses.
[b] Estimate obtained from a 'leave-one-out' cross-validation.
[c] (R)-N-1-(α-naphthyl)ethylaminocarbonyl-(S)indoline-2-carboxylic acid
[d] (R)-N-1-(α-naphthyl)ethylaminocarbonyl-(S)-tert-leucine
[e] (R)-N-1-(α-naphthyl)ethylaminocarbonyl-(S)-proline
[f] (S)-N-1-(α-naphthyl)ethylaminocarbonyl-(S)-proline
[g] (R)-N-(3, 5-dinitrobenzoyl)naphthylglycine
[h] No clauses were induced for two of the partitions for this selector; an accuracy of 0% was assigned to these partitions when estimating the test accuracy.

5 Conclusions

A scheme for data mining a relational database of published enantioseparations has been described. As far as this author is aware, this is the first paper to describe the application of Progol to enantioseparations.

The scheme was applied to published data concerning 197 attempted separations on seven CSP chiral selectors. Progol induced a set of clauses for each of five of these selectors. All of these clauses are very concise which facilitates both their interpretation and the comprehension of their coverage. The two sets of clauses that were induced from the two training sets with a significant number of positives have some chemical justification because some aspects of these clauses reflect advice given in a booklet produced by a company that supplies CSPs. The training accuracy and test accuracy for the union of these two datasets are 93% and 61% respectively.

The results suggest that the application of ILP to enantioseparations may prove fruitful and that this line of research should be pursued further.

6 Acknowledgements

The funding was provided by the EPSRC, under the remit of the Total Technology programme, and by Zeneca Pharmaceuticals. C.H.Bryant should like to thank Dr A.Srinivasan of the Oxford University Computing Laboratory and Mr R.Soloman of Phenomenex UK Ltd for their help.

References

1. Bratko, I., Muggleton, S.: Applications of Inductive Logic Programming. *Communications of the ACM* **38**(11) (1995) 65-70
2. Bryant, C.H.: Data Mining for Chemistry: the Application of Three Machine Induction Tools to a Database of Enantioseparations. Ph.D. Thesis. University of Manchester Institute of Science and Technology, UK. 1996.
3. Bryant, C.H., Adam, A.E., Taylor, D.R., Rowe, R.C.: Towards an Expert System for Enantioseparations: Induction of Rules Using Machine Learning. *Chemometrics and Intelligent Laboratory Systems* **34** (1996) 21-40
4. Bryant, C.H., Adam, A.E., Taylor, D.R., Rowe, R.C.: Using Inductive Logic Programming to Discover Knowledge Hidden in Chemical Data. *Chemometrics and Intelligent Laboratory Systems*, **36** (1997) 111-123
5. *Chirex. The Innovative Direction in Chiral Separations.* Phenomenex Ltd. UK, Macclesfield, Cheshire, UK.
6. Cleveland, T.: Pirkle-Concept Chiral Stationary Phases for the HPLC Separation of Pharmaceutical Racemates. *Journal of Liquid Chromatography* **18**(4) (1995) 649-671
7. Dzeroski, S., Schulze-Kremer, S., Heidtke, K.R., Siems: K., Wettschereck, D.: Applying ILP to Diterpene Structure Elucidation from ^{13}C NMR Spectra. *Presented at a workshop in Bari, Italy on 2nd July 1996 entitled 'Data Mining with Inductive Logic Programming' associated with the 13th International Conference on Machine Learning.*
8. Muggleton, S.: Inverse Entailment and Progol. *New Generation Computing* **13**(3-4) (1995) 245-286
9. Muggleton, S., Feng, C.: Efficient Induction of Logic Programs, in: Arikawa, S., Goto, S., Ohsuga, S., Yokomori, T. (eds.), Proc. 1st Conf. on Algorithmic Learning Theory, Japanese Society for Artificial Intelligence, Tokyo, 1990
10. Quinlan, J.R.: Learning Logical Definitions from Relations. *Machine Learning* **5** (1990) 239-266
11. Taylor, D.R., Maher, K.: Chiral Separations by High-Performance Liquid Chromatography. *Journal of Chromatographic Science* **30** (1992) 67-85

Part-of-Speech Tagging Using Progol

James Cussens

Oxford University Computing Laboratory
Wolfson Building, Parks Road
Oxford OX1 3QD, UK
Tel: +44 1865 283520   Fax: +44 1865 273839
james.cussens@comlab.ox.ac.uk

Abstract. A system for 'tagging' words with their part-of-speech (POS) tags is constructed. The system has two components: a lexicon containing the set of possible POS tags for a given word, and rules which use a word's context to *eliminate* possible tags for a word. The Inductive Logic Programming (ILP) system Progol is used to induce these rules in the form of definite clauses. The final theory contained 885 clauses. For background knowledge, Progol uses a simple grammar, where the tags are terminals and predicates such as nounp (noun phrase) are non-terminals. Progol was altered to allow the caching of information about clauses generated during the induction process which greatly increased efficiency. The system achieved a per-word accuracy of 96.4% on known words drawn from sentences without quotation marks. This is on a par with other tagging systems induced from the same data [5, 2, 4] which all have accuracies in the range 96–97%. The per-sentence accuracy was 49.5%.

1   Introduction

In part-of-speech disambiguation or 'tagging', the aim is to classify word tokens according to their part of speech. This is non-trivial because many words are ambiguous. For example, in the sentence "Jane sat on the table", "table" is a noun, yet in the sentence "James decided to table the motion", "table" is a verb. Once disambiguation has been carried out, the word can be 'tagged' with its correct part of speech (POS) tag. As Daelemans et al [5] note: "Automatic tagging is useful for a number of applications: as a preprocessing stage to parsing, in information retrieval, in text to speech systems, in corpus linguistics, etc."

A variety of approaches, both inductive and non-inductive, have been used to attack the tagging problem. In [7] a Hidden Markov model (HMM) was used to create the well-known Xerox tagger [4] which correctly tagged 96% of word instances on a subset of the Brown corpus.

In [2], Brill induces a rule-based tagger based on transformations. Words are initially tagged with their most common tag according to the training corpus. If a word is not in the corpus, a tag is guessed according to a number of features of the word such as capitalisation. Brill then considers 11 rule templates dictating when a word should have its tag changed. For example, the first rule template

is: "Change tag *a* to tag *b* when the preceding (following) word is tagged *z*."
Lexicalized rules are included such as: "Change tag *a* to tag *b* when one of the
two preceding (following) words is *w*." With this approach 267 transformation
rules were induced, and an accuracy of 96.5% was achieved on a subset of the
Wall Street Journal

A notable non-inductive tagger is EngCG, the English Constraint Grammar,
which is a "rule-based framework for morphological disambiguation and shallow
syntactic parsing, where the rules are hand-coded by a linguistic expert" [8].
EngCG achieved a per-word accuracy of 99.7%, albeit with each word receiving
on average 1.04–1.09 tags, so some ambiguity remains [9].

Daelemans et al [5] take a memory-based approach to the tagging problem,
implemented via *IG Tree*, a tree-based approach for efficient indexing and searching of large case base. Together with a method for handling unknown words,
Daelemans et al achieved an accuracy of 96.4% overall, and 96.7% on known
words. (Known words are those that have occurred at least once in the training
data.) Training was performed on 2 million words from the Wall Street Journal,
and testing on the remaining one million.

Tapanainen and Voutilainen [9] *combined* the inductively constructed Xerox
tagger and the hand-crafted EngCG to produce a system which achieved an
accuracy of 98.5% with no remaining ambiguities on test data of 26,711 words
of newspaper text taken from the Bank of English corpus from the University
of Birmingham. The motivation for such a combination was that when EngCG
performs a disambiguation it is almost always correct. However, EngCG does
not disambiguate all words, so these remaining ambiguities are passed to the
Xerox tagger, which always makes some decision.

There are two dichotomies in the work just described: that between inductive and non-inductive approaches and that between statistical and rule-based
approaches. EngCG, the only non-inductive approach described, does have the
best accuracy figures, but was "developed and debugged over several years". All
the inductive approaches have accuracies around 96%, but these systems can
rapidly be produced from pre-tagged training corpora.

A useful discussion of the relative merits of statistical and rule-based approaches can be found in [1]. Those rule-based taggers tend to be more compact,
faster and more comprehensible. A HMM tagger has two notable advantages.
Firstly, it can be trained using *untagged* text, although better performance is
possible using tagged text. Secondly, HMM taggers can perform tagging on a
sentence-by-sentence basis, using the entire sequence of words in the sentence
to find the most likely sequence of tags. Such a system should be able to cope
when the correct tag can only be decided with reference to words some distance
away: the problem of *long-distance dependency*. Rule-based approaches which
consider a small window of words on either side of the word to be tagged (the
focus word), will be in trouble in such cases.

Given the complementary strengths of the various approaches just outlined,
some sort of hybrid system, such as that in [9], is attractive. Here, we report
on the application of the Inductive Logic Programming (ILP) system Progol [6]

to the tagging problem. Since the brunt of the work involves inducing rules, in the form of definite clauses, for *eliminating* possible tags, our work falls mainly into the inductive+rule-based category. However, we employ a simple statistical method for those ambiguities left unresolved by the elimination rules and employ hand-crafted (and fairly complex) background knowledge. This means that the complete tagging system is hybrid in nature.

The plan of this report is as follows. In Section 2, we describe the two components of our tagging system. Section 3 describes the core of the work: the use of Progol to induce tag elimination rules. In Section 4, we describe how Progol was altered to handle large data sets in a reasonable amount of time. Results and conclusions are in Sections 5 and 6.

2 Combining lexical-statistical information and tag elimination rules

2.1 Creating a lexicon

The data used in this work was the 3 million word tagged Wall Street Journal corpus[1]. The first tagged sentence from the corpus is: Pierre_NP Vinken_NP ,_, 61_CD years_NNS old_JJ ,_, will_MD join_VB the_DT board_NN as_IN a_DT nonexecutive_JJ director_NN Nov._NP 29_CD ._. So that tags could be represented as Prolog constants, without the need for messy quoting, the original tags were translated into strings of lower-case letters. The tag set used in the corpus, together with the Prolog translations and frequencies, is given in Table 1.

After splitting the corpus into 2/3 train and 1/3 test set, the first step taken was to create a *lexicon* which records the frequency with which words in the training set are given different tags. An excerpt from the lexicon is given in Fig 1. Despite its simplicity, the lexicon is the most powerful single element of our tagging system, since it gives us (according to the training data) the set of possible tags for a given word: the word's *ambiguity class*. In many cases there is, according to the training data, only one possible tag for a word.

The entry for "New" in Fig 1 shows the problem of rare tags: out of 2574 occurrences "New" is tagged as nps (plural proper noun) only twice. From such statistics one might infer that these two occurrences are due to noise in the training set, Also, intuitively, "New" is not plural. However, the tagging here is correct, both occurrences are part of the noun phrase "New Yorkers", where "New" is correctly tagged as a plural noun. On the other hand the nn tagging *is* incorrect.

Noise-handling is a particularly important issue when one is chasing accuracies in excess of 96%. In this work, we simply deleted a tag from a word's ambiguity class if it occurred less than 5% of the time. This crude approach is a weakness, since, for example, the correct nps and even the jj tagging for "New" were deleted. Future work will concentrate on improved noise-handling, but there are some advantages to this approach. Firstly, most incorrect tags are

---

[1] ACL Data Collection Initiative CD-ROM 1, September 1991

Table 1. Penn Treebank Part of Speech Tags.

Tag	Prolog	Meaning	Frequency
#	pnd	£	538
$	dlr	"$"	21242
"	lqt	" " " or " ' "	23789
"	rqt	" " " or " ' "	23427
(	lpn	"("	4647
)	rpn	")"	4552
,	cma	","	163227
.	stp	"."	127640
:	cln	";" or ":"	8806
CC	cc	Coordinating Conjunction	67833
CD	cd	Cardinal number	112565
DT	dt	Determiner	263125
EX	ex	Existential "there"	2826
FW	fw	Foreign word	705
IN	in	Preposition or Subordinating conjunction	321687
JJ	jj	Adjective	197118
JJR	jjr	Adjective, comparative	10574
JJS	jjs	Adjective, superlative	6104
LS	ls	List item marker	109
MD	md	Modal	31516
NN	nn	Noun, singular or mass	424605
NNS	nns	Noun, plural	192883
NP	np	Proper noun, singular	304396
NPS	nps	Proper noun, plural	8778
PDT	pdt	Predeterminer	1075
POS	pos	Possessive ending	28090
PP	pp	Personal pronoun	56094
PP$	ppz	Possessive pronoun	27378
RB	rb	Adverb	99788
RBR	rbr	Adverb, comparative	5482
RBS	rbs	Adverb, superlative	1436
RP	rp	Particle	5391
SYM	sym	Symbol	91
TO	to	"To"	72202
UH	uh	Interjection	328
VB	vb	Verb, base form	86049
VBD	vbd	Verb, past tense	96504
VBG	vbg	Verb, gerund or present participle	48325
VBN	vbn	Verb, past participle	65663
VBP	vbp	Verb, non 3rd-person, singular present	40099
VBZ	vbz	Verb, 3rd person singular present	70394
WDT	wdt	Wh-determiner	14300
WP	wp	Wh-pronoun	7771
WP$	wpz	Possessive wh-pronoun	587
WRB	wrb	Wh-adverb	6829

```
New nps 2 jj 61 nn 1 np 2501
...
bears vbz 16 nns 10
beast nn 1
beasties nns 1
beasts nns 3
beat vbd 11 vbp 4 jj 1 nn 5 vb 30
beat-up jj 1
```

Fig. 1. An excerpt from the lexicon (before noise elimination).

eliminated, secondly, those correct tags that are deleted are necessarily rare so their deletion will not cause a substantial decrease in accuracy.

2.2 The tagging system

Our basic approach combines features of [8] and [9]. As in [8], we learn rules for *eliminating* possible tags, but our possible tags are taken from the lexicon, not the EngCG. As in [9], we use a statistical approach if and only if the rule-based approach does not resolve all ambiguities, except here, rather than use the Xerox tagger, we simply choose the most frequent possible tag for a word according to the lexicon.

The central issue of inducing tag elimination rules is detailed in Section 3. Here, by way of motivation, we show, via an example, how the completed system operates. The system works on a sentence-by-sentence basis. Suppose the sentence to be tagged was:

A House-Senate conference last week accepted the provision with no discussion of the potential cost to the government.

The lexicon then replaces each word with its ambiguity class. Note that for this to be possible the word must appear in the lexicon; the word must be one of the 66,024 'known' words in the lexicon. Consequently, our system is restricted to sentences containing only known words. Future work will use morphological analysis of unknown words to overcome this restriction.

Each tag in a non-singleton ambiguity class is paired with the relative frequency with which it appeared in the lexicon after noise pre-processing. This gives us:

```
[[[dt,0.947],[np,0.053]], [[jj,0.268],[np,0.732]], nn, jj, nn,
[[vbn,0.523],[vbd,0.477]], dt, nn, in, [[dt,0.873],[rb,0.127]],
nn, in, dt, [[jj,0.784],[nn,0.216]], [[nn,0.790],[vb,0.210]],
to, dt, nn, stp]
```

We then use induced clauses to eliminate tags. The first elimination is that of the vbn (past participle) tagging for "accepted". This is due to the following induced clause:

```
rmv(A,B,vbn) :- dt(B,C), nounp1(A,D).
```

Here A is the left context of "accepted" and B is the right context. dt(B,C) holds if B starts with a dt (determiner) and the remainder of B is C. This rule eliminates the possibility that "accepted" is a past participle because it is sandwiched between the noun phrase "week" and the determiner "the". Note that vbn is the more likely tag for "accepted" without contextual information, so here the elimination rules have (correctly) overridden the lexical-statistical information.

Using the following rule, the rb (adverb) tagging for "no" is eliminated because "no" is followed by the noun "discussion":

```
rmv(A,B,rb) :- noun(B,C).
```

The vb (infinitive) tag for "cost" has also been eliminated, because it is followed by "to" and preceded by "potential" which may be a noun or an adjective. If "potential" is a noun and hence, in our grammar, a noun phrase, it allows the following rule to fire:

```
rmv(A,B,vb) :- to(B,C), nounp1(A,D).
```

If instead "potential" is an adjective, then the following rule fires:

```
rmv(A,B,vb) :- adjp1(A,C).
```

Either way the vb tagging for "cost" is eliminated.

Since no more tag elimination rules can fire, the lexical statistics take over and eliminate the very unlikely np tagging for "A". Returning to the rules, this allows us to knock out the np tagging for "House-Senate", since the following rule can now fire.

```
rmv(A,B,np) :- dt(A,C), cnoun(B,D), nounp(D,E), sverb(E,F)
```

The final ambiguity caused by the word "potential" is then resolved using the lexical statistical information, giving us the (correct) final sequence of tags:

```
[dt, jj, nn, jj, nn, vbd, dt, nn, in, dt, nn, in, dt, jj, nn,
to, dt, nn, stp]
```

3 Eliminating tags by partial parsing

3.1 Generating examples for Progol

It was decided to learn rules for eliminations on a tag by tag basis. In other words, Progol learnt rules for eliminating cc, cd, dt, etc from separate data sets, one data set for each tag. Positive and negative examples were generated as follows. The corpus was scanned a sentence at a time. For each word which has an ambiguous tag according to the lexicon, one negative example, and one or more positive examples of tag elimination were created. The negative example records which tag it would not be correct to eliminate, i.e. the correct tag. The positive examples record which tags might have been correct, since they are members of the word's ambiguity class, but are, in fact, incorrect in the current context. The example contains the tag to be removed and its entire left and right context. The left context is reversed so that the start of the tag list representing the left context contains those tags nearest to the focus word. For example, the second sentence from the corpus produces the positive and negative examples given in Table 2.

Table 2. Creating examples from a sentence.

Mr. Vinken is chairman of Elsevier N.V., the **Dutch** publishing group.
:- rmv([dt,cma,np,np,in,nn,vbz,np,np],[vbg,nn,stp],np).
rmv([dt,cma,np,np,in,nn,vbz,np,np],[vbg,nn,stp],jj).
rmv([dt,cma,np,np,in,nn,vbz,np,np],[vbg,nn,stp],nps).
Mr. Vinken is chairman of Elsevier N.V., the Dutch **publishing** group.
:- rmv([np,dt,cma,np,np,in,nn,vbz,np,np],[nn,stp],vbg).
rmv([np,dt,cma,np,np,in,nn,vbz,np,np],[nn,stp],nn).

Since it was possible to create vast numbers of examples (at least for the more important tags), we could afford to be quite restrictive about which examples to include in training. Firstly, only sequences which (i) began with a word with an initial capital letter, (ii) ended in a full stop and (iii) *contained no quotes* were used. This had the effect of filtering out some noisy sentences but meant that certain sorts of sentence were never used to generate training examples. The no-quote restriction is a considerable one, and further work will have to drop it. It was used in this preliminary work since it made it easier to identify where sentences began and ended and because the lack of embedded speech in sentences simplified their structure.

For many tags, this produced many thousands of examples (positive and negative). In the future, it may be possible to develop Progol to cope with such vast example sets. Although Progol was altered to speed up learning on large data sets, it was still thought necessary here to sample from the full training set for each tag. So in this work we used only the first 6000 examples found for each tag. Details of the various training sets so produced can be found in [3].

3.2 Using a partial grammar as background knowledge

A subset of the background knowledge is given in Fig 2. The background predicates fall into three sets: 'tag' predicates, such as cc/2, forward parsing predicates and backward parsing predicates. The background knowledge defines a grammar where the 43 POS tags are terminals and there are 22 nonterminals defining such grammatical constructs as noun phrase (nounp) and adjectival phrase (adjp). There is also a number of 'utility predicates' such as adjp_rest which are used for efficiency.

```
cc([cc|S],S).      cd([cd|S],S).      dt([dt|S],S).
ex([ex|S],S).      fw([fw|S],S).      in([in|S],S).

cncy([pnd|S],S) :- !. cncy([dlr|S],S).

cds([cd|X],S2) :- cd(S1,X), (X=S2 ; cds(X,S2)).

noun([nn|S],S) :- !. noun([np|S],S) :- !.
noun([nns|S],S) :- !. noun([nps|S],S).

snp(L1,L2) :- noun(L1,X), (X=L2 ; snp(X,L2)).

dtz([dt|S],S) :- !. dtz([ppz|S],S).

nounp(L1,L2) :- noun(L1,X), !, (X=L2 ; snp(X,L2)). % "Pierre Vinken"
nounp([pp|S],S) :- !. % "us, him"
nounp(L1,L2) :- dtz(L1,L3), !, (snp(L3,L2) ; adjp(L3,L4), snp(L4,L2)).
nounp(L1,L2) :- cncy(L1,L3), !, cds(L3,L2). % "$ 20 billion "
nounp([cd|Y],L2) :- !, (X=Y ; cds(Y,X)), (X=L2 ; snp(X,L2)). % "20, 20%"
nounp(L1,L2) :- adjp(L1,L3), snp(L3,L2). % "green men"

nounp1([pp|S],S) :- !. % "us, him"
nounp1([cd|S1],S2) :- !, (S3=S1 ; cds(S1,S3)), (S3=S2 ; cncy(S3,S2)).
nounp1(S1,S2) :- snp(S1,S3), nounp1_rest(S3,S2).

nounp1_rest(S,S).
nounp1_rest(S1,S2) :- dtz(S1,S2), !.
nounp1_rest([cd|S1],S2) :- !, (S1=S2 ; cds(S1,S2)).
nounp1_rest(S1,S2) :- adjp1(S1,S3), (S3=S2 ; dtz(S3,S2)).
```

Fig. 2. A subset of the background knowledge.

Because the terminals of the grammar are the tags which do not represent all the information there is about the underlying words, the grammar so defined is very 'sloppy'. For example, the definition of simple verb phrase svp allows that the tag sequence [vbz,vbg] constitutes a simple verb phrase. This means that in any case where a gerund or past participle follows a 3rd person singular present verb, then this is counted as a simple verb phrase. *The singular present verb is not constrained to be an auxiliary verb.* The tag set used here does not distinguish auxiliary verbs. For example, the phrase "is wandering" will be translated, via the lexicon, into [vbz,vbg] (neither word is ambiguously tagged in the lexicon, although "wandering" can be a noun). It will then be correctly recognised as a simple verb phrase. However, the fragment "wanders being" which is nonsense, will also be marked as a simple verb phrase.

The grammar defined in the background knowledge is clearly over-general, but we are not using it to determine whether sentences are grammatical, or to generate new sentences. We have chosen the definitions of the 22 background predicates in the hope that these will be relevant to the task of tag elimination. The clauses produced show this to be the case.

As well as the terminals and the 'forward parsing' predicates we have defined 4 predicates for parsing backwards. We parse the left context of the focus word backwards on the grounds that the most useful part of the context is that nearest to the focus word. Consequently, we work from right-to-left through the left context, i.e. backwards. This can best be done by reversing the the context to the left of the focus word, and then parsing taking the reversal into account. Consequently, a simple verb phrase in the left context can be a sequence [vbg,vbz] ("walking is").

Although all background predicates were defined for all Progol runs, not all were allowed to appear in bodies of induced tag elimination clauses. The basic set of 38 background predicates that were allowed to appear in clause bodies can be found in [3]. The intuition for doing this was that for many of the tags, the missing background predicates were irrelevant. For example, knowing whether a particular tag was an nn, nns, np or nps was thought not to be that helpful in eliminating the possibility that a certain word could be a dt—it is enough to know that it is a noun or indeed a noun phrase. When learning elimination rules for certain tags: jj, jjr, jjs, nn, nns, np, nps, vb, vbg, vbn, vbp, vbz it was judged that extra background predicates should be allowed to appear in clause bodies. The details are given in [3].

4 Speeding up Progol with caching

The combination of four factors meant that inducing a theory for tag elimination involved a heavy computational burden. These are: the size of the example sets, the complexity and size of the background knowledge, the non-heuristic nature of Progol's search and the fact that positive examples covered by induced clauses were not removed from the training set. Given the scale of the induction problem a more heuristically based ILP approach has attractions. However the very high accuracy figures required motivate a complete search ILP algorithm, such as Progol. Although this can lead to long computation times (e.g. 19.8 hours for rp), computation still comprised a very small fraction of the total time committed to the problem. (The Prolog implementation of the Progol algorithm, called P-Progol, was used in all the work reported here. P-Progol is available, for academic research, via anonymous ftp from ftp.comlab.ox.ac.uk in the directory pub/Packages/ILP.)

In Progol, a 'bottom' clause is produced from a 'seed' positive example, which is the most specific clause which covers that example, given the declarative bias. Progol then carries out an *admissible* top-down search of the subsumption lattice of clauses which subsume the bottom clause (and are in the hypothesis language). Progol is *guaranteed* to find a clause which has maximal compression in this lattice. In this work the following search strategy was employed: once a positive example became covered by an induced clause it was removed from the set of possible seeds. However, it was *not* removed from the example set. This ensured that the correct positive (P) and negative cover (N) of induced clauses is always available, allowing a training set estimate of the accuracy of a clause: $|P|/(|P| + |N|)$. This was required to exceed 0.95 for all induced clauses.

The computational problem was tackled in two ways. Firstly, search constraints were used: clauses were constrained to have at most 5 literals and cover at least 15 positive examples ($|P| > 15$). This last constraint plays a dual role. Firstly, it ensures that our crude and generally over-optimistic clause accuracy estimate is unlikely to be too inaccurate. But it is also particularly useful in Progol's top-down search; if a clause covers less than 15 positive examples, then so will all its refinements and so the search can be pruned at this clause. One final syntactic constraint pruned out clauses with redundant literals: for example, if a clause contains the literals adjp(B,C), jjs(B,C) then adjp(B,C) is redundant since all superlative adjectives are also adjectival phrases.

These constraints alone were insufficient to allow learning in a reasonable amount of time. To speed up learning further, we traded space for time by caching the positive and negative cover of clauses which Progol produced during its search. If a clause appears again in a subsequent search, we can avoid doing any theorem-proving by simply recovering its cover from the cache. This approach was extended by having a 'prune cache'. If a clause is such that, for any search in which it appears, the search can be pruned at that clause, then it is added to the prune cache. For each clause produced by Progol during its search, we then check to see if it is in the prune cache, and prune the search if it is. (Details of the caching method are in [3]. Caching is now implemented in the ftp-able version of P-Progol.)

Caching brought a large speed-up. A few comparative experiments have been done to measure this speed-up. In one experiment we induced the sub-theory for eliminating rp, with and without caching. With caching Progol took 19.8 hours, which is the longest time for any theory. Without caching, Progol took 312 hours and then stalled, for reasons unknown. This means we have a speed up factor in excess of 15.75. However, even for small data sets the improvements are significant, for the rbs theory (1784 examples) Progol without caching took 17,403 seconds. With caching, the same theory was induced in 1,620 seconds, a speed-up factor of 10.74. Using a very recent version of Progol with additional efficiency improvements the rbs theory was induced in only 641 seconds, which is over 27 times quicker than the original non-caching version of Progol.

5   Results

5.1   Computation times

Details of the computation times for inducing tag elimination theories for each tag are given in Table 3. The n/a entries for jj, nn, nns, np and nps are because the theories for these tags were produced over a number of runs, where many of the same clauses were found in the different runs. The "Searches" column records the number of bottom clauses and hence subsumption lattices searches undertaken. The "Mean" column gives the mean time taken over all these searches. All times are in seconds.

Table 3. Theory size and search computation times for each tag.

Tag	Pos	Neg	Searches	Mean	Search time	Total time (est.)	Clauses
cc	1192	338	539	10.61	5717	6417	28
cd	780	2312	780	26.47	20650	21664	0
dt	3825	2175	385	53.83	20724	21225	42
ex	182	660	101	2.85	288	419	2
fw	331	162	294	7.31	2148	2530	2
in	2292	3708	1186	20.75	24605	26146	22
jj	3216	2784	n/a	n/a	n/a	n/a	47
jjr	2624	3376	1101	49.06	54012	55444	39
jjs	879	1068	426	7.98	3401	3955	19
md	209	102	35	0.19	7	52	4
nn	3025	2975	n/a	n/a	n/a	n/a	61
nns	2266	3734	n/a	n/a	n/a	n/a	48
np	2647	3353	n/a	n/a	n/a	n/a	31
nps	3773	2227	n/a	n/a	n/a	n/a	47
pdt	3231	470	21	58.41	1227	1254	14
pos	448	448	21	110.05	2311	2338	6
pp	511	168	32	2.32	74	116	18
ppz	152	511	84	0.41	35	144	2
rb	4182	1818	1305	19.63	25622	27318	87
rbr	3850	2150	1727	21.08	36400	38645	45
rbs	1064	720	250	4.04	1009	1334	25
rp	4539	1461	1883	36.31	68371	71259	48
rqt	1043	0	1	4.65	5	6	1
stp	11	1	10	0.01	0	13	0
sym	11	18	10	0.01	0	13	0
uh	195	33	42	0.21	9	64	3
vb	3566	2434	180	44.09	7935	8169	35
vbd	3294	2706	545	37.35	20354	21062	20
vbg	3192	2808	1589	22.24	35335	37401	44
vbn	3087	2913	881	28.92	25482	26627	57
vbp	4328	1672	222	38.39	8522	8811	25
vbz	4925	1075	462	62.90	29061	29661	83
wdt	4433	1567	5	115.83	579	586	3
wp	10	5	10	0.01	0	13	0
Total	73313	51952	14127	n/a	n/a	n/a	908

5.2 Structure of the induced theory

Because of the search strategy used, it is possible to have redundant clauses in the induced sub-theories. We call a clause redundant if all the positive examples it covers are covered by other clauses in the theory. Removing such clauses make the theory simpler and may reduce the negative cover, rendering it more likely to be accurate.[2] It does not specialise the theory according to the training data. Redundant clauses were removed by a companion program to P-Progol called T-Reduce. T-Reduce reduced the final theory from the original 908 clauses to 885 clauses. The two big reductions were for the nn subtheory (from 61 to 54 clauses) and nps (from 47 to 41 clauses). This was probably because these theories were produced over several runs leading to large overlap over clauses. (T-Reduce is available from Ashwin Srinivasan at the same address as the current author.)

One of the features of ILP is that the first-order representation often allows an easily intelligible induced theory. Examining the theory induced here, an extract of which is shown in Fig 3, we see that each individual clause *is* easy to understand, although not all are intuitive. So, although, it seems intuitive that no word preceding "to" should be a co-ordinating conjunction (second rule) rules such as

```
rmv(A,B,in) :- cma(A,C), cds(C,D), nounp1(D,E), cln(E,F).
```

are not so obvious.

The number of 2,3,4 and 5 literal clauses is 103, 251, 276 and 254 respectively. The number of clauses of depth 0,1,2,3 and 4 is 1, 242, 322, 228 and 92 respectively. The induction of a large number of depth 4 and 5 clauses is significant. This shows that our approach performs disambiguation based on long-distance dependencies, which was one of the motivations for using ILP. The most commonly appearing background predicates are: nounp (15.4%), nounp1 (12.1%), in (10.4%), noun (8.0%) dt (6.5%), cma (5.2%), vp (4.0%), vp1 (3.1%), adjp (3.1%) and advp (2.9%). The importance of complex background predicates such as nounp demonstrate the utility of background knowledge for the tagging problem.

Taking the theory as a whole, there is the intelligibility problem of the sheer number of clauses. In future work, we will induce both tag elimination *and* tag identification rules which may lead to a more compact theory. However, it should be noted that overriding goal in tagging is to produce a tagging system of very high accuracy, and given the complexity of the problem it is probably over-optimistic to hope that accurate theories will also be simple ones. (The full (unreduced) theory and extensive analysis of the results can be found in [3]. The reduced theory is available from the author on request.)

5.3 Accuracy on test data

The central results of this work are summarised in Tables 4-7. These show the results of testing the tagging system on an independent test set of 5000 sen-

---

[2] In fact, accuracy was only increased from 106718/110716 to 106719/110716!

```
rmv(A,B,cc) :- nounp(B,C), in(A,D), noun(D,E), in(E,F).
rmv(A,B,cc) :- to(B,C).

rmv(A,B,dt) :- in(B,C), noun(C,D), nounp(D,E), vp1(A,F).
rmv(A,B,dt) :- in(B,C), nounp(C,D), vp(D,E), vp1(A,F).
rmv(A,B,dt) :- noun(B,C), noun(C,D), vp1(A,E), advp(E,F).
rmv(A,B,dt) :- nounp(B,C), advp(C,D), vp(D,E), vp1(A,F).
rmv(A,B,dt) :- nounp(B,C), noun(C,D), pos(D,E), nounp(E,F).

rmv(A,B,in) :- cma(A,C), cds(C,D), nounp1(D,E), cln(E,F).
rmv(A,B,in) :- dt(A,C), in(C,D).

rmv(A,B,jj) :- cc(A,C), prnoun(B,D).
rmv(A,B,jj) :- cma(B,C), vp(C,D).
rmv(A,B,jj) :- dt(A,C), in(B,D), dt(D,E).

rmv(A,B,nn) :- advp(A,C), nounp1(C,D).
rmv(A,B,nn) :- cc(A,C), dt(B,D).
rmv(A,B,nn) :- cc(B,C), nounp(C,D), prnoun(A,E).

rmv(A,B,rp) :- dt(B,C), nounp1(A,D).
rmv(A,B,rp) :- in(A,C).
rmv(A,B,rp) :- in(B,C), adjp(C,D), noun(D,E), nounp1(A,F).

rmv(A,B,vb) :- cc(B,C), vp(C,D).
rmv(A,B,vb) :- cma(A,C), nounp1(C,D), nounp1(D,E).
```

Fig. 3. Subset of theory of tag elimination.

tences consisting of 110,716 words. This preliminary system is only applicable
to sentences starting with a capital letter, ending with a full stop, not containing quotes and which are composed entirely of words which have occurred at
least once in the training set. Only sentences which met these restrictions were
included in the test set.

As well as overall accuracy figures, we give accuracies on just the ambiguous
words and also accuracies excluding lexical errors. A lexical error occurs when
the correct tag for a word is not in the lexicon. This can arise either because of
our crude noise-handling approach or simply because not all of the correct tags
for a word were seen in the training data. We also compare tagging using the tag
elimination theory with tagging just using the lexical statistics. The per-word
difference between 94.1% and 96.4% given in Table 5 may seem insignificant.
But when we compare on a sentence by sentence basis we see (in Table 7) that
the rules increase accuracy from 30.4% to 49.5%.

Finally, in Table 8, we show the results of testing the tag elimination theory
in isolation. As expected, the theory is seriously under-general: only 62% of
tags that should be eliminated are eliminated. However, tags are very rarely

Table 4. Per-word tagging accuracy.

Lexical errors?	Ambiguous				Overall			
	Correct	Total	Lex-Errs	Acc	Correct	Total	Lex-Errs	Acc
Included	19495	22956	247	84.9%	106719	110716	783	96.4%
Excluded	19495	22709	0	85.8%	106719	109933	0	97.1%

Table 5. Per-word tagging accuracy with and without rules.

Theory	Ambiguous				Overall			
	Correct	Total	Lex-Errs	Acc	Correct	Total	Lex-Errs	Acc
Full	19495	22956	247	84.9%	106719	110716	783	96.4%
Empty	16937	22956	247	73.8%	104161	110716	783	94.1%

incorrectly eliminated. In this application we are *not* invoking the Closed World Assumption as is often done in ILP. If we can not prove that a tag should be eliminated, we do not assume it is the correct tag; instead we ask the lexicon to do the necessary disambiguation. This accounts for the large discrepancy between an accuracy of 77.4% for the rules in isolation and a system accuracy of 96.4%.

6 Conclusions and future work

The most important figure is that of overall 96.4% per-word tagging accuracy. Given our restrictions it is difficult to compare with other approaches, given the absence of many 'known' words results. Daelemans et al [5] achieve 96.7% on known words, but do not have our 'no quotes' restrictions. We conjecture that including sentences with quotes will not cause us too many problems, indeed will increase accuracy since quotes themselves are unambiguous and such sentences generally include the word "said" which is almost always a vbd. We conclude that the system produced here achieved a respectable result for a first application of Progol to the tagging problem, but that better results using an unrestricted system are required in the future.

Apart from the reasonable accuracy achieved, important features of this work include the combination of induced clauses and lexical statistics, the capturing of long-term dependencies, the construction of a reasonably comprehensible theory and the successful incorporation of caching.

Table 6. System tagging accuracy for sentences.

Lexical errors?	Correct	Total	Lex-Errs	Acc
Included	2475	5000	698	49.5%
Excluded	2475	4302	0	57.6%

Table 7. System tagging accuracy for sentences with and without rules.

Theory	Correct	Total	Lex-Errs	Acc
Full	2475	5000	698	49.5%
Empty	1520	5000	698	30.4%

Table 8. Contingency table for complete theory

Predicted↓	Actual Pos	Neg	Total
Pos	3439	146	3585
Neg	2111	4304	6415
Total	5550	4450	10000

True positives = 62.0%
True negatives = 96.7%
Overall accuracy = 77.4%

Having said this, our approach could be improved in a number of ways. We finish by listing, in order of importance, necessary future work.

Unknown words At present, we have *no* method of dealing with words that have not occurred in the training set. This means that the present system is not yet a practical tagging system. There is nothing to stop us "bolting on" a sensible method of dealing with unknown words which takes an unknown word and returns a tag ambiguity class. Brill [2] and Daelemans et al [5] both have methods for dealing with unknown words; these techniques could be incorporated into future work.

Noise handling Noisy data is particularly problematic when one is aiming for accuracies of over 96%. [8] used two linguists to pore over the training data to weed out noise. Our crude method of noise-handling is the single biggest cause of inaccuracy. Future work should use a Bayesian approach to take into account the absolute frequency with which a tag appears for a particular word, rather than the simply the proportion (relative frequency) with which it appears.

Combining rules and lexical statistics Our system uses two sources of information to tag a word:

1. The frequencies with which the word has been given particular tags, irrespective of context.
2. The context of the word in terms of the tags of the other words in the sentence.

Essentially, we are trying to find $\arg\max_{tag} P(tag|word, context)$. At present, we use the lexicon to estimate $P(tag|word)$ and have a collection of rules, such that if a rule of the form $remove(tag) \leftarrow context$ is present, then we assume, sometimes incorrectly, that $P(tag|context) < 0.05$ and also that if this inequality holds then *tag* has a lower probability than any other tag. If no elimination rule covers the word then we simply use $P(tag|word)$ to estimate $P(tag|word, context)$. A better approach would be to *label* induced clauses with estimates of their accuracy and to allow (labelled) clauses with much lower estimated accuracy to be included in the final theory, essentially using induced clauses as the structural component of a suitable probability distribution.

Including quotes The avoidance of sentences with quotes is a non-essential restriction and is primarily a matter of convenience. This should be dropped in future work.

Acknowledgements This work was supported by ESPRIT IV Long Term Research Project ILP II (No. 20237). The author would like to thank Walter Daelemans, Ashwin Srinivasan, David Page, Stephen Muggleton and two anonymous reviewers.

References

1. Steven Abney. Part-of-speech tagging and partial parsing. In Ken Church, Steve Young, and Gerrit Bloothooft, editors, *Corpus-Based Methods in Language and Speech*. Kluwer, Dordrecht, 1996.
2. Eric Brill. Some advances in transformation-based part of speech tagging. In *AAAI94*, 1994.
3. J. Cussens. Part-of-speech disambiguation using ILP. Technical Report PRG-TR-25-96, Oxford University Computing Laboratory, 1996.
4. Doug Cutting, Julian Kupiec, Jan Pedersen, and Penelope Sibun. A practical part-of-speech tagger. In *Third Conference on Applied Natural Linguistic Processing (ANLP-92)*, pages 133–140, 1992.
5. W. Daelemans, J. Zavrel, P. Berck, and S. Gillis. MBT: A memory-based part of speech tagger-generator. In *Proceedings of the Fourth Workshop on Very Large Corpora,*, pages 14–27, Copenhagen, 1996.
6. S. Muggleton. Inverse entailment and Progol. *New Generation Computing Journal*, 13:245–286, 1995.
7. Lawrence R. Rabiner. A tutorial on hidden Markov models and selected applications in speech recognition. *Proceedings of the IEEE*, 77(2):257–285, February 1989.
8. Christer Samuelsson, Pasi Tapanainen, and Atro Voutilainen. Inducing constraint grammars. In Laurent Miclet and Colin de la Higuera, editors, *Grammatical Inference: Learning Syntax from Sentences*, volume 1147 of *Lecture Notes in Artificial Intelligence*, pages 146–155. Springer, 1996.
9. Pasi Tapanainen and Atro Voutilainen. Tagging accurately – Don't guess if you know. In *Proc. ANLP94*, 1994.

Maximum Entropy Modeling with Clausal Constraints

Luc Dehaspe

Katholieke Universiteit Leuven, Department of Computer Science,
Celestijnenlaan 200A, B-3001 Heverlee, Belgium
email : Luc.Dehaspe@cs.kuleuven.ac.be
fax : ++ 32 16 32 79 96; telephone : ++ 32 16 32 75 67

Abstract. We present the learning system MACCENT which addresses the novel task of stochastic MAximum ENTropy modeling with Clausal Constraints. Maximum Entropy method is a Bayesian method based on the principle that the target stochastic model should be as uniform as possible, subject to known constraints. MACCENT incorporates clausal constraints that are based on the evaluation of Prolog clauses in examples represented as Prolog programs. We build on an existing maximum-likelihood approach to maximum entropy modeling, which we upgrade along two dimensions: (1) MACCENT can handle larger search spaces, due to a partial ordering defined on the space of clausal constraints, and (2) uses a richer first-order logic format. In comparison with other inductive logic programming systems, MACCENT seems to be the first that explicitly constructs a conditional probability distribution $p(C|I)$ based on an empirical distribution $\tilde{p}(C|I)$ (where $p(C|I)$ ($\tilde{p}(C|I)$) equals the induced (observed) probability of an instance I belonging to a class C). First experiments indicate MACCENT may be useful for prediction, and for classification in cases where the induced model should be combined with other stochastic information sources.

Keywords: stochastic modeling, inductive logic programming

1 Introduction

Bayesian probability theory permits one to use prior knowledge for making rational inferences about the behavior of a random process. *Maximum Entropy* [15] method is a Bayesian method based on the principle that the target stochastic model should be as uniform as possible, subject to constraints extracted from the training distribution. This principle is not new, it can in fact be traced back to Laplace, and beyond, but relatively recent developments in computer science have boosted its popularity and have enabled its application to real-world problems, mainly in physics (cf. [14]). As a starting point for our research we used the paper by Berger, Della Pietra, and Della Pietra [1], which presents a maximum-likelihood approach to the construction of maximum entropy models of natural language.

We have combined the statistical approach of [1] with techniques from the field of inductive logic programming to build the relational learner MACCENT that addresses the task of MAximum ENTropy modeling with Clausal Constraints. The adjective "clausal" here refers to the fact that in MACCENT the constraints, which are the building blocks of maximum entropy modeling, are based on the evaluation of Prolog clauses in examples represented as Prolog programs. The integration of probabilistic methods with inductive logic programming has recently become a popular research topic (cf. [5, 16, 19, 21, 22]), but, to the best of our knowledge, MACCENT is the first inductive logic programming algorithm that explicitly constructs a conditional probability distribution $p(C|I)$ based on an empirical distribution $\tilde{p}(C|I)$ (where $p(C|I)$ $(\tilde{p}(C|I))$ gives the induced (observed) probability of an instance I belonging to a class C).

We start our discussion with a brief introduction to the logical and mathematical foundations (Section 2). In the two next parts we then present the task addressed by MACCENT (Section 3), and the algorithm itself (Section 4). Finally, we report on classification and prediction experiments with a prototypical implementation of MACCENT (Section 5), and conclude (Section 6). Though throughout the paper we have restricted the logical notation to a minimum, we do assume some familiarity with the programming language Prolog [3].

2 Logical and statistical background

2.1 Logical paradigm: learning from interpretations

animal	has_covering	has_legs	habitat	homeothermic	class
dog	hair	yes	land	yes	mammal
dolphin	none	no	water	yes	mammal
trout	scales	no	water	no	fish
shark	none	no	water	no	fish
herring	scales	no	water	no	fish
eagle	feathers	yes	air	yes	bird
penguin	feathers	yes	water	yes	bird
lizard	scales	yes	land	no	reptile
snake	scales	no	land	no	reptile
turtle	scales	yes	land	no	reptile

Table 1. The animals domain

Consider the data in Table 1, which presents instances of four classes of animals. Traditional attribute-value learners represent each animal and candidate classification rule as a set of attribute-value pairs, such that simple subset test suffices in order to verify if a rule covers an instance. Alternatively, one can store the information available about a single animal in a Prolog knowledge base, encode candidate rules as Prolog queries, and apply the Prolog execution mechanism to verify whether or not a rule covers an instance. If the query succeeds, the rule covers the instance. If the query fails[1], the rule does not cover the instance. For example, the logical conjunction *has_legs* ∧ *habitat(land)* covers instance *dog* because the Prolog query ← *has_legs* ∧ *habitat(land)* succeeds in the Prolog program dog:

```
animal(dog). has_covering(hair). has_legs. habitat(land).
homeothermic. class(mammal).
```

Notice that the attribute-value and Prolog representations are equivalent in standard propositional domains. In Prolog notation however instances can be Prolog programs of deliberate size and complexity, rather than fixed-length vectors of attribute-value pairs. As a consequence, background knowledge can be added in a natural way as Prolog code shared by all instances. For example, with Prolog clause *kids_love_it* ← *homeothermic* ∧ *habitat(water)* added as background knowledge to Table 1, rule *has_covering(none)* ∧ *kids_love_it* exclusively covers instance dolphin.

The above alternative and flexible Prolog based representation and verification method fits in the *learning from interpretations* paradigm, introduced by [9] and related to other inductive logic programming settings in [7]. This paradigm provides a convenient environment for upgrading attribute-value learners to first order logic, witness ICL [10] and TILDE [2] which are first order equivalents of respectively CN2 and C4.5.

2.2 Statistical paradigm: maximum entropy

Let us reconsider the data in Table 1, and interpret them as as a sample of an expert biologist's decisions concerning the class of animals. The observed behavior of the biologist can be summarized as an empirical conditional distribution $\tilde{p}(C|I)$ that, given the description of an instance in I in the first five columns, assigns probability 1 to the class specified in the last column, and 0 to all other classes. Sample $\tilde{p}$ can be used to support the construction of a stochastic model p to predict the behavior of the biologist. Given an instance I, this target model will assign to each class C_j an estimate $p(C_j|I)$ of the conditional probability that the biologist would classify I as C_j.

"Relevant" facts (statistics) extracted from the empirical distribution $\tilde{p}$ are the building blocks of the target distribution p. For example, with sample Table 1, $\tilde{p}$ assigns conditional probability 1 to exactly four classes C. If we are convinced this fact captures relevant information about the sample, we can construct our model p such that, for all instances I it meets the following constraint:

$$p(mammal|I) + p(fish|I) + p(bird|I) + p(reptile|I) = 1 \qquad (1)$$

There is of course a whole family of models that meet constraint (1). However, some members of this family seem more justified than others, given the limited

---

[1] Termination can be guaranteed by employing a depth-bound on the depth of the proof tree.

empirical evidence (1) we have gathered so far. More specifically, the model p_{mfbr} that assigns equal 0.25 probability to all four classes seems intuitively more reasonable than a model p_{mf} that grants probability 0.5 to *mammal* and *fish*, and 0 to the other classes. Though model p_{mf} agrees with what we know, it contains information for which we have – as yet – no evidence. A stochastic model that avoids such bold assumptions, should be as "uniform" as possible, subject to the known constraints.

In the maximum entropy paradigm [15] conditional entropy

$$H(p) \equiv -\frac{1}{N} \sum_{C,I} p(C|I) \log p(C|I) \qquad (2)$$

is used to measure uniformity[2], with N the number of instances in the sample. For example, if we apply the conditional entropy metric to the two alternative models introduced in the previous paragraph for the animals domain, we obtain:

$$H(p_{mfbr}) = -\frac{1}{10} * 10 * 4 * 0.25 * \log(0.25) = -\log(0.25) \simeq 1.39$$

$$H(p_{mf}) = -\frac{1}{10} * 10 * 2 * 0.50 * \log(0.50) = -\log(0.50) \simeq 0.69$$

The *Maximum Entropy Principle* then states that, from the family of conditional probability distributions allowed by an empirically compiled set of constraints, we should elect the model with maximum conditional entropy $H(p)$. In the example, $H(p_{mfbr}) > H(p_{mf})$, therefore, in accordance with our intuitions, p_{mfbr} is preferable.

3   Maximum entropy modeling with clausal constraints

3.1   The building blocks: clausal constraints

As indicated in the previous section, the building blocks of a maximum entropy model are constraints such as Equation (1). MACCENT incorporates constraints based on *boolean clausal indicator functions* $f(I, C)$ with general form:

$$f_{j,k}(I, C) = \begin{cases} 1 & \text{if } C = C_j, \text{ and} \\ & \quad \text{Prolog query} \leftarrow Q_k \text{ succeeds in instance } I \\ 0 & \text{otherwise} \end{cases} \qquad (3)$$

A clausal[3] indicator function $f_{j,k}$ gives rise to a *clausal constraint* of the form

$$CC_{j,k} : p(f_{j,k}) = \tilde{p}(f_{j,k}) \qquad (4)$$

---

[2] Throughout the paper log denotes natural logarithm.

[3] Recall that Prolog queries are a special type of Prolog *clauses* with **false** in the conclusion part.

where $p(f_{j,k})$ is the *expected value* of $f_{j,k}(I,C)$ in the target distribution, and $\tilde{p}(f_{j,k})$ is the expected value of $f_{j,k}(I,C)$ in the empirical distribution. For any $f_{j,k}(I,C)$, the calculation of its expected value with respect to a conditional (target or empirical) distribution proceeds as follows.

First, we count the number of instances in which Prolog query $\leftarrow Q_k$ succeeds. We can obtain this number by taking the sum over all instances $\sum_I f_{j,k}(I,C_j)$. For example, given the data in Table 1, and

$$C_1 = fish$$
$$Q_1 = \neg has\_legs \wedge habitat(water),$$

such that,

$$f_{1,1}(I,C) = \begin{cases} 1 & \text{if } C = fish, \text{ and} \\ & \leftarrow \neg has\_legs \wedge habitat(water) \text{ succeeds in } I \\ 0 & \text{otherwise} \end{cases}$$

we find that $\leftarrow Q_1$ succeeds in four instances. Accordingly, the set of (*instance, class*) tuples for which $f_{1,1}$ evaluates to one is

$$\{(dolphin, fish), (trout, fish), (shark, fish), (herring, fish)\}.$$

All other combinations evaluate to zero, either because the class is not fish, or because query $\leftarrow \neg has\_legs \wedge habitat(water)$ does not succeed in the instance. Hence,

$$\#\{\text{instances in which} \leftarrow Q_1 \text{ succeeds}\} = \sum_I f_{1,1}(I,C_1) = 4.$$

Next, we normalize the summation with constant N, the number of instances in the sample, for example $1/10 \sum_I f_{1,1}(I,C_1) = 0.4$. Finally, to obtain the expected value $p(f_{j,k})$ of $f_{j,k}(I,C)$ in model p, we multiply $f_{j,k}(I,C_j)$ by $p(C_j|I)$. Thus, instead of adding 1 for each instance in which $\leftarrow Q_k$ succeeds, we add the number between 0 and 1 model p assigns to the conditional probability of class C_j given instance I. For the expected value of $f_{j,k}(I,C)$ in empirical distribution $\tilde{p}$, and in target distribution p this yields the equations

$$\tilde{p}(f_{j,k}) \equiv \frac{1}{N} \sum_I \tilde{p}(C_j|I)f_{j,k}(I,C_j) \tag{5}$$

$$p(f_{j,k}) \equiv \frac{1}{N} \sum_I p(C_j|I)f_{j,k}(I,C_j) \tag{6}$$

For example, reconsider the uniform conditional distribution p_{mfbr} introduced above. We know that $p_{mfbr}(fish|I) = 0.25$ for all ten instances in Table 1. As $f_{1,1}(I,fish)$ evaluates to one for the four instances dolphin, trout, shark, herring, and zero for all other instances, the expected value $p_{mfbr}(f_{1,1})$ of indicator function $f_{1,1}(I,C)$ in model p_{mfbr} is

$$p_{mfbr}(f_{1,1}) = \frac{1}{10} * (0.25 + 0.25 + 0.25 + 0.25) = 0.1.$$

On the other hand, in the sample we find that $\tilde{p}(fish|I) = 1$ for the three instances trout, shark, and herring, and $\tilde{p}(fish|I) = 0$ for all other instances, including dolphin. Hence,

$$\tilde{p}(f_{1,1}) = \frac{1}{10} * (1 + 1 + 1) = 0.3.$$

Function $f_{1,1}$, through its expected value, thus reveals a discrepancy between the empirical distribution $\tilde{p}$ and target distribution p_{mfbr}:

$$p_{mfbr}(f_{1,1}) + 0.2 = \tilde{p}(f_{1,1}).$$

This discrepancy disappears if we add the clausal constraint

$$CC_{1,1} : p_{mfbr}(f_{1,1}) = \tilde{p}(f_{1,1}) = 0.3$$

to our initial constraint Equation (1), and construct a new target model that maximizes conditional entropy subject to both constraints.

As a second example, consider $f_{2,2}$ defined by:

$$C_2 = reptile$$
$$Q_2 = \neg has\_covering(hair) \wedge \neg has\_legs$$

The expected values are $p_{mfbr}(f_{2,2}) = 0.125$, and $\tilde{p}(f_{2,2}) = 0.1$. Notice that with respect to the sample the expected value $p_{mfbr}(f_{2,2})$ is 0.025 units too high, whereas $p_{mfbr}(f_{1,1})$ is 0.2 units too low. Later, where we discuss the construction of the new target model, we will see that a model that incorporates $CC_{1,1}$ assigns a positive weight to $f_{1,1}$, whereas a model that incorporates $CC_{2,2}$ assigns a negative weight to $f_{2,2}$. The intuition behind these weights is that Q_1 is a better indication for *fish*, and Q_2 a worse indication for *reptile* than is assumed in model p_{mfbr}.

3.2 Problem specification

Now that we have described the building blocks, we can formulate the task of *maximum entropy modeling with clausal constraints*:

- *Given*: A set $\mathcal{I}$ of N training instances, represented as Prolog programs;
- *Given*: An empirical conditional distribution $\tilde{p}(C|I)$, with $I \in \mathcal{I}$;
- *Given*: A language $\mathcal{L}$ of clausal constraints $CC_{j,k} : p(f_{j,k}) = \tilde{p}(f_{j,k})$;
- *Find*: An optimal set $CC \subseteq \mathcal{L}$ of clausal constraints;
- *Find*: A stochastic model $p^{CC}(C|I)$ that maximizes conditional entropy $H(p)$ subject to the clausal constraints in CC.

To restate, algorithms that address this task receive as input training instances, an empirical conditional distribution that relates training instances to classes, and a set of clausal constraints. In response, they must (1) select an "optimal" subset of clausal constraints, and (2) with these constraints build a model for use in classifying new instances.

3.3 Model selection

We come back to the selection of CC later, and first concentrate on the modeling subtask. Given set $CC = \{CC_{j_1,k_1}, CC_{j_2,k_2}, \ldots, CC_{j_M,k_M}\}$ of M clausal constraints, the method of Lagrange multipliers from the theory of constrained optimization produces the model p that maximizes conditional entropy $H(p)$. As discussed thoroughly in [12, 1], the model in question has the parametric form

$$p_\Lambda(C|I) = \frac{1}{Z_\Lambda(I)} \exp\left(\sum_{m=1}^{M} \lambda_m f_{j_m,k_m}(I, C)\right). \tag{7}$$

In parameter set $\Lambda = \{\lambda_1, \lambda_2, \ldots, \lambda_M\}$, each of the M parameters (Lagrange multipliers) λ_m corresponds to a clausal constraint $CC_{j_m,k_m} \in CC$ based on clausal indicator function f_{j_m,k_m}. The optimal parameter set Λ can be determined by maximizing the log-likelihood $L_{\tilde{p}}(p_\Lambda)$ of the empirical distribution $\tilde{p}$, which is defined by

$$L_{\tilde{p}}(p_\Lambda) = -\frac{1}{N} \sum_I \log Z_\Lambda(I) + \sum_{m=1}^{M} \lambda_m \tilde{p}(f_{j_m,k_m}) \tag{8}$$

where $Z_\Lambda(I)$ is a normalization constant:

$$Z_\Lambda(I) = \sum_C \exp\left(\sum_{m=1}^{M} \lambda_m f_{j_m,k_m}(I, C)\right) \tag{9}$$

If we apply these equations to our running example, we obtain, after reduction,

$$L_{\tilde{p}}(p_{\{\lambda_1\}}) = -0.4 * \log(e^{\lambda_1} + 3) - 0.6 * \log(4) + 0.3 * \lambda_1$$
$$L_{\tilde{p}}(p_{\{\lambda_2\}}) = -0.5 * \log(e^{\lambda_2} + 3) - 0.5 * \log(4) + 0.1 * \lambda_2$$

where λ_1 and λ_2 correspond to $f_{1,1}$ and $f_{2,2}$. The graph of these two log-likelihood functions is plotted in Figure 1. On the X axis of this graph, we find the λ values, on the Y axis the log-likelihood of the Table 1 training set. The graph shows that with $CC = \{CC_{1,1}\}$, the optimal parameter set $\{\lambda_1\}$ is obtained with a positive value close to two for λ_1. This agrees with the earlier finding that in the uniform distribution, $p_{mfbr}(f_{1,1}) < \tilde{p}(f_{1,1})$. The intuition here is that the appropriateness of $CC_{1,1}$ has been underestimated in p, and a positive weight λ_1 is required to correct this. The opposite holds for $CC = \{CC_{2,2}\}$, where the optimum for λ_2 is reached in a negative value close to zero. Notice both graphs intersect on the Y axis. The point of intersection $(0, -1.39)$ corresponds to the case where no constraints apart from Equation (1) are added (i.e. the weights are set to zero).

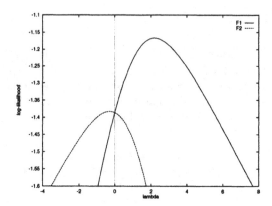

Fig. 1. The log-likelihood functions $F1 = L_{\tilde{p}}(p_{\{\lambda_1\}})$ and $F2 = L_{\tilde{p}}(p_{\{\lambda_2\}})$.

3.4 Feature selection

Let us now return to the selection of an optimal set $CC \subset \mathcal{L}$. For the time being we assume an exhaustive search through $2^{\mathcal{L}}$ and focus on an evaluation function for $S \subset \mathcal{L}$. Notice that maximum entropy and maximum likelihood are dual problems and that, of all models of parametric form (7), the maximum entropy model is the one that maximizes the likelihood of the sample. As might be clear from the above discussion of Figure 1, this maximum is function of the set S of clausal constraints. We are interested in the set S that produces the highest likelihood of the training sample $\tilde{p}$. Formally, if we let p^S denote the maximum entropy model obtained with a set S of clausal constraints then

$$CC \equiv \operatorname*{argmax}_{S \subset \mathcal{L}} L_{\tilde{p}}(p^S) \tag{10}$$

For an illustration of this evaluation function consider again Figure 1. The graph shows that with $\{CC_1\}$ we can obtain log-likelihood around -1.17, whereas with $\{CC_2\}$ we only reach -1.38. Therefore, of these two sets, $\{CC_1\}$ is to be preferred. In Table 2 the conditional probabilities are shown for the two models $p^{\{CC_1\}}$ and $p^{\{CC_2\}}$. Notice $p^{\{CC_1\}}$ is indeed closer to Table 1 than $p^{\{CC_2\}}$.

4 The MACCENT Algorithm

In this section we present the learning system MACCENT which addresses the task of MAximum ENTropy modeling with Clausal Constraints. The task as described in the previous section does not directly translate to a tractable algorithm. Usually, with millions of clausal constraints in $\mathcal{L}$, it is prohibitive to inspect all subsets of $\mathcal{L}$ in search for the optimal one. In our description of MACCENT we will gradually abandon the request for optimality of CC. We first discuss a greedy search method and an approximate gain evaluation function, both due

animal	$p = p^{\{CC_1\}}$				$p = p^{\{CC_2\}}$			
	$p(m\|I)$	$p(f\|I)$	$p(b\|I)$	$p(r\|I)$	$p(m\|I)$	$p(f\|I)$	$p(b\|I)$	$p(r\|I)$
dog	0.25	0.25	0.25	0.25	0.25	0.25	0.25	0.25
dolphin	0.08	0.76	0.08	0.08	0.26	0.26	0.26	0.22
trout	0.08	0.76	0.08	0.08	0.26	0.26	0.26	0.22
shark	0.25	0.25	0.25	0.25	0.26	0.26	0.26	0.22
herring	0.08	0.76	0.08	0.08	0.26	0.26	0.26	0.22
eagle	0.25	0.25	0.25	0.25	0.25	0.25	0.25	0.25
penguin	0.25	0.25	0.25	0.25	0.25	0.25	0.25	0.25
lizard	0.25	0.25	0.25	0.25	0.25	0.25	0.25	0.25
snake	0.25	0.25	0.25	0.25	0.26	0.26	0.26	0.22
turtle	0.25	0.25	0.25	0.25	0.25	0.25	0.25	0.25

Table 2. Two target distributions for the animals domain

to [1]. In addition, we then propose a structure on $\mathcal{L}$ that one can use to organize the search process.

As shown in Algorithm 1, MACCENT carries out a greedy search, adjoining clausal constraints one at a time, using an evaluation function to select the next constraint at each step. Given a set S of constraints collected so far, a natural evaluation function for a candidate clausal constraint $\widehat{cc}$ returns the gain $\triangle L_{\tilde{p}}(S, \widehat{cc})$ in the log-likelihood of the training data obtained by that adding $\widehat{cc}$ to S:

$$\triangle L_{\tilde{p}}(S, \widehat{cc}) \equiv L_{\tilde{p}}(p^{S \cup \widehat{cc}}) - L_{\tilde{p}}(p^{S}). \tag{11}$$

As $L_{\tilde{p}}(p^{S})$ remains constant, this comes down to adding at each step the constraint CC that maximizes $L_{\tilde{p}}(p^{S \cup CC})$. We have thus reduced the selection task to the discovery of the best $CC \in \mathcal{L}$. For instance, consider again our running example and the graph in Figure 1. Knowing that $L_{\tilde{p}}(p^{\theta}) = -\log(4) \simeq -1.39$, we can compute that the gain obtained by adding $CC_{1,1}$ and $CC_{2,2}$ is something round 0.22 and 0.01 respectively. Therefore, $CC_{1,1}$ is a better initial choice.

Algorithm 1 : MACCENT

Inputs: Language $\mathcal{L}$; empirical distribution $\tilde{p}(C|I)$
Outputs: Set CC of clausal constraints; model p^{CC}

1. Start with $CC = \emptyset$; thus p^{CC} is uniform
2. Select next clausal constraint $\widehat{cc}$ from $\mathcal{L}$ using Algorithm 2
3. Check the termination condition
4. Adjoin $\widehat{cc}$ to CC
5. Compute p^{CC} using Equation (7)
6. Go to step 2

Still, given the "old" set $S = \{CC_1, \ldots, CC_n\}$, log-likelihood gain requires for each candidate $\hat{cc} \in \mathcal{L}$ the computation of the set of parameters $\Lambda = \{\lambda_1, \ldots, \lambda_n, \alpha\}$ that maximizes $L_{\tilde{p}}(p_\Lambda)$, where α is the parameter that corresponds to $\hat{cc}$. Various numerical methods have been applied to this problem, including problem specific algorithms such as BROWN [4] or ITERATIVE SCALING [6]. However, none of these methods allow for a sufficiently efficient computation of gain $\Delta L_{\tilde{p}}(\mathcal{S}, \hat{cc})$. As a remedy, [1] introduce the notion of *approximate gain* which no longer requires the computation of $n + 1$ parameters. The "old" parameter set $\{\lambda_1, \ldots, \lambda_n\}$ is retained, and the approximation is made that the addition of constraint $\hat{cc}$ affects only parameter α. Given candidate constraint $\hat{cc}$ derived from indicator function $\hat{f}$, Equation (8) then reduces to

$$G_{S,f}(\alpha) = -\frac{1}{N} \sum_{I,C} \log \left(p^S(C|I) e^{\alpha \hat{f}(I,C)} \right) + \alpha \tilde{p}(\hat{f}) \qquad (12)$$

Equation (12) in turn simplifies the computation of the *approximate gain*

$$\sim \Delta L_{\tilde{p}}(\mathcal{S}, \hat{cc}) \equiv \max_\alpha G_{S,f}(\alpha) \qquad (13)$$

to a one-dimensional optimization problem which can be solved, for instance, with Newton's method.

Though [1] has shown one can implement a high-performance algorithm on the basis of the above approximations, we still assume an exhaustive search through a flat, unstructured space $\mathcal{L}$ of clausal constraints. To further speed up the search, and enable the exploration of bigger search spaces, MACCENT extends these approximations with classical machine learning techniques. The key observation here is that generality imposes a partial ordering on $\mathcal{L}$:

$CC_{j,k}$ is more general than $CC_{j',k'}$ if and only if
$C_j \leftarrow Q_k$ is logically more general than $C_{j'} \leftarrow Q_{k'}$.

One can specify a lattice for clausal constraints with a set of most general descriptions $\{CC_{j,k} \in \mathcal{L} | Q_k = true\}$ at the top, and a specialisation operator for top-down exploration of this lattice. In MACCENT we handle both tasks, language specification and specialisation, with the declarative language bias formalism DLAB [11], which is based on θ subsumption (cf. [20]).

As shown in Algorithm 2, MACCENT exploits the lattice structure of $\mathcal{L}$ to carry out a general-to-specific heuristic beam search for clausal constraints with satisfactory, rather than optimal, approximate gain. At each level of its search, MACCENT considers all specialisations of clausal constraints in the beam, and if necessary updates the current best solution.

We still have to specify a stopping criterion (Algorithm 1, step 3) and a procedure for pruning *Beam* (Algorithm 2, step 5). For our stopping criterion we use Equation (8) to calculate the log-likelihood $L_{\tilde{p}}(p^{CC \cup \hat{cc}})$ of a separate empirical distribution $\bar{p}$. If the log-likelihood of this witheld portion of the training set decreases[4] with the addition of $\hat{cc}$, this is taken as an indication of overtraining, and MACCENT terminates.

---

[4] A delay is built in to allow recovery from a temporary decrease.

Algorithm 2 : Select next clausal constraint

Inputs: Language $\mathcal{L}$; empirical distribution $\tilde{p}(C|I)$; current set CC
Outputs: Clausal constraint $\widehat{cc}$

1. Initialize current best approximate gain $Best := -1$
2. Initialize $Beam := \{CC_{j,k} \in \mathcal{L}|Q_k = true\}$
3. For each cc in $Beam$, and for each specialisation $cc' \in \mathcal{L}$ of cc:
   (a) Compute $Gain = \triangle L_{\tilde{p}}(CC, cc')$ using Equation (13),
   (b) If $Gain > Best$ then update $Best := Gain$ and $\widehat{cc} := cc'$,
   (c) Add cc' to $Beam$
4. Prune $Beam$
5. If $Beam$ is not empty, go to step 3

Given a beam size BS, the default strategy for pruning $Beam$ is to rank the clausal constraints cc' in $Beam$ according to their $Gain$ and keep at most BS of the best scoring constraints. However, in cases where the input empirical distribution assigns only probabilities 1 and 0, as for instance in Table 1, we can apply a more sophisticated heuristic. Thereto, we define the notion of *potential approximate gain* as an upper bound to the maximum $Gain$ that can be obtained via further specialisation of cc'. We cannot go into details here, but under the circumstances mentioned, potential approximate gain can easily be computed. One has to select the instances for which $\tilde{p}(C'|I) = 1$, compute the approximate gain counting only this subset, do the same for the complementary subset, and take the maximum of both computations. The potential approximate gain upper bound allows a branch-and-bound search in which clausal constraints are pruned that after specialisation can never produce an approximate gain above the current best. Apart from that, potential approximate gain can also be used in combination with actual approximate gain to better rank the constraints in $Beam$[5].

5   Experiments

In this section we report on some first classification and prediction experiments with a prototypical Prolog implementation of MACCENT. Both classification and numeric prediction could in fact be considered as special cases of the task of learning from a conditional probability distribution $\tilde{p}(C|I)$: with classification $\tilde{p}(C|I)$ only takes values 0 and 1; with numeric prediction there are only two classes C. We would like to stress that the full power of MACCENT should best be demonstrated on the general case of multi-class datasets where $\tilde{p}$ can take any real value between 0 and 1 (e.g. distribution of votes for more than two

---

[5] MACCENT mainly employs the average of the actual and the potential approximate gain.

candidates in different districts). At present however, such data do not seem to be readily available.

First, we round off the running example with the application of MACCENT to the multi-class animals domain. With the hold-out stopping criterion suppressed, MACCENT found 13 constraints before the log-likelihood of Table 1 was reduced to 0. The components C_j and Q_k of the indicator functions $f_{j,k}$ on which these clausal constraints are based are shown, in order of discovery, in Table 3. The approximate gain, best λ, and log-likelihood of the sample are listed in columns 3, 4, and 5 respectively.

C_j	Q_k	gain	λ	llh
reptile	has_covering(scales) ∧ habitat(land)	0.266	1.59	-1.114
fish	¬has_legs ∧ ¬homeothermic	0.227	1.56	-0.883
bird	has_covering(feathers)	0.177	1.59	-0.702
mammal	¬has_covering(feathers) ∧ homeothermic	0.177	1.59	-0.520
fish	¬has_covering(none) ∧ ¬habitat(water)	0.107	-36.98	-0.414
bird	¬has_covering(feathers)	0.118	-36.97	-0.296
mammal	¬homeothermic	0.104	-36.86	-0.192
reptile	true	0.092	-1.56	-0.099
fish	homeothermic	0.033	-37.10	-0.066
mammal	has_covering(feathers)	0.036	-36.09	-0.030
reptile	true	0.022	-1.46	-0.007
reptile	¬habitat(land)	0.005	-37.21	-0.002
reptile	¬has_covering(scales)	0.002	-35.89	0

Table 3. Output of MACCENT on the animals domain

5.1 Classification

When compared to other inductive logic programming classifiers, MACCENT has the advantage that it induces a conditional probability distribution that can directly be combined with other stochastic information sources. To illustrate this point we conducted a relatively small experiment with natural language data extracted from the Wall Street journal corpus [18].

In this corpus the words are tagged with so-called Parts-of-Speech (POS). We grouped the tags into 16 classes, the most important of which are noun, adjective, verb, punctuation, determiner, pronoun, adverb. Next, based on frequency counts in the corpus, we set up a dictionary that, given a word w assigns to each class POS a lexical probability $p_{dict}(POS|w)$. For instance, $p_{dict}(adjective|cross) = 0.03$, $p_{dict}(noun|cross) = 0.69$, $p_{dict}(verb|cross) = 0.28$. Then we selected from the corpus the first 1000 occurrences of words, such as cross, that are ambiguous between exactly the three classes noun, adjective, and verb. We stored each word, with its class label, and the tagged left and right context in a separate instance. As background knowledge we specified Prolog predicates $left(Index, Limit, POS)$, and $right(Index, Limit, POS)$ that check whether a certain tag POS appears in the context of a word within distance $Limit$, where $Index$ is the position the word in the sentence. In the language $\mathcal{L}$, with a size of order 10^{15}, we allowed combinations of these two predicates, with $Limit$ taking values 1, 2, 3, 4, 5, and *unlimited*, and with POS instantiated to one of the 16 morphological categories. Finally, we ran MACCENT on this 3-class problem to construct a probability distribution $p_{context}(POS|w)$ based on the context of the word.

Classifying words into the class with highest probability as predicted by the model we ran a 10-fold crossvalidation based on a random partition over 1000 instances, and each time measured the performance in terms of classification accuracy. The model $p_{context}(POS|w)$ induced by MACCENT achieved an average accuracy of 70.4%($\pm$4.8). The model $p_{dict}(POS|w)$ based on the dictionary had a much better score of 81.2($\pm$3.0). The best score however was obtained from the combination of the two models $p_{context}(POS|w) * p_{dict}(POS|w)$ which achieved an accuracy of 85.4($\pm$3.0).

Though MACCENT by itself is likely to perform better in the presence of more sophisticated background knowledge, this initial experiment with POS-tagging demonstrates the (poor) output of MACCENT can successfully be combined with other stochastic information sources. For a more mature application of maximum entropy method to the general POS-tagging problem, we refer to [23].

5.2 Numeric prediction

Recall that one of the inputs to MACCENT is an empirical distribution $\tilde{p}(C|I)$. In the previous examples, $\tilde{p}$ took only the values 0 and 1. Multi-class datasets where $\tilde{p}$ can take any real value between 0 and 1, do not seem to be readily available. There are however enough tasks available that involve regression, the prediction of a numeric value. These values can always be projected onto a scale from 0 to 1. With some abuse of the intuitions behind a conditional probability model, MACCENT can now interpret the rescaled values as estimates of the probability that the example belongs the single "positive" class. The inverse "unscaling" projection allows one to calculate predictions from the induced model. Like FORS [16], which incorporates linear regression techniques, SRT [17], which builds structural regression trees, and C0.5 [8] which builds first order clusters, MACCENT can then perform first order regression from positive data only.

We applied this technique to two benchmark domains well known in the inductive logic programming community: mutagenicity [25], and mesh design [13].

In the first domain the task is to predict the log mutagenicity of molecules on the basis of structural information on the compounds. We used the full set of available background predicates and defined a language $\mathcal{L}$ with size order 10^{24}. With a 10-fold crossvalidation we obtained an average standard error of 1.38($\pm$0.18), with log-mutagenicity ranging from -3 to 5.39.

The second domain requires a prediction about the coarseness of a mesh model used to approximate physical structures. For every edge of the structure one has to decide on the number, ranging from 1 to 17, of subedges on the basis of properties of the edge and of related edges. We focused our experiments on the 5 structure (A,B,C,D,E) dataset. With a language $\mathcal{L}$, with size of order 10^7, we tried both a 5-fold leave-one-structure-out (mesh-xv5) and a random 10-fold crossvalidation (mesh-xv10). We calculated standard error of the estimate, and accuracy. For accuracy we rounded MACCENT's predictions to the nearest class. Table 4 summarizes results for MACCENT and ICL [10].

	Accuracy		Standard error	
Algorithm	mesh-xv5	mesh-xv10	mesh-xv5	mesh-xv10
ICL	0.50	0.70(±0.05)	2.82(±1.19)	1.84(±1.03)
MACCENT	0.25	0.44(±0.11)	2.83(±0.42)	1.54(±0.33)

Table 4. Performances on the mesh domain

The above table shows roughly the same picture for mesh-xv5 and mesh-xv10: MACCENT scores a lot worse on accuracy, but comparable on standard error. We take this as an indication that the scaling technique indeed makes sense, and that MACCENT can be considered for solving regression tasks.

6 Conclusion and future work

We have presented a framework for combining maximum entropy modeling with inductive logic programming techniques, and a number of approximations that led to the definition and implementation of the MACCENT algorithm. First experiments indicate the first order statistical modeling algorithm MACCENT may be useful for prediction, and for classification in cases where the induced model should be combined with other stochastic information sources.

Further experiments are required on more appropriate multi-class datasets where empirical conditional probability $\tilde{p}$ can take any real value between 0 and 1. For these experiments we intend to make use of the Maximum Entropy Modeling Toolkit [24] to improve our initial prototypical implementation. Future theoretical research should clarify the relationship between MACCENT and (more) standard inductive logic programming approaches to classification and regression.

Acknowledgements

This research is sponsored by the ESPRIT IV project no. 20237 on Inductive Logic Programming II (ILP^2). I would like to thank Walter Daelemans for his crucial pointer to the Maximum Entropy literature; Adam Berger, Vincent Della Pietra, Stephen Della Pietra, and Adwait Ratnaparkhi for their inspiring papers; Bojan Dolsak and Ashwin Srinivasan for the mesh and mutagenicity data; Hendrik Blockeel and Dirk Roose for mathematical assistance; Bart Demoen and

Wim Van Laer for their contributions to the implementation of MACCENT; and finally, Luc De Raedt and Maurice Bruynooghe for the stimulating (logical) context for this research.

References

1. A.L. Berger, V.J. Della Pietra, and S.A. Della Pietra. A maximum entropy approach to natural language processing. *Computational Linguistics*, 22(1):39–71, 1996.
2. H. Blockeel and L. De Raedt. Experiments with top-down induction of logical decision trees. Technical Report CW 247, Dept. of Computer Science, K.U.Leuven, January 1997. Also in Periodic Progress Report ESPRIT Project ILP2, January 1997. http://www.cs.kuleuven.ac.be/publicaties/rapporten/CW1997.html.
3. I. Bratko. *Prolog Programming for Artificial Intelligence*. Addison-Wesley, 1986.
4. D. Brown. A note on approximations to discrete probability distributions. *Information and Control*, 2:386–392, 1959.
5. J. Cussens. Baysian inductive logic programming with explicit probabilistic bias. Technical Report PRG-TR-24-96, Oxford University Computing Laboratory, 1996.
6. J. N. Darroch and D. Ratcliff. Generalized Iterative Scaling for Log-linear Models. *Annals of Mathematical Statistics*, 43:1470–1480, 1972.
7. L. De Raedt. Induction in logic. In R.S. Michalski and Wnek J., editors, *Proceedings of the 3rd International Workshop on Multistrategy Learning*, pages 29–38, 1996.
8. L. De Raedt and H. Blockeel. Using logical decision trees for clustering. In *Proceedings of the 7th International Workshop on Inductive Logic Programming*. Springer-Verlag, 1997.
9. L. De Raedt and S. Džeroski. First order jk-clausal theories are PAC-learnable. *Artificial Intelligence*, 70:375–392, 1994.
10. L. De Raedt and W. Van Laer. Inductive constraint logic. In *Proceedings of the 5th Workshop on Algorithmic Learning Theory*, volume 997 of *Lecture Notes in Artificial Intelligence*. Springer-Verlag, 1995.
11. L. Dehaspe and L. De Raedt. DLAB: A declarative language bias formalism. In *Proceedings of the International Symposium on Methodologies for Intelligent Systems (ISMIS96)*, volume 1079 of *Lecture Notes in Artificial Intelligence*, pages 613–622. Springer-Verlag, 1996.
12. S.A. Della Pietra, V.D. Della Pietra, and J. Lafferty. Inducing features of random fields. Technical Report CMU-CS-95-144, Carnegie-Mellon University, Pittsburgh, PA, 1995.
13. B. Dolšak and S. Muggleton. The application of Inductive Logic Programming to finite element mesh design. In S. Muggleton, editor, *Inductive logic programming*, pages 453–472. Academic Press, 1992.
14. S.F. Gull and G.J. Daniell. Image Reconstruction from Incomplete and Noisy Data. *Nature*, 272:686, 1978.
15. E.T. Jaynes. Notes on present status and future prospects. In W.T Grandy and L.H. Schick, editors, *Maximum Entropy and Bayesian Methods*, pages 1–13. Kluwer Academic Publishers, 1990.
16. A. Karalič and I. Bratko. First order regression. *Machine Learning*, 1997. To appear.

17. S. Kramer. Structural regression trees. In *Proceedings of the 13th National Conference on Artificial Intelligence (AAAI-96)*, 1996.

18. M.P. Marcus, B. Santorini, and M. A. Marcinkiewicz. Building a large annotated corpus of English: the Penn Treebank. *Computational Linguistics*, 19(2):313–330, 1993.

19. S. Muggleton. Stochastic logic programs. *Journal of Logic Programming*, 1997. submitted.

20. G. Plotkin. A note on inductive generalization. In *Machine Intelligence*, volume 5, pages 153–163. Edinburgh University Press, 1970.

21. U. Pompe and I. Kononenko. Naive bayesian classifier within ILP-R. In L. De Raedt, editor, *Proceedings of the 5th International Workshop on Inductive Logic Programming*, pages 417–436, 1995.

22. U. Pompe and I. Kononenko. Probabilistic first-order classification. In *Proceedings of the 7th International Workshop on Inductive Logic Programming*. Springer-Verlag, 1997.

23. A. Ratnaparkhi. A maximum entropy part-of-speech tagger. In *Proceedings of the Empirical Methods in Natural Language Processing Conference*. University of Pennsylvania, 1996.

24. E.S. Ristad. Maximum entropy toolkit, release 1.5 beta. Technical report, Princeton Univ., January 1997. ftp://ftp.cs.princeton.edu/pub/packages/memt.

25. A. Srinivasan, S.H. Muggleton, M.J.E. Sternberg, and R.D. King. Theories for mutagenicity: A study in first-order and feature-based induction. *Artificial Intelligence*, 85, 1996.

Mining Association Rules in Multiple Relations

Luc Dehaspe and Luc De Raedt

Katholieke Universiteit Leuven, Department of Computer Science,
Celestijnenlaan 200A, B-3001 Heverlee, Belgium
email : {Luc.Dehaspe, Luc.DeRaedt}@cs.kuleuven.ac.be
fax : ++ 32 16 32 79 96; telephone : ++ 32 16 32 75 67

Abstract. The application of algorithms for efficiently generating association rules is so far restricted to cases where information is put together in a single relation. We describe how this restriction can be overcome through the combination of the available algorithms with standard techniques from the field of inductive logic programming. We present the system WARMR, which extends APRIORI [2] to mine association rules in multiple relations. We apply WARMR to the natural language processing task of mining part-of-speech tagging rules in a large corpus of English. be applied to further constrain the space of *interesting* ARMR's.

Keywords: association rules, inductive logic programming

1 Introduction

Association rules are generally recognized as a highly valuable type of regularities and various algorithms have been presented for efficiently mining them in large databases (cf. [1, 7, 2]). To the best of our knowledge, the application of these algorithms is so far restricted to cases where information is put together in a single relation. We describe how this restriction can be overcome through the combination of the available algorithms with standard techniques from the field of inductive logic programming [6, 3, 8].

In Section 2, we first formalize the concept of association rules over multiple relations and the task of mining them in a deductive relational database. In Section 3, we present the algorithm WARMR, which extends APRIORI [2] to mine association rules in multiple relations. WARMR is applied in Section 4 to a database of Wall Street Journal articles.

2 Representation and Problem specification

We first recapitulate some original concepts of association rules over a single relation, and then generalize these to the case of association rules over multiple relations.

2.1 Association Rules

Agrawal, Imielinski, and Swami [1] define association rules as expressions of the form $X \Rightarrow Y$, where X and Y are itemsets, i.e. sets of attributes. Association rules are evaluated with respect to a relation $\mathcal{R}$ over a set $\mathcal{I}$ of binary attributes. Each example in $\mathcal{R}$ is associated with a unique key, below called the ExampleKey $ExKey$, and with an itemset $E \subseteq \mathcal{I}$ that contains all attributes with value 1. A rule $X \Rightarrow Y$ over relation $\mathcal{R}$ then holds with *confidence c* if $c\%$ of the itemsets in $\mathcal{R}$ that are supersets of X are also supersets of Y. The *support* of this rule equals s, if $s\%$ of the examples in $\mathcal{R}$ are supersets of $X \cup Y$.

For instance, given the relation kid(KID, Piglet, Dolphin, Icecream), the rule piglet, icecream $\Rightarrow$ dolphin (c:85,s:9) states that 85% of the kid-examples that like Piglet and icecream, also like dolphins, and that 9% of the kid-examples are fond of Piglet, icecream and dolphins.

The task of discovering association rules in a single relation $\mathcal{R}$ is to generate all association rules over $\mathcal{R}$ with confidence and support above given thresholds, below called *minconf* and *minsup* respectively. Efficient algorithms for solving this task proceed in two stages (cf. [1]). First, all *large* itemsets are generated, i.e. all itemsets with support above *minsup*. Second, the itemsets found large in the first stage are used to generate the target association rules without further consideration of the data in $\mathcal{R}$. This second step is based on the observation that $X \Rightarrow Y$ holds if and only if X and $X \cup Y$ are amongst the large itemsets, and $support(X \cup Y)/support(Y) \geq minconf$.

2.2 Association Rules over Multiple Relations

Let us now modify the original concepts, so as to make them operational in the context of a deductive relational database $\mathcal{D}$ composed of multiple relations.

As before, each example in $\mathcal{D}$ is identified by a unique ExampleKey $ExKey$. Furthermore, all relations in $\mathcal{D}$ have exactly one attribute that corresponds to $ExKey$. The idea is that the $ExKey$ then partitions the tuples in a deductive relational database into disjoint subsets with identical $ExKey$. An example identified by ExampleKey i is then the set of all tuples in the database with $ExKey = i$. Notice the ExampleKey is somewhat similar to notion of a clustering field as used in the database literature. The idea of partitioning the database also fits in the *learning from interpretations* paradigm (an interpretation here corresponds to a partition), introduced by [5] and related to other inductive logic programming settings in [4]. From a practical point of view a significant speed up can be obtained if the partioning scheme creates examples that fit in main memory. As we will see later, the algorithm for efficiently mining association rules over multiple relations exploits and crucially depends on the fact that an example can be singled out from the database.

Association rules over multiple relations (ARMR's) are expressions of the form $X \Rightarrow Y$, where X and Y are atomsets, i.e. sets of logical atoms of the form $p(t_1, \ldots, t_n)$, where each term t_i is a variable V or a function $f(t_1, \ldots, t_k)$ (if k=0, f is a constant). Given an atomset $A = \{A_1, \ldots, A_m\}$, and an example

LIKES		HAS		PREFERS		
KID	OBJECT	KID	OBJECT	KID	OBJECT	TO
joni	icecream	joni	icecream	joni	icecream	pudding
joni	dolphin	joni	piglet	joni	pudding	raisins
elliot	piglet	elliot	icecream	joni	giraffe	gnu
elliot	gnu			elliot	lion	icecream
elliot	lion			elliot	piglet	dolphin

Fig. 1. A sample from the KIDS database

E_i with $ExKey = i$ we will associate with the couple (A, E_i) an existentially quantified conjunction (eqc) of the form

$$eqc(A, E_i) = \exists(ExKey = i \wedge A_1 \wedge \ldots \wedge A_m).$$

We say that an atomset A *covers* an example E_i if $eqc(A, E_i)$ is true in $\mathcal{D}$. Several strategies are available to verify truth of $eqc(A, E_i)$ in $\mathcal{D}$. One possibility is to convert $eqc(A, E_i)$ into an SQL-query. In our implementation, we have opted for a conversion of $eqc(A, E_i)$ to a Prolog query $\leftarrow eqc(A, E_i)$. If this Prolog query succeeds in $\mathcal{D}$, the atomset A covers example E_i, if the query fails[1], the atomset does not cover example E_i.

An ARMR $X \Rightarrow Y$ then holds in $\mathcal{D}$ with *confidence* c if $c\%$ of the examples in $\mathcal{D}$ that are covered by X are also covered by $X \cup Y$[2]. The *support* of this ARMR equals s, if $s\%$ of the examples in $\mathcal{D}$ are covered by $X \cup Y$.

Consider for instance the KIDS database in Figure 1. Let the ExampleKey be *KID*. Notice the relations likes(KID, Object), has(KID, Object), and prefers(KID, Object, Above) each have multiple entries per ExampleKey.

As shown in Figure 2, the ExampleKey *KID*, indeed partitions the KIDS database in disjoint examples for *ExKey = joni* and *ExKey = elliot*. With this representation, the running example rule would take the form

```
likes(KID, piglet), likes(KID, icecream) ⇒ likes(KID, dolphin)
(c:85,s:9).
```

A new rule over all three relations might be

```
likes(KID, A), has(KID, B) ⇒ prefers(KID, A, B) (c:98, s:70).
```

This new rule states that 98% of the kids who like something and have something prefer a thing they like over a thing they have. Furthermore, 70% of the kids like and have something and prefer the first over the second.

The task of discovering ARMR's in a deductive relational database $\mathcal{D}$ is then to generate all ARMR's over $\mathcal{D}$ with confidence above *minconf* and support above *minsup*. In the next section we show how the two-phased algorithm of [1] summarized above can be modified for solving this task.

---

[1] Termination can be guaranteed by employing a depth-bound on the depth of the proof tree.

[2] Notice we evaluate $X \cup Y$, rather than just Y, to allow variables occurring in Y to be bound in X.

LIKES		HAS		PREFERS		
KID	OBJECT	KID	OBJECT	KID	OBJECT	TO
joni	icecream	joni	icecream	joni	icecream	pudding
joni	dolphin	joni	piglet	joni	pudding	raisins
				joni	giraffe	gnu

LIKES		HAS		PREFERS		
KID	OBJECT	KID	OBJECT	KID	OBJECT	TO
elliot	piglet	elliot	icecream	elliot	lion	icecream
elliot	gnu			elliot	piglet	dolphin
elliot	lion					

Fig. 2. Two disjoint examples from the KIDS database.

3 Mining Large Atomsets: Algorithm WARMR

In this section we demonstrate how an existing algorithm for mining large itemsets, i.e. itemsets with support above *minsup*, can be modified to mine large atomsets over multiple relations. As a starting point we take the APRIORI algorithm by Agrawal, Mannila, Srikant, Toivonen, and Verkamo [2]. We will stick as closely as possible to the notation introduced by these authors.

Essentially APRIORI (WARMR) exploits the lattice structure the subset relation imposes on the space of itemsets (atomsets[3]) to perform a breadth-first search. The symbol $\mathcal{L}_k$ is used to refer to the set of large k-itemsets mined at depth k in this lattice. Given $\mathcal{L}_{k-1}$ the next search level k is prepared with the generation of all potentially large candidates C_k. The general idea here is to prune the set of k-itemsets, from what we know of the large $(k-1)$-itemsets. Initial candidate set C_1 is to be specified by the user. The actual support of all sets in C_k is then calculated during a single pass over the data. From C_k we can select the sets with minimum support into $\mathcal{L}_k$, and move on to the next level.

The main loop of WARMR is formalized in Algorithm 1. The original algorithm APRIORI has been modified in two places. First, at step (3.a) an explicit reference is added to the fact that an example E is singled out from the database. This step is trivial in APRIORI where an example is simply a tuple. As described in Section 2.2, when mining ARMR's this step involves selecting from all relations the tuples with a given value for the ExampleKey. In our implementation the main loop is executed in Prolog and an example is loaded in Prolog (and main memory) from an $Oracle7^{TM}$ database. Alternative implementations should somehow succeed in isolating (activating) a single example, such that rules are evaluated with respect to the (small) example instead of the (large) database.

Step (3.b) is the second location where WARMR deviates from the original: a coverage test involving theorem proving replaces the original subset check. An important observation here is that in case atoms share variables apart from

---

[3] In the case of atomsets the subset relation can be interpreted as a special case of the θ-subsumption relation [10] frequently used in inductive logic programming.

Algorithm 1 : WARMR

Inputs: Set of candidate 1-atomsets C_1; database $\mathcal{D}$; *minsup*
Outputs: All queries with minimum support $\bigcup_k \mathcal{L}_k$

1. Initialize $k := 1$
2. For each candidate $C_i \in C_k$, initialize support counter $sup_i := 0$
3. For each example $E \in \mathcal{D}$, do the following:
   (a) load E
   (b) For each candidate k-atomset $C_i \in C_k$, do the following:
       If atomset C_i covers E, increment support counter sup_i
4. Let set of large k-atomsets $\mathcal{L}_k := \{(C_i, sup_i) \in C_k \times [0, 100] | sup_i \geq minsup\}$
5. Compute new candidates C_{k+1} from $\mathcal{L}_k$ using WARMR-gen
6. If C_{k+1} is not empty, increment k and go to step 2

---

the ExampleKey, the coverage test should be executed on the full atomset, not on single atoms. As a consequence, the use of (an adaptation of) algorithm APRIORITID [2] (which passes through the data only once), is restricted to the case where the only shared variable is the ExampleKey.

Algorithm 2 : WARMR-gen

Inputs: Set of large k-atomsets $\mathcal{L}_k$; clausal theory $\mathcal{T}$
Outputs: Set of candidate (potentially large) $(k+1)$-atomsets C_{k+1}

1. $C_{k+1} := \{\{p_1, \ldots, p_k, q_k\} | \ (\{p_1, p_2, \ldots, p_{k-1}, p_k\}, s_1) \in \mathcal{L}_k;$
$(\{p_1, p_2, \ldots, p_{k-1}, q_k\}, s_2) \in \mathcal{L}_k;$
$p_k < q_k\}$
2. Delete all $(k+1)$-atomsets $C = \{p_1, \ldots, p_k, q_k\}$ from C_{k+1} with:
   (a) some k-subset of C is not in $\mathcal{L}_k$; or
   (b) $\mathcal{T} \wedge \exists (p_1 \wedge p_2 \wedge \ldots \wedge p_k \wedge q_k) \models \Box$ (C is contradictory); or
   (c) $\mathcal{T} \wedge \exists (p_1 \wedge p_2 \wedge \ldots \wedge p_k \wedge \neg q_k) \models \Box$ (C is redundant)

The procedure WARMR-gen for the generation of all potentially large candidates C_k is presented in Algorithm 2. This procedure consists of a join-step (1) followed by a prune-step (2). In the join-step we assume that atomsets are kept sorted in their lexicographic order. The condition $p_k < q_k$ is added to preserve this property. From this initial set C_{k+1}, we then, following APRIORI-gen [2], prune the atomsets that have a subset with no minimum support. New with respect to APRIORI-gen is that we have added two pruning conditions. These extra tests involve running a theorem prover to verify whether the atomsets are contradictory (2.b) or redundant (2.c) with respect to a user-specified clausal theory $\mathcal{T}$. Clausal theory $\mathcal{T}$ provides the user with a powerful tool to specify taxonomies, mutual exclusion relations, and other types of information which is

WSJ_CORPUS

SID	WID	WORD	TAG
77	1	champagne	nn
77	2	and	cc
77	3	dessert	nn
77	4	followed	vbd
77	5	.	.

Fig. 3. A sample from the WSJ database

known to hold in the database. Pruning steps (2.b) and (2.c) may thus contribute not only to the efficiency of the algorithm, but also to the quality of the output (cf. the *novelty* requirement frequently mentioned in definitions of KDD).

For the generation of ARMR's we refer to the algorithm described in [2]. The procedure **ap-genrules** described there for large itemsets, with minor modifications, applies to large atomsets.

4 Application: Part-of-Speech tagging

To apply WARMR, we established a connection between an $Oracle7^{TM}$ database and ProLog by BIM on a SPARCstation 20, to obtain the full power of a deductive relational database. We performed two experiments on the tagged Wall Street Journal (WSJ) corpus provided by the Penn Treebank Project [9]. In this corpus of Wall Street Journal articles, each of the (close to 3 million) words is associated with a so-called part-of-speech tag, chosen from set of about 50 tags. The corpus is frequently used for inductive experiments typically aimed at the (semi-) automatic construction of part-of-speech taggers.

We stored the raw WSJ data in a single-relation $Oracle7^{TM}$ database as shown in Figure 3. SID refers to the sequence number of the sentence in the corpus, and WID to the sequence number of the word in the sentence. The TAG column shows the part-of-speech assigned to WORD in that sentence. The main problem of automated tagging is that words may get different tags in different contexts (e.g. the word "plans" can be a noun or a verb). Therefore it is useful to mine the corpus for rules that might help to resolve ambiguity of a word given its context.

4.1 Discovering properties of sentences

In a first experiment, we let SID be the ExampleKey, such that we obtained about 125000 examples (= sentences), for the full WSJ database ($\approx$ 3 million words). The set of candidate atomsets was initialized to $C_1 = \{\{\texttt{determiner(SID,A,B)}\},$ $\{\texttt{adjective(SID,C,D)}\}, \{\texttt{adjective(SID,B,D)}\}, \{\texttt{noun(SID,E,F)}\},$ $\{\texttt{noun(SID,D,F)}\}, \{\texttt{noun(SID,B,F)}\}\}$. The relations in C_1 are defined intensionally in a straightforward manner. The second argument each time corresponds to WID in WSJ_CORPUS, and the third argument is simply the second argument plus 1. The name of the relation refers to the fact a number of tags are grouped. For instance, a tuple noun(SID, X, (X+1)) exists for each tuple wsj_corpus(SID, X, W, Tag) with Tag $\in$ {nn,nns,prp,wp,nnp,nnps}. In about 48h, WARMR found all atomsets with support above 10%, on the basis of which we could generate ARMR's such as:

    determiner(SID,A,B),adjective(SID,B,D) $\Rightarrow$ noun(SID,D,F)
    (c:81,s:32)

In words, this rule says that in 81% of the sentences in which a determiner occurs followed by an adjective, there is also a sequence determiner, adjective, noun. Furthermore, the latter sequence occurs in 32% of the sentences.

4.2 Inducing frequent binary features

All work on induction of part-of-speech taggers is based on the assumption that the context of target word is a good indicator for the target tag. In its most basic form, the context is simply the words in the sentence that precede and follow the target. As combinations of more than two words are typically very rare, even in huge corpora, it is common practise to generalize over word sequences and consider the more frequent (disambiguated) tag sequences (typically to the left of the target). We take this idea one step further and consider sequences of constituents, where constituents (e.g. noun phrase) generalize over tag sequences (e.g. determiner + 0 or more adjectives + noun). Constituents are of variable length (unlike tags, which all have length 1), such that we need a first order language for representing sequences of constituents.

In a second experiment we deployed WARMR to the discovery of frequent sequences of constituents. These can later be used as binary features (a constituent sequence precedes the target or not) in standard propositional approaches. We used an elementary phrase structure grammar for building constituents over tag sequences. The combination SID, WID served as ExampleKey, and we retained only the first 100000 examples (= words = starting points for a constituent sequence). The support threshold was lowered to 0.5%. In about 5 days WARMR discovered all 783 constituent sequences that occur at least 500 times in a 100000 word corpus, such as[4]:

constituent sequence	frequency
np(WID, B)	36310
np(WID, B), vp(B,C)	7842
np(WID, B), vp(B,C), np(C,D)	2165
np(WID, B), vp(B,C), np(C,D), prep(D,E)	995
np(WID, B), vp(B,C), np(C,D), prep(D,E), np(E,F)	644

For instance, the last line says that 644 words in the corpus are starting points for the sequence noun phrase + verb phrase + noun phrase + preposition + noun phrase.

---

[4] To simplify matters, the ExampleKey has been left out in the presentation of the sequences.

5 Concluding remarks

We have introduced association rules over multiple relations (ARMR's) as a novel class of regularities, and presented and applied an algorithm WARMR for mining these regularities in deductive relational databases. Characteristic for WARMR is that examples are disjoint subsets of the database. The efficiency of WARMR derives from, and crucially depends on the possibility to cache a single example in main memory.

Acknowledgements

This research is part of the ESPRIT IV project no. 20237 on Inductive Logic Programming II (ILP^2), and FWO project no. 8.0157.97 (LINGUADUCT). Luc De Raedt is supported by the Fund for Scientific Research, Flanders. The authors would like to thank Walter Daelemans and Arno Knobbe for inspiring discussions on respectively part-of-speech tagging and mining association rules.

References

1. R. Agrawal, T. Imielinski, and A. Swami. Mining assosiation rules between sets of items in large databases. In *Proceedings of the 1993 International Conference on Management of Data (SIGMOD 93)*, pages 207–216, May 1993.
2. R. Agrawal, H. Mannila, R. Srikant, H. Toivonen, and A.I. Verkamo. Fast discovery of association rules. In U. Fayyad, G. Piatetsky-Shapiro, P. Smyth, and R. Uthurusamy, editors, *Advances in Knowledge Discovery and Data Mining*, pages 307–328. The MIT Press, 1996.
3. L. De Raedt, editor. *Advances in Inductive Logic Programming*, volume 32 of *Frontiers in Artificial Intelligence and Applications*. IOS Press, 1996.
4. L. De Raedt. Induction in logic. In R.S. Michalski and Wnek J., editors, *Proceedings of the 3rd International Workshop on Multistrategy Learning*, pages 29–38, 1996.
5. L. De Raedt and S. Džeroski. First order jk-clausal theories are PAC-learnable. *Artificial Intelligence*, 70:375–392, 1994.
6. S. Džeroski. Inductive logic programming and knowledge discovery in databases. In U. Fayyad, G. Piatetsky-Shapiro, P. Smyth, and R. Uthurusamy, editors, *Advances in Knowledge Discovery and Data Mining*, pages 118–152. The MIT Press, 1996.
7. M. Houtsma and A. Swami. Set-oriented mining of assocation rules. Technical Report RJ 9567, IBM Almaden Research Center, San Jose, Calif., 1993.
8. N. Lavrač and S. Džeroski. *Inductive Logic Programming: Techniques and Applications*. Ellis Horwood, 1994.
9. M.P. Marcus, B. Santorini, and M. A. Marcinkiewicz. Building a large annotated corpus of English: the Penn Treebank. *Computational Linguistics*, 19(2):313–330, 1993.
10. G. Plotkin. A note on inductive generalization. In *Machine Intelligence*, volume 5, pages 153–163. Edinburgh University Press, 1970.

Using Logical Decision Trees for Clustering

Luc De Raedt and Hendrik Blockeel

Department of Computer Science, Katholieke Universiteit Leuven,
Celestijnenlaan 200A, B-3001 Heverlee, Belgium
email: {Luc.DeRaedt,Hendrik.Blockeel}@cs.kuleuven.ac.be

Abstract. A novel first order clustering system, called C 0.5, is presented. It inherits its logical decision tree formalism from the TILDE system, but instead of using class information to guide the search, it employs the principles of instance based learning in order to perform clustering. Various experiments are discussed, which show the promise of the approach.

1 Introduction

A decision tree is usually seen as representing a theory for classification of examples. If the examples are positive and negative examples for one specific concept, then the tree defines these two concepts. One could also say, if there are k classes, that the tree defines k concepts.

Another viewpoint is taken in Langley's *Elements of Machine Learning* [11]. Langley sees decision tree induction as a special case of the induction of *concept hierarchies*. A concept is associated with each node of the tree, and as such the tree represents a kind of taxonomy, a hierarchy of many concepts. This is very similar to what many clustering algorithms do (e.g. COBWEB, [9]).

Concept hierarchies can be induced in a supervised or unsupervised manner. Decision trees are an example of the former, while typical clustering algorithms are unsupervised.

The ILP system TILDE [2] induces first order logical decision trees from classified examples. In this paper, we show how to adapt the TILDE system to perform clustering, resulting in the C 0.5 system. To realize this, principles from instance based learning are employed. More specifically, we assume that a distance measure is given that computes the distance between two examples. Furthermore, in order to compute the distance between two clusters (i.e. sets of examples), we employ a function that computes a prototype of a set examples. A prototype can be regarded as an example. The distance between two clusters is then defined as the distance between the prototypes of the two clusters. Now, the distance measure employed determines whether the learning process is supervised or unsupervised. If the distance measure employs class information, learning is supervised, if no class information is employed, learning is unsupervised.

All logical aspects of TILDE are inherited by C 0.5. This includes the logical representation of binary decision trees and the learning from interpretations setting (in which examples are logical interpretations).

2 The problem

We use the *learning from interpretations* setting. In this setting, each example is a Prolog program encoding the specific properties of the example. See [5, 3] for more details on learning from interpretations.

For instance, examples for the well-known mutagenesis problem [14] can be described by interpretations. Here, an interpretation is simply an enumeration of all the facts we know about one single molecule: its class, *lumo* and *logp* values, the atoms and bonds occurring in it, certain high-level structures, ... We can represent it e.g. as follows: { logmutag(-0.7), lumo(-3.025), logp(2.29), atom(d189_1,c,22,-0.11), bond(d189_2,d189_3,7), ... }.

A logical decision tree is a binary decision tree in which each node contains a conjunction of literals. This conjunction may share variables with nodes above it in the tree. The test that is to be performed at the node consists of its conjunction, together with the conjunctions on the path from the root of the tree to this node that share variables with this node or with other nodes sharing variables with it. This test has two possible outcomes (it may fail or succeed), upon which the splitting of a cluster of examples into two subclusters is based.

The format of logical decision trees makes them perfectly fit as a representation for a cluster hierarchy. Each node in the tree corresponds to a cluster of examples, and the hierarchical structure of the tree shows how clusters are split into subclusters. The test in a node can be seen as a discriminant description of the two clusters in which the current cluster of examples is divided. One cluster is described by saying that the test succeeds, the other by saying that it fails.

This view is in correspondence with Langley's viewpoint that a test in a node is not just a decision criterion, but also a description of the subclusters formed in this node. In [2], we have shown how a logical decision tree can be transformed into an equivalent logic program. This procedure can be used to obtain descriptions of the clusters.

The purpose of conceptual clustering is to obtain clusters such that intra-cluster distance (i.e. the distance between examples belonging to the same cluster) is as small as possible and the inter-cluster distance (i.e. the distance between examples belonging to different clusters) is as large as possible.

In this paper, we assume that a distance measure d that computes the distance $d(e_1, e_2)$ between examples e_1 and e_2 is given. Furthermore, there is also a need for measuring the distance between different clusters (i.e. between sets of examples). Therefore we will assume as well the existence of a prototype function p that computes the prototype $p(E)$ of a set of examples E. The distance between two clusters C_1 and C_2 is then defined as the distance $d(p(C_1), p(C_2))$ between the prototypes of the clusters. This shows that the prototype should be considered as (possibly) partial example descriptions.

For instance, on the mutagenesis problem, the distance could be the Euclidean distance d_1 between the activities of the two compounds, or the Euclidean distance d_2 between the points in the three-dimensional space corresponding to the *lumo, logp* and *activity* values of the two compounds, or it could be the distance d_3 as measured by a first order distance measure.

Given the distance at the level of the examples, the principles of instance based learning can be used as to compute the prototypes. E.g. on the mutagenesis problem, d_1 would result in a prototype function p_1 that would simply compute the average activity of the compounds in the cluster, d_2 would result in a prototype function p_2 that would compute the average instance along the *lumo, logp* and *activity* values of the compounds in the cluster, whereas d_3 could result in function p_3 that would compute the (possibly reduced) least general generalisation[1] of the compounds in the cluster.

Notice that although we employ - in this paper - only propositional distance measures, we obtain first order descriptions of the clusters through the representation of logical decision trees. Hence, one could say that we realize 0.5th order Clustering, which explains the name of our system C 0.5.

By now we are able to formally specify the clustering problem:

Given

- a set of examples E (each example is a definite clause theory),
- a background theory B in the form of a definite clause theory,
- a distance measure d that computes the distance between two examples or prototypes,
- a prototype function p that computes the prototype of a set of examples,

Find: clusters in the form of a logical decision tree.

Notice that in this problem-setting, the interpretation i corresponding to an example e is the least Herbrand model of $B \wedge e$. So, conceptually, the clustering process learns from interpretations. This is similar to the Claudien [4], ICL [6] and TILDE [2] systems.

3 C 0.5 : Clustering of order 0.5

C 0.5 employs the basic TDIDT framework as it is also incorporated in TILDE. The only point where our algorithms C 0.5 and TILDE differ from the propositional TDIDT algorithm is in the computation of the tests to be placed in a node. To this aim, we employ a classical refinement operator under θ-subsumption [12],see [2] for details.

Another point where C 0.5 deviates from the classical TDIDT algorithm is in its heuristics. TDIDT algorithms typically use two heuristics: a splitting criterion to select the best test in a node, and a stopping criterion to decide whether a given node or cluster should be turned into a leaf or should be split further.

The splitting criterion used in C 0.5 works as follows. For a given a cluster C, and a test T that will result in two disjoint subclusters C_1 and C_2 of C, C 0.5 computes the distance $d(p(C_1), p(C_2))$. The best test T is then the one

---

[1] Using Plotkin's [12] notion of θ-subsumption or the variants corresponding to structural matching [1, 13].

that maximizes this distance. This reflects the principle that the inter-cluster distance should be as large as possible.

Stopping criteria for conceptual clustering are usually less clear. Typically, the stopping criterion depends on the number and size of clusters one wants to obtain. In C 0.5, we consider right now only that each leaf of the tree should contain a minimal number of examples.

4 Applications of Clustering in ILP

We see a number of interesting applications of clustering in ILP. We will divide these into characterisation, classification and regression tasks. But first, we make an observation that will be important to all these tasks.

Once a decision tree has been induced, there can be two separate arguments for saying that an example belongs to a cluster. One is based on the tests in the tree. If an example is sorted into a specific node based on those tests, one has reason to say that the example really belongs to the cluster corresponding to that node. A second argument is based on the distance metric. Without performing any tests in the tree, one can still say that an example belongs to a cluster because it is close to the examples in that cluster. Both arguments are quite independent from one another (cf. also [10]).

This means that information can flow in two opposite directions. One can assign an example to a cluster based on the tree, and predict that its distance to the examples in that cluster will be small; or one can assign it to a cluster based on its distance to the examples in the cluster, and predict that it will satisfy the description of that cluster that the tree gives. While the first information flow has a flavour of classification, the second comes closer to characterisation (although the difference between the two is not always very clear-cut).

4.1 Characterisation of clusters

The fact that logical decision trees offer a first order description of clusters makes it possible to perform a kind of abduction. Based on the fact that an example belongs to a specific cluster (according to the distance metric that is used), one can predict that it fulfills the intensional description of that cluster.

4.2 Classification

It is quite clear that first order clustering can be used for classification; in fact, the original TILDE system is such a classification system. Following Langley's viewpoint, it is basically a clustering system where the "distance" metric is the class entropy within the clusters : lower class entropy within a cluster means that the examples in that cluster are more similar with respect to their classes.

Since TILDE needs information about the classes of its training examples, it is a supervised learning system. However, clustering can also be done in an unsupervised manner. The distance metric used to form clusters may or may not use information about the classes of the examples. Even if it does not use class information, clusters may be coherent with respect to the class of the examples in them. This will be illustrated in our experiments.

This principle leads to a classification technique that is very robust with respect to missing class information. Indeed, even if only a small percentage of the examples is labelled with a class, one could perform unsupervised clustering, and assign to each leaf in the concept hierarchy the majority class in that leaf. If the leaves are coherent with respect to classes, this method would yield high classification accuracy with a minimum of class information available. This is similar to Emde's method for learning from few classified examples, implemented in the COLA system [7].

4.3 Regression

The above shows that first order clustering can be used for characterisation of clusters in the data, as well as for classification. An application that has a flavour of both, is predicting numerical values. If clusters are coherent with respect to some numerical attribute of the examples, one can compute the average value for a cluster of examples and use this to predict the value of unseen examples. This is basically what Kramer's SRT system [10] does. SRT builds so-called structural regression trees: trees in which each leaf predicts a numerical value instead of a symbolic class and the tests in the nodes are conjunctions of literals.

5 Experiments

We have evaluated some of the ideas proposed in this paper using a preliminary implementation of C 0.5. Concerning the evaluation of a clustering system, there is the fundamental problem of how to evaluate the quality of a set of clusters as there is no clear and objective criterion to measure this. The situation is different in concept-learning, where the quality of the output of a system is measured in terms of accuracy. Therefore, as frequently done in conceptual clustering (cf. [9]), we will measure the quality of the obtained clusters using the accuracy with which these clusters can be used for prediction.

5.1 Experimental setup

Originally, mutagenicity was represented by a number on a logarithmic scale. For prediction purposes, a molecule is considered to be of class *positive* if this number is positive, and is of class *negative* otherwise. In all experiments we use euclidean distance metrics based on the numerical information about molecules, i.e. their *logp*, *lumo* and *logm* (which stands for *log-mutagenicity*, the number describing the activity of the molecule) values. Several distance metrics have been tried out. First of all, supervised learning (using *logm* for distance computation) was compared to unsupervised learning (using *logp* and *lumo*). This was done for three different hypothesis languages corresponding to the background knowledges BG1-BG3 as defined in [14]. BG1 contains only structural information (atoms and bonds), BG2 adds to this the charges of each individual atom, BG3 adds to BG2 the *lumo* and *logp* values of each molecule.

In order to evaluate the results of the clustering algorithm, we have computed accuracies as follows. For a whole cluster the *logm* value of the prototypical element is computed. If this is a positive number, then the whole cluster is predicted to be positive, otherwise negative. The observed class of an example is then compared with the class of its cluster. Classification accuracy on the regression-friendly set is based on tenfold crossvalidation, for the regression-unfriendly set a leave-one-out procedure was adopted.

5.2 Classification Accuracy

In a first experiment we compare supervised and unsupervised clustering, on both the regression-friendly and regression-unfriendly datasets. Table 1 shows the results of our experiments. The results for supervised learning can be compared with results obtained with other systems (Progol, TILDE), but for unsupervised learning this comparison is harder in the case of BG1 and BG2, since C 0.5 does use *logp* and *lumo* information during the induction process, even if the theories that are derived do not use them. For the regression-friendly data we have included results obtained with the TILDE system. The refinement operator and other parameters were exactly the same in C 0.5 as in TILDE, only the minimal coverage of clusters was higher (10 examples for the regression-friendly data, 4 for the regression-unfriendly data) because C 0.5 does not have a good stopping criterion yet. We have not tried to find an optimal value for the minimal coverage, but consistently used 10 (or 4).

Table 1 shows that the results of both supervised and unsupervised learning are comparable with results for TILDE (with the exception of BG3 where a significantly lower score is obtained). Especially for unsupervised learning this is a surprise. It shows that *lumo* and *logp* are very closely related to the class; examples with similar *lumo* and *logp* values often have the same class. This explains in part why FOIL, on the Mutagenesis dataset with BG3, finds a theory simply consisting of a large number of intervals for *logp* and *lumo* (see [14]).

In order to check this out in more detail, we have additionally experimented (on BG2) with distances based on *logp* only, on *lumo* only, and on the three numerical values together. Results are shown in Table 2 (first row). There are no significant differences for the different distance functions.

The results on the regression-unfriendly set (Table 1) are much harder to explain. The expected behaviour (less accuracy for unsupervised than for supervised learning) occurs clearly in BG3, but not in BG1 and BG2. We do not have an explanation for this.

5.3 Learning From Incomplete Examples

Next to comparing different distance functions, Table 2 also shows what happens if numerical information is missing. The dataset was changed so that the *lumo* information was removed in approximately 50% of the models, chosen at random (every model has probability 0.5 of having this value removed), and the same was done independently for *logp* and *logm* values. This was repeated with removal of 75% or 90% of the information.

Table 2 shows that in the absence of a lot of information, classification accuracy slowly decreases. However, when using a distance measure that combines several numerical attributes, prototypes can be computed more accurately than if only one numerical attribute is used. Absence of information about one attribute can be compensated for by knowledge of another value. This causes the distance function using all three attributes (*lumo, logp, logm*) to be very robust w.r.t. missing information; predictive accuracy decreases more slowly.

These results suggest that even if more complicated distance functions do not yield higher accuracy when all information is present, they make learning from incomplete examples more feasible.

	Regression friendly			Regression unfriendly		
	unsupervised	supervised	TILDE	unsupervised	supervised	TILDE
BG1	0.73	0.74	0.75	0.76	0.76	0.83
BG2	0.81	0.80	0.79	0.74	0.76	0.83
BG3	0.79	0.78	0.85	0.71	0.86	0.79

Table 1. Comparison of supervised and unsupervised clustering on both regression-friendly and unfriendly data; results with TILDE included for reference.

available numerical data	lumo	logp	lumo+logp	logm	lumo+logp+logm
100%	0.79	0.79	0.81	0.80	0.81
50%	0.77	0.79	0.81	0.78	0.79
25%	0.73	0.72	0.73	0.72	0.77
10%	0.65	0.65	0.67	0.67	0.74

Table 2. Classification accuracies obtained on BG2 with several distance functions, and on several levels of missing information.

6 Related Work

Our work is related to KBG [1], which performs first order agglomerative clustering but employs a first order distance measure, to RIBL [8], a first order instance based learner, and to Kramer's SRT [10], which builds first order regression trees. Our work also exploits many of the ideas contained in Langley's book, as he makes the link between TDIDT and clustering.

Acknowledgements

Luc De Raedt is supported by the Fund for Scientific Research, Flanders. Hendrik Blockeel is supported by the Flemish Institute for the Promotion of Scientific and Technological Research in the Industry (IWT). This work is also part of the European Community Esprit project no. 20237, ILP2. The authors wish to thank Luc Dehaspe, Wim Van Laer and Nico Jacobs for proofreading this text.

References

1. G. Bisson. Conceptual clustering in a first order logic representation. In *Proceedings of the 10th European Conference on Artificial Intelligence*, pages 458–462. John Wiley & Sons, 1992.
2. H. Blockeel and L. De Raedt. Experiments with top-down induction of logical decision trees. Technical Report CW 247, Dept. of Computer Science, K.U.Leuven, January 1997. Also in Periodic Progress Report ESPRIT Project ILP2, January 1997.
3. L. De Raedt. Induction in logic. In R.S. Michalski and Wnek J., editors, *Proceedings of the 3rd International Workshop on Multistrategy Learning*, pages 29–38, 1996.
4. L. De Raedt and L. Dehaspe. Clausal discovery. *Machine Learning*, 26:99–146, 1997.
5. L. De Raedt and S. Džeroski. First order jk-clausal theories are PAC-learnable. *Artificial Intelligence*, 70:375–392, 1994.
6. L. De Raedt and W. Van Laer. Inductive constraint logic. In *Proceedings of the 5th Workshop on Algorithmic Learning Theory*, volume 997 of *Lecture Notes in Artificial Intelligence*. Springer-Verlag, 1995.
7. W. Emde. Inductive learning of characteristic concept descriptions. In S. Wrobel, editor, *Proceedings of the 4th International Workshop on Inductive Logic Programming*, volume 237 of *GMD-Studien*, pages 51–70, Sankt Augustin, Germany, 1994. Gesellschaft für Mathematik und Datenverarbeitung MBH.
8. W. Emde and D. Wettschereck. Relational instance-based learning. In L. Saitta, editor, *Proceedings of the 13th International Conference on Machine Learning*, pages 122–130. Morgan Kaufmann, 1996.
9. D. H. Fisher. Knowledge acquisition via incremental conceptual clustering. *Machine Learning*, 2:139–172, 1987.
10. S. Kramer. Structural regression trees. In *Proceedings of the 13th National Conference on Artificial Intelligence (AAAI-96)*, 1996.
11. P. Langley. *Elements of Machine Learning*. Morgan Kaufmann, 1996.
12. G. Plotkin. A note on inductive generalization. In *Machine Intelligence*, volume 5, pages 153–163. Edinburgh University Press, 1970.
13. L. De Raedt, P. Idestam-Almquist, and G. Sablon. Theta-subsumption for structural matching. In *Proceedings of the 9th European Conference on Machine Learning*, 1997.
14. A. Srinivasan, S.H. Muggleton, and R.D. King. Comparing the use of background knowledge by inductive logic programming systems. In L. De Raedt, editor, *Proceedings of the 5th International Workshop on Inductive Logic Programming*, 1995.

Induction of Slovene Nominal Paradigms

Sašo Džeroski and Tomaž Erjavec

Department of Intelligent Systems, Jožef Stefan Institute
Jamova 39, SI 1000 Ljubljana, Slovenia

Abstract. The paper presents results of using FOIDL, an inductive logic programming system, to learn the inflectional paradigms of Slovene nouns. FOIDL learns first-order decision lists, defined as ordered list of clauses; it has been previously tested on the problem of inducing rules for forming the past tense of English verbs. Slovene, unlike English, has rich inflectional morphology, and the paper reports the result of applying FOIDL over a large lexicon of Slovene word-forms to induce rules for the synthesis and analysis of the full inflectional paradigms of Slovene nouns.

1 Introduction

The Slovene language belongs to the South-Slavic family of languages; with the other Slavic languages it shares a rich system of inflections. Nouns in Slovene are lexically marked for gender (3), and inflect for number (3) and case (6), which gives 18 morphologically distinct forms comprising the paradigm of a noun. The situation is complicated, much as in Latin, by nouns belonging to various paradigm classes (declensions); inflected forms can also exhibit alternations from their canonical declensions, either by stem and/or ending modification. These alternations can be determined by the morphophonological makeup of the word, by its morphosyntactic properties, by its declension, or are simply idiosyncratic to the word in question.

In the scope of the MULTEXT-East project [1] an (orthographic) lexicon for the Slovene language was developed, which comprises all the inflectional word-forms (paradigms) of approximately 15.000 lemmas appearing in the corpus of the project. The lexicon has 560.000 entries and 200.000 distinct word-forms. Each lexicon entry is composed of three fields: (1) the word-form, (2) the lemma (base form), and (3) the morphosyntactic description. Two example entries are given below:

```
golobu    golob   Ncmsd (Noun common masculine singular dative)
golobu    golob   Ncmsl (Noun common masculine singular locative)
```

This paper is concerned with the problem of learning morphological rules for producing the inflectional forms of nouns given the base form (nominative singular), and of deducing the base form from these inflectional forms, i.e., of learning rules for morphological synthesis and analysis.

In our setting, a particular morphosyntactic description (such as ncmsg) is considered a concept. Examples corresponds to pairs of lemmas and word-forms.

For example, the fact ncmsg([g,o,l,o,b], [g,o,l,o,b,u]) is a positive example for the concept Ncmsg, represented by the predicate ncmsg. Because the formation of the word-forms of a noun is not affected by whether it is common or proper (Nc or Np), these morphosyntactic descriptions were collapsed to the common N*, denoted by nx.

For our experiments, 37 such nx predicates were constructed from the lexicon so as to cover all the inflections of Slovene nouns that have distinct forms. Namely, although the total number of inflectional noun concepts is 54 (3 genders × 3 numbers × 6 cases), some concepts are syncretic and thus omitted. In other words, certain forms are always identical to some other forms, e.g., the dual genitive to the plural genitive and the neuter accusative to the neuter nominative. As such, they were defined as e.g., nxmdg(X,Y):- nxmpg(X,Y).

The numbers of distinct examples in the datasets for each concept learned averaged 2808 for the 13 masculine, 2650 for the 13 feminine and 1286 for the 11 neuter concepts. The numbers for different concepts for a gender differ because nouns can have defective paradigms (e.g., proper nouns having no plural) or free variations in a form (e.g., *kmeti/kmetje* 'peasants', both Ncmpn), or are due to the quirks of lexicon design.

In this paper, FOIDL [4] is used to learn rules for synthesizing and analyzing the noun forms. A brief overview of FOIDL and its application to learning the English past tense is given in Section 2. Section 3 describes the set up for the experiments with FOIDL. Discussed here are the induced rules for the synthesis and the analysis tasks and their performance on unseen cases. Section 4 concludes with a discussion and some directions for further work.

2   FOIDL and Learning Past Tense

FOIDL [4] is an inductive logic programming (ILP) [3] system. Unlike most other ILP approaches that learn unordered sets of Horn clauses, FOIDL learns first-order decision lists, i.e., ordered lists of clauses. First-order decision lists seem to be a very appropriate formalism for representing linguistic knowledge, as they allow for an elegant way of representing exceptions to general rules. The exceptions are placed before the general rules in a decision list: the first applicable rule from the list is used when treating new cases. The data structure produced by FOIDL thus implements a version of the Elsewhere Condition, well known in morphological theory [2].

Another important feature of FOIDL is its ability to learn decision lists from positive examples only. Most other ILP systems rely on negative examples to avoid overly general hypotheses. FOIDL, on the other hand, uses an output completeness assumption. It states that the training set contains all of the corresponding output patterns for every unique input pattern that it contains. The ability to learn from positive data only is also very important for almost all linguistic applications of ILP.

Like all ILP systems, FOIDL can use background knowledge defining predicates relevant for learning the target predicate. While some ILP systems, e.g., FOIL [5], can only use extensional background knowledge (consisting of ground facts), FOIDL can use intensional background knowledge consisting of PROLOG clauses. Predicates for list processing, relevant for learning linguistic concepts, can thus be represented concisely and efficiently.

FOIDL has been successfully applied to the problem of learning rules for forming the past tense of English verbs [4]. Three different variants of the problem have been addressed: phonetic representation, phonetic representation of regular verbs only, and orthographic representation. For illustration, a positive example for the last case is past([s,l,e,e,p],[s,l,e,p,t]). In all three cases, the list processing predicate split(A,B,C), which splits a list A into two nonempty lists B and C, was used as background knowledge. This predicate is defined as:

```
split([X,Y|Z],[X],[Y|Z]).
split([X|Y],[X|Z],W) :- split(Y,Z,W).
```

The first argument (present tense of the verb) of the target predicate past is an input argument and the second (past tense) is an output argument. FOIDL was given the opportunity to use constant prefixes and suffixes in its rules. An excerpt from a first-order decision list learned by FOIDL from 250 examples is given below.

```
past(A,B) :- split(A,C,[e,p]), split(B,C,[p,t]), !.
...
past(A,B) :- split(B,A,[d]),    split(A,C,[e]), !.
past(A,B) :- split(B,A,[e,d]).
```

Note the ! (cut) in the clauses: this indicates that only the first applicable clause from the list should be used when treating new examples. The FOIDL output, however, does not list the cuts; the FOIDL output in the next Section is shown in its original form, thus without cuts. When treating new cases, it is interpreted as a decision list, i.e., as if the cuts were there.

Given 1392 examples of the English past tense, FOIDL used up to 500 examples for learning and the remainder for testing. Given 500 examples for learning, FOIDL achieved an accuracy of approximately 85% on the testing set. The running time on a SUN SPARC 10 was approximately 8 hours.

3   Experiment and Results

Our decision to use FOIDL for learning Slovene declensions was based on its properties listed in the previous Section and its success on the English past tense learning problem. FOIDL was run 37 times for synthesis and 37 times for analysis, i.e., twice for each target concept. The training sets sizes were chosen with regard to FOIDL's computational efficiency limits, i.e., given the large number of relations to be induced, at 200 examples. The remainder of the data was used to test the performance of the rules induced by FOIDL. The training sets were obtained by random sampling of the concept data sets.

The set-up for the experiment was as for the orthographic past tense experiment, i.e., for synthesis the training data was encoded as PROLOG facts of the form[1] nxfsg([b,o,l,e,cx,i,n,a],[b,o,l,e,cx,i,n,e]). The first argument of each target predicates (the lemma) is an input argument and the second is an output argument. The only difference between the analysis and synthesis tasks was that the arguments were switched. The predicate split is used as background knowledge. Constant prefixes and suffixes are allowed in the rules.

3.1 Synthesis Results

The 37 programs generated for the synthesis concepts show varying degrees of success in capturing the relevant morphological generalizations. First, it should be noted that due to the random sampling of the dataset some low-frequency alternations were not included in the training sets. The rules to generate such forms could obviously not be discovered by FOIDL. Second, as has been already mentioned, FOIDL works only with the orthographic representation of the words, which does not contain enough information to predict the correct rule for synthesizing or analyzing the paradigm forms in all cases.

Table 1. Accuracy and complexity of FOIDL synthesis rules

nxmsg = 89.1% 27/18	nxfsg = 99.2% 4/1	nxnsg = 97.7% 9/4
nxmsd = 86.5% 30/19	nxfsd = 99.1% 4/1	nxnsd = 98.3% 9/3
nxmsa = 49.6% 74/50	nxfsa = 97.5% 8/4	
nxmsl = 88.1% 32/21	nxfsl = 99.1% 4/1	nxnsl = 98.3% 9/3
nxmsi = 84.5% 28/14	nxfsi = 99.0% 3/0	nxnsi = 97.7% 6/4
nxmpn = 80.5% 29/19	nxfpn = 97.9% 8/5	nxnpn = 96.0% 6/2
nxmpg = 80.2% 34/19	nxfpg = 93.5% 16/8	nxnpg = 91.0% 21/10
nxmpd = 80.0% 28/15	nxfpd = 95.9% 9/5	nxnpd = 97.1% 5/4
nxmpa = 83.5% 25/11	nxfpa = 99.0% 5/1	
nxmpl = 85.2% 27/17	nxfpl = 95.8% 8/4	nxnpl = 96.8% 7/2
nxmpi = 76.6% 35/20	nxfpi = 99.1% 4/1	nxnpi = 96.9% 7/2
nxmdn = 83.0% 27/18	nxfdn = 99.1% 5/2	nxndn = 97.7% 8/4
nxmdd = 79.5% 31/13	nxfdd = 97.0% 9/7	nxndd = 98.8% 6/4

Table 1 gives the accuracy of the programs on the testing set, followed by the number of clauses that FOIDL induced for the concept. The testing cases where no rules for the corresponding concept apply are counted as errors. The total number of clauses is followed by the number of exceptions, i.e., ground facts that cover only one lexical item; the difference between the two would give the number of generalizations, which attempt synthesis via the split predicate.

---

[1] The Slovene characters č, š, ž are encoded as cx, sx, and zx respectively.

Given that FOIDL generates forms without the support of the lexicon and without any additional constraints, the results are relatively good. The average accuracy over all the 37 concepts is 91.4%, the feminine gender leading with the average of 97.8%, followed by the neuter with 96.9% and the masculine gender with 80.5%. The average number of rules is 16.4, with 9.1 exceptions and 7.3 generalizations.

First, we should note the masculine singular accusative, where FOIDL achieves only a 49.55% accuracy with 74 induced rules. This is, in fact, a case of blind guessing as this form is, like the forms that we leave out of the paradigm altogether, a syncretic form. However, unlike the other syncretisms the referred to rule is not constant. If a masculine noun has the 'animate' subgender, then the singular accusative is identical to the singular genitive, if 'inanimate', then to the singular nominative. As the lexicon does not contain the animate attribute FOIDL cannot induce any useful rules for the synthesis of this concept.

We now examine one induced concept in more detail, namely the singular genitive case of masculine nouns. It has the relatively low accuracy of 89.1% and needs 27 (=18+9) rules to describe the complete training set. The rules for this concept must cover three different declensions, as well as numerous alternations and idiosyncratic nouns. A number of cases (18) were treated by FOIDL as exceptions, and some examples are given in Table 2. The first two cases are, respectively, an example of the second and third masculine declensions. Here FOIDL is correct in postulating them as exceptions, as insufficient information is available in the base form to correctly predict the genitive. The next two cases are examples of an ending alternation (-u instead of -a) which affects some short masculine nouns. As there is no rule that would predict which nouns fall in this class, FOIDL is, again, correct in treating them as exceptions. The same holds for the next case, which covers the rare and unpredictable case of -a- elision. The last two groups are, however, different. Both contain examples of a productive alternation (-e- elision and stem lengthening with -j-) which are, furthermore, also encompassed in the generalization rules that follow.

The nine generalization rules are given in Table 3. The first covers masculine nouns whose base form ends in -a and are inflected according to the first masculine declension.[2] The second case covers first declension nouns which end in -o. The third group tries to model the -e- elision alternation, by listing the possible end-strings of the base forms where it occurs. The fourth group models stem lengthening by -j-. Finally, the last group takes canonical nouns and appends to them the regular first declension ending -a.

3.2 Analysis Results

In general, it is more useful to analyze word-forms than synthesize them. To this end, an additional experiment was performed with FOIDL, where the input and

---

[2] Such masculine nouns actually fall outside the scope of the FOIDL induction algorithm, which presupposes that the mapping is a function: Slovene nouns ending in -a can be declined both according to the first and to the second masculine declension. In other words, they exhibit free variation in the oblique forms.

Table 2. FOIDL rules for synthesis of the masculine genitive: exceptions

```
nxmsg([t,e,s,l,a],[t,e,s,l,e]).
nxmsg([m,o,sx,k,i],[m,o,sx,k,e,g,a]).
...
nxmsg([s,a,d],[s,a,d,u]).
nxmsg([l,e,d],[l,e,d,u]).
...
nxmsg([d,o,p,o,l,d,a,n],[d,o,p,o,l,d,n,e,v,a]).
...
nxmsg([o,v,e,n],[o,v,n,a]).
nxmsg([s,t,e,b,e,r],[s,t,e,b,r,a]).
...
nxmsg([h,e,l,i,k,o,p,t,e,r],[h,e,l,i,k,o,p,t,e,r,j,a]).
nxmsg([a,t,a,sx,e],[a,t,a,sx,e,j,a]).
```

Table 3. FOIDL rules for synthesis of the masculine genitive: generalizations

```
nxmsg(A,B) :- split(A,C,[a]),       split(B,C,[a]).

nxmsg(A,B) :- split(A,C,[o]),       split(B,C,[a]).

nxmsg(A,B) :- split(A,C,[z,e,m]),   split(B,C,[z,m,a]).
nxmsg(A,B) :- split(A,C,[e,k]),     split(B,C,[k,a]).
nxmsg(A,B) :- split(A,C,[e,c]),     split(B,C,[c,a]).

nxmsg(A,B) :- split(B,A,[j,a]),     split(A,C,[r]),     split(A,[k],D).
nxmsg(A,B) :- split(B,A,[j,a]),     split(A,C,[r]),     split(A,[t],D).
nxmsg(A,B) :- split(B,A,[j,a]),     split(A,C,[r]),     split(A,D,[a,r]).

nxmsg(A,B) :- split(B,A,[a]).
```

output arguments were switched; the task of FOIDL was to learn rules to generate the base form of the noun given the oblique form. Apart from exchanging the input and the output, the set-up for this experiment was identical to the synthesis one. Table 4 gives the accuracy of the programs, followed by the number of clauses (total/exceptions) that FOIDL produced for each concept.

The average accuracy over all the above concepts is 91.5%, which is almost identical to the synthesis accuracy (91.4%). Here neuter scores highest 95.9%, while feminine scores 94.8% and masculine 84.5%. The average number of rules is 19.5 (16.4 for synthesis), with average 10.5 exceptions and 9.1 generalizations.

As can be seen there is no great systematic difference between the synthesis and analysis tasks. The differences are in general due to the different informativeness of the base form compared to the singular genitive form.

Table 4. Accuracy and complexity of FOIDL analysis rules

nxmsg = 87.5% 29/21	nxfsg = 98.9% 6/2	nxnsg = 94.8% 17/11
nxmsd = 88.5% 29/20	nxfsd = 88.4% 35/13	nxnsd = 95.9% 13/5
nxmsa = 85.9% 32/10	nxfsa = 97.5% 8/4	
nxmsl = 87.5% 34/19	nxfsl = 88.4% 35/13	nxnsl = 95.9% 13/5
nxmsi = 84.5% 27/13	nxfsi = 88.0% 21/4	nxnsi = 98.0% 5/3
nxmpn = 84.0% 23/14	nxfpn = 97.7% 8/5	nxnpn = 94.2% 12/5
nxmpg = 83.9% 33/22	nxfpg = 94.9% 14/8	nxnpg = 94.1% 16/8
nxmpd = 83.6% 28/15	nxfpd = 97.7% 8/4	nxnpd = 97.1% 4/2
nxmpa = 84.2% 30/19	nxfpa = 97.7% 9/6	
nxmpl = 81.3% 35/26	nxfpl = 97.7% 8/4	nxnpl = 95.2% 13/4
nxmpi = 82.0% 31/19	nxfpi = 97.7% 6/4	nxnpi = 95.1% 12/3
nxmdn = 83.6% 33/24	nxfdn = 88.3% 31/14	nxndn = 95.7% 13/5
nxmdd = 82.1% 39/27	nxfdd = 99.2% 8/5	nxndd = 99.2% 5/2

4 Discussion

We have presented the results of learning rules for synthesizing and analyzing inflectional forms of Slovene nouns. In particular, FOIDL was applied to learn synthesis and analysis rules for 37 non-syncretic inflectional concepts of proper and common nouns belonging to three different genders and three numbers. Taking into account that FOIDL was given very limited background knowledge, the results obtained are quite satisfactory: the average accuracy of the induced rules for synthesis was 91.4%, and for analysis 91.5%.

The errors can be traced to two causes, both having to do with insufficient information available to FOIDL. First, the information available in the orthographical representation is at times insufficient to predict whether a certain phonologically determined alternation should take place or not. To cover such cases, a phonological representation would have to be substituted for, or added to the orthographic one. Furthermore, the background knowledge of FOIDL could in such a set-up be extended to take phonological regularities into account, by e.g., distinguishing vowels from consonants etc., thus leading to better generalizations. Second, FOIDL makes use only of the form of the lemma. Additional background knowledge on lexical morphosyntactic information should be incorporated into the lexicon and made use of by the induction algorithm. The most obvious example is to add the declension to the lexical entries, but other necessary information includes animacy for masculine nouns and the origin of the noun, i.e., whether it is of native or foreign origin.

Several other directions for further work can be pointed out. As regards the induction methodology, at least two improvements of FOIDL seem to be needed. Efficiency seems to be a major problem, effectively limiting the size of training sets that can be considered to approximately 500 examples. Post-processing of the induced decision lists is also needed in order to remove irrelevant literals.

The final direction for further work concerns the use of the analysis rules induced by FOIDL. Up to now the test of the induced rules was in trying to produce the correct base form given the concept and the oblique form, corresponding to a syntax driven morphological analysis. As morphological analysis is rather a first step in text processing, it is more interesting to see whether the correct base form is obtained with the concept being any of the possible 54 nx concepts. In other words, given a noun in a running text, how accurate is FOIDL in giving it the correct morphosyntactic interpretation and deducing its base form?

For a test we took the form 'golobu', which was not a member of the training set, and has the two lexical entries (Ncmsd and Ncmsl). With the induced analysis rules FOIDL proposes only 11 concepts containing 4 different lemmatizations. The induced morphological rules thus eliminate four fifths of the possible concepts. Employing a simple phonological constraint of Slovene, which forbids a word ending in two vowels, the hypotheses are reduced to 7 concepts with two lemmatizations. If, finally, a lexicon of base forms constrains the output of analysis, three concepts are left, two of which are correct, and only the correct lemmatization is proposed. The results are thus quite promising.

In summary, we have successfully applied the ILP system FOIDL to learn rules for synthesis and analysis of inflectional forms of Slovene nouns. Further work will focus on improving the induced rules by using additional linguistic background knowledge and using the improved rules to perform preliminary analysis of word forms appearing in corpora, producing input for further text processing, e.g., part-of-speech tagging.

Acknowledgements

This work was supported in part by the projects ESPRIT IV 20237 ILP2 and COPERNICUS COP 106 MULTEXT-East.

References

1. T. Erjavec, N. Ide, V. Petkevič, and J. Véronis. MULTEXT-East: Multilingual text tools and corpora for Central and Eastern European languages. In *Proceedings of the First TELRI European Seminar: Language Resources for Language Technology*, pages 87–98, 1996.
2. P. Kiparsky. "Elsewhere" in phonology. In Steven R. Anderson, editor, *Festschrift for Morris Halle*, pages 93–106. Holt, Rinehart and Winston, New York, 1973.
3. N. Lavrač and S. Džeroski. *Inductive Logic Programming: Techniques and Applications*. Ellis Horwood, Chichester, 1994.
4. R.J. Mooney and M.-E. Califf. Induction of first-order decision lists: Results on learning the past tense of English verbs. *Journal of Artificial Intelligence Research*, (3):1–24, 1995.
5. J.R. Quinlan. Learning logical definitions from relations. *Machine Learning*, 5(3): 239–266, 1990.

Normal Forms for Inductive Logic Programming

Peter A. Flach

Infolab, Tilburg University
POBox 90153, 5000 LE Tilburg, the Netherlands
email `Peter.Flach@kub.nl`

Abstract. In this paper we study induction of unrestricted clausal theories from interpretations. First, we show that in the propositional case induction from complete evidence can be seen as an equivalence-preserving transformation from DNF to CNF. From this we conclude that induction is essentially a process of determining what is false in the domain of discourse. We then proceed by investigating dual normal forms for evidence and hypotheses in predicate logic. We define *evidence normal form* (ENF), which is Skolemised existential DNF under a Consistent Naming Assumption. Because ENF is incomplete, in the sense that it does not have the expressive power of clausal logic, ENF evidence requires the identification of Skolem terms. The approach is partly implemented in the PRIMUS system.

1 . Introduction

In this paper we study induction of unrestricted clausal theories from interpretations. In the propositional case, this setting amounts to learning a Boolean function from verifying and falsifying truthvalue assignments. If we are given all verifying truthvalue assignments, the problem can be mapped to the problem of DNF to CNF conversion, followed by a minimisation step. We explore the prospects of such a reformulation approach for inducing universal CNF formulae (first-order clausal theories) from evidence expressed in a suitable normal form.

The outline of the paper is as follows. In Section 2 we discuss the learning from interpretations setting, and introduce the reformulation approach. In Section 3 we introduce DNF to CNF conversion and minimisation. In Section 4 we proceed to predicate logic. We define *evidence normal form* and discuss how hypotheses can be constructed from ENF evidence. In Section 5 we discuss related work. The paper is ended with a discussion.

2 . The learning setting: learning from interpretations

A central problem in computational learning theory is learning a Boolean function from evidence consisting of verifying and falsifying truthvalue assignments (also called positive and negative interpretations, or models and countermodels). This setting was upgraded to ILP by De Raedt & Dzeroski (1994), who introduced the term *learning from interpretations*.

We introduce the propositional setting by means of an example. Consider the following evidence:

woman ∧ ¬man ∧ human	% Mary
¬woman ∧ man ∧ human	% John
¬woman ∧ ¬man ∧ ¬human	% thing

Part of this work was supported by Esprit IV Long Term Research Project 20237 (ILP II). Thanks are due to Luc De Raedt for inspiring discussions and useful suggestions.

Our task is to find a set of clauses that is verified by each of these models. The following theory is a solution:

human → woman ∨ man
man → human
woman → human
woman ∧ man →

Notice that this theory is falsified by each of the 5 remaining interpretations over the same alphabet. In other words, this solution assumes that the evidence is *complete*, in the sense that it lists all models of the target theory. In section 3 we will present a way to construct this theory from the given interpretations.

The task of learning from complete evidence expressed as models was termed *identification* by Dechter & Pearl (1992). Due to the completeness of the evidence, identification is a relatively straightforward task. However, in general an identification task has many logically equivalent solutions. Finding non-redundant theories is a major concern for practical ILP systems. We will call the identification of minimal theories from interpretations *reformulation*.

3. Induction as reformulation

An alternative representation for the set of models of a theory utilises disjunctive normal form (DNF). For instance, in the running example we have seen a woman, a man, and something not human — if these are the only three posibilities, then the following DNF formula is valid:

woman∧¬man∧human ∨ ¬woman∧man∧human ∨
¬woman∧¬man∧¬human

The reformulation task is then to convert this DNF formula to CNF, followed by a minimisation step. Conversion of a propositional DNF formula to its CNF equivalent is relatively straightforward, using some concepts from switching theory (see for instance (Friedman, 1986)).

DEFINITION 1 (*Canonical DNF/CNF*). Given a fixed alphabet of proposition symbols, a *minterm* (*maxterm*) is a conjunction (disjunction) of literals in which each proposition symbol occurs exactly once. A *canonical DNF* (*CNF*) *formula* is a disjunction (conjunction) of minterms (maxterms).

PROPOSITION 2. *Each propositional formula is logically equivalent to a canonical DNF (CNF) formula, which is unique (modulo the order of minterms (maxterms) and literals).*

Clearly, the canonical DNF form of a formula F corresponds to the set of its models. Somewhat more interestingly, the canonical CNF form of F can be mapped to the set of *countermodels* of F: by negating this canonical CNF representation of F and pushing the negation symbol inside, we obtain a canonical DNF representation of $\neg F$, which corresponds to the set of countermodels of F. Conversely, we can obtain a canonical CNF representation of F by first determining its countermodels, and then turning every countermodel into a true clause by flipping its truthvalue and interpreting the expression disjunctively.

To continue the running example, the canonical DNF formula representing the evidence corresponds to rows 1, 4 and 6 of the following truth table:

woman	man	human
−	−	−
−	−	+
−	+	−
−	+	+
+	−	−
+	−	+
+	+	−
+	+	+

From the countermodels (the remaining 5 rows) we obtain the following canonical CNF theory:

human → woman ∨ man
man → woman ∨ human
woman → man ∨ human
woman ∧ man → human
woman ∧ man ∧ human →

From this analysis the view emerges that *induction is the process of determining what is false in the domain of discourse.* In the idealised case of complete evidence the countermodels are uniquely determined and construction of the inductive hypothesis proceeds deterministically. In the non-ideal case of daily life we must make assumptions about what are the countermodels.

Since a canonical CNF theory is a set of maxterms, it contains (generally speaking) a lot of redundancy. For instance, the above theory can be compressed by resolving the second and fourth clause, the third and fourth clause, and the fourth and fifth clause, which yields the logically equivalent theory that we have seen before:

human → woman ∨ man
man → human
woman → human
woman ∧ man →

These clauses are called *prime implicates*, since they are the most general clauses (under subsumption) entailed by the original set of clauses.

PROPOSITION 3. *Every clausal theory is logically equivalent to its set of prime implicates.*

The process by which the canonical CNF formula was compressed is known in switching theory as *Quine-McCluskey minimisation.* The idea is to look for clauses that assign opposite sign to exactly one literal, which can then be resolved away to produce an implicate. The fact that all the remaining literals have the same sign in both original clauses guarantees that no information is lost in the process. Equivalently, we can look for all pairs of countermodels in the truth table that differ only in one proposition symbol, and add a new countermodel with a don't care truthvalue for that proposition symbol (also called an *implicant*). This process is then repeated for all countermodels with 1 don't care, and so on. The output of this iterative process consists of all countermodels (with or without don't cares) that were never combined with another countermodel (also called *prime implicants*). Notice that the final set of prime implicants may still be redundant in the sense that it is logically equivalent with a proper subset — we will not deal with this prime implicant covering problem in this paper. Minimisation algorithms are described in full detail in (Friedman, 1986).

We have just demonstrated that, in the ideal case of complete evidence, learning from interpretations can be viewed as a reformulation process in which a DNF formula is converted to a logically equivalent minimal CNF formula. Just as CNF is a natural normal form for inductive hypotheses, DNF is a natural normal form for the evidence fed to the inductive agent. Using this normal form, *anything that is expressible as an inductive hypothesis is equivalently expressible as a set of examples.* We may therefore say that DNF is a *complete* representation for evidence in learning from interpretations. This completeness property is lost when moving from propositional logic to predicate logic. However, also in predicate logic there exists a normal form for evidence with considerable expressive power, as will be demonstrated in the next section.

4. Lifting it to predicate logic

We proceed to extend the foregoing analysis to predicate logic. In Inductive Logic Programming (ILP), inductive hypotheses are expressed in *universal* CNF or clausal form (that is, all quantifiers are universal and precede a wff in CNF). Clausal logic is slightly less expressive than predicate logic, because it requires that all objects are named (no existential quantifiers) and that each object has a unique name (semantic equality is reduced to syntactic equality, i.e. unification). We will now investigate the corresponding normal form for the evidence.

4.1 Skolem DNF

As in the propositional case, an equally expressive normal form for evidence is obtained by negating the normal form for hypotheses. This results in *existential* DNF as normal form for the examples, which is the dual of universal CNF. For instance, the negation of the clause $\forall X : \text{woman}(X) \rightarrow \text{human}(X)$ is the existential conjunction $\exists X : \text{woman}(X) \land \neg\text{human}(X)$, which can be viewed as a 'countermodel' in existential DNF. Evidence and counter-evidence may be expressed by a disjunction of such existential conjunctions, which establishes a normal form for evidence with the same expressiveness as clausal logic.

However, in ILP the use of existential quantifiers in the evidence is usually excluded. Instead of existentially quantified variables the evidence contains constants or terms, naming the objects known to exist (skolemisation). So, the above countermodel is expressed as a ground conjunction of literals, say $\text{woman}(a) \land \neg\text{human}(a)$.

DEFINITION 4. A formula is said to be in *Skolem DNF* (SDNF) if it is a disjunction of conjunctions of ground literals.

Unfortunately, skolemisation is *not* an equivalence-preserving transformation: the negation of the latter conjunction is the clause $\text{woman}(a) \rightarrow \text{human}(a)$. If we do not take Skolem terms into account, the clauses corresponding to counter-models are always ground. Without explicit existential quantification, Skolem DNF is an essentially incomplete representation for evidence. Hence, the fundamental problem of ILP can be paraphrased as *the problem of recognising Skolem terms in the evidence.*

As an illustration, consider the countermodel $\text{member}(2,[2]) \land \neg\text{member}(2,[1,2])$. If we choose all occurrences of 2 as representing the same Skolem constant and 1 as representing another, then the corresponding clause is $\forall X \forall Y : \text{member}(X,[X]) \rightarrow \text{member}(X,[Y,X])$. If we want to resurrect the more general clause we must additionally recognise the two occurrences of the list [2] as Skolem terms.

4.2 The Consistent Naming Assumption

Skolem DNF does not exhaust the expressive power of predicate logic. A considerable advantage of predicate logic over propositional logic is that it permits us to formulate statements about different objects in a syntactically different way. For instance, the evidence from the running example would be expressed in predicate logic as the SDNF formula

$$woman(mary) \wedge \neg man(mary) \wedge human(mary) \vee$$
$$\neg woman(john) \wedge man(john) \wedge human(john) \vee$$
$$\neg woman(thing) \wedge \neg man(thing) \wedge \neg human(thing)$$

In this formula, the statements about Mary are distinguished syntactically from the statements about John. As a consequence, literals like $\neg man(mary)$ are also meaningful (and true) outside the context of the DNF formula. This stands in contrast with the propositional formulation, in which $\neg man$ in the first disjunct refers to Mary not being a man, while man in the second disjunct expresses that John is a man.

Predicate logic does not enforce this use of different names for different objects; the assumption that this is indeed the case will be termed the *Consistent Naming Assumption (CNA)*.

DEFINITION 5. Let F be a formula in Skolem DNF, and let G be the conjunction of the disjuncts in F. F is said to satisfy the *Consistent Naming Assumption* (CNA) iff G is logically consistent. We also say that F is in *evidence normal form* (ENF).

Notice that G itself a formula in SDNF, representing the domain of discourse in its entirety. In fact, under the CNA we may transform any SDNF formula F into another SDNF formula G by combining some of its models. Clearly G entails F, but since hypothesis construction proceeds through the negation of the evidence G contains actually *less* information than F. Therefore, hypothesis construction will still be based on F rather than G — the sole purpose of the latter is to test whether F employs names in a consistent way throughout all models.

4.3 Hypothesis construction

It has been noted previously that SDNF is inherently incomplete when compared to the expressive power of the hypothesis language. In other words, constructing countermodels from the evidence is problematic. The Consistent Naming Assumption increases the expressive power of Skolem DNF, since it aids us in constructing countermodels, as will be explained presently.

In the running example, one of the models in the evidence contains the facts $woman(mary)$ and $human(mary)$. From the CNA we infer that both statements are true in the domain of discourse, and therefore changing the truthvalue of one of them results in a countermodel. The question is: which literal to negate? This question seems crucial, since the countermodel $woman(mary) \wedge \neg human(mary)$ corresponds, after hypothesising that $mary$ is a Skolem constant, to the (correct) clause $\forall X : woman(X) \rightarrow human(X)$, while the countermodel $\neg woman(mary) \wedge human(mary)$ corresponds to the (incorrect) clause $\forall X : human(X) \rightarrow woman(X)$. We will show that this choice can in fact be avoided by a simple truth table method.

Taking the two unsigned literals woman(mary) and human(mary), we hypothesise that mary is a Skolem constant, and construct a table with columns for woman(X) and human(X), also called *features*, and an additional column for the variable X. For each possible assignemnt of truthvalues, we then try to find a substitution for X such that the assignment agrees with the evidence. This results in the following table, which we call a *feature table*.

X	woman(X)	human(X)
mary	+	+
john	−	+
thing	−	−

The fourth possible truthvalue assignment is not supported by the evidence, which means that $\exists X : \text{woman}(X) \land \neg\text{human}(X)$ is an existential DNF countermodel, corresponding to the clause $\forall X : \text{woman}(X) \to \text{human}(X)$.

This example suggests the following three-step approach to hypothesis construction: (*i*) select a set of unsigned literals from one of the models in the evidence; (*ii*) construct the features by identifying Skolem terms; (*iii*) determine the signs of the features by constructing the feature table. The third step is deterministic, as has just been illustrated. Feature construction is indeterministic, and should be guided by heuristics.

4.4 Implementation

The approach outlined above is currently being implemented in the PRIMUS (prime implicants uncovering system) system. At present, PRIMUS implements the construction of countermodels (represented as bit-vectors) via the feature table, determination of prime implicants by means of Quine-McCluskey minimisation, and conversion to clausal form. Feature construction is done top-down by means of a (rudimentary) refinement approach. In addition to extensionally specified evidence, PRIMUS can make use of intensionally defined background knowledge and built-in predicates. We are currently working on heuristic methods for bottom-up detection of Skolem constants.

5. Related work

Countermodels and normal form conversions appear in various guises in the learning and reasoning literature. The Horn theory learning algorithm of Angluin, Frazier & Pitt (1992) constructs hypothesis clauses from countermodels: for instance, the countermodel $\neg a \land b \land \neg c \land d$ is transformed into the Horn clauses $b \land d \to \text{false}$, $b \land d \to a$, and $b \land d \to c$. Khardon & Roth (1994) investigate efficient reasoning with models rather than theories. The idea is to reason with a selected set of *characteristic models*, rather than with all satisfying truthvalue assignments. In turn, the characteristic models can be reconstructed from a set of selected countermodels called a *basis* (Bshouty, 1993). Kautz, Kearns & Selman (1995) study reasoning with models in the context of Horn clause theories. The set of models of a Horn theory T can be reconstructed from its characteristic models by model intersection. If T is not Horn, then this process gives us the models of the *Horn approximation* of T. The authors show how the Horn approximation of a given set of models can be computed using Angluin *et al.*'s algorithm, in which the equivalence oracle is replaced by a sampling strategy.

Claudien (De Raedt & Dehaspe, 1997) is an ILP system that operates in the learning from interpretations setting, which induces non-Horn clausal theories from examples using a top-down refinement approach. Claudien constructs all most general clauses that are verified by the given positive interpretations, which effectively means that the remaining interpretations are considered countermodels. As such, it fits in the reformulation framework described in this paper. PRIMUS could also use a refinement operator as feature enumerator; the difference with Claudien is that the signs of literals are determined later through the feature table method. This means that one set of features could give rise to several clauses; for instance, the following theory could be constructed at once from appropriate evidence:

```
daughter(Y,X):-parent(X,Y),female(Y)
female(X):-daughter(X,Y)
parent(Y,X):-daughter(X,Y)
```

This method of delayed signing of literals is related to the multiple predicate learning approach of (De Raedt *et al.*, 1993): their MPL algorithm constructs clause bodies separately, dynamically deciding with which clause head to combine.

Finally, we mention that (De Raedt, 1996) also discusses the duality between DNF and CNF as representations for hypotheses. A CNF learning problem can be transformed to a DNF learning problem by switching the positive and negative interpretations, and negating the result. The ICL system (De Raedt and Van Laer, 1995) employs this duality between CNF and DNF by implementing a dual form of the propositional classification-oriented learning algorithm CN2 (Clark and Niblett, 1989).

6. Conclusions

In this paper we viewed induction as a two-step process: (*i*) determining false evidence from true evidence; (*ii*) determining a true hypothesis from the false evidence. The justification of this perspective is that evidence and hypothesis are most naturally expressed in normal forms that are each other's dual through negation. In propositional logic, the normal form for evidence (DNF) has the same expressive power as the normal form for hypotheses (CNF). This means that, in the idealised case of complete evidence, hypothesis construction proceeds deterministically by negating the evidence, converting it to CNF, and minimise the resulting expression. In this context, complete evidence means simply that all models of the intended hypothesis have been included. So, if we want to learn that all ravens are black, we must have observed at least one black raven, one black non-raven, and one non-black non-raven. (It has frequently been argued that this viewpoint is paradoxical, since it forces us to treat non-ravens as confirming evidence for the hypothesis 'all ravens are black'. However, we believe the raven paradox to be a problem of *representation* rather than a problem of reasoning.)

If we switch to predicate logic, the universal quantifiers in clausal logic require existential quantifiers in the evidence in order to achieve completeness. Since these are normally not available and replaced by Skolem terms, this introduces a fundamental incompleteness in induction. We need an additional Consistent Naming Assumption in order to be able to construct countermodels from the evidence. We have suggested a three-step approach to construction of countermodels, of which the first two steps (selecting a set of ground literals and selecting the Skolem terms) are basically equivalent to bottom-up ILP techniques such as inverse substitutions and anti-unification. Alternatively, we may adapt a top-down technique such as refinement operators. The reason that these classification-oriented methods can be upgraded to a non-classificatory context is that the feature table technique, by which one determines the signs of the literals in the hypothesis, is applicable in each case. The fact that the signs of literals are determined in the last step of hypothesis construction means that we can use the same learning algorithm for construction of Horn clauses as well as indefinite clauses, denials, predicate completions, integrity constraints, multiple predicate definitions, and so on.

In the course of this research we are developing the PRIMUS system. Currently, PRIMUS is an experimental testbed for hypothesis construction implementing the following steps: construction of the feature table and determination of the countermodels, determination of prime implicates by means of Quine-McCluskey minimisation, and conversion to clausal form. We are currently working on upgrading PRIMUS to an ILP system, by introducing heuristics that can guide hypothesis construction.

References

D. Angluin, M. Frazier & L. Pitt. Learning conjunctions of Horn clauses. *Machine Learning*, 9(2/3):147–164, 1992.

N.H. Bshouty. Exact learning via the monotone theory. *Proc. IEEE Symp. on Foundations of Computer Science*, pp.302–311. 1993.

P. Clark & T. Niblett. The CN2 induction algorithm. *Machine Learning*, 3(4):261–283, 1989.

R. Dechter & J. Pearl. Structure identification in relational data. *Artificial Intelligence*, 58:237–270, 1992.

L. De Raedt. Induction in logic. *Proc. 3d Multistrategy Learning Workshop*, pp.29–38. 1996.

L. De Raedt & L. Dehaspe. Clausal discovery. *Machine Learning*, 26(2/3):99–146, 1997.

L. De Raedt & W. Van Laer. Inductive Constraint Logic. *Proc. 6th Workshop on Algorithmic Learning Theory*, pp.80–94. Springer, 1995.

L. De Raedt, N. Lavrac & S. Dzeroski. Multiple predicate learning. *Proc. 13th Int. Joint Conf. on Artificial Intelligence*, pp.1037–1042. Morgan Kaufmann, 1993.

A. Friedman. *Fundamentals of Logic Design and Switching Theory*. Computer Science Press, 1986.

R. Khardon & D. Roth. *Reasoning with models*. Technical Report TR-1-94, Center for Research in Computing Technologies, Harvard University, 1994.

H. Kautz, M. Kearns & B. Selman. Horn approximations of empirical data. *Artificial Intelligence*, 74:129–145, 1995.

On a Sufficient Condition for the Existence of Most Specific Hypothesis in Progol

Koichi FURUKAWA[1], Tomoko MURAKAMI[1], Ken UENO[1],
Tomonobu OZAKI[1] and Keiko SHIMAZU[1]

Graduate School of Media and Governance, Keio University
5322 Endo, Fujisawa, Kanagawa 252, JAPAN

Abstract. In this paper, we give a sufficient condition for the existence of the most specific hypothesis (MSH) in Progol. Muggleton [2] showed that for any first order theory (background knowledge) B and a single clause (a positive example) E, there exists the most specific hypothesis $\neg bot(B, E)$ which satisfies $B \wedge \neg bot(B, E) \models E$ and for any hypothesis H satisfying $B \wedge H \models E$, H entails $bot(B, E)$ assuming that hypotheses are all single clauses. Yamamoto[8] gave a counter example and indicated that Muggleton's proof contains error. He also gave a sufficient condition under which the MSH exists. In this paper, we give another and more realistic sufficient condition to guarantee the existence of the MSH.

1 Introduction

Recently, inductive logic programming (ILP) has been paid a big attention as a framework of supervised learning in first order logic. Decision tree making systems such as ID3[5], CART[1], and C4.5[6] are well known as supervised learning systems in propositional logic. An advantage of ILP over these systems is its capability of utilizing background knowledge. On the other hand, there is a trade-off between the expressiveness and its performance. One of the most well known forerunners of the ILP is Shapiro's Model Inference System (MIS)[7]. Since MIS provided a uniform framework for solving different problems such as grammatical inference, program synthesis, and concept formation, it received a high reputation as an elegant system. However, it could not treat problems with more or less complex problems because of the combinatorial explosion and therefore researches in that direction could not be developed any more. The reason why MIS failed is its way of searching the hypothesis space. Essentially, it adopted the enumeration method and it searched the concept lattice in a top down manner, that is, from general to specific. MIS identified a cause of error in a hypothesis and tried to modify the hypothesis to remove the error by a back-tracing algorithm. This strategy worked very well in simple problems but it could overcome the problem of combinatorial explosion.

Muggleton, on the other hand, pursued bottom up search methods to solve this problem. One of his solutions is a method based on Plotkin's **Relative Least General Generalization (RLGG)** [4]. It picks up two positive examples of a target concept and tries to generalize them by RLGG. Since it searches the concept lattice from very specific nodes (the examples themselves) to more general nodes, it can be regarded as a bottom up search. Furthermore, since it tries to generalize examples in relative to background knowledge, the framework naturally includes the utilization of background knowledge. Muggleton developed a system called GOLEM[3] based on RLGG. GOLEM has been paid an attention as the first inductive inference system which can utilize background knowledge. However, since RLGG can only treat the case where background knowledge is given as a conjunction of ground unit clauses, we cannot use arbitrary background knowledge in the form of, say, a Prolog program unless we expand it as a conjunction of ground unit clauses; thus it again confronted the problem of complexity in representation.

Muggleton proposed another method to solve this problem based on **inverse entailment** [2]. Let B be background knowledge, E a positive example, and H a hypothesis. Then, H should satisfy the condition $B \wedge H \models E$ when B alone cannot explain E. Then, this condition can be expressed as

$$B \wedge \neg E \models \neg H$$

which we call inverse entailment. Based on this formula, Muggleton developed a very efficient algorithm to compute the best hypothesis given background knowledge and a set of positive examples, and implemented a system called Progol[2]. Progol algorithm is based on the "fact" that if we restrict both a hypothesis and a positive example to be a single clause, then there exists the **most specific hypothesis (MSH)** which any hypothesis H satisfying $B \wedge H \models E$ entails and furthermore can be computed very easily. However, Yamamoto[8] disproved the above "fact" by showing a counter example. He gave a sufficient condition for the existence of the MSH; that is, background knowledge be a set of reduced ground clauses. He proposed a revised algorithm of GOLEM based on this condition.

This paper gives another sufficient condition for the existence of the MSH. The condition is "background knowledge must be a clausal form consisting of definite clauses which do not contain any negative literals having the target predicate symbol." This condition is more realistic than that given by Yamamoto [8] and is directly applicable to Progol. Actually this condition does not significantly violate the standard usages of Progol.

The configuration of this paper is as follows. In Section 2, we give terminology and lemmas to be used later. In Section 3, we give the counter example against the Muggleton's theorem of the existence of MSH by Yamamoto [8]. In Section 4, we identify the error of the proof by Muggleton. In Section 5, we show a new sufficient condition for the existence of the MSH and prove its correctness. Finally, we compare our condition with Yamamoto's one and give further researches to be done in future.

2 Preliminaries

This section introduces terminology, concepts and lemmas needed later to prove our theorem.

2.1 Terminology and Lemmas in Logic

Definition 1. Let $A_i, B_j (i = 1, \ldots, n, j = 1, \ldots, m)$ be atoms. Then a universally quantified disjunction $A_1 \vee \ldots \vee A_n \vee \neg B_1 \vee \ldots \vee \neg B_m$ is called a **clause** where all universal quantifiers are omitted for the simplicity. A clause which has exactly one positive literal is called a **definite clause**.

Definition 2. Let $C_1, C_2, \ldots$ be clauses. Then a conjunction $C_1 \wedge C_2 \wedge \ldots$ is called **a clausal form**.

Definition 3. A clausal form which consists of only definite clauses is called a **difinite clausal form**.

Here we define several new terms.

Definition 4. Let S be a set of all conjuncts P_i in a given conjunction $P_1 \wedge P_2 \wedge \ldots$. Then a conjunction which consists of a subset of S is called a **sub-conjunction** of the original conjunction.

Definition 5. Let P be a logical formula and l a literal. A partial model $\mathcal{M}$ of P such that the truth value for l is not assigned yet is called a **partial model of P with respect to l**.

Definition 6. Let P be a logical formula, l a literal and $\mathcal{M}$ a partial model of P with respect to l. It is said that P **covers (does not cover)** $\neg l$ **in the partial model** $\mathcal{M}$ if $\neg l$ logically follows (does not follow) from the partial model. It is said that P does not cover $\neg l$ if P does not cover $\neg l$ in any partial model of P with respect to l.

Next, we need two lemmas necessary to to prove our main theorem appeared later.

Lemma 7. *Let C be a clausal form. If any clause in C other than tautology does not contain any literals unifiable to a negative literal $\neg l$, then C does not cover $\neg l$.*

Proof.
Assume that it is not the case that C never covers $\neg l$. Then there should exist a partial model $\mathcal{M}$ of C with respect to l which covers $\neg l$. Then, $\neg l$ should be refuted by all model elements of $\mathcal{M}$ together with C. However, since the resolution proof strategy is refutation complete, the refutation proof should be done by resolution proof strategy. Then, there should exist a model element or a literal in a clause other than tautology in C which can be unifiable with $\neg l$. This contradicts the assumption of the lemma. □

Lemma 8. *Let $\mathcal{M}$ be an Herbrand partial model of a given logical formula P with respect to a positive literal l. If P does not cover a negative literal $\neg l$, then $\mathcal{M} \cup \{l\}$ is a model of P.*

Proof.
Since P does not cover $\neg l$ in any partial model of P with respect to l, $\mathcal{M}$ does not contradict against l. From this fact and the monotonicity of first order logic, $\mathcal{M} \cup \{l\}$ becomes a model of P. □

2.2 Terminology in Inductive Logic Programming

Logical setting of ILP

Components in the logical setting of ILP are positive examples, background knowledge and hypotheses generated from them. We assume that background knowledge B, a hypothesis H, and a positive example E are all in clausal form. Then the following relations hold:

1. For a positive example E and background knowledge B, $B \not\models E$ holds.
2. A hypothesis H should satisfy $B \wedge H \models E$.

1. states that background knowledge B alone cannot explain a positive example E, whereas 2. states that B plus H can explain E.

Definition 9. The second formula in the logical setting of ILP can be transformed to
$$B \wedge \neg E \models \neg H.$$
Be interchanging the both sides of this formula, we obtain
$$B \to E \models^{-1} H.$$
We call this formula as the **inverse entailment** of the original formula.

The inverse entailment expression suggests a possibility that a hypothesis can be deduced from background knowledge and a positive example.

Definition 10. We denote the conjunction of all (positive and negative) ground literals which are true in all Herbrand models of $B \wedge \neg E$ by $\neg bot(B, E)$.

Definition 11. A predicate which represents the target concept of learning is called a **target predicate**. Positive examples are represented by a target predicate.

Assuming that both a hypothesis and an example be a single clause, Muggleton [2] "proved" that the negation of conjunction of all ground literals which are true all models of $B \wedge \neg E$ is the most specific hypothesis, which we denote $bot(B, E)$. However, it turned out that his proof contained error as show later.

3 A Counter Example against Muggleton's Proof

Let us define:
$$\begin{cases} B_1 = even(0) \leftarrow \\ \quad\quad even(s(x)) \leftarrow odd(x) \\ E_1 = odd(s(s(s(0)))) \leftarrow \\ H_1 = odd(s(x)) \leftarrow even(x) \end{cases}$$

Then,
$$bot(B_1, E_1) = odd(s(s(s(0)))) \leftarrow even(0).$$

In this example, H_1 is a correct hypothesis because it explains E_1 together with B_1. However, it cannot be computed from $bot(B_1, E_1)$ since $H_1 \models bot(B_1, E_1)$ does not hold.

4 Errors in Muggleton's Proof

First, we show Muggleton's proof of the theorem on the existence of the MSH.

Muggleton's "MSH Existence Theorem"
Let B be a clausal form, and E be a single clause. Let $\neg bot(B, E)$ be a conjunction of literals which are true in all models of $B \wedge \neg E$. Then, any single clause hypothesis H which satisfies $B \wedge H \models E$ entails $bot(B, E)$.

Proof:
Since both H and E are single clauses, their negations are both a conjunction of Skolemized ground unit clauses. Then, since $\neg H$ is true in all models of $B \wedge \neg E$, it must be a sub-conjunction of $\neg bot(B, E)$. Therefore

$$B \wedge \neg E \models \neg bot(B, E) \models \neg H$$

holds and thus for all H,

$$H \models bot(B, E).$$

$\square$

Now, let us consider this proof for Yamamoto[8]'s counter example. Then,
$$\neg bot(B_1, E_1) = even(0) \wedge \neg odd(s(s(s(0))))$$
and thus
$$bot(B_1, E_1) = odd(s(s(s(0)))) \leftarrow even(0).$$
On the other hand, the negation of H_1 is expressed as:
$$\neg H_1 = \neg odd(s(a)) \wedge even(a),$$
where a is a Skolem constant. The problem is that although H_1 satisfies the condition $B_1 \wedge H_1 \models E_1$, $\neg H_1$ is not a sub-conjunction of $\neg bot(B_1, E_1)$.

By considering the second clause of B_1:
$$even(s(x)) \leftarrow odd(x),$$
it turns out that every model of $B_1 \wedge \neg E_1$ either contains $\{\neg odd(s(0))\}$ or $\{odd(s(0)), even(s(s(0)))\}$. Therefore, in both cases, $\neg H_1 = \neg odd(s(a)) \wedge even(a)$ becomes true by simply assigning $a = s(s(0))$ and $a = 0$ respectively.

Thus, when $\neg H$ contains Skolem constants, $\neg H$ need not be a sub-conjunction of $\neg bot(B, E)$ even if it is true for all models of $B \wedge \neg E$. Muggleton[2]'s proof was wrong because it did not take into account the fact that Skolem constants can take different constants in different models.

5 A new sufficient condition for the existence of MSH

Yamamoto gave a sufficient condition for $bot(B, E)$ be a most specific correct hypothesis. The condition requires that the background knowledge be a ground reduced logic programs, an example be a ground unit clause and hypotheses be single clauses[8]. The condition is too strict to be applied to Progol and therefore Yamamoto only applied his results to improve GOLEM. In this paper, we give a better sufficient condition which can be fit to the current implementation of Progol. Our new sufficient condition is stated as a theorem:

Theorem 12. *Let B be a conjunction of definite clauses whose bodies do not contain any literals having the target predicate symbol h, and E be a ground unit clause with h as its predicate symbol. Then any single clause hypothesis H which satisfies $B \wedge H \models E$ and has h as its head predicate symbol entails bot(B, E).*

We need the following lemma to prove the theorem:

Lemma 13. *If $B \not\models E$, then the least model $\mathcal{M}_0$ of B is also a model of $B \wedge \neg E$.*

Proof:
¿From the assumption, $\mathcal{M}_0$ does not contain E. Therefore $B \wedge \neg E$ is true in $\mathcal{M}_0$. Hence $\mathcal{M}_0$ is a model of $B \wedge \neg E$. □

Next, we prove the main theorem.
Proof of Theorem 12
Let an arbitrary single definite clause hypothesis H be

$$h(X) \leftarrow b_1(X_1, Y_1) \wedge \cdots \wedge b_i(X_i, Y_i) \wedge \cdots$$

where X represents a variable vector in the head h, and $X_k, k = 1, 2, \cdots$ be (possibly empty) sub-vectors of X. Then $\neg H$ becomes

$$\neg h(s) \wedge b_1(s_1, t_1) \wedge \cdots \wedge b_i(s_i, t_i) \wedge \cdots$$

where $s, s_k, t_k, k = 1, 2, \cdots$ are Skolem constants vector corresponding to X, X_k, Y_k, respectively.

In the following, we deduce contradiction by assuming that $\neg H$ is true in all Herbrand models of $B \wedge \neg E$ and it is not included in $\neg bot(B, E)$. Then, from the assumption, it must be true that there exists a literal l_0 in $\neg H$ which does not belong to $\neg bot(B, E)$.

First, we show that l_0 is not equal to $h(s)$ by proving only $\neg E$ in $\neg bot(B, E)$ contributes to the entailing of a conjunct $\neg h(s)$ of $\neg H$.

Let $\mathcal{M}_0$ be the least model of B. By applying Lemma 13 to $\mathcal{M}_0$, we conclude that $\mathcal{M}_0$ is a model of $B \wedge \neg E$.

Since the target predicate h does not appear in antecedent parts of any clauses in B, there are no negative literals having h as their predicate symbols in B. Let $h(c)$ be an arbitrary element other than E with h as its predicate symbol in the Herbrand Base (a set of all possible atoms) of $B \wedge \neg E$. Then, from Lemma 7, $B \wedge \neg E$ does not cover $\neg h(c)$.

By applying Lemma 8 to the above result, it is shown that

$$\mathcal{M} = \mathcal{M}_0 \cup \{h(c)\}$$

is a model of $B \wedge \neg E$. Therefore, the conjunct $\neg h(s)$ of $\neg H$ cannot be true in all Herbrand models when the Skolem constant s is equal to c. Hence, $\neg h(s)$ coincides to a unique negative literal $\neg E$ in $\neg bot(B, E)$.

Since l_0 is not equal to $h(s)$, it must be one of the remaining positive literals. Let $b_i(s_i, t_i)$ be the literal. The Skolem constants vector s_i is assigned to constants in Herbrand universe since its all components appear in $\neg h(s)$ which in turn is equal to $\neg E$. On the other hand, t_i may be assigned to different constants for different models. Let the set of all possible values be $\{t_{i1}, t_{i2}, \cdots\}$ and let $\mathcal{M}^-$ be defined as follows:

$$\mathcal{M}^- = \mathcal{M}_0 - \{b(s_i, t_{i1}), b(s_i, t_{i2}), \cdots\}.$$

Then, $\neg H$ does not hold in $\mathcal{M}^-$ since $b_i(s_i, t_i)$ is false for every possible values of t_i. Thus, $\mathcal{M}^-$ should not be a model of $B \wedge \neg E$ since $\neg H$ must be true for all Herbrand models of $B \wedge \neg E$.

However, $\mathcal{M}^-$ turns out to be a model of $B \wedge \neg E$ as shown below.

At first, $\neg b_i(s_i, t_{ik})$ does not contradict to $B \wedge \neg E$ and hence to $\mathcal{M}_0$, because each $b(s_i, t_{ik})$ does not belong to $\neg bot(B, E)$.

Then, we prove that $\{\neg b_i(s_i, t_{i1}), \neg b_i(s_i, t_{i2}), \cdots\}$ does not contradict by itself. Since B consists of only definite clauses, it does not contain any clauses of the form

$$p \leftarrow \neg q \wedge \neg r \wedge \cdots$$

where $p, q, r, \cdots$ are positive literals. That is, no positive literals are derived from any conjunction of negative literals. Therefore $\{\neg b(s_i, t_{i1}), \neg b(s_i, t_{i2}), \cdots\}$ does not contradict to each other. Thus, M^- becomes a model of $B \wedge \neg E$. □

6 Comparison with Yamamoto's sufficient condition

Yamamoto's sufficient condition[8] for the existence of the MSH requires that background knowledge be ground reduced clausal form which means that there is no redundant clauses such that their removal does not affect the least Herbrand model. His condition guarantees that the resulting most specific hypothesis be a finite conjunction of literals whereas our new sufficient condition does not guarantee it. On the other hand, Yamamoto's condition requires background knowledge to be ground whereas our condition does not require it. These two conditions therefore mutually do not include the other. In summary, Yamamoto's condition could only give some improvements to GOLEM, whereas our condition fits to current implementation of Progol very well and it does not restrict the standard usage of Progol. In that sense, our sufficient condition is much acceptable than Yamamoto's one.

7 Conclusion

In this paper, we gave a sufficient condition for the existence of the most specific hypothesis which plays a crucial rule in inducing the best hypothesis to explain a given example together with given background knowledge. The condition is summarized as "background knowledge is a conjunction of definite clauses whose bodies do not contain any literals having the target predicate symbol, and positive examples are ground unit clauses." We further restrict that hypotheses are single clauses whose head predicate symbol is the same as that of examples. The condition fits to the current implementation of Progol and therefore does not restrict the application domains. This is an advantage of our sufficient condition compared with Yamamoto's condition.

The latter condition for background knowledge which excludes any negative literals with target predicate symbols in background knowledge does not allow recursive clauses under learning to be added to background knowledge. This restriction may now allow to induce some interesting hypotheses. But this restriction seems to be intuitively natural.

For background knowledge including disjunctive clauses, there might be a sub-class that exists the MSH. Another direction of the possible extension of our result is to investigate "negation as failure" since it has useful database applications. These are future research topics to be done.

Acknowledgement

This research was strongly inspired by Yamamoto[8]. Fundamental hints are obtained from the paper. At the same time, Prof. Yamamoto were very kind in carefully reading the manuscript and giving many useful suggestions to improve the paper. Prof. Mukai also kindly read our manuscript and gave useful suggestions. We would like to express our deep thanks to both of them.

References

1. Breiman, L., Friedman, j. H., Olshen, R. A. and Stone, C. J.: Classification and Regression Trees. Wadsworth, Belmont (1984).
2. Muggleton, S.: Inverse Entailment and Progol. New Generation Computing, Vol.13, pp.245-286 (1995).
3. Muggleton, S. and Feng, C.: Efficient induction of logic programs. In *Proc. First Conference on Algorithmic Learning Theory*, pp.368-381, Ohmsha, Tokyo (1990).
4. Plotkin, G.D.: A note on inductive generalization. In Meltzer, B. and Michie, D. editors, *Machine Intelligence 5*, pp.153-163, Edinburgh University Press (1970).
5. Quinlan, J.R.: Induction of decision trees. Machine Learning, 1(1), pp.81-106 (1986).
6. Quinlan, J.R.: C4.5: Programs for Machine Learning. Morgan Kaufmann, San Mateo, CA (1993).
7. Shapiro, E.: Inductive Inference of Theories from Facts. Research Report 192, Department of Computer Science, Yale University (1981).
8. Yamamoto, A.: Improving Theories for Inductive Logic Programming Systems with Ground Reduced Programs. Technical Report, Forschungsbericht AIDA-96-19 FG Intellektik FB Informatik TH Darmstadt (1996).

Induction of Logic Programs with More Than One Recursive Clause by Analyzing Saturations

Mitsue Furusawa[1], Nobuhiro Inuzuka[2], Hirohisa Seki[2] and Hidenori Itoh[2]

[1] Mitsubishi Electric Engineering, Higashi-ozone, Kita-ku, Nagoya 462, Japan
[2] Nagoya Institute of Technology, Gokiso-cho, Showa-ku, Nagoya 466, Japan
E-mail: {inuzuka,seki,itoh}@ics.nitech.ac.jp

Abstract. This paper describes a bottom-up ILP algorithm called MRI, which induces recursive programs with one or more recursive clauses from a few of examples. It analyzes saturations using path structures, which express streams of terms processed by predicates and was originally introduced by Identam-Almquist. We introduce extension and difference of path structures. Recursive clauses can be expressed as a difference among path structures. The paper also shows experimental results.

1 Introduction

Induction of logic programs from small sample sets is an interesting topic in inductive logic programming (ILP), because in applying ILP to automatic programming, it is very annoying when large sample sets must be supplied. Recursive programs have been a target of ILP. Systems such as FOIL[1, 2], Progol[3] and GOLEM[4] induce recursive programs, but need many examples. Structural analysis has succeeded. LOPSTER[5] and its successor CRUSTACEAN[6, 7] induce recursive programs very efficiently from small sample sets. TIM[8] induces recursive programs by analyzing saturations, also very efficiently.

Programs induced by these systems, however, are very restricted. LOPSTER and CRUSTACEAN induce only programs with one unit clause and one two-literal recursive clause, which only has a head literal and a recursive literal. TIM has more ability. It learns logic programs with one base clause and one tail recursive clause. The class of programs that these systems induce is computationally important. It is not flexible enough for practical use, however. This paper gives an efficient method which can learn programs that have one or more recursive clauses, which are not restricted to tail recursion.

2 Preliminary definitions

We consider only two classes of predicates. A class includes predicates all of whose arguments are input arguments. The other class includes determinate predicates with exactly one input argument. We call predicates in the former class *check predicates* and call ones in the latter class *path predicates*. A literal with a check (path) predicate is called a *check (path) literal*.

We use the words, *saturation*, *path*, and *path structure* after the manner of [8] with slight changes. A *saturation* of a positive example E wrt a theory T is a clause F that satisfies:

1. $T \wedge E \equiv T \wedge F$,
2. if a clause F' satisfies that $T \wedge F' \equiv T \wedge F$ then $F' \Rightarrow F$, and
3. E and F have the same head literal.

For a positive example E and its saturation F, if a sequence of literals $(l_1, l_2, \cdots, l_t)$ satisfies the following conditions, we call the sequence a *path* of E wrt T, which is denoted by $P = [p_1-b_1, p_2+a_2-b_2, \cdots, p_t+a_t-b_t]$, where p_i is a predicate symbol of the literal l_i.

1. l_1 is the head literal of F and $l_2, \cdots, l_t$ are body literals of F,
2. $l_i (i = 2, \cdots, t)$ has a path predicate, and a_i and b_i are an input argument and an output argument of the path predicate, respectively, and
3. l_i and l_{i+1} $(i = 1, \cdots, t-1)$ have a common term in the b_i-th argument of l_i and in the a_{i+1}-th argument of l_{i+1}.

A term in the b_t-th argument of l_t is called a *value* of the path and is denoted by $P[E]$. For an ordered set of n paths, which is called a (an) $(n\text{-})path$ *tuple*, $\mathcal{P} = (P_1, \cdots, P_n)$ and an n-ary predicate q, $q(\mathcal{P}[E])$ denotes a literal $q(P_1[E], \cdots, P_n[E])$.

For a k-ary positive example E, a k-path tuple $\mathcal{PS} = (P_1, \cdots, P_k)$ is called a *path structure* of E if P_i is a path that starts with p–i, where p is a predicate symbol of E $(i = 1, \cdots, k)$. In this case, $p(\mathcal{PS}[E])$ denotes $p(P_1[E], \cdots, P_k[E])$.

If two paths P and P' are

$$P = [p_1-b_1, p_2+a_2-b_2, \cdots, p_t+a_t-b_t]$$
$$P' = [p_1-b_1, p_2+a_2-b_2, \cdots, p_t+a_t-b_t, p_{t+1}+a_{t+1}-b_{t+1}, \cdots, p_{t+s}+a_{t+s}-b_{t+s}],$$

we say that P' is an extension of P or that P' extends P. Then we call

$$D = [p_1-b_1, p_{t+1}+a_{t+1}-b_{t+1}, \cdots, p_{t+s}+a_{t+s}-b_{t+s}]$$

a *difference* of P' from P. We also say that a path tuple $\mathcal{P}$ extends a path structure $\mathcal{PS}$, if every path in $\mathcal{P}$ extends a path in $\mathcal{PS}$. If a path structure $\mathcal{PS}$ (i.e., a path tuple) extends another path structure $\mathcal{PS}'$, $\mathcal{PS}$ is called an *extension* of $\mathcal{PS}'$ or $\mathcal{PS}'$ is called a *sub-path structure* of $\mathcal{PS}$. If $\mathcal{P} = (P_1, \cdots, P_n)$ extends $\mathcal{PS} = (P_1', \cdots, P_k')$, we call $(D_1, \cdots, D_n)$ a *difference* of $\mathcal{P}$ from $\mathcal{PS}$ to be denoted by $\mathcal{P} - \mathcal{PS}$, where D_i is a difference of P_i from a path in $\mathcal{PS}$ extended by P_i.

```
1  ← remove(a, [a, b], [b])
2       ← decomp([a, b], a, [b])
3       ← eq(a, a)
4       ← remove(a, [b], [b])
5            ← decomp([b], b, [])
6            ← decomp([b], b, [])
7            ← eq(b, b)
8            ← remove(a, [], [])
9                 ← nil([])
10                ← nil([])
```

Fig. 1. An execution trace

3   Analysis of execution trace using path structures

Let us consider the following logic program, which has two recursive clauses. Predicates used in the program are defined in Table 1.

$$\text{remove}(A, B, C) \leftarrow \text{nil}(B), \text{nil}(C). \tag{1}$$

$$\text{remove}(A, B, C) \leftarrow \text{decomp}(B, B_1, B_2), \text{eq}(A, B_1), \text{remove}(A, B_2, C). \tag{2}$$

$$\text{remove}(A, B, C) \leftarrow \text{decomp}(B, B_1, B_2), \text{decomp}(C, C_1, C_2), \tag{3}$$
$$\text{eq}(C_1, B_1), \text{remove}(A, B_2, C_2).$$

Table 1. Background knowledge

predicates	check or path	explanation
decomp$(+A, -B, -C)$	path	$A = [B|C]$
nil$(+A)$	check	$A = []$
eq$(+A, +B)$	check	$A = B$
large$(+A, +B)$	check	$A \geq B$
father$(+A, -B)$, etc.	path	A is father of B

An execution trace of the program with a goal $\leftarrow$remove$(a, [a, b], [b])$ is shown in Fig. 1. When we regard the goal as a positive example E of remove, this example E and the literals remove$(a, [b], [b])$ and remove$(a, [], [])$ in the trace can be expressed using path structures of E as remove$(\mathcal{PS}_1[E])$, remove$(\mathcal{PS}_2[E])$, and remove$(\mathcal{PS}_3[E])$, where

$$\mathcal{PS}_1 = ([\mathsf{remove-1}], [\mathsf{remove-2}], [\mathsf{remove-3}]),$$
$$\mathcal{PS}_2 = ([\mathsf{remove-1}], [\mathsf{remove-2}, \mathsf{decomp+1-3}], [\mathsf{remove-3}]),$$
$$\mathcal{PS}_3 = ([\mathsf{remove-1}], [\mathsf{remove-2}, \mathsf{decomp+1-3}, \mathsf{decomp+1-3}], [\mathsf{remove-3}, \mathsf{decomp+1-3}]).$$

$\mathcal{PS}_1$ is a sub-path structure of $\mathcal{PS}_2$, and also a sub-path structure of $\mathcal{PS}_3$.

Let us consider differences $\mathcal{PS}_2 - \mathcal{PS}_1$ and $\mathcal{PS}_3 - \mathcal{PS}_2$.

$$\mathcal{PS}_2 - \mathcal{PS}_1 = ([\mathsf{remove-1}], [\mathsf{remove-2}, \mathsf{decomp+1-3}], [\mathsf{remove-3}]), \tag{4}$$
$$\mathcal{PS}_3 - \mathcal{PS}_2 = ([\mathsf{remove-1}], [\mathsf{remove-2}, \mathsf{decomp+1-3}], [\mathsf{remove-3}, \mathsf{decomp+1-3}]). \tag{5}$$

The recursive literals can be expressed using these differences as remove$(a, [b], [b]) =$ remove$((\mathcal{PS}_2 - \mathcal{PS}_1)[E])$ and remove$(a, [], []) =$ remove$((\mathcal{PS}_3 - \mathcal{PS}_2)[E'])$, respectively, where $E' = \mathcal{PS}_2(E) =$ remove$(a, [b], [b])$. In general, if $\mathcal{PS}$ and $\mathcal{PS}'$ are path structures of an example E with a predicate p and $\mathcal{PS}'$ extends $\mathcal{PS}$, it is true that

$$p(\mathcal{PS}'[E]) = p((\mathcal{PS}' - \mathcal{PS})[\mathcal{PS}[E]]).$$

Differences include all the information required to construct recursive literals.

Finally, let us consider check literals in the trace. Literal eq(b, b) (line 7 in the trace) is expressed in eq$(b, b) =$ eq$(\mathcal{P}[E])$, where

$$\mathcal{P} = ([\mathsf{remove-2}, \mathsf{decomp+1-3}, \mathsf{decomp+1-2}], [\mathsf{remove-3}, \mathsf{decomp+1-2}]).$$

$\mathcal{P}$ extends $\mathcal{PS}_2$, which expresses the precedent recursive literal remove$(a, [b], [b])$ (line 4 in the trace). A difference

$$\mathcal{P} - \mathcal{PS}_2 = ([\mathsf{remove-2}, \mathsf{decomp+1-2}], [\mathsf{remove-3}, \mathsf{decomp+1-2}]) \tag{6}$$

includes all the information of literals to prepare terms for the check literal. Figure 2 illustrates the situation that has been described.

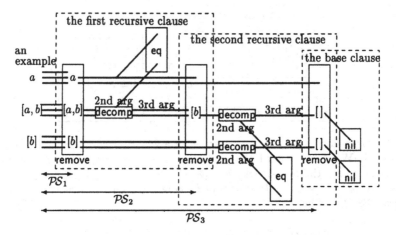

Fig. 2. Stream of terms and path structures

4 MRI Algorithm

Our observations are summarized as follows:

1. Recursive literals in a series in which the literals are nested in an order are expressed by path structures extended in the order.
2. In case 1, the difference of a path structure expressing a recursive literal from a path structure expressing the preceding recursive literal in the order includes path literals followed by the recursive literal.
3. A check literal followed by a recursive literal expressed by a path structure can be written using a path tuple extending the path structure.
4. In case 3, a difference of the path tuple from the path structures includes a literal to generate information for check literals.

As we summarized above, a path tuple which extends a path structure corresponds to literals. For example, $\mathcal{PS}_2-\mathcal{PS}_1$ in (4) corresponds with $\{\text{decomp}(x_2, x_4, x_5), \text{remove}(x_1, x_5, x_3)\}$, if a head literal is $\text{remove}(x_1, x_2, x_3)$. Indeed, Clause (2) includes them. Similarly, $\mathcal{PS}_3 - \mathcal{PS}_2$ in (5) corresponds with $\{\text{decomp}(x_2, x_4, x_5), \text{decomp}(x_3, x_6, x_7), \text{remove}(x_1, x_5, x_7)\}$, which are included in Clause (3).

We can give a formal correspondence. Let us consider a path structure $\mathcal{PS}$ of an example E and a path tuple $\mathcal{P}$ that extends $\mathcal{PS}$. If $q(\mathcal{P}[E])$ is in a saturation of E, then there is a difference $\mathcal{P} - \mathcal{PS}$ and it is generally written as follows:

$$(\; [p-i_1, p_{11}+a_{1\,1}-b_{11}, p_{12}+a_{1\,2}-b_{12}, \cdots, p_{1n_1}+a_{1n_1}-b_{1n_1}],$$
$$\cdots, [p-i_l, p_{l1}+a_{l1}-b_{l1}, p_{l2}+a_{l2}-b_{l2}, \cdots, p_{ln_l}+a_{ln_l}-b_{ln_l}] \;)$$

In this case, we can have a set of literals corresponding with $\mathcal{P} - \mathcal{PS}$ as follows:

$$\{p_{11}(\cdots x_{i_1}\cdots y_{11}\cdots), \; p_{12}(\cdots y_{11}\cdots y_{12}\cdots), \cdots, p_{1n_1}(\cdots y_{1(n_1-1)}\cdots y_{1n_1}\cdots),$$

where the superscripts are $a_{11}^{\text{-th}}\, b_{11}^{\text{-th}}$, $a_{12}^{\text{-th}}\, b_{12}^{\text{-th}}$, $a_{1n_1}^{\text{-th}}\, b_{1n_1}^{\text{-th}}$

$$\cdots$$

$$p_{l1}(\cdots x_{i_l}\cdots y_{l1}\cdots), \; p_{l2}(\cdots y_{l1}\cdots y_{l2}\cdots), \cdots, p_{ln_l}(\cdots y_{l(n_l-1)}\cdots y_{ln_l}\cdots), \; q(y_{1n_1}, \cdots, y_{ln_l}) \; \}.$$

where the superscripts are $a_{l1}^{\text{-th}}\, b_{l1}^{\text{-th}}$, $a_{l2}^{\text{-th}}\, b_{l2}^{\text{-th}}$, $a_{ln_l}^{\text{-th}}\, b_{ln_l}^{\text{-th}}$

This set of literals is denoted by $q(\mathcal{P} - \mathcal{PS})$.

The MRI algorithm is shown in Fig. 3. It treats literals of a clause by classifying them into two groups: literals for conditions and literals for preparing terms to a recursive call. If a recursive literal l is represented by a path structure $\mathcal{PS}$, the conditional part of a clause that processes l consists of $q(\mathcal{P} - \mathcal{PS})$ for a check predicate q and a path tuple $\mathcal{P}$ extending $\mathcal{PS}$. The other part, which prepares terms for the succeeding recursive call, is $p(\mathcal{PS}' - \mathcal{PS})$ for a path structure $\mathcal{PS}'$ extending $\mathcal{PS}$, where p is a target predicate. A base clause only has the former part, which is denoted by condition^{base} in the algorithm. A recursive clause has both parts, which are denoted by condition^{recur} and pass^{recur}, respectively.

The algorithm has three parts following its initialization, where several positive examples are chosen and their saturations are calculated. **Select** is a nondeterministic command, which selects an object from choices, and so the algorithm is nondeterministic.

The first part generates a path structure of the last recursive call for each example. The last call should be processed by a base clause. Its conditional part is calculated by enumerating all path tuples that extend the path structure for each example. Only the common part of the conditional parts is considered, because we assume that there is only a base clause.

The second part extracts candidates of recursive clauses. This is done by generating sub-path structures of the path structure generated previously for a base clause, and calculating the difference between them. A conditional part is generated to collect all path tuples that extend the path structure. To avoid collecting the same path tuple twice for an example, the variable used$_i$ is used.

The third part refines the base clause by a greedy search. It collects only necessary literals from the literals generated previously. This part also constructs a program by collecting clauses from candidates by a greedy search. It takes recursive clauses in order of the numbers of examples explained by the clauses.

5 Implementation and Experiments

The MRI algorithm was implemented using Quintus prolog 3.2. The algorithm is nondeterministic, and thus was implemented to enumerate all solutions.

Modes and types of predicates are used to reduces the size of saturations. The algorithm assumes that all arguments of a target predicate are input. However, the implementation also treats output arguments. For output arguments, the input (output) modes of path predicates are considered as output (input, respectively).

Table 2 shows some predicates that MRI can induce and some of their associated samples which MRI can induce the predicates with. Predicates used in the definitions are shown in Table 1. Some predicates have two recursive clauses, and ancstr-in-law, which is very artificial, has four recursive clauses.

Table 3 shows the results of induction from two positive and one negative examples, selected randomly. Inductin is tried using fifty different samples for each predicate. Results are compared with CRUSTACEAN. MRI gives higher correct rates and has a moderate runtime. It also induces predicates with two recursive clauses. MRI may induce more than one definition and uses negative

Table 2. Target predicates and their definitions

definitions of target predicates	Examples(pos:+,neg:−)
reverse(A, A)←nil(A). reverse($A, [B|C]$)←last(A, D, B),reverse(D, C).	+($[3, 1, 2], [2, 1, 3]$) +($[a, a, b], [b, a, a]$) −($[a, y], [a, y]$)
append(A, B, B)←nil(A). append($A, B, [C|D]$)←decomp(A, C, E),append(E, B, D).	+($[], [], []$) +($[a, b], [], [a, b]$)
last-of(A, B)←decomp(A, B, C),nil(C). last-of(A, B)←decomp(A, C, D),last-of(D, B).	+($[d,e,a],a$) +($[d,b],b$) −($[x, y, d], x$)
remove(A, B, B) ←nil(B). remove($A, B, [C|D]$)←decomp(B, C, E),remove(A, E, D). remove(A, B, C)←decomp(B,D,E),remove(A,E,C),eq(A,D).	+($c, [d], [d]$) +($1, [1, 1], []$)
merge(A, B, B) ←nil(A). merge($A, B, [C|D]$)←decomp(B, C, E),merge(A, E, D). merge($A, B, [C|D]$)←decomp(A, C, E),merge(E, B, D).	+($[d],[],[d]$) +($[d],[b],[b,d]$) −($[d], [e], [d, e, f]$) −($[a], [], []$)
max(A, B)←decomp(A, B, C),nil(C). max(A, B)←decomp(A, C, D),max(D, B),large(B, C). max(A, B) ←decomp(A, B, C),max(C, D),large(B, D).	+($[3, 4, 2], 4$) +($[5, 2], 5$) −($[3, 4, 5], 2$)
ancstr-in-law(A, B)←eq(A, B). ancstr-in-law(A, B)←father(A, C),ancstr-in-law(C, B). ancstr-in-law(A, B)←mother(A, C),ancstr-in-law(C, B). ancstr-in-law(A,B)←father-in-law(A,C),ancstr-in-law(C,B). ancstr-in-law(A,B)←mother-in-law(A,C),ancstr-in-law(C,B).	

Table 3. Results of MRI and CRUSTACEAN(CRU)

	Correct		Number		Time	
	CRU	MRI	CRU	MRI	CRU	MRI
reverse	100	100	5.2	2.0	0.7	0.6
append	22	100	4.9	2.0	0.4	1.6
last-of	46	90	1.8	2.2	0.2	0.8
remove	-	96	-	2.7	-	1.8
merge	-	78	-	2.6	-	4.2
max	-	36	-	1.1	-	0.8

Correct: Rate of correct answers (%)
Number: Average of the number of induced programs
Time: Runtime (sec.)

Definitions are induced from two positive examples and a negative example, selected randomly.

examples to prune solutions. Table 3 also shows the average number of definitions induced. The rate of correct definitions is the proportion of cases where one of the definitions induced is the intended one.

6 Discussions

This paper has already described an induction method for logic programs based on the structural analysis of saturations. The analysis uses path structures, which was originally proposed in [8]. The main contribution of this paper is to show the differential analysis of path structures and the correspondence between difference and literals. The results show that the method induces programs with more than one recursive clause from a few positive and negative examples.

Now, we describe the ability of MRI. It induce a recursive definition which includes exactly one base clause and recursive clauses. A recursive clause has exactly one recursive literal whose i-th input argument depends only on the i-th argument of a head literal. Background knowledge includes only check predicates and path predicates. If these conditions are satisfied, the recursive definition is one of the solutions found by MRI with appropriate examples.

We analyze the time complexity using a result given in [8], which uses the same situation as MRI. The result states that the number of literals in a saturation is bounded by $O((kjm)^{j^i})$ and the number of possible path structures is bounded by $O((kjm)^{j^i ik})$, where k is the arity of positive examples, j is the maximum arity of predicates in the background knowledge, m is the number of predicates in the background knowledge, and i is the maximum length of paths considered. Let the number of saturations be s, and the number of path structures p. The most time-expensive routines involve gathering the conditional part of a base clause (lines 5–11 in the algorithm) and generating candidates of recursive clauses (lines 21–32). Both routines try to make a match between path structures, at most, sn times. An attempt at matching takes $O(i)$, and so the routines take $O(ins) = O(in(kjm)^{j^i})$, where n is the number of positive examples chosen. This bounds the time complexity of a trial of MRI: MRI tries all of the lines, at most, p times, and so the total time complexity is bounded by $O(in(kjm)^{j^i} \cdot p) = O(in(kjm)^{j^i ik})$. If we can assume i, j, and k are constants, the algorithm works in a polynomial time of m and n.

References

1. Quinlan, J. R.: "Learning logical definitions from relations", *Machine Learning*, **5**, pp.239–266 (1990).
2. Quinlan, J. R., Cameron-Jones, R. M.: "FOIL: A midterm report", In P. Brazdil, editor, *Proc. 6th European Conf. on Machine Learning*, LNAI **667**, Springer-Verlag, pp.3–20 (1993).
3. Muggleton, S.: "Inverse entailment and progol", *New Generation Computing*, **3+4**, pp.245–286 (1995).
4. Muggleton, S., Feng, C.: "Efficient induction of logic programs", Proc. Workshop on Algorithmic Learning Theory, Ohmsma, Tokyo, pp.368–381 (1990).
5. Lapointe, S., Matwin, S.: "A tool for efficient induction of recursive programs", Proc. 11th Int'l Conf. on Machine Learning, Morgan Kaufmann, pp.273–281 (1992).
6. Aha, D. W., Lapointe, S., Ling, C. X., Matwin, S.: "Inverting Implication with Small Training Sets", Proc. 7th European Conf. on Machine Learning, LNAI **784**, Springer-Verlag, pp.31–48 (1994)
7. Aha, D. W., Lapointe, S., Ling, C. X., Matwin, S.: "Learning Recursive Relations with Randomly Selected Small Training Sets", Proc. 11th Int'l Conf. on Machine Learning, Morgan Kaufmann, pp.12–18 (1994).
8. Idestam-Almquist, P.: "Efficient Induction of Recursive Definitions by Structural Analysis of Saturations", in Advances in Inductive Logic Programming, L.De Raedt (ed.), IOS Press Ohmsha, pp.192–205 (1996).

Input a set of positive examples $\mathcal{E}^+$ of a predicate p with arity k
           a set of negative examples $\mathcal{E}^-$ of p
           a background theory T

Output a program base $\cup$ recursion

 # Initialization

1   Select a set of several examples $\{E_1^+, \cdots, E_n^+\}$ from $\mathcal{E}^+$
2   **For** $i = 1$ **to** n **do**
3          $F_i :=$ saturation of E_i^+ wrt T
4          $used_i := \emptyset$

 # Select path structures for a base clause

5   **For** $i = 1$ **to** n **do**
6   Select a path structure $\mathcal{PS}_i$ of E_i^+ wrt T
7          $condition_i^{base} := \emptyset$
8   **For every** check predicate q of T and **every** path tuple $\mathcal{P}$ that extends
          $\mathcal{PS}_i$ and satisfies $q(\mathcal{P}[E_i^+]) \in F_i$ **do**
9              $condition_i^{base} := condition_i^{base} \cup \{q(\mathcal{P} - \mathcal{PS}_i)\}$
10            $used_i := used_i \cup \{(q, \mathcal{P})\}$
11   **If** $condition_1^{base} \cap \cdots \cap condition_n^{base} = \emptyset$ **go to 5**
12     $condition^{base} := \emptyset$
13   **For every** set of literals $\mathcal{L} \in condition_1^{base} \cap \cdots \cap condition_n^{base}$ **do**
14         $condition^{base} := condition^{base} \cup \mathcal{L}$
15   **For** $i = 1$ **to** n **do**
16   **For every** $(q, \mathcal{P}) \in used_i$ **do**
17   **If** $q(\mathcal{P} - \mathcal{PS}_i) \notin condition_1^{base} \cap \cdots \cap condition_n^{base}$
                then $used_i := used_i - \{(q, \mathcal{P})\}$
18     $base' :=$ "$p(x_1, \cdots, x_k) \leftarrow condition^{base}$"

 # Generate candidates of recursive clauses

19     $candidates := \emptyset$
20   **For** $i := 1$ **to** n **do**
21   **Repeat**
22   Select a sub-path structure $\mathcal{PS}_i'$ of $\mathcal{PS}_i$
23            $condition^{recur} := \emptyset$
24   **For every** check predicate q of T and **every** path tuple $\mathcal{P}$ that
            extends $\mathcal{PS}_i'$ and satisfies $q(\mathcal{P}[E_i^+]) \in F_i$ and $(q, \mathcal{P}) \notin used_i$ **do**
25               $condition^{recur} := condition^{recur} \cup q(\mathcal{P} - \mathcal{PS}_i)$
26               $used_i := used_i \cup \{(q, \mathcal{P})\}$
27            $pass^{recur} := p(\mathcal{PS}_i - \mathcal{PS}_i')$
28            $candidates := candidates \cup \{$"$p(x_1, \cdots, x_k) \leftarrow condition^{recur} \cup pass^{recur}$"$\}$
29            $\mathcal{PS}_i := \mathcal{PS}_i'$
30   **Until** $p(\mathcal{PS}_i[E_i^+]) = E_i^+$

 # Select recursive clauses which are consistent with examples

31     $base :=$ a minimal set of literals that is consistent with $\mathcal{E}^+$ and $\mathcal{E}^-$,
        the literals which are collected by a greedy search from $base'$
32     $recursion :=$ a minimal set of recursive clauses that is consistent with $\mathcal{E}^+$ and
        $\mathcal{E}^-$, the clauses which are collected by a greedy search from $candidates$

Fig. 3. MRI algorithm

A Logical Framework for Graph Theoretical Decision Tree Learning

Peter Geibel and Fritz Wysotzki

Methods of Artificial Intelligence, Computer Science Department, Sekr. Fr 5–8
Technical University Berlin, Franklinstr. 28/29, D-10587 Berlin, Germany
Email {geibel|wysotzki}@cs.tu-berlin.de

Abstract. We present a logical approach to graph theoretical learning that is based on using alphabetic substitutions for modelling graph morphisms. A classified graph is represented by a definite clause that possesses variables of the sort *node* for representing nodes and atoms for representing the edges. In contrast to the standard logical semantics, different node variables are assumed to denote different objects. The use of an alphabetical subsumption relation (α-subsumption) implies that the least generalization of clauses (α-generalization) has different properties than Plotkin's least generalization (*lgg*). We present a method for constructing optimal α-generalizations from Plotkin's least generalization. The developed framework is used in the relational decision tree algorithm TRITOP.

1 Introduction

In this paper, we present a logical approach to graph theoretical decision tree learning that is based on using alphabetic substitutions for modelling graph morphisms. The nodes of a graph are represented by variables of the sort (type) *node* while atoms are used for representing the edges. A classified graph is this way represented by a definite clause. In contrast to the standard logical semantics, different node variables are assumed to denote different objects which is quite natural in many, e.g. technical application domains.

To compare the generality of clauses in this framework, we will introduce an alphabetical subsumption relation (α-subsumption) that relies on alphabetical substitutions (α-substitutions) and preserves the distinctness of node variables. In [5], N. Helft uses inequalities to express the distinctness of variables. Though we also use inequalities for defining the meaning of clauses containing node variables, we propose a different notion of least generalization. In contrast to Plotkin's (and Helft's) least generalization (*lgg*, see [10]), each such least α-generalization is reduced, has less literals than the original clauses, but is not unique. Nevertheless, optimal α-generalizations with a high structural complexity can be constructed from Plotkin's least generalization. We will show that the α-generalization algorithm can also be used for testing α-subsumption, as well as for computing the number of possible embeddings of one structure into another, which is crucial for defining relational decision trees.

In this framework, domain theories can be included by a modified version of saturation ([13]). This approach is similarly used in the system CILGG ([7]) and can be shown to be equivalent to a modified version Buntine's generalized subsumption ([1]).

For showing the feasibility of our approach, it is used in the learning system TRITOP that induces relational decision trees that contain complex structural (relational) attributes as tests. TRITOP is based on the decision tree algorithms CAL3 ([16]) and ID3 ([12]). In TRITOP, the relational attributes are constructed from the examples by combining the computation of α-generalizations with the application of refinement operators. In contrast to the graph based decision tree learner INDIGO ([4]), the attributes are not computed before, but during the construction of the tree which leads to smaller and more accurate decision trees.

This article is organized as follows. In section 2, the representation of classified relational structures and of attributes by definite clauses is discussed, and α-subsumption is introduced. In section 3 we describe an approach to using domain theories. In section 4 an algorithm for computing optimal α-generalizations is given. In section 5 the learning system TRITOP is sketched. Section 6 concludes.

2 Training Examples and Attributes

For learning a n-ary relational concept, a training set $\mathcal{E} = \{E_i \mid 1 \leq i \leq e\}$ is given, that contains $e \geq 0$ definite clauses $E_i = class(x_1^i, \ldots, x_n^i, c^i) \leftarrow a_1^i, \ldots, a_{m^i}^i$ from a function free and sorted logical language ([9]). In each example E_i, the body $a_1^i, \ldots, a_{m^i}^i$ is a conjunction of atoms a_j^i containing the classified objects $x_1^i, \ldots, x_n^i$ and contextual objects as variables of the sort *node*. The class value c^i of the tuple $x_1^i, \ldots, x_n^i$ stems from the set $\{c_1, \ldots, c_v\}$ of class constants that posses the sort *Class*. The concept to be learned is characterized by the predicate symbol *class* with type *node* $\times \ldots \times$ *node* $\times$ *Class* whose arity $n + 1$ determines the arity n of the concept.

In the following, we will use the relations $b(x)$ ("x is a block"), $s(x,y)$ ("x supports y") and $d(x,y)$ ("x does not touch y") for describing blocks world situations. Suppose that we want to learn the binary relation *passage* that is true for two objects that both support the roof of a blocks world arch. We will consider the training set $\mathcal{E} = \{E_1, E_2, E_3, E_4\}$ that contains the following examples and counterexamples for the concept *passage*: $E_1 = class(x_1, x_2, 1) \leftarrow b(x_1), b(x_2), b(x_3), s(x_1, x_3), s(x_2, x_3), d(x_1, x_2), E_2 = class(x_1, x_2, 1) \leftarrow b(x_1), b(x_2), b(x_3), b(x_4), s(x_1, x_3), s(x_2, x_3), s(x_4, x_3), d(x_1, x_2), d(x_2, x_4), E_3 = class(x_1, x_2, 0) \leftarrow b(x_1), b(x_2), b(x_3), s(x_1, x_3), s(x_2, x_3), E_4 = class(x_1, x_2, 0) \leftarrow b(x_1), b(x_2), b(x_3), b(x_4), s(x_1, x_3), s(x_2, x_3), d(x_1, x_2), s(x_4, x_1), s(x_4, x_2)$.

To construct a relational decision tree, we can use relational attributes that are implicitly given by the set of all substructures of the examples in the training set $\mathcal{E}$. For example, the attribute $A = class(y_1, y_2, y) \leftarrow s(y_1, y_3), s(y_2, y_3), d(y_1, y_2)$ describes the objects y_1 and y_2 by their relation to a third contextual object y_3. A occurs as a substructure in the examples E_1, E_2, and E_4 but not in E_3. Because attributes are *not* assigned to a specific class, the class value of A is given by the dummy class variable y.

In the blocks world example, we intuitively require y_1, y_2, and y_3 to denote different objects, i.e. the logical meaning of A is described by the less general attribute $\Phi(A) = class(y_1, y_2, y) \leftarrow s(y_1, y_3), s(y_2, y_3), d(y_1, y_2), \neg y_1 = y_2,$ $\neg y_2 = y_3, \neg y_1 = y_3$ whose inequalities enforce y_1, y_2 and y_3 to be bound to different objects.

Generally, for a clause (example or attribute) $C = class(x_1, \ldots, x_n, y) \leftarrow a_1, \ldots, a_m$ we will use its **expanded clause** $\Phi(C) = class(x_1, \ldots, x_n, y) \leftarrow a_1, \ldots, a_m, Ineq(C)$ with inequalities $Ineq(C) = \{\neg x = y \mid x, y \in vars(C), x, y \in node, x \neq y\}$ to describe its logical meaning. The conjunction $Ineq(C)$ expresses that distinct variables x and y of sort *node* denote different objects.

Subsumption is used to compare the generality of attributes and to check, if an attribute occurs in a classified object. A clause C_1 **subsumes** a clause C_2 – $C_1 \vdash_\theta C_2$ – if $C_1\theta \subseteq C_2$ holds for a substitution θ. In contrast, α-**subsumption** requires different node variables to be mapped to different objects in the subsumed structure. Formally, a clause C_1 α-subsumes a clause C_2 – $C_1 \vdash_\theta^\alpha C_2$ – iff $\Phi(C_1) \vdash_\theta \Phi(C_2)$ holds.

A substitution θ is called an α-**substitution** (with respect to a variable set V), iff for node variables $x, y \in node$ with $x \neq y$ the relation $\theta(x) \neq \theta(y)$ holds. If $\Phi(C_1) \vdash_\theta \Phi(C_2)$ holds, then each inequality in $\Phi(C_1)$ has to be mapped to an inequality in $\Phi(C_2)$, obliging θ to be an α-substitution for which $C_1 \vdash_\theta C_2$ holds. Therefore the following proposition holds.

Proposition 2.1 *For clauses C_1 and C_2 the relation $C_1 \vdash_\theta^\alpha C_2$ holds, iff $C_1 \vdash_\theta C_2$ holds for θ being an α-substitution.*

The blocks world example, the attribute A α-subsumes the example E_1 using the α-substitution $\theta = \{y_1 \leftarrow x_1, y_2 \leftarrow x_2, y_3 \leftarrow x_3, y \leftarrow 1\}$. Similar to α-substitutions we can define α-variable bindings that can be used to define α-models of logical formulae. α-models can be used to define the notions of α-**correctness** and α-**completeness**. It can be shown, that $\vdash_\theta^\alpha$ is correct, α-correct, α-complete (because of our language restrictions) but not complete in general.

As an extension to first order formalisms, we define $n^\alpha(C_1, C_2) = \|\{\theta \mid C_1 \vdash_\theta^\alpha C_2\}\|$ as the **multiplicity** of C_1 in C_2. In the above example, $n^\alpha(A, E_1) = 1$ holds.

3 Using Domain Theories

We allow a domain theory $\mathcal{T}$ to comprise general or application specific knowledge in form of *class*-free generative definite clauses (remember that the example specific knowledge is contained in the examples). In a generative clause, each head variable occurs also in the body of the clause, i.e. the rule does not introduce new variables. Similar to CILGG ([7]), the relation $\vdash_\theta^\alpha$ can be extended to include a domain theory $\mathcal{T}$ by using α-saturation which is equivalent to a modified version of Buntine's generalized subsumption $\vdash_{gen}$ ([1]) and therefore correct.

The definite clause C_1 subsumes the definite clause C_2 with respect to a definite program $\mathcal{T} - C_1 \vdash_{gen} (\mathcal{T}) C_2$ – if every ground atom that follows from C_2 in a Herbrand model of $\mathcal{T}$ follows also from C_1. Similar to α-subsumption, we define $C_1 \vdash_{gen}^{\alpha} (\mathcal{T})C_2$ to mean $\Phi(C_1) \vdash_{gen} (\Phi(\mathcal{T})) \Phi(C_2)$.

Jung shows in [6] that the generalized subsumption can be tested by computing the **saturation** ([13]) of the clause C_2, if the saturation exists. In this case $C_1 \vdash_{gen} (\mathcal{T}) C_2$ iff $C_1 \vdash_{\theta} C_2 \downarrow \mathcal{T}$. The saturation of a clause $C_2 = H_2 \leftarrow B_2$ is defined by $C_2 \downarrow \mathcal{T} = H_2 \leftarrow [\mathcal{T}]B_2$ where $[\mathcal{T}]B_2$ is the deductive closure of B_2 with respect to the elementary saturation with clauses from $\mathcal{T}$. The clause $H_2 \leftarrow B_2, H_3\theta$ is an **elementary saturation** of C_2 with $C_3 = H_3 \leftarrow B_3 \in \mathcal{T}$, if the relation $B_3 \vdash_{\theta} B_2$ holds.

The α-**saturation** of a rule C_2 with respect to a theory $\mathcal{T}$ is defined by $C_2 \downarrow^{\alpha} \mathcal{T} = \Phi(C_2) \downarrow \Phi(\mathcal{T})$. Because $\mathcal{T}$ is generative and function free, $C_2 \downarrow^{\alpha} \mathcal{T}$ is finite. Again, instead of using the inequalities, the α-saturation can be computed directly by using elementary α-saturation steps, i.e. $\vdash_{\theta}$ is replaced by $\vdash_{\theta}^{\alpha}$. Because each elementary α-saturation step does not introduce new variables, the equation $\Phi(C_2 \downarrow^{\alpha} \mathcal{T}) = \Phi(C_2) \downarrow \Phi(\mathcal{T})$ holds. The following theorem states that using α-saturation is equivalent to generalized α-subsumption and thus correct (and because of our language restrictions even α-complete, see also [7]).

Proposition 3.1 $C_1 \vdash_{gen}^{\alpha} (\mathcal{T})C_2$ iff $C_1 \vdash_{\theta}^{\alpha} C_2 \downarrow^{\alpha} \mathcal{T}$.

Proof: $C_1 \vdash_{gen}^{\alpha} (\mathcal{T}) C_2$ is by definition equivalent to $\Phi(C_1) \vdash_{gen} (\Phi(\mathcal{T})) \Phi(C_2)$. Because $\mathcal{T}$ and $\Phi(\mathcal{T})$ are both generative, $\Phi(C_2) \downarrow \Phi(\mathcal{T})$ exists. Therefore $\Phi(C_1) \vdash_{gen} (\Phi(\mathcal{T})) \Phi(C_2)$ holds iff $\Phi(C_1) \vdash_{\theta} \Phi(C_2) \downarrow \Phi(\mathcal{T})$ holds, due to [6]. Due to the equality $\Phi(C_2 \downarrow^{\alpha} \mathcal{T}) = \Phi(C_2) \downarrow \Phi(\mathcal{T})$ this is equivalent to $\Phi(C_1) \vdash_{\theta} \Phi(C_2 \downarrow^{\alpha} \mathcal{T})$ which is by definition equivalent to $C_1 \vdash_{\theta}^{\alpha} C_2 \downarrow^{\alpha} \mathcal{T}$.

In the example of section 2, the modified attribute $A' = class(y_1, y_2, y) \leftarrow s(y_1, y_3), s(y_2, y_3), d(y_2, y_1)$ does not α-subsume the example E_1. Using the theory $\mathcal{T} = \{d(x_1, x_2) \leftarrow d(x_2, x_1)\}$ we construct the α-saturated clause $E_1 \downarrow^{\alpha} \mathcal{T} = class(x_1, x_2, 1) \leftarrow s(x_1, x_3), s(x_2, x_3), d(x_1, x_2), d(x_2, x_1)$ that is α-subsumed by A'.

4 α-Generalizations

In the following we will consider only clauses, that posses node variables as the only terms (except the class constant or variable in the head). Then $C_1 \vdash_{\theta}^{\alpha} C_2$ implies that θ is an injective mapping of variables of C_1 to variables in C_2. Therefore, different literals $l, l' \in C_1$ are mapped to different literals $\theta(l)$ and $\theta(l')$. **Therefore each genuine generalization C_1 of C_2 possesses at least one literal less than C_2. This means that there are only finitely many clauses C, for which $C_1 \vdash_{\theta}^{\alpha} C$, $C \vdash_{\theta}^{\alpha} C_2$ holds.**

Now the least (i.e. least general, or most specific) α-generalizations can be defined as follows.

Definition 4.1 (α-generalization) *The clause C is an α-generalization of C_1 and C_2, if $C \vdash^\alpha_\theta C_1$ and $C \vdash^\alpha_\theta C_2$ holds. C is a least generalization, if for every other α-generalization $C_3 \neq C$ the relation $C \vdash^\alpha_\theta C_3$ does not hold.*

In contrast to Plotkin's least generalizations, the least α-generalization is shorter than the original clauses, and reduced, but not unique. It can be shown that Plotkin's least generalization of C_1 and C_2 is equivalent to the conjunction of all least α-generalizations of C_1 and C_2.

Least α-generalizations may differ in the number of variables and literals and may be not comparable with respect to $\vdash^\alpha_\theta$. Therefore we define heuristically a **node optimal α-generalization** as an α-generalization that possesses the maximum number of node variables possible together with the maximum number of literals with respect to the set of all generalizations with the maximum number of nodes.

In the following we use Plotkin's *lgg* algorithm ([10]) as a starting point for constructing optimal α-generalizations. Due to [10] there are substitutions μ_1 and μ_2 such that $lgg(C_1, C_2)\mu_1 \subseteq C_1$ and $lgg(C_1, C_2)\mu_2 \subseteq C_2$ holds. The substitutions μ_1 und μ_2 are not injective in general.

Least α-generalizations can be computed from $lgg(C_1, C_2)$ by determining maximal substructures $L \subseteq lgg(C_1, C_2)$, for which both μ_1 and μ_2 are injective. Two variables $w, w' \in vars(lgg(C_1, C_2))$ are called **compatible** – $k(w, w')$ –, if $w \neq w'$, $w\mu_1 \neq w'\mu_1$ and $w\mu_2 \neq w'\mu_2$ holds.

The following algorithm is adapted from the dynamic programming maximum clique algorithm of Carraghan and Pardalos ([2]) that is used in [14] for efficiently deciding $\vdash_\theta$. Roughly speaking, it computes all node optimal generalizations restricted to such generalizations that contain a head literal (step 1 of alg. 4.1) by determining largest, maximal cliques in the graph formed by the relation k. The cliques are additionally required to posses the maximum number of literals with respect to the set of all maximum cliques.

Let the set $vars(lgg(C_1, C_2))$ be arbitrarily ordered. For variables $V \subseteq vars(lgg(C_1, C_2))$ and literals $L \subseteq lgg(C_1, C_2)$ let $restr(L, V)$ contain those literals in L, that posses only variables in V. Let $\mathcal{H} = vars(lgg(H_1, H_2))$ be the set of the head variable generalizations. The global variable $CBCS$ contains the list of the current best cliques, $CBCN$ is the number nodes in every clique of $CBCS$, and $CBCL$ is the number of literals for every clique in $CBCS$.

Algorithm 4.1 $gen^\alpha_{opt}(C, V, L)$: *The variable sets C and V are disjoint and comprise the variables of the literals in L. All variables in C are compatible with each other and with all variables in V.*

1. *if $\neg (\mathcal{H} \subseteq C \cup V)$ holds, or $\|C \cup V\| < CBCN \vee (\|C \cup V\| = CBCN \wedge \|L\| < CBCL)$, i.e. the clique is not good enough, then return*
2. *If there are incompatible Variables in V, then choose a minimal $x \in V$ and construct the set $N := \{v \mid v \in V \wedge k(x, v)\}$. Set $V_1 = \{x\} \cup C \cup N$, $L_1 = restr(L, V_1)$, $V_2 = C \cup V - \{x\}$, $L_2 = restr(L, V_2)$ and recursively compute $gen^\alpha_{opt}((\{x\} \cup C) \cap vars(L_1), N \cap vars(L_1), L_1)$ and $gen^\alpha_{opt}(C \cap vars(L_2), (V - \{x\}) \cap vars(L_2), L_2)$. Then return.*

3. *Otherwise the new clique $C \cup V$ is found that yields the α-generalization L. Retain, augment or replace CBCS according to the values $\|C \cup V\|$ and $\|L\|$, and update the values CBCN and CBCL if necessary. Then return.*

After termination of $gen_{opt}^\alpha(\emptyset, vars(lgg(C_1, C_2)), lgg(C_1, C_2))$ with the initial values $CBCS = \emptyset$, $CBCN = 0$ and $CBCL = 0$, the set $CBCS$ contains all node optimal cliques with $CBCN$ variables and $CBCL$ literals that posses a head literal. After termination of $gen_{opt}^\alpha(\emptyset, vars(lgg(C_1, C_2)), lgg(C_1, C_2))$ with the initial values $CBCS = \emptyset$, $CBCN = \|vars(C_1)\|$ and $CBCL = \|C_1\|$, the equality $\|CBCS\| = n^\alpha(C_1, C_2)$ holds. If.e. The algorithm can also be used for computing $C_1 \vdash_\theta^\alpha C_2$ and $n^\alpha(C_1, C_2)$.

Let us consider the example of section 2 again. Using the variables $v_1 = x_1 = lgg(x_1, x_1)$, $v_2 = lgg(x_1, x_2)$, $v_3 = lgg(x_1, x_4)$, $v_4 = lgg(x_2, x_1)$, $v_5 = x_2 = lgg(x_2, x_2)$, $v_6 = lgg(x_2, x_4)$, $v_7 = v_3 = lgg(x_3, x_3)$ we construct the Plotkin-generalization $lgg(E_1, E_2) = class(v_1, v_5, 1) \leftarrow b(v_1), b(v_2), b(v_3), b(v_4), b(v_5), b(v_6), b(v_7), s(v_1, v_7), s(v_2, v_7), s(v_3, v_7), s(v_4, v_7), s(v_5, v_7), s(v_6, v_7), d(v_1, v_5), d(v_2, v_6)$. There are two maximal and optimal cliques $\{v_1, v_5, v_7\}$ and $\{v_2, v_6, v_7\}$. Because the second clique does not contain the head variables v_1 and v_2, $\{v_1, v_5, v_7\}$ Is the only valid clique. The only node and as well literal optimal α-generalization of E_1 and E_2 is $class(v_1, v_5, 1) \leftarrow b(v_1), b(v_5), b(v_7), s(v_1, v_7), (v_5, v_7), d(v_1, v_5)$. Because this generalization has the same number of variables and literals as S_1, we know that there is exactly one embedding of E_1 into E_2, i.e. $n^\alpha(E_1, E_2) = 1$ and $E_1 \vdash_\theta^\alpha E_2$.

5 The Learning Algorithm TRITOP

Relational concepts can be expressed by relational decision trees, that contain relational attributes as tests. In the blocks world example of section 2 we can use the attribute $A_1 = class(y_1, y_2, y) \leftarrow s(y_1, y_3), s(y_2, y_3), d(y_1, y_2)$ to separate E_3 from E_1, E_2 and E_4. The latter set is split into the pure subsets $\{E_1, E_2\}$ and $\{E_4\}$ using the second test $A_2 = class(y_1, y_2, y) \leftarrow s(y_4, y_1), s(y_4, y_2)$ that occurs only for E_4. Theses decisions can be expressed by the compound relational decision tree $D = A_1[0 \rightarrow 0, 1 \rightarrow A_2[0 \rightarrow 1, 1 \rightarrow 0]]$.

More formally, we define a **relational decision tree** D to be either a class constant c or of the form $D = A[v_1 \rightarrow D_1, \ldots, v_n \rightarrow D_n]$ with a relational attribute A, natural numbers $v_1, \ldots, v_n$ and decision trees $D_1, \ldots, D_n$. A $(0, 1)$-decision tree has the form $D = A[0 \rightarrow D_0, 1 \rightarrow D_1]$.

A tree D constitutes a classification function $\phi(D)$ in an obvious way. For an example $E = class(x_1, \ldots, x_n, y) \leftarrow a_1, \ldots, a_m$ to be classified, we define $\phi(D)(E) = c$, if $D = c$ is a leaf. For a compound tree D, we set $\phi(D)(E) = \phi(D_i)(E)$ if $n^\alpha(A, E) = v_i$ for an index i and $\phi(D)(E) = \star$ otherwise (rejection). The interpretation of a $(0, 1)$-tree tests for existence of A in E only.

Relational decision trees can be constructed using the system **TRITOP**. The tree building algorithm of TRITOP is a top down algorithm, similar to the one used in ID3, combined with a CAL3 style ([16]) pre-pruning to prevent overfitting in the presence of noise. In every recursive learning step, TRITOP selects a discriminating relational attribute A and partitions the current training set T according to the different attribute values by computing $n^\alpha(A, E)$ for each $E \in T$. Then the algorithm is applied to each nonempty subset until a stopping criterion is fulfilled, i.e. the training set is sufficiently pure.

The crucial point of the algorithm is the construction of a discriminating relational attribute A from the current dataset T. In a first step, a set of initial attributes is constructed from T. This set is allowed to comprise the **empty attributes** $\{class(x_1, \ldots, x_n, y) \leftarrow \mid class(x_1, \ldots, x_n, c) \leftarrow s \in \mathcal{E}\}$ that can be specialized by adding literals. We also allow **generalized contextual attributes** inspired by the ones known from INDIGO ([4]). E.g. computing the depth 1 context of (x_1, x_2) in the additional training example $E_5 = class(x_1, x_2, 1) \leftarrow b(x_1), b(x_2), b(x_3), b(x_4), b(x_5), s(x_1, x_3), s(x_2, x_3), s(x_4, x_3), s(x_5, x_3), d(x_1, x_2), d(x_2, x_4), d(x_4, x_5)$, leads to the contextual attribute $class(y_1, y_2, y) \leftarrow b(y_1), b(y_2), s(y_1, y_3), s(y_2, y_3), d(y_1, y_2), d(y_2, y_4)$ that has a **smaller** structural complexity as compared to E_5. Contextual attributes are optimized by dropping irrelevant literals and by adding missing discriminating literals. We also allow **user defined attributes** and the training examples $\mathcal{E}$ as initial attributes.

Now, the set $\mathcal{A}$ of initial attributes is augmented by computing optimal α-generalizations of the initial attributes using the algorithms in section 4. The new set $\mathcal{A}_1$ is sorted by the value of the transinformation attribute selection measure $T(A) = H(C) - H(C|A)$, where $H(C)$ is the entropy of the classes, and $H(C|A)$ is the conditional entropy. Instead of expensively computing generalizations of 3 and more objects, the best attributes in $\mathcal{A}_1$ are optimized by removing irrelevant and adding discriminating literals and a systematic way. For an attribute $A = H \leftarrow B \in \mathcal{A}_1$ to be optimized we obtain the set $O^-(A) = \{H \leftarrow (B - \{a\}) \mid a \in B\}$ by removing literals a from the body of A. Accordingly we construct the set $O^+(A) = \{H \leftarrow (B, a) \mid E \in \mathcal{E}, A \vdash_\theta^\alpha E, a \in \theta^{-1}(E - \theta(A))\}$ by adding exactly one literal to the body of A. The best attribute from $O^-(A) \cup O^+(A)$ is chosen for further optimization. Deletion of literals is preferred over the addition of literals. The complete optimization of all best attributes in $\mathcal{A}_1$ yields the new test attribute.

The System TRITOP was implemented in Eclipse Prolog. First experiments with the system were promising. On the **mutagenesis data set**, the accurracy of TRITOP is comparable to INDIGO with 86% on the 188 dataset (10fold cross validation, version B2 according to [15]) and 89% on the 42 dataset (leave one out method, also version B2), and is slightly better than PROGOL and FOIL on the same version of the dataset. The performance of TRITOP is increased significantly by using contextual attributes.

On the **mesh design data**, TRITOP performs with 37% predictive accuracy **better** than the systems FOIL (12%), MFOIL (21%), GOLEM (19%), Claudien (28%, [3]), MILP (32%), FOSSIL (32%), FORS (31%), SRT (24%, [8]), CILLG (22%, [7]), and INDIGO (34%) on the deterministic data.

When learning **illegal chess end game positions** (e.g. [11]), TRITOP reaches an accuracy of 99.3% on a 1000 instance training set using a 10-fold cross validation. In accuracy TRITOP is comparable to the systems FOIL (99.4%), LINUS (99.7%), and STRUCT (99.3%). INDIGO (73%) performed much worse than TRITOP, because it produces overly specific decision trees.

6 Concluding Remarks

In this article, we presented a framework for graph theoretical learning that was embodied in the relational decision tree algorithm TRITOP. First experiments showed, that with respect to accuracy TRITOP can keep up with most other learning systems or is even better. The experiments showed also, that using contextual attributes together with attribute optimization increases the accuracy significantly.

References

1. W. Buntine. Generalized subsumtion and its applications to induction and redundancy. *Artificial Intelligence*, 36:149–176, 1988.
2. R. Carraghan and M. P Pradalos. An exact algorithm for the maximum clique problem. *Operations Research Letter*, 9:375–382, 1990.
3. L. Dehaspe, W. van Laer, and L. De Raedt. Applications of a logical discovery engine. In *Proc. 4th Int. Workshop on ILP, GMD-Studien Nr. 237*, 1994.
4. Peter Geibel and Fritz Wysotzki. Learning relational concepts with decision trees. In Lorenza Saitta, editor, *Machine Learning: Proceedings of the Thirteenth International Conference*. Morgan Kaufmann Publishers, San Fransisco, CA, 1996.
5. N. Helft. Inductive generalization: A logical framework. In *Proceedings of the Second Working Session on Learning*, pages 149–157, 1987.
6. B. Jung. On inverting generality relations. In S. Muggleton, editor, *Proc. of the 3rd Int. Workshop on ILP*, pages 87–102. J. Stefan Institute, 1993.
7. J. Kietz. *Induktive Analyse relationaler Daten*. PhD thesis, Technische Universität Berlin, 1996.
8. S. Kramer. Structural regression trees. Technical Report TR-95-35, Oesterreichisches Forschungsinstitut fuer Artificial Intelligence, 1995.
9. J. W. LLoyd. *Foundations of Logic Programming*. Springer-Verlag, 1987.
10. G. D. Plotkin. A note on inductive generalization. In *Machine Intelligence*, pages 153–164. Edinburgh University Press, 1969.
11. J. R. Quinlan. Learning Logical Definitions from Relations. *Machine Learning*, 5:239 – 266, 1990.
12. J.R. Quinlan. Induction of Decision Trees. *Machine Learning*, 1(1):82 – 106, 1986.
13. C. Rouveirol. Semantic model for induction of first order theories. In *Proceedings of the 12th IJCAI*, pages 685–691. Morgan Kaufmann, 1991.
14. T. Scheffer, H. Herbrich, and F. Wysotzki. Efficient theta-subsumtion based on graph algorithms. In *Proceedings of the International Workshop on ILP*, 1996.
15. A. Srinivasan and S. H. Muggleton. Comparing the use of background knowledge by two inductive logic programming systems. In *Proceedings ILP 1995*, 1995.
16. S. Unger and F. Wysotzki. *Lernfähige Klassifizierungssysteme*. Akademie-Verlag, Berlin, 1981.

Learning with Abduction

A.C. Kakas[1], F. Riguzzi[2]

[1] Department of Computer Science, University of Cyprus
75 Kallipoleos str., CY-1678 Nicosia, Cyprus
antonis@turing.cs.ucy.ac.cy
[2] DEIS, Università di Bologna
Viale Risorgimento 2, 40136 Bologna, Italy
friguzzi@deis.unibo.it

Abstract. We investigate how abduction and induction can be integrated into a common learning framework through the notion of Abductive Concept Learning (ACL). ACL is an extension of Inductive Logic Programming (ILP) to the case in which both the background and the target theory are abductive logic programs and where an abductive notion of entailment is used as the coverage relation. In this framework, it is then possible to learn with incomplete information about the examples by exploiting the hypothetical reasoning of abduction.
The paper presents the basic framework of ACL with its main characteristics. An algorithm for an intermediate version of ACL is developed by suitably extending the top-down ILP method and integrating this with an abductive proof procedure for Abductive Logic Programming (ALP). A prototype system has been developed and applied to learning problems with incomplete information.

1 Introduction

The problem of integrating abduction and induction in Machine Learning systems has recently received renewed attention with several works on this topic [5, 2, 1]. In [5] the notion of Abductive Concept Learning (ACL) was proposed as a learning framework based on an integration of Inductive Logic Programming (ILP) and Abductive Logic Programming (ALP) [8].

Abductive Concept Learning is an extension of ILP that allows us to learn abductive logic programs of ALP with abduction playing a central role in the covering relation of the learning problem. The abductive logic programs learned in ACL contain both rules for the concept(s) to be learned as well as general clausal theories called integrity constraints. These two parts are synthesized together in a non-trivial way via the abductive reasoning of ALP which is then used as the basic covering relation for learning. In this way, learning in ACL synthesizes discriminant and characteristic induction to learn abductive logic programs.

This paper presents the basic framework of ACL with its main characteristics and demonstrates its potential for addressing the problem of learning from an incomplete background knowledge and of classifying new cases that again could be incompletely specified.

An algorithm is presented that performs a simpler version of ACL called Intermediate ACL (I-ACL): new rules are learned but not new integrity constraints and learned programs must satisfy a weaker condition on negative examples.

Integrity constraints can be learned externally to the I-ACL to solve the full ACL problem. The algorithm has been implemented in a new system also called I-ACL that constitutes the first building block of a system for performing full ACL. Integrity constraints are learned externally to this system using the Claudien [12] system together with additional data generated by the I-ACL system when this has finished. Several initial experiments are presented that demonstrate the ability of I-ACL and ACL to learn with incomplete information.

2   Abductive Logic Programming

In this section we very briefly present some of the elements of Abductive Logic Programming (ALP) needed for the formulation of the learning framework of Abductive Concept Learning (ACL). For more details the reader is referred to the survey [8] and the technical report [10].

Definition 1. An **abductive theory** T in ALP is a triple $\langle P, A, I \rangle$, where P is a normal logic program, A is the set of predicates called *abducible predicates*, and I is a set of first-order closed formulae called *integrity constraints*[3].

The semantics of an abductive theory is formalized through the notion of a Generalized Stable Model (for details see [8]). With this we define the notion of an abductive explanation and abductive entailment as follows. Given an abductive theory $T = \langle P, A, I \rangle$ and a formula G, the goal of abduction is to find a set of ground atoms Δ (*abductive explanation*) on the set of predicates in A which together with P entails G, i.e. $P \cup \Delta \models G$. It is also required that the program $P \cup \Delta$ is consistent with respect to I, i.e. $P \cup \Delta \models I$. When there exists an abductive explanation for e from T we say that T *abductively entails* e and we write $T \models_A e$.

These definitions can be extended (see [10]) to allow in Δ negative abducible assumptions for the falsity (or absence) of an abducible assumption. Such negative assumptions will be denoted by not_p where p is an abducible.

3   Learning with Abduction

Abductive Concept Learning can be defined as a case of discriminant concept learning but which contains in it also a characteristic learning problem. It thus combines discriminant and characteristic learning in a non-trivial way using the abductive entailment relation as the covers relation for the training examples.

The language of hypotheses is that of Abductive Logic programming as is also the language of background knowledge. The language of the examples is simply that of atomic ground facts.

---

[3] In practice, integrity constraints are restricted to be range-restricted clauses.

Definition 2. Abductive Concept Learning (ACL)
Given

- a set of positive examples E^+ of a concept C,
- a set of negative examples E^- of a concept C,
- an abductive theory $T = \langle P, A, I \rangle$ as background theory.

Find
A new abductive theory $T' = \langle P', A, I' \rangle$ with $P' \supseteq P$ and $I' \supseteq I$, such that

- $T' \models_A E^+$,
- $\forall e^- \in E^-, T' \not\models_A e^-$.

Therefore, ACL differs from ILP because both the background knowledge and the learned program are abductive logic programs. As a consequence, the notion of deductive entailment of ILP is substituted with the notion of abductive entailment ($\models_A$) in ALP.

Note that whereas for positive examples it is sufficient for the learned theory to provide an explanation of these, for the negative examples there should not exist a single abductive explanation in the learned theory that covers any of the negative examples.

It is often useful for practical reasons to initially relax this strong requirement on the negative examples and consider an **intermediate** problem, denoted by **I-ACL**, where the negative examples are also only required to be credulously uncovered i.e. that there exits in the learned theory at least one abductive explanation where the negative examples can not be covered (and of course in this extension it is also possible to cover the positive examples). Moreover, in this intermediate problem we are not interested in learning new integrity constraints. To this end we define the intermediate problem where the two conditions in the above definition are replaced by:
Find
A new abductive theory $T' = \langle P', A, I \rangle$ with $P' \supseteq P$, such that

- $T' \models_A E^+ \cup not\_E^-$, where $not\_E^- = \{not\_e^- | e^- \in E^-\}$.

where we use the notation $T' \models_A not\_e^-$ to mean that there exists at least one abductive sets of hypotheses such that, when added to P', then e^- would fail. We can then solve first this simpler problem and then use the explanations for the examples as input for further learning in order to satisfy the full ACL problem. The following example illustrate how it is possible to solve an ACL problem by first solving an I-ACL problem and then learning the integrity constraints.

Example 1. Suppose we want to learn the concept *father*. Let the background theory be $T = \langle P, A, \emptyset \rangle$ where:
$P = \{parent(john, mary), male(john),$
$parent(david, steve),$
$parent(kathy, ellen), female(kathy)\}$

$A = \{male/1, female/1\}$
and let the training data be:

$E^+ = \{father(john, mary), father(david, steve)\}$

$E^- = \{father(kathy, ellen), father(john, steve)\}$

In this case, a possible hypotheses $T' = \langle P', A, I \rangle$ learned by I-ACL would contain in P' the rule

$father(X, Y) \leftarrow parent(X, Y), male(X).$

under the abductive assumptions

$\Delta = \{male(david), not\_male(kathy)\}.$

The positive assumption comes from the requirement to cover the positive examples while the negative assumption from the requirement to cover the default negation of negative examples. In addition, by considering the background knowledge together with the positive assumption $male(david)$ from Δ, we could learn (using characteristic induction) the integrity constraint:

$\leftarrow male(X), female(X).$

Note that this integrity constraint provides independent support for the negative assumption $not\_male(kathy)$ in Δ thus ensuring that the corresponding negative example can not be abductively covered by the learned hypothesis. Therefore, the final theory containing the rule and the constraint satisfies the full ACL problem definition.

4 Algorithm

In this section we present an algorithm for I-ACL. This algorithm is based on the generic top-down algorithm (see e.g. [11]) suitably adapted to deal with the incompleteness of the abducible predicates and to take into account the integrity constraints in the background theory. It incorporates (and adapts) algorithms for abductive reasoning from ALP [9], extending the algorithm in [6]. We will not consider here fully the problem of integrating the learning of integrity constraints in this algorithm but rather we will assume that these exist (or have been learned) in the background theory. For lack of space, we outline a version of I-ACL for the case of single predicate learning, however I-ACL is able to perform effectively multiple predicate learning (see the technical report [10] for this extension).

The I-ACL algorithm differs from the basic top-down algorithm in the following respects. In the specialization loop, instead of a greedy search in the space of possible clauses, a best-first search is performed using an heuristic evaluation function that will be defined below.

The evaluation of a clause is done by starting and abductive derivation for each e^+ and each not_e^-, using the procedure defined in [9]. This procedure takes as input the goal to be derived, the abductive theory, the set of previous assumptions and, if it succeeds, produces as output the set of assumptions extended with the atoms abduced during the derivation. The set of assumptions abduced for earlier examples is also considered as input to ensure that the assumptions made during the derivation of the current example are consistent with the ones made before. Thus, we can test each positive and negative example separately and be sure that the clause will abductively derive $e_1^+ \wedge \ldots \wedge e_n^+ \wedge not\_e_1^- \wedge \ldots \wedge not\_e_m^-$.

The heuristic function of a clause is an *expected classification accuracy* [11] in which we need to take into account the relative strength of covering an example with abduction (i.e. some assumptions are needed and the strength of those assumptions) or without assumption (i.e. no assumption is needed) and similarly for the failure to cover negative examples with or without assumptions. The heuristic function used is

$$A = \frac{n^\oplus + k^\oplus \times n_A^\oplus}{n^\oplus + n^\ominus + k^\oplus \times n_A^\oplus + k^\ominus \times n_A^\ominus}$$

where $n^\oplus, n_A^\oplus, n^\ominus, n_A^\ominus$ are:

$n^\oplus$ number of pos. ex. covered by the clause without abduction,

$n_A^\oplus$ number of pos. ex. covered by the clause with abduction,

$n^\ominus$ number of neg. ex. covered by the clause (not_e^- has failed),

$n_A^\ominus$ number of neg. ex. uncovered by the clause with abduction.

The coefficients $k^\oplus$ and $k^\ominus$ are introduced in order to take into account the uncertainty in the coverage of the positive examples and in the failure to cover the negative examples when abduction is necessary for this to occur. Further details on these coefficients and the heuristic function can be found in [10].

The algorithm described above is sound but not complete for the intermediate problem I-ACL. Its soundness is ensured by the soundness of the abductive proof procedure and its extensions developed for the learning algorithm.

The algorithm is not complete because the search space is not completely explored. In particular, there are two choice points which are not considered in order to reduce the computational complexity of the algorithm. The first choice point is related to the greedy search in the space of possible programs (clauses are never retracted). The second choice point concerns the abductions that are made in order to cover the examples. In fact, an example can be abductively derived with different sets of assumptions. Depending on which set of assumptions we choose, this can change the outcome of the algorithm later on.

5 Experiments

We have performed several experiments to test the ability of I-ACL and ACL to learn from incomplete data. One set of experiments centered around the problem of learning family relations under different degree of incompleteness in the background knowledge. The I-ACL system was able to learn correctly from data which was only 80 % complete (20 % of the data was randomly removed) and, when integrity constraints were introduced, the system learned correctly with the missing data approaching 40 % of the initially complete data. Also multiple predicate learning experiments were carried out. The I-ACL system was able to handle this problem using the abductive data generated for one predicate while learning another predicate.

More details on these experiments can be found in [10]. Here we describe in some detail a series of experiments on the multiplexer problem [13] and compare the results of I-ACL with those of ICL-Sat.

5.1 Multiplexer

The multiplexer problem consists in learning the definition of a 6 bits multiplexer, starting from a training set where each example is composed by 6 bits, where the first two bits are interpreted as the address of one of the other four bits. If the bit at the specified address is 1 (regardless of the values of the other three bits), the example is considered positive, otherwise it is considered negative. For example, consider the example 10 0110. The first two bits specify that the third bit should be at 1, so this example is positive. We represent it by adding the positive example $mul(e1)$ to the training set and by including the following facts in the background knowledge

$bit1at1(e1)$. $bit2at0(e1)$. $bit3at0(e1)$.
$bit4at1(e1)$. $bit5at1(e1)$. $bit6at0(e1)$.

For the 6-bit multiplexer problem we have $2^6 = 64$ examples, 32 positive and 32 negative. We performed three experiments using the same datasets as in [13]: the first on the complete dataset, the second on an incomplete dataset and the third on the incomplete dataset plus some integrity constraints. The incomplete dataset was obtained by considering 12 examples out of 64 and by specifying for them only three bits where both the examples and bits were selected at random. E.g. the above example 10 0110 could have been replaced by 1? 0?1?. The incomplete example is still in the set of positive examples and its description in the background knowledge would be

$bit1at1(e1)$. $bit3at0(e1)$. $bit5at1(e1)$.

Now, all the predicates $bitNatB$ are abducibles and integrity constraints of the form below are added to the background theory

$\leftarrow bitNat0(X), bitNat1(X)$.

The dataset of the third experiment is obtained by including additional integrity constraints to the incomplete dataset. For each of the incomplete examples, an attempt was made to add constraints so that 1) the value of unknown attributes was still unknown (could still be 1 or 0); 2) some combination of values incompatible with the known class was now made impossible.

I-ACL was run on all the three datasets. The measure of performance that was adopted is accuracy, defined as the number of examples correctly classified over the total number of examples in the testing set, i.e. the number of positive examples covered plus the number of negative examples not covered over 64. The theory was tested on complete examples. The result are summarized in the following table:

Experiments	I-ACL	ICL- Sat
Complete background	100 %	100 %
Incomplete background	98.4 %	82.8 %
Incomplete background plus constraints	96.9 %	92.2 %

The theories learned by I-ACL were also tested on the incomplete examples and other randomly generated incomplete testing data to see how these could classify incomplete examples. The accuracy of this classification remained at approximately the same level as with the complete testing examples shown above.

Finally, we performed an experiment where more information was taken out. In this case we have taken out completely from the training data some of the negative examples. The I-ACL system learned rules that are incorrect (i.e. cover negative examples) as they are too general, e.g. the rule:

$mul(X) \leftarrow bit1at1(X), bit2at1(X).$

Extending the I-ACL algorithm, we run Claudien to learn clauses (integrity constraints) that hold on the positive examples. In this way we generate several constraints amongst which is

$\leftarrow mul(X), bit1at1(X), bit2at1(X), bit6at0(X)$

which effectively corrects the rule above by preventing the negative examples to be abductively classified as positive even when the rule succeeds. This experiment illustrates the potential of ACL to integrate characteristic with discriminant induction.

6 Conclusions and Related Work

We have studied the new learning framework of Abductive Concept Learning developing a first system for an intermediate version of it, I-ACL. Initial experiments with this system have demonstrated I-ACL as a suitable framework for learning with incomplete information.

Abduction has been incorporated in many learning systems (see e.g. [5, 2, 1]) but in most cases this is seen as a useful mechanism that can support some of the activities of the learning systems. For example, in multistrategy learning (or theory revision) abduction is identified as one of the basic computational mechanisms (revision operators) for the overall learning process. A notable exception is that of [15] where a simple form of abduction is used as the covering relation in the context of a particular application of learning theories for diagnosis. Also recently, the deeper relationship between abduction and induction has been the topic of study of an ECAI96 workshop [3]. Our work builds on earlier work in [5] and [6] for learning simpler forms of abductive theories. Finally, the issue of integrating discriminant (or explanatory) and characterizing ILP systems has also been put forward in [4].

Recently, there have been several other proposals for learning with incomplete information. The FOIL-I system [7] learns from incomplete information in the training examples set but not in the background knowledge. In [16] the authors propose several frameworks for learning from partial interpretations. A framework that can learn form incomplete information and is closely related to ACL is that of learning from satisfiability [13].

Further development of the I-ACL system is needed to integrate in it the characteristic induction process of learning integrity constraints and thus solving directly the full ACL problem. An interesting approach for this is to use existing

ILP systems for characteristic learning such as Claudien and Claudien-Sat, but also discriminant systems like ICL [14] and ICL-Sat for learning integrity constraints that discriminate between positive and negative abductive assumptions generated by ACL. We have also began to investigate the application of I-ACL to real-life problems in the area of analyzing market research questionnaires where incompleteness of information occurs naturally by unanswered questions or do not know and undecided answers.

References

1. H. Adé and M. Denecker. RUTH: An ILP theory revision system. In *Proceedings of the 8th International Symposium on Methodologies for Intelligent Systems*, 1994.
2. H. Adé and M. Denecker. AILP: Abductive inductive logic programming. In *Proceedings of the 14th International Joint Conference on Artificial Intelligence*, 1995.
3. M. Denecker, L. De Raedt, P. Flach, and A. Kakas, editors. *Proceedings of ECAI96 Workshop on Abductive and Inductive Reasoning*. Catholic University of Leuven, 1996.
4. Y. Dimopoulos, S. Džeroski, and A.C. Kakas. Integrating explanatory and descriptive learning in ILP. In *Proceedings of the 15th International Joint Conference on Artificial Intelligence*, 1997.
5. Y. Dimopoulos and A. Kakas. Abduction and inductive learning. In L. De Raedt, editor, *Advances in Inductive Logic Programming*, pages 144–171. IOS Press, 1996.
6. F. Esposito, E. Lamma, D. Malerba, P. Mello, M. Milano, F. Riguzzi, and G. Semeraro. Learning abductive logic programs. In Denecker et al. [3].
7. N. Inuzuka, M. Kamo, N. Ishii, H. Seki, and H. Itoh. Top-down induction of logic programs from incomplete samples. In S. Muggleton, editor, *Proceedings of the 6th International Workshop on Inductive Logic Programming*, pages 119–136. Stockholm University, Royal Institute of Technology, 1996.
8. A.C. Kakas, R.A. Kowalski, and F. Toni. Abductive logic programming. *Journal of Logic and Computation*, 2:719–770, 1993.
9. A.C. Kakas and P. Mancarella. On the relation between truth maintenance and abduction. In *Proceedings of the 2nd Pacific Rim International Conference on Artificial Intelligence*, 1990.
10. A.C. Kakas and F. Riguzzi. Learning with abduction. Technical Report TR-96-15, University of Cyprus, Computer Science Department, 1996.
11. N. Lavrač and S. Džeroski. *Inductive Logic Programming: Techniques and Applications*. Ellis Horwood, 1994.
12. L. De Raedt and M. Bruynooghe. A theory of clausal discovery. In *Proceedings of the 13th International Joint Conference on Artificial Intelligence*, 1993.
13. L. De Raedt and L. Dehaspe. Learning from satisfiability. Technical report, Katholieke Universiteit Leuven, 1996.
14. L. De Raedt and W. Van Lear. Inductive constraint logic. In *Proceedings of the 5th International Workshop on Algorithmic Learning Theory*, 1995.
15. C. Thompson and R. Mooney. Inductive learning for abductive diagnosis. In *Proceedings of the 12th National Conference on Artificial Intelligence*, 1994.
16. S. Wroble and S. Džeroski. The ILP description learning problem: Towards a genearl model-leve definition of data mining in ILP. In *Proceedings of the Fachgruppentreffen Maschinelles Lernen*, 1995.

Systematic Predicate Invention in Inductive Logic Programming

Lionel Martin and Christel Vrain

LIFO - université d'Orléans
BP 6759 - 45067 Orléans cedex 02 - France
email : {martin,cv}@lifo.univ-orleans.fr

Abstract. We propose in this paper a new approach for learning predicate definitions from examples and from an initial theory. The particularity of this approach consists in inventing both a new predicate symbol and a specification for this predicate at most steps of learning. The specifications that are built are incomplete and imprecise, what is modelized by introducing the notion of σ-interpretation. At the end of the learning task, some invented predicates are removed by unfolding techniques. The remaining predicates either enable to simplify the program, or are defined by recursive programs. In the second case, the program could not have been learned without inventing these predicates.

The method has been implemented in a system, called SPILP, which has been successfully tested for inventing predicates which simplify the learned programs as well as for inventing recursively defined predicates. Let us point out that the introduction of σ-interpretations gives us a general framework for dealing with imprecise specifications and that SPILP can work, even when the target concepts are also incompletely defined by σ-interpretations.

1 Introduction

In this paper, we propose a new method for Constructive Learning which is based on a systematic use of predicate invention. Constructive Learning is an active research topic in Machine Learning and in Inductive Logic Programming (**I.L.P.**) [2, 4, 7, 8, 9, 18], and it is defined as the capacity to extend a fixed initial representation by adding new non-observational representation primitives [4]; in I.L.P., these new primitives are mainly predicate symbols. This enables to overcome the limitation of most classical approaches, as for instance Foil [14] or ICN [6], that restrict the language of hypotheses to the target predicates and to the basic predicates occurring in the initial theory $\mathcal{T}$.

Example. To illustrate this point, let us consider a domain of 9 cities and 2 basic predicates fl and tr such that $fl(X,Y)$ is true iff there exists a direct flight from X to Y, and $tr(X,Y)$ is true iff there exists a train going from X to Y. Let us consider the target predicate p defined by: $p(X,Y)$ is true iff both, there exists a direct flight from X to Y and it is possible to go from X to Y by train. This concept cannot be learned without introducing a predicate $by\_train(X,Y)$, representing the transitive closure of tr. In other words, systems like Foil [14] or ICN [6] are unable to learn a definite logic program defining the predicate p. The system $SPLIP$ that we present here learns the program given in the last column of Table 1. It contains predicates, as for instance R_1 and R_2, which are both invented and defined during the learning process. Let us notice that the last two clauses can be simplified into $R1(X,Y) \leftarrow tr(X,Z), R2(Z,Y)$, and thus, the invented predicate R_1 represents the transitive closure of tr.

Basic predicates	Target predicate	Learned program
$tr(d,a), tr(a,b), tr(b,c),$		$p(X,Y) \leftarrow fl(X,Y), R1(X,Y).$
$tr(e,f), tr(f,g), tr(h,i),$	$p(d,a), p(a,c),$	$R1(X,Y) \leftarrow tr(X,Y).$
$tr(b,e), fl(a,c), fl(e,d),$	$p(b,g), p(b,c),$	$R1(X,Y) \leftarrow tr(X,Z), R2(X,Y,Z).$
$fl(b,c), fl(c,g), fl(h,i),$	$p(e,g), p(h,i),$	$R2(X,Y,Z) \leftarrow R1(Z,Y).$
$fl(b,g), fl(e,g), fl(d,a)$		

Table 1. example of predicate invention.

Predicate invention has two main advantages:

simplicity/comprehensibility: In the best case, invented predicates correspond to predicates that were missing in the initial theory and which have a particular meaning on the domain.
completeness: Some learning problems can be solved only if the description language is widened by the invention of predicates. In that sense, learning with predicate invention enables to increase the completeness of the learning process.

These two advantages have already been mentioned in [4], where predicates which do not affect the learnability are called *useful* and the other ones are called *necessary*.

Two types of approaches have been proposed for predicate invention in ILP: on one hand, the systems DUCE [7] and CIGOL [9] introduce the intra-construction operator in the framework of inverse resolution, which allows to introduce only *useful* predicates simplifying the program. On the other hand, the algorithm of CILP [4] is based on the notion of *sub-unification* of terms in the context of inverting implication. This allows to produce a particular form of recursive clauses by analysing terms containing function symbols and therefore inventing *necessary* predicates defined recursively. In this paper, we propose a new approach for predicate invention which is based neither on inverse resolution, nor on inverse implication. The approach proposes a uniform method to learn both target predicates and invented predicates. The basic operation consists in introducing a new predicate and building its specification; invented predicates are then considered as target predicates. The definitions learned for both kinds of predicates may be recursive. This differs from [16, 19], since we do not use folding techniques to introduce new predicates, but unfolding ones in order to remove useless invented predicates. For the time being, our approach is restricted to function free logic programs.

The paper is organized as follows. Section 2 introduces the basic mechanism of our approach. Section 3 presents the system SPILP that we have developed based on this method and Section 4 gives examples of learned programs. Finally, we conclude with a discussion of the complexity and a presentation of further developments.

2 σ-interpretation and invention of predicates

In the following, $\mathcal{T}$ represents an initial theory, defining a set of basic predicates (denoted by $p_1, p_2, \ldots$); $I_\mathcal{T}$ denotes a finite set of ground atoms, true in $\mathcal{T}$; R_0 denotes the target predicate and R_i, $i > 0$ denotes an invented predicate.

The specification of a target predicate is usually given by two sets of ground atoms: the set of positive examples and the set of negative ones. This is too restrictive in our framework. In fact, invented predicates are incompletely specified: the positive examples of an invented predicate R_i is determined according to the way R_i helps covering positive examples of $R_j, j \neq i$, but in general there are several ways of achieving this, as shown in the introductory example of Section 2.1, and this leads to imprecision. To handle this, we introduce the notion of σ-interpretation:

Definition 1. A σ-interpretation is a pair $< E_\sigma^+, E^- >$ where E^- is a finite set of ground atoms and E_σ^+ is a set $\{\sigma_1, \ldots, \sigma_n\}$ where each σ_i is a finite set of ground atoms.

Given a σ-interpretation $E = < E_\sigma^+, E^- >$ for the target predicate, our goal is to build a program $\mathcal{P}$ which is consistent, i.e., no negative example of E^- is true for $\mathcal{P}$, and σ-complete, i.e. each $\sigma_i \in E_\sigma^+$ contains an atom true for $\mathcal{P}$. This acceptability criterion can be formulated as follows:

σ-**completeness:** $\forall \sigma_i \in E_\sigma^+, \exists l \in \sigma_i$ such that $\mathcal{P}, \mathcal{T} \models l$,
consistency: $\forall e \in E^-$, $\mathcal{P}, \mathcal{T} \not\models e$.

Remarks:
1. For sake of simplicity, we suppose that the initial target predicate is defined by a set $\{e_1, \ldots, e_n\}$ of positive examples and a set $\{e'_1, \ldots, e'_m\}$ of negative ones. Let us point out that this is a particular case of a σ-interpretation E by taking $E_\sigma^+ = \{\{e_1\}, \ldots, \{e_n\}\}$ and $E^- = \{e'_1, \ldots, e'_m\}$. The method that we propose can be applied, even when the target predicate is specified with a σ-interpretation.
2. Let us notice that the notion of σ-interpretation goes beyond the problem of predicate invention, addressed in this paper, since it can be compared to other learning problems in the context of incomplete specifications, such as for instance [1].

Notations: $P(\vec{Y})$ denotes the atom $P(Y_1,\ldots,Y_n)$ and $P(\vec{c})$ denotes the ground atom $P(c_1,\ldots,c_n)$.

2.1 Introductory Example

Let us consider the basic predicates *father* and *mother* defined by the ground atoms:

$$\{father(a,c), father(c,e), father(a,d), mother(b,c),$$
$$mother(b,d), mother(d,f), mother(d,g)\}$$

The target predicate $R_0 = grand - father$ is defined by:

$$E_{\sigma,0}^{+} = \{\{R_0(a,e)\}, \{R_0(a,f)\}, \{R_0(a,g)\}\}$$

and E_0^{-} is a set of negative examples containing at least $R_0(a,b)$ but eventually incomplete.

The search strategy is similar to the strategy used in FOIL [14]. The learned program is initially empty and we have to build a clause defining $R_0(X,Y)$. Let us assume that the first selected literal for the definition of R_0 is $father(X,Z)$. The clause:

(i) $R_0(X,Y) \leftarrow father(X,Z)$.

covers the negative example $R_0(a,b)$. In Foil, the clause would be specialized by introducing a literal built with a predicate among *father*, *mother* and R_0. Our approach is completely different: we introduce a new symbol of predicate, called R_1, we add the clause:

(ii) $R_0(X,Y) \leftarrow father(X,Z), R_1(X,Y,Z)$.

to the program $\mathcal{P}$ and we build a σ-interpretation of R_1, so that the clause covers the positive examples of R_0 and rejects all negative examples.

The set E_1^{-} contains $R_1(a,b,c)$, since $R_0(a,b) \leftarrow father(a,c)$ is a ground instance of the clause (i), $R_0(a,b)$ is a negative example of R_0 and $father(a,c)$ is true in $\mathcal{T}$. For similar reasons, it contains also $R_1(a,b,d)$.

Concerning the set $E_{\sigma,1}^{+}$, let us consider, for instance, the positive example $R_0(a,e)$ given in $E_{\sigma,0}^{+}$. Since $father(a,c)$ and $father(a,d)$ are true in $\mathcal{T}$, a sufficient condition to ensure that $R_0(a,e)$ is true in the learned program is that either $R_1(a,e,c)$, or $R_1(a,e,d)$ is true. This is expressed by adding to the positive specification $E_{\sigma,1}^{+}$ of R_1 the set $\{R_1(a,e,c), R_1(a,e,d)\}$. By considering all positive examples of R_0, we get:

$$E_{\sigma,1}^{+} = \{\{R_1(a,e,c), R_1(a,e,d)\}, \{R_1(a,f,c), R_1(a,f,d)\},$$
$$\{R_1(a,g,c), R_1(a,g,d)\}\}.$$

Once the clause (ii) has been built, the learned program is completed by adding either a definition for the predicate R_0, or for the predicate R_1. Since R_1 is not already defined, it seems natural to first search for a definition for R_1 that will enable to precise it. Let us assume that the learned clause is then:

(iii) $R_1(X, Y, Z) \leftarrow mother(Z, Y)$.

Since the program is not complete, a new clause is built:

(iv) $R_1(X, Y, Z) \leftarrow father(Z, Y)$.

The program is now complete; the variable X does not appear in the body of the clauses defining R_1, we can drop it in the definition of R_1 and we obtain the program

$R_0(X, Y) \leftarrow father(X, Z), R_1(Y, Z)$.
$R_1(X, Y) \leftarrow mother(Y, X)$.
$R_1(X, Y) \leftarrow father(Y, X)$.

It is important to notice that the invented predicate R_1 represents the concept *parent*, which was not given in the initial theory. Next section formalizes the process for building clauses, inventing predicates and building their σ-interpretations.

2.2 Induction process

Let us consider the problem of finding a consistent and σ-complete definition for the target predicate R_0, specified by a σ-interpretation E_0. Moreover let us suppose that the learning process has already introduced some new predicates $R_j, j > 0$ and that it has built a σ-interpretation $E_j = <E_{\sigma,j}^+, E_j^- >$ specifying R_j, for each $R_j, j > 0$. Let us consider now the problem of finding a clause defining a predicate $R_i, i \geq 0$. A literal $P(\vec{Y})$, where P is either a basic predicate or a predicate $R_j, j \geq 0$, is selected, according to its relevance to the predicate R_i [1]. Two situations are distinguished:

- The clause
$$(*)\ \ R_i(\vec{X}) \leftarrow P(\vec{Y}).$$
covers no negative examples of R_i (i.e., no elements of E_i^-). In this case, the clause (*) is added to the program. Moreover, this clause enables to deduce more precise information about R_i and about predicates depending [2] on R_i. Intuitively, each ground instance $R_i(\vec{c}) \leftarrow P(\vec{c'})$ of (*) such that $P(\vec{c'})$ is true implies that $R_i(\vec{c})$ is true, which can in turn be used in clauses depending on R_i. Therefore, the set I_i^+ (initially empty) of such ground atoms is computed and this operation is repeated for each predicate depending on R_i;
- The previous clause (*) covers some negative examples of R_i. In this case, instead of adding the clause (*), we add the clause
$$(**)\ \ R_i(\vec{X}) \leftarrow P(\vec{Y}), R_k(\vec{Z}).$$
where R_k is a new predicate symbol and $\vec{Z}$ is the union of the variables occurring in $\vec{X}$ and $\vec{Y}$. The σ-interpretation E_k, specifying the predicate R_k is then computed.

---

[1] We describe in Section 3 the way this literal is selected.

[2] A predicate P depends on a predicate Q for a program $\mathcal{P}$ if there exists a clause $P(\vec{X}) \leftarrow \ldots R(\vec{Y}) \ldots$ in $\mathcal{P}$ such that $R = Q$ or R depends on Q.

To sum up, we propose to build the program by iteratively adding either a clause of the form (*) or a clause of the form (**), which introduces a new predicate; the form of the clause (* or **) is determined by the selected literal. For each predicate R_i $i \geq 0$ (the target predicate or an invented one), two kinds of information are used: on one hand, the σ-interpretation E_i gives an imprecise but complete specification of the positive and negative examples of R_i; on the other hand, I_i^+ gives a precise but incomplete interpretation of R_i since it is a set of positive examples which grows during the learning process. We now describe the way E_i and I_i^+ are computed.

Computation of I_i^+: Initially, $I_i^+ = \emptyset$. Let us consider the case when a clause

$$(*) \ \ R_i(\vec{X}) \leftarrow P(\vec{Y}).$$

is added to the program, which means that the clause covers no negative examples of R_i. If P is a basic predicate or a predicate R_j which does not depend on R_i, then for each ground instance $R_i(\vec{c}) \leftarrow P(\vec{c'})$ of (*) such that $P(\vec{c'})$ is true in T (if P is a basic predicate) or in I_j^+ (if $P = R_j$), $R_i(\vec{c})$ is added to I_i^+. The set I_i^+ increases as well as the sets I_k^+, for the predicates R_k that depend on R_i.

More generally, when a clause (*) is added, we compute the semantics of $\mathcal{P} \cup T$, where $\mathcal{P}$ is the learned program and we update all the sets I_k^+ according to the new ground atoms that are deduced.

Since the learned program is function symbol free, its semantics is a finite set; it can be obtained by computing the least fixed point of the immediate consequence operator T_P [5].

Computation of E_k: When the selected literal $P(\vec{Y})$ is such that the clause (*) covers some negative examples of R_i, we build the clause

$$(**) \ \ R_i(\vec{X}) \leftarrow P(\vec{Y}), R_k(\vec{Z}).$$

where R_k is a new predicate.

Since this predicate has to ensure the consistency of the learned program, the negative examples of R_k are built from the ground instances of this clause which cover negative examples of R_i: let θ be a substitution such that $R_i(\vec{X})\theta \leftarrow P(\vec{Y})\theta$ is a ground instance of (*), $R_i(\vec{X})\theta$ is a negative example of R_i and $P(\vec{Y})\theta$ is true in T (if P is a basic predicate) or in I_j^+ (if P is a predicate R_j, $j \geq 0$). To ensure $R_i(\vec{X})\theta$ to be false in the learned program, $R_k(\vec{Z})\theta$ must be expected to be false. It must therefore be a negative example of the invented literal R_k. We obtain the set of negative examples of R_k:

$$E_k^- = \{R_k(\vec{c''}) \mid R_i(\vec{c}) \leftarrow P(\vec{c'}), R_k(\vec{c''}) \text{ is a ground instance of } (**),$$
$$R_i(\vec{c}) \in E_i^- \text{ and } P(\vec{c'}) \text{ is true in } T \text{ (if } P \text{ is a basic pred-}$$
$$\text{icate) or in } I_j^+ \text{ (if } P = R_j)\}$$

Let us notice that when P is an invented predicate R_j, more information about R_j can be deduced later by adding new clauses. Therefore, I_j^+ can increase. It explains why in SPILP, we check the consistency of the program each time a new clause (*) is added (see Section 3).

The predicate R_k must enable to achieve the σ-completeness of the learned program $\mathcal{P}$, concerning the predicate R_i. This enables to define the set $E^+_{\sigma,k}$ defining the positive examples of R_k, based on the following idea: let $\sigma \in E^+_{\sigma,i}$, an element of σ will be true in $\mathcal{P}$ if there exists a ground substitution θ such that $R_i(\vec{X})\theta \in \sigma$, $P(\vec{Y})\theta$ is true in T (if P is a basic predicate) or in I^+_j (if $P = R_j$) and $R_k(\vec{Z})\theta$ is true in $\mathcal{P}$. If $E^+_{\sigma,i} = \{\sigma_1, \ldots, \sigma_n\}$, the set $E^+_{\sigma,k}$ is then defined by $\{\sigma'_1, \ldots, \sigma'_n\}$ where

$$
\begin{aligned}
\sigma'_p = \{R_k(\vec{c''}) | R_i(\vec{c}) &\leftarrow P(\vec{c'}), R_k(\vec{c''}) \text{ is a ground instance of } (**), \\
R_i(\vec{c}) &\in \sigma_p \text{ and } P(\vec{c'}) \text{ is true in } T \text{ (if } P \text{ is a basic predi-} \\
&\text{cate) or in } I^+_j \text{ (if } P = R_j)\}
\end{aligned}
$$

Nevertheless, let us notice that the learned program has to be σ-complete only w.r.t. E_0. It may exist a substitution $\sigma \in E^+_{\sigma,k}$, $k > 0$, such that no elements of σ is true for $\mathcal{P}$. This means that we have hypothesized a positive example for R_k, incompletely defined by σ, which appears to be irrelevant for the learning process.

3 The system SPILP

We present now the system SPILP which relies on the notions introduced in Section 2. The algorithm adds iteratively either a clause of the form:

(*) $R_i(\vec{X}) \leftarrow P(\vec{Y})$.

or a clause of the form:

(**) $R_i(\vec{X}) \leftarrow P(\vec{Y}), R_k(\vec{Z})$.

Two steps determine the behaviour of the system:

- the choice of the next predicate R_i which will be defined by a new clause,
- the selection of the literal $P(\vec{Y})$ that will be added to the body of the clause defining R_i.

Once $P(\vec{Y})$ is chosen, the form of the clause is automatically deduced: if no negative example of R_i is covered by the clause (*), then this clause is added to the program under construction, otherwise the clause (**) is added. In this last case, the σ-interpretation of R_k is then computed.

In order to choose the next predicate R_i to learn, we use two heuristics. First, we add a clause for each predicate R_i, for which there exists no clause defining it, i.e., having as head $R_i(\vec{X})$. This leads to the building of series of clauses, like:

$R_i(\vec{X_0}) \leftarrow P_0(\vec{Y_0}), R_{i+1}(\vec{Z_0})$.
$R_{i+1}(\vec{X_1}) \leftarrow P_1(\vec{Y_1}), R_{i+2}(\vec{Z_1})$.
...

$$R_{i+j+1}(\vec{X_{j+1}}) \leftarrow P_{j+1}(\vec{Y_{j+1}}).$$

Such a series is called an *informative definition for R_i*.

A second heuristic for choosing the next predicate R_i to learn is applied when all predicates have an informative definition and when the learned program is not yet σ-complete. It will be discussed in Section 3.1.

> $\mathcal{P} \leftarrow \emptyset$
> While $\mathcal{P}$ is not σ-complete
> $(\exists \sigma \in E_{\sigma,0}^+ \ s.t. \ \sigma \cap I_0^+ = \emptyset)$ do
>   choose a predicate R_i to define
>   build an informative definition for R_i .
> done

Main loop of SPILP

Once a predicate R_i has been chosen, the following procedure, called *informative*, builds an informative definition for R_i from its σ-interpretation E_i:

> procedure $informative(\mathcal{P}, R_i, E_i)$
> begin
>   select a literal $P(\vec{Y})$
>   if $R_i(\vec{X}) \leftarrow P(\vec{Y})$ covers $e \in E_i^-$
>   then add $R_i(\vec{X}) \leftarrow P(\vec{Y}), R_k(\vec{Z})$ to $\mathcal{P}$ (R_k *is a new predicate*)
>   build E_k (*see Section 2.2*)
>   call $informative(\mathcal{P}, R_k, E_k)$
>   else add $R_i(\vec{X}) \leftarrow P(\vec{Y})$ to $\mathcal{P}$
>   compute I_i^+ and I_j^+ for each R_j depending on R_i (*see Section 2.2*)
> end

Construction of an informative definition for R_i

SPILP can back-track (on the choice of the predicate R_i and on the selection of the literal $P(\vec{Y})$): before adding the clause $R_i(\vec{X}) \leftarrow P(\vec{Y})$, all sets I_j^+ are updated; if a set I_k^+ is not consistent w.r.t. E_k^- or if the program does not allow to deduce enough information, the algorithm back-tracks on another literal $P(\vec{Y})$.

3.1   Selection of the literal $P(\vec{Y})$

As most systems in ILP, SPILP is based on the notion of coverage which enables to guide the search: the selected literal is the one which covers as many positive examples as possible and which covers as few negative examples as possible. Nevertheless, in our framework, two kinds of information are available for each predicate R_i, $i \geq 0$: the σ-interpretation E_i and the set I_i^+ of atoms true for the learned program. Moreover, our description of the positive examples of R_i is given by a set $E_{\sigma,i}^+$ containing sets σ_j of ground atoms, each σ_j containing at least a positive example. The program has to be σ-complete only w.r.t. $E_{\sigma,0}^+$. We define two notions of covering, adapted to our framework, based either on true information defined by I_i^+ or on expected information given in $E_{\sigma,i}^+$:

Definition 2. Let e be a ground atom and let $\mathcal{P}$ be the program under construction;

- e is I-*covered* by the clause
  $$C = R_i(\vec{X}) \leftarrow P(\vec{Y}).$$
  iff there exists a ground instance $C\theta$ of C such that $e = R_i(\vec{X})\theta$ and $P(\vec{Y})\theta$ is true in $\mathcal{T}$ (if P is a basic predicate) or in I_j^+ (if $P = R_j$).
- e is I-*covered* by the clause
  $$C' = R_i(\vec{X}) \leftarrow P(\vec{Y}), R_k(\vec{Z}).$$
  iff there exists a ground instance $C'\theta$ of C' such that $e = R_i(\vec{X})\theta$, $P(\vec{Y})\theta$ is true in $\mathcal{T}$ (if P is a basic predicate) or in I_j^+ (if $P = R_j$) and $R_k(\vec{Z})\theta$ is true in I_k^+.

Let us notice that the notion of I-covering depends only on information that are deduced from the program $\mathcal{P} \cup \mathcal{T}$. Therefore, we have the following result: an example which is I-covered is true for $\mathcal{P} \cup \mathcal{T}$.

Definition 3. Let e be a ground atom and let $\mathcal{P}$ be the program under construction;

- e is E-*covered* by the clause
  $$C = R_i(\vec{X}) \leftarrow P(\vec{Y}).$$
  iff e is not I-covered by C and there exists a ground instance $C\theta$ of C such that $e = R_i(\vec{X})\theta$ and $P(\vec{Y})\theta$ belongs to an element of $E_{\sigma,j}^+$ $(P = R_j)$.
- e is E-*covered* by the clause
  $$C' = R_i(\vec{X}) \leftarrow P(\vec{Y}), R_k(\vec{Z}).$$
  iff e is not I-covered by C' and there exists a ground instance $C'\theta$ of C' such that $e = R_i(\vec{X})\theta$, $P(\vec{Y})\theta$ is true in $\mathcal{T}$ (if P is a basic predicate) or belongs to an element of $E_{\sigma,j}^+$ (if $P = R_j$) and $R_k(\vec{Z})\theta$ belongs to an element of $E_{\sigma,k}^+$ or is true in I_k^+.

When an atom e is E-covered by a clause of $\mathcal{P}$, it is not sure that it will be true for $\mathcal{P} \cup \mathcal{T}$.

Definition 4. The notions of I-covering and E-covering are extended to sets of ground atoms as follows: a set σ of ground atoms is I-covered (resp. E-covered) iff there exists at least an atom of σ which is I-covered (resp. E-covered).

These notions are used to choose the literal $P(\vec{Y})$ which is added to the body of the clause defining $R_i(\vec{X})$. We have adapted the information gain used in FOIL [14] to our framework, in order to take into account not only E-covered atoms, but also I-covered ones and we choose the literal which has the largest information gain among all possible literals.

Let $E_{\sigma,i}^+ = \{\sigma_1, \dots, \sigma_n\}$ and $\Sigma_i = \sigma_1 \cup \sigma_2 \cup \dots \cup \sigma_n$. Let C be the clause $R_i(\vec{X}) \leftarrow P(\vec{Y})$. We define:

- n_I^+: the number of ground atoms in $\Sigma_i - I_i^+$,
- n_I^-: the number of ground atoms of E_i^-,
- $\tilde{n}_I^+$: the number of ground atoms of $\Sigma_i - I_i^+$, which are I-covered by C,
- $\tilde{n}_I^-$: the number of ground atoms of E_i^- which are I-covered by C,
- $\tilde{c}_I^+$: the number of σ_i such that $\sigma_i - I_i^+ \neq \emptyset$, $\sigma_i - I_i^+$ is I-covered by C and $\sigma_i \in E_{\sigma,i}^+$.

The information gain of $P(\vec{Y})$ w.r.t the notion of I-covering is defined by:

$$\text{gain}_I(P(\vec{Y})) = \tilde{c}_I^+ \times (log_2(\frac{\tilde{n}_I^+}{\tilde{n}_I^+ + \tilde{n}_I^-}) - log_2(\frac{n_I^+}{n_I^+ + n_I^-}))$$

We define in the same way

- $\tilde{n}_E^+$: the number of ground atoms of $\Sigma_i - I_i^+$ which are E-covered by C,
- $\tilde{n}_E^-$: the number of ground atoms of E_i^- which are E-covered by C,
- $\tilde{c}_E^+$: the number of σ_i such that $\sigma_i - I_i^+ \neq \emptyset$, $\sigma_i - I_i^+$ is E-covered by C and $\sigma_i \in E_{\sigma,i}^+$.

The information gain of $P(\vec{Y})$ w.r.t the notion of E-covering is defined by

$$\text{gain}_E(P(\vec{Y})) = \tilde{c}_E^+ \times (log_2(\frac{\tilde{n}_E^+}{\tilde{n}_E^+ + \tilde{n}_E^-}) - log_2(\frac{n_I^+}{n_I^+ + n_I^-}))$$

The total information gain is defined by:

$$\boxed{\text{gain}(P(\vec{Y})) = \omega_I * \text{gain}_I(P(\vec{Y})) + \omega_E * \text{gain}_E(P(\vec{Y}))}$$

where ω_I and ω_E are such that $\omega_I + \omega_E = 1$. These coefficients allow to control the influence of the information contained in the σ-interpretations: the higher ω_I is, the more SPILP uses information deduced from the previous learned clauses; it is better to choose a ω_I which is high when the target predicate is defined with an incomplete specification. On the other hand, the higher ω_E is, the more the selected literal will build clauses which do not enable to deduce new information and the algorithm might back-track more often. Practically, we use the values $\omega_I = 0.8$ and $\omega_E = 0.2$. A similar idea was developed in [15], although it was in a different context.

3.2 Choice of the predicate R_i

Once an informative definition has been built for the target predicate R_0, SPILP chooses a predicate for which a new informative definition will be built and this choice must be repeated until the program is σ-complete w.r.t E_0.

To determine the next predicate R_i, the total information gain in the clause

$$R_j(\vec{X}) \leftarrow P_{j_k}(\vec{Y}).$$

is computed for each possible R_j, $j \geq 0$ and for each possible literal $P_{j_k}(\vec{Y})$. This gives the information gain for each pair $(R_j(\vec{X}), P_{j_k}(\vec{Y}))$. The predicate R_i that is chosen is the one that maximizes the gain of the pairs $(R_j(\vec{X}), P_{j_k}(\vec{Y}))$. When a large number of predicates has been invented, this choice is time-consuming but it gives both the predicate and the selected literal $P(\vec{Y})$. As has already been mentioned, the clause that must be added is then automatically determined, depending on whether negative examples are covered.

A particular case When an informative definition for R_i already exists and when information has already been deduced for R_i, it may happen that the pair having the best gain has the form $(R_i(\vec{X}), R_i(\vec{Y}))$. If we add the clause:

$$\text{(i)} \quad R_i(\vec{X}) \leftarrow R_i(\vec{Y}), \ldots.$$

to the program, and if another clause defining R_i has been previously added, the clause (i) may allow to build new negative examples of R_i, which can make previous clauses inconsistent. For this reason, we introduce a new predicate R_k, the clauses defining R_i

$$R_i(\vec{X}) \leftarrow B_1.$$

$\ldots$

$$R_i(\vec{X}) \leftarrow B_n.$$

are replaced by the clauses

$$R_k(\vec{X}) \leftarrow B_1.$$

$\ldots$

$$R_k(\vec{X}) \leftarrow B_n.$$
$$R_i(\vec{X}) \leftarrow R_k(\vec{X}).$$

and the pair $(R_i(\vec{X}), R_k(\vec{Y}))$ is then considered to be the pair that maximizes the gain.

An illustration of this case is given in Section 4, when learning the predicate ancestor.

3.3 Biases and simplifications

A first bias has been mentioned above: it consists in choosing values for the parameters ω_I and ω_E. The selection of the literal $P(\vec{Y})$ is also biased when several literals have the same information gain: SPILP prefers basic predicates in order to increase the simplicity of the learned program and in order to complete the definition of non-basic predicates. Finally, SPILP uses two biases which limit the number of new variables. When a clause

$$R_i(\vec{X}) \leftarrow P(\vec{Y}), R_k(\vec{Z}).$$

is built, the set of variables in $\vec{Z}$ is the union of the variables appearing in $\vec{X}$ and $\vec{Y}$. Each new variable introduced in $\vec{Y}$ increases the arity of R_k. Moreover, when defining R_k, the complexity of the selection of a literal $P'(\vec{Y})$ depends mainly on the arity of R_k since SPILP explores the space of all possible predicates and all possible variabilizations for finding $P'(\vec{Y})$. For these reasons, SPILP uses the 2 following biases:

- the number of new variables in a variabilization of a predicate R_i is limited to 2,

- the information gain is divided by (2+New), where New is the number of variables introduced by the literal.

To conclude this section, let us consider the way the learned programs can be simplified, even though it is not yet implemented:

- if an invented predicate is defined by only one clause, it is removed by unfolding,
- for the remaining invented predicates, if a variable appears in the head of the definition of a R_i and if it does not appear in the body of any clauses defining R_i, this variable is removed, which reduces the arity of R_i. This operation is repeated for all invented predicates depending on R_i.

In next section, we present some programs learned by SPLIP.

4 Examples

The algorithm SPILP has been written in Prolog, the following programs have been built in 5 up to 20 seconds on a Sparc 4. We give first the programs built by SPILP and then we rewrite them using simplifications given in Section 3.3 and renaming the invented predicates. The 3 following programs have been learned on a family containing 11 people $\{a, b, \ldots, k\}$; the basic predicates are *father* and *mother*, *parent* is a basic predicate only in the third example. The initial theory T is defined by:

$$\{father(a, c), father(a, d), father(c, e), father(g, j), father(g, i), father(h, k),$$
$$mother(b, c), mother(b, d), mother(d, f), mother(d, g), mother(e, h)\}$$

4.1 Learning grand-father

The first example is the example proposed in Section 2; the target predicate is $grand - father$ (written gf) and the predicate *parent* is not given in T. The program learned by SPILP is given in fig. 4.1a. As mentioned in Section 3, R_1 can be simplified and renamed with *parent* and we get the program of fig 4.1b ($parent(X, Y)$ is true here if Y is a parent of X).

fig. 4.1a:
```
R0(X,Y) <- father(X,Z), R1(X,Y,Z).
R1(X,Y,Z) <- mother(Z,Y).
R1(X,Y,Z) <- father(Z,Y).
```

fig. 4.1b:
$$gf(X, Y) \leftarrow father(X, Z), parent(Y, Z).$$
$$parent(X, Y) \leftarrow mother(Y, X).$$
$$parent(X, Y) \leftarrow father(Y, X).$$

4.2 Learning ancestor

This example illustrates the particular case of predicate invention discussed in Section 3.2: SPILP has to learn *ancestor* (*anc*) with the basic predicates *father* and *mother*. It first builds the 2 clauses:

$$R_0(X,Y) \leftarrow father(X,Y).$$
$$R_0(X,Y) \leftarrow mother(X,Y).$$

When SPILP tries to build a new clause defining $R_0(X,Y)$, the selected literal is $R_0(X,Z)$; this can easily be explained since the choice mainly relies on information of I_0^+. We can notice, although SPILP does not know this, that at this level, information known about R_0 are information defining *parent*. Since the system cannot build the clause $R_0(X,Y) \leftarrow R_0(X,Z),\ldots$, it renames the learned concept R_0 in R_1 and finally, we get the program of fig 4.2a. R_2 is defined by just one clause, so it can be deleted by unfolding techniques; then if R_1 is renamed by *parent*, we get the program of fig 4.2b.

fig. 4.2a :
```
R0(X,Y) <- R1(X,Y).
R0(X,Y) <- R1(X,Z), R2(X,Y,Z).
R1(X,Y) <- father(X,Y).
R1(X,Y) <- mother(X,Y).
R2(X,Y,Z) <- R0(Z,Y).
```

fig. 4.2b :
$$
\boxed{
\begin{array}{l}
anc(X,Y) \leftarrow parent(X,Y). \\
anc(X,Y) \leftarrow parent(X,Z), anc(Z,Y). \\
parent(X,Y) \leftarrow mother(X,Y). \\
parent(X,Y) \leftarrow father(X,Y).
\end{array}
}
$$

4.3 Learning male-ancestor

The goal here is to find a definition for *male − ancestor* (*ma*) with the basic predicates *father, mother* and *parent*. In this problem, the invention of a new predicate such as *female − ancestor* or *ancestor* is essential. The learned program is given in fig. 4.3a. In this program, R_2 can be removed by unfolding; then the variable X does not appear in the body of the definitions of R_1 which is simplified and renamed with *ancestor* (*anc*). We obtain the program of fig. 4.3b ($anc(Y,Z)$ is true if Z is an ancestor of Y):

fig. 4.3a :
```
R0(X,Y) <- father(X,Y).
R0(X,Y) <- father(X,Z), R1(X,Y,Z).
R1(X,Y,Z) <- parent(Z,Y).
R1(X,Y,Z) <- parent(Z,T), R2(X,Y,Z,T).
R2(X,Y,Z,T) <- R1(Z,Y,T).
```

$$
\begin{array}{l}
ma(X,Y) \leftarrow father(X,Y). \\
ma(X,Y) \leftarrow father(X,Z), anc(Y,Z). \\
anc(Y,Z) \leftarrow parent(Z,Y). \\
anc(Y,Z) \leftarrow parent(Z,T), anc(Y,T).
\end{array}
$$

fig. 4.3b:

4.4 Learning path-2

The last example illustrates another case when the invented predicate is defined recursively. Let us consider the example given in introduction, specified by a domain of 9 cities and 2 basic predicates fl and tr such that $pl(X,Y)$ is true iff there exists a direct flight from X to Y, and $tr(X,Y)$ is true iff there exists a train going from X to Y. These concepts are defined by the true ground atoms:

$\{tr(d,a), tr(a,b), tr(b,c), tr(b,e), tr(e,f), tr(f,g), tr(h,i), fl(d,a),$
$fl(a,c), fl(e,d), fl(b,g), fl(e,g), fl(b,c), fl(c,g), fl(h,i)\}$

We want to learn the concept p defined by: $p(X,Y)$ is true iff both, there exists a direct flight from X to Y and it is possible to go from X to Y by train. In our domain, p is defined by:

$E_{\sigma,0}^{+} = \{p(d,a), p(a,c), p(b,g), p(b,c), p(e,g), p(h,i)\}$

SPILP learns the program:

```
          R0(X,Y) <- fl(X,Y), R1(X,Y).
          R1(X,Y) <- tr(X,Y).
fig. 4.4a:  R1(X,Y) <- tr(X,Z), R2(X,Y,Z).
          R2(X,Y,Z) <- R1(Z,Y).
```

After unfolding R_2, we obtain the program:

$$
\begin{array}{l}
p(X,Y) \leftarrow fl(X,Y), R1(X,Y). \\
R1(X,Y) \leftarrow tr(X,Y). \\
R1(X,Y) \leftarrow tr(X,Z), R1(Z,Y).
\end{array}
$$

fig. 4.4b:

where R_1 is the transitive closure of the relation tr.

5 Complexity - Further works

We propose in this paper a new system, called SPILP, for constructive learning of predicate definitions. This system performs empirical learning of function free logic programs and it is able to invent both predicates simplifying the learned program and predicates defined recursively. Moreover, the framework that we have developed enable to learn even when the specification of the target predicate is both incomplete and imprecise, since SPILP relies both on information from the specification and on information deduced from the learned clauses.

SPILP can be compared with FOIL algorithm [14]. Nevertheless, four main differences can be noted, namely the ability to deal with imprecise information, the systematic invention of new predicates which reduces the size of clauses to at most 2 literals in their bodies, the computation of the gain and the fact that

SPILP always builds a consistent and complete program whereas FOIL produces a program which covers all the positive examples and no negative ones.

Since when building a clause, FOIL and SPILP explore the space of all possible literals, we can compare the complexity of SPILP with the one of FOIL which is known to be a fast algorithm. At the beginning of learning, the complexity is the same, but once a predicate is invented by SPILP, the search space of all the possible literals is widened by new predicates. The bias which limits the number of introduced variables in the variabilization of an invented predicate reduces this search space to a reasonable size.

Future works include:

- handling negation by building clauses of the form: $R_i(\vec{X}) \leftarrow P(\vec{Y}), \neg R_k(\vec{Z})$.
- extending the form of the learned clauses: once an informative definition is built for the target predicate, the clause
$$R_0(\vec{X}) \leftarrow P(\vec{Y}), R_1(\vec{Z}).$$
could be transformed into
$$R_0(\vec{X}) \leftarrow R_k(\vec{Y}), R_1(\vec{Z}).$$
$$R_k(\vec{X}) \leftarrow P(\vec{Y}).$$
where R_k is a new predicate. It could then be possible to learn a concept defined as the conjunction of several concepts, defined recursively.

References

1. Dietterich T.G., Lathrop R.H., Lozano-Perez T., 1996. Solving the Multiple-Instance Problem with Axis-Parallel Rectangles. to be published in Artificial Intelligence Journal.
2. Kijsirikul B., Numao M. et al, 1992. Discrimination-based Constructive Induction of Logic Programs, Procs. of AAAI-92, San Jose, pp.44-49, 1992.
3. Lavrač N., Džeroski S., 1992. Inductive Learning of Relations from Noisy Examples. Inductive Logic programming. The A.P.I.C. Series N° 38, S. Muggleton (Ed.), Academic Press, pp.495-516.
4. Lapointe S., Ling C., Matwin S., 1993. Constructive Inductive Logic Programming. Procs. of the Sixteenth International Joint Conference on Artificial Intelligence (IJCAI-93), pp. 1030-1036, 1993.
5. J. W. Lloyd. Foundations of Logic Programming. *Springer Verlag*, 1987.
6. Martin L., Vrain C., 1996. Induction of Constraint Logic Programs. Procs. of the Seventh International Whorkshop on Algorithmic Learning Theory, Lecture Notes in Artificial Intelligence
7. Muggleton S., 1987. Duce, an oracle based approach to constructive induction, Procs. of the Tenth International Joint Conference on Artificial Intelligence (IJCAI-87), Milan, pp. 287-292, 1987.
8. Muggleton S., 1988. A strategy for constructing new predicates in first order logic. Procs. of the 3rd European Working Session on Learning, Pitman, pp. 123-130, 1988.
9. Muggleton S., Buntine W. (1988) Machine invention of first order predicates by inverting resolution. Procs. of the Fifth Internationnal Conference on Machine Learning, pp. 339-351, 1988.

10. Muggleton S., Feng C., 1992. Efficient Induction of Logic Programs". Inductive Logic programming. The A.P.I.C. Series N° 38, S. Muggleton (Ed.), Academic Press. pp. 281-298.

11. Muggleton S., de Raedt L., 1994. Inductive Logic Programming: Theory and Methods. Journal of Logic programming, vol. 19/20, May/July 94, pp. 629-680.

12. Plotkin G., 1970. A note on inductive generalization. Machine Intelligence, Vol. 5, Edinburgh University Press, Edinburgh.

13. Plotkin G.. 1971. A further note on inductive generalization. Machine Intelligence, Vol. 6, Edinburgh University Press, Edinburgh.

14. Quinlan J.R., 1990. Learning Logical Definitions from Relations. Machine Learning Journal, Vol. 5, Kluwer Academic Publishers, pp. 239-266.

15. de Raedt L., Lavrac N., Dzeroski S., 1993. Multiple Predicate Learning. Procs. of the Thirteen International Joint Conference on Artificial Intelligence, Chambéry, France, August 28 - September 3, 1993, Vol. 2, pp. 1037-1043.

16. Sommer E., 1994. Rulebase Stratification: an Approach to theory restructuring. Proceedings of the Fourth International Workshop on Inductive Logic Programming, Germany, GMD-Studien Nr. 237.

17. Vrain C., Martin L., 1994. Inductive learning of normal clauses. Machine Learning: ECML-94, Lecture Notes in Artificial Intelligence 784, F. Bergadano, L. De Raedt (Eds.), Springer Verlag, pp. 435-438.

18. Wirth R., O'Rorke P., 1991. Constraints on predicate invention. Procs. of the Eighth International Workshop on Machin Learning, Evanston, pp. 457-461, Morgan-Kaufmann, 1991.

19. Wrobel S., 1994. Concept Formation and Knowledge Revision. Kluwer Academic Publishers, Netherlands.

Learning Programs in the Event Calculus

Stephen Moyle and Stephen Muggleton *

Oxford University Computing Laboratory,
Wolfson Building,
Parks Road,
Oxford, OX1 3QD,
United Kingdom.
{sam, steve}@comlab.ox.ac.uk

Abstract. The event calculus is a formalism for reasoning about actions and change in dynamic systems. It has been used in diverse areas including planning and communications protocol specification. Writing event calculus programs requires the construction of domain specific axioms (DSAs) - a programming task which is non-trivial, and one that hinders the broader use of the event calculus. This work demostrates that such axioms can be learned from temporal observations using Inductive Logic programming (ILP) techniques, in particular theory completion. The theory of logical back-propagation as a mechanism for theory completion is described and its implementation in the ILP system Progol is used here. These techniques were used to investigate learning DSAs for the traditional AI blocks world. In the experiments Progol, utilising logical back-propagation, learned correct DSAs. These results provide encouragement and highlight the possibility of discovering causal relationships from data in temporal databases, and also learning the domain specific knowledge necessary in the development of plans.

1 Introduction

The amount of data recorded electronically continues to grow. It is common for the time that the data was collected to be recorded along with the data, therefore classifying it as temporal. In both science and commerce the requirements are to analyse and understand patterns in temporal data. However, increasingly human analysts are overwhelmed by the quantities of data involved. An automated method of generating knowledge from temporal data is required.

The event calculus [6] is a declarative formalism that represents time implicitly by describing the relationships between actions and change. It provides a notion of default persistence which enable the derivation of properties that are unaffected by actions. Event calculus programs are typically normal logic programs with a fixed clausal structure. An event calculus program T_{EC}, is composed of two non-intersecting sets of clauses; (1) the immutable core axioms

---

* Address for correspondence: Department of Computer Science, University of York, Heslington, York, YO1 5DD.

T_{Core}, and (2) the domain specific axioms T_{DSA}. Together they allow future states of the program to be derived.

The structural components of an event calculus program are common in the field of *theory revision* [3]. The learning of event calculus programs from examples can be stated as: *given* a set of integrity constraints I, a theory $T_{EC} = T_{Core} \cup T_{DSA}$, and evidence E (observations of dynamic behaviour); *find* a theory $T'_{EC} = T_{Core} \cup T'_{DSA}$ obtained by applying transformations on T_{DSA} such that T'_{EC} explains E and is consistent with I.

Any ILP technique applied to learning event calculus programs must contend with the nature of the observations provided relative to the clauses to be constructed. It is common within ILP for single predicate learning to produce definitions for predicates of the examples. This is not the case for the event calculus where the observations are recorded by different predicates from those used to define legitimate DSAs.

Theory revision attempts to address both incompleteness and incorrectness in a theory. This paper aims solely at the incompleteness problem. The theory completion mechanism that is applied to learning event calculus programs in this paper is provided by logical back-propagation which makes use of a general form of inverting entailment [8].

The contribution of this paper is the extension and application of ILP techniques to generate event calculus programs for dynamic systems from temporal observations of system properties. It is organised as follows - the event calculus is introduced and a version suitable for ILP described. The theory of logical back-propagation as a method for theory completion is introduced in section 3. This is followed by experimental results of applying logical back-propagation to the induction of DSAs. Section 5 presents a discussion of the findings and suggests areas for future research. Readers unfamiliar to the event calculus can find an example in the appendix.

2 The Event Calculus

An event calculus [6] program allows a dynamic system to be modelled so that future states of the system can be determined, thus enabling the derivation of system values that *hold at* future times based upon events that have *happened* at previous times. It formalises the notion that properties remain constant unless effected by the action of an event. Events are related to system properties if they initiate (or terminate) periods in which the properties hold (or do not hold). DSAs relate events to property initiation/termination. Codification of DSAs is difficult, and exacerbated by the non-monotonicity of the formalism. A possible source of relief is to induce DSAs from observed time traces of property values from an existing dynamic system.

The ontological primitives used by the event calculus are *events* and *fluents*. Fluents are time-varying properties of the world, which may have different values at different times. Events are instantaneous and may cause change in the values of fluents. A set of events is called a *narrative*. A *dependent fluent* is one that is assumed to rely on the properties of the world around it, while *independent fluents* are assumed fiat. A *fluent trace* is the collection of fluent values for the same fluent at different times. *Trace constraints* represent the periods in which the values of the fluent trace must remain constant. *Up* and *down* transitions are the time points at which fluents change value.

The event calculus used here departs from the more often used Simplified Event Calculus (SEC) (see [10]) in two ways. First, the truth value of a fluent is reified within the `holds_at` predicate[2], which enables the derivation of negative fluent values. The second alteration to the SEC is the replacement of definitions for `initiates/3` and `terminates/3` predicates with a single predicate `flips/4`, with an intended meaning that an event flips the fluent into the specified truth state. This allows the ILP techniques to focus on learning a single target predicate. The complete definition of the core Flip-Clip event calculus (FC EC) appears in the example in the appendix.

The event calculus is being used to describe an increasing number of domains and include: an Air Traffic Control system [12]; a decision support system for vascular surgery [1]; modelling a communications protocol [4].

3 Theory completion by Logical Back-propagation

The theory completion mechanism that is applied to learning event calculus programs in this paper is provided by logical back-propagation, a form of generalised inverse entailment [8]. The problem specification for ILP is: *given* background knowledge B and examples E; *find* the simplest consistent hypothesis H s.t. $B \land H \models E$. In the case that both E and H are single Horn clauses then by inverse entailment it is possible to generate the conjunction of all ground literals that are true in all models of $B \land \overline{E}$, denoted by $\bot$ (i.e. $B \land \overline{E} \models \bot \models \overline{H}$). In logical back-propagation examples of an observational predicate are used to augment the definition of a related theoretical predicate. In the following, examples of sentences (predicates for s) are used to augment a definition for noun phrase (np).

Example 1 Natural language processing. Given background knowledge

$$B = \begin{cases} s(A,B) \leftarrow np(A,C), vp(C,D), np(D,B) \\ np(A,B) \leftarrow det(A,C), noun(C,B) \end{cases}$$

example $E = s([the, nasty, man, hit, the, dog], [])$, and a prior hypothesis $H = np(A,D) \leftarrow det(A,B), adj(B,C), noun(C,D)$ then by inverse entailment

$$\bot = \tilde{\ } s([the, nasty, man, hit, the, dog], [])$$
$$\land \tilde{\ } np([the, nasty, man, hit, the, dog], [hit, the, dog])$$
$$\land det([the, nasty, man, hit, the, dog], [nasty, man, hit, the, dog])$$
$$\land \ldots \land np([the, dog], [])$$

---

[2] A similar notion of reificaion can be found in Kakas and Miller's Language $\mathcal{E}$ [5].

The most specific (non-definite) clause that results from variablising terms (guided by mode declarations) is

$$\perp = s(A, B); np(A, C) \leftarrow det(A, D), adj(D, E), noun(E, C), vp(C, F), np(F, B)$$

The generation of $\perp$ in the above example requires derivation of $\tilde{}s$ and $\tilde{}vp$, which leads to obvious difficulties when using a Horn clause theorem prover. To overcome this the implementation of logical back-propagation makes use of mechanisms from Stickel's Prolog Technology Theorem Prover [13]. Clauses are constructed to provide definitions for negated literals. For example, for the clause $p \leftarrow q$, the extra clause $\tilde{}q \leftarrow \tilde{}p$ is added, allowing the possibility of $\tilde{}q$ being derived using a Prolog interpreter.

Not all clauses of a theory need be Stickelised when implementing generalised inverse entailment. A relevance map based on the calling diagram among predicates is used to determine the additional Stickel clauses required (see Fig. 1). The Stickel clause required to generate $\perp$ for the example is $\tilde{}np(A, C) \leftarrow \tilde{}s(A, B), vp(C, D), np(D, B)$. This enables the derivation of $\tilde{}np$ for the generation of $\perp$. The theoretical and observational predicates involved in the generalisations are communicated by the user to CProgol5.0 by way of mode declarations.

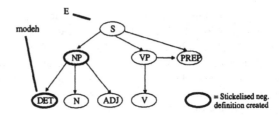

Fig. 1. Relevance map for natural language processing example.

4 Learning Event Calculus Programs

The aim of the experiments was to induce domain specific axioms for event calculus programs of dynamic systems from observed system properties using ILP techniques. The general procedure used is: (1) select a complete and working event calculus program; (2) generate a narrative of events; (3) execute the event calculus program from an initial state and record time traces for all observables; (4) remove the domain specific axioms; (5) input to Progol - core event calculus axioms, narrative, some (possibly all) of the fluent traces, other background knowledge; (6) induce domain specific axioms using Progol5.0

The full experimental method used in this paper can be found in [7]. A brief summary follows. Independent fluent trace data was transformed so that it did not participate as a target observation, nor in the scoring of hypotheses. The induction problem was decoupled into two separate problems, one for learning *up* transitions, and one for *down* transitions. Opposite fluent data was treated as a constraint to prevents over generalisation.

4.1 Experiment - the blocks world

The complete FC EC program for the blocks world (see appendix Fig. 2) provides answers to queries about the state of the blocks at different times. These were the source of observed trace information used for induction. The usual ILP inputs were provided to CProgol5.0: *examples* were specified in terms of the fluent observations (e.g. holds_at(on(block_b, block_c),+, 1)); *background knowledge* including the core event calculus axioms(FC1 and FC2), the narrative (e.g. happens(move(block_a,block_d),5).) and other background relations (e.g. diff(block_a,block_d)); *constraints* as a means for representing the fluent values that are not observed in time periods (e.g. :- clipped(1,on(block_c, table),+, 15).); and *mode declarations*. For a complete description see [7].

Logical back-propagation generated the most specific clauses using one example of holds_at/3 and the core axioms. For example

```
flips(move(A,B),on(A,B),+,C) :-
     holds_at(clear(A),+,C), holds_at(clear(B),+,C), diff(A,block_b),
     diff(A,block_d), diff(A,table), diff(A,block_c),
     diff(A,B), diff(B,block_b), diff(B,table),
     diff(B,block_a), diff(B,block_c), diff(B,A).
```

from which Progol produced the following clause.

```
flips(move(A,B),on(A,B),+,C) :-
     holds_at(clear(A),+,C), holds_at(clear(B),+,C),
     diff(A,table), diff(A,B).
```

This clause is identical (modulo variable renaming) to the original domain specific axiom for the up transition, and includes literals that relate both temporal and static relationships between the objects in the domain. The hypotheses generated by Progol for the down transitions of the fluent on/2 were as follows.

$$flips(move(A, B), on(A, C), -, D) : - holds\_at(on(B, C), +, D).$$

```
flips(move(A,B),on(A,C),-,D) :-
     holds_at(on(A,C),+,D), holds_at(clear(A),+,D),
     holds_at(clear(B),+,D).
```

The first clause was not part of the original set of domain specific axioms for the blocks world program, and trivially states that moving one block to another will not make the first be on a third if there is already the second on the third. The second clause, although not identical to the original domain specific axiom for the up transition, does imply the original.

5 Discussion

The experimental evidence presented demonstrates that it is possible to induce domain specific axioms for event calculus programs using temporal observations of system properties. By employing logical back-propagation, Progol was able to learn the domain specific axioms to describe the dynamics of the blocks world from observations of the world over time.

The core event calculus axioms play an important role in the theory completion process. They participate in the induction in two ways, (1) for generating a most specific hypothesis, and (2) searching the subsumption lattice of possible clauses. First, attempts to generalise examples (holds_at/3) do not succeed directly as no modeh definition for holds_at/3 exists. The logical back propagation algorithm searches for predicate definitions having a modeh and also holds_at/3 in its ancestor set. One such predicate is flips/4, which appears in core axiom FC1. A Stickel transformation is applied to the axiom, and an extra clause is added. This allows negated atoms of ~flips/4 to be tested for derivability. Successful bindings returned are used as part of the start set for inverse entailment, leading to the generation of the most specific clause. Second, the core axioms aid in constraining the search for the most compressive hypothesis. The search for consistent hypothesis clauses makes use of core axiom (FC2) and the ground trace constraints of the form : $-clipped(Time_1, Fluent, -, Time_2)$. This core axiom contains flips/4 as a body literal, via which every clause considered in the subsumption lattice is checked for constraint satisfaction.

Although the possibility of learning causal rules in the event calculus is mentioned by Kakas and Miller [5], this work is the first to achieve it. Previous researchers have studied ILP in temporal domains although only [9] has used the event calculus. Within ILP formalisms based on qualitative models have been used (e.g.[2]), as have systems employing regression techniques (e.g. [11]).

Future work should consider domains where the effects of events are delayed. Another alternative area for future research would be the extension of the event calculus formulation to include continuous change (see [10]). Learning rules about action and change may also be possible using an analogous logic programming implementation of the situation calculus[3].

References

[1] Abeysinghe, G. K.: Event Calculus to Support Temporal Reasoning in a Clinical Domain, Ph.D. thesis, University of Southampton (1993).

[2] Bratko, I., Muggleton, S., Varsek, A.: Learning Qualitative Models of Dynamic Systems, in Inductive Logic Programming, S. Muggleton, Editor. (1992) Academic Press: London. p. 437-452.

[3] De Raedt, L.: Interactive Theory Revision: An Inductive Logic Programming Approach. (1992), London: Academic Press.

[4] Denecker, M., et al.: A Realistic Experiment in Knowledge Representation in Open Event Calculus: Protocol Specification in Proceedings of JICSLP'96, the Joint International Conference and Symposium on Logic Programming. (1996) Bonn, Germany: MIT Press.

---

[3] This was suggested by Murray Shanahan.

[5] Kakas, A. C., Miller, R. S.: A Simple Declarative Language for Describing Narratives with Actions. Journal of Logic Programming: Special Issue on Reasoning about Action and Change (1997).

[6] Kowalski, R., Sergot, M.: A Logic-based Calculus of Events. New Generation Computing **4** (1986) 67 - 95.

[7] Moyle, S., Muggleton, S.: Experiments in Learning Event Calculus Programs, Oxford University Computing Laboratory PRG-TR-23-97 (1997).

[8] Muggleton, S.: Inverse Entailment and Progol. New Generation Computing **13**(3 and 4) (1995) 245–286.

[9] Sablon, G.: Iterative Versionspaces with an application in Inductive Logic Programming, Ph.D. thesis, Katholic University of Leuven (1995).

[10] Shanahan, M.: Solving the Frame Problem: A Mathematical Investigation of the Common Sense Law of Inertia. (1997), MIT Press.

[11] Srinivasan, A., Camacho, R.: Numerical reasoning in ILP in Machine Intelligence 15. (1995), Oxford.

[12] Sripada, S. M.: Efficient Implementation of the Event Calculus for Temporal Database Applications in Proceedings of the 12th International Conference on Logic Programming. (1995), Japan.

[13] Stickel, M. E.: A Prolog technology theorem prover: a new exposition and implementation in Prolog. Theoretical Computer Science **104**(1) (1992) 109–128.

A An Introduction to the Event Calculus: a Blocks World Example

This appendix presents an event calculus program that permits reasoning about what fluents hold at different times in the blocks world[4]. Reasoning is based on a narrative of events, and for this example, the process of moving the two blocks shown in Fig. 2 individually requires that block A is first moved (first event), and then block B is moved (second event).

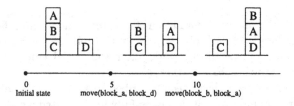

Fig. 2. The Blocks World Narrative

The state of the blocks world is represented by `holds_at/2` facts. Examples from the initial state are `holds_at(clear(block_a),+,0)` and `holds_at(on(block_b,block_a),+,0)`. The narrative is given by the two facts `happens(move(block_a,block_d),5)` and

---

[4] This example is adapted from [10].

`happens(move(block_b,block_a),10)`. To derive information about the state of the world at later times the *core axioms* and the *domain specific axioms* must be included. The *core axioms* of the event calculus consist of the following normal program clauses.

```
holds_at(Fluent,State,Time2) :-
    happens(Event,Time1), Time1<Time2,
    flips(Event,Fluent,State,Time1),                    (FC1)
    not clipped(Time1,Fluent,State,Time2).

clipped(Time1,Fluent,State1,Time2) :-
    happens(Event,Time), flips(Event,Fluent,State2,Time),
    switch(State1,State2), Time1=<Time, Time<Time2.     (FC2)
```

The clause FC1 means that a fluent value holds at a later time $Time_2$, if an event happens at an earlier time $Time_1$ initiates the fluent value (i.e. flips it into the + state), provided that the fluent value is not clipped between those two times. A fluent value is *clipped* (FC2) between times $Time_1$ and $Time_2$ if there is an event that occurs at some time in between the two that terminates the fluent value (i.e. flips it into the - state).

The DSAs determine which events trigger the state of particular fluents. DSAs for relating *move* events to both *on* and *clear* fluents are required. As an example the DSAs for *move* and *on* in the blocks world are

```
flips(move(X,Y),on(X,Y),+,Time) :-
    holds_at(clear(X),+,Time), holds_at(clear(Y),+,Time),
    diff(X,Y), diff(X,table).                           (BDSA1)

flips(move(X,Y),on(X,Z),-,Time) :-
    holds_at(clear(X),+,Time), holds_at(clear(Y),+,Time),
    holds_at(clear(Z),+,Time), diff(X,Y),
    diff(X,table).                                      (BDSA2)
```

From all of the above information (and some additional facts relating to the uniqueness of objects) it is possible to derive statements about the state of the blocks world after the initial configuration (e.g. `holds_at(on(block_a,block_d),+,6)`).

More elaborate domains have been described using the event calculus (e.g. [12]). Researchers in Leuven have successfully implemented a sliding window protocol with go-back-n in the event calculus [4], from which they were able to prove that the communications system as modelled was deadlock free.

Distance Between Herbrand Interpretations:
A Measure for Approximations to a Target Concept

Shan-Hwei Nienhuys-Cheng
cheng@cs.few.eur.nl

Department of Computer Science, H4-19
Erasmus University Rotterdam
P.O. Box 1738, 3000DR, Rotterdam, the Netherlands

Abstract. We can use a metric to measure the differences between elements in a domain or subsets of that domain (i.e. concepts). Which particular metric should be chosen, depends on the kind of difference we want to measure. The well known Euclidean metric on $\Re^n$ and its generalizations are often used for this purpose, but such metrics are not always suitable for concepts where elements have some structure different from real numbers. For example, in (Inductive) Logic Programming a concept is often expressed as an Herbrand interpretation of some first-order language. Every element in an Herbrand interpretation is a ground atom which has a tree structure.

We start by defining a metric d on the set of expressions (ground atoms and ground terms), motivated by the structure and complexity of the expressions and the symbols used therein. This metric induces the Hausdorff metric h on the set of all sets of ground atoms, which allows us to measure the distance between Herbrand interpretations. We then give some necessary and some sufficient conditions for an upper bound of h between two given Herbrand interpretations, by considering the elements in their symmetric difference.

Keywords: metric space, inductive logic programming, logic programming.

1 Introduction

An important problem in Inductive Logic Programming is the following *model inference problem* [18]. Suppose we have a first-order language and an interpretation T which is a subset of the set of all ground atoms $\mathcal{B}$ (*Herbrand base*). Our aim is to find a definite program H, (*target program*), whose least Herbrand model M_H equals T (*target interpretation*). If $M_H = T$, we will call H *correct w.r.t.* T. For example, given $T = \{P(a), P(f^2(a)), \ldots, P(f^{2k}(a)), \ldots\}$ (where $f^2(a)$ abbreviates $f(f(a))$, etc.), a correct program is

$P(a)$

$P(f^2(x)) \leftarrow P(x)$

However, a correct program may not always be found, and often we need to approximate it by other programs, for the following reasons:

1. A correct program w.r.t. a taregt T may not exist. As noted in [13, 14], the set of Herbrand interpretations is uncountable, while the set of programs is only countable. Hence for many interpretations T, there is no program H with $M_H = T$, and the best we can do is to find some kind of approximately correct program.

2. In general we are not given a complete interpretation $T \subseteq B$ but some $E^+ \subset T$ as a set of positive examples and some $E^- \subset (B \setminus T)$ as a set of negative examples. We want to find a program which implies all atoms in E^+ and none in E^-. Such a correct program H w.r.t. $E = E^+ \cup E^-$ may not be correct w.r.t. T. The idea of machine learning is to use H to predict the truth values of new examples in $B \setminus E$. Since the information about T is incomplete, there is no way to know the correctness of H w.r.t. T and hence no way to guarantee correct predictions. However, there may be some way to estimate the closeness of M_H to T.

   Even if we are only interested in finding a correct program H w.r.t. the given examples E, we may still for efficiency reasons have to settle for an approximation H' which is not totally correct w.r.t. E. Thus we also want to know how close H' is to a correct program w.r.t. E.

3. The examples will sometimes not give us correct information about T because of *noise*. From noisy data it is difficult to find a correct program. Moreover, a program that is correct w.r.t. noisy examples may be inadequate, while a program that is incorrect w.r.t. noisy examples may be adequate.

For these reasons, a way to measure the 'quality' of an approximation to a correct program is needed. How can we make this notion of 'approximation' precise, so we can use it in theoretical and practical analysis? Given some examples (ground atoms) from T, we may be satisfied with a program that covers only 90% of the examples correctly. This, however, is rather crude; for instance, all different examples are then considered equally important. A more sophisticated way is used in the framework of Probably Approximately Correct learning [10]. Here the examples are drawn according to an unknown probability distribution $\mathcal{P}$, and the induced M_H would be considered approximately correct if the probability (according to $\mathcal{P}$) of getting examples from the symmetric difference $M_H \triangle T = (M_H \setminus T) \cup (T \setminus M_H)$ is less than a user-specified ϵ.

In ILP, we usually do not consider the probability distributions on the examples. Thus we will take a different viewpoint towards approximation than the one adopted in PAC-learning. We compare two ground expressions by their tree structures. For differences between trees, the nodes close to the root count the most. This measure of difference is given by a metric d defined on the set $\mathcal{E}$ of ground atoms and ground terms. For example, $P(a)$ and $Q(a)$ are considered quite different by our definition of d, and the difference between $P(a)$ and $P(f(a))$ is considered larger than the difference between $P(f(a))$ and $P(f^2(a))$. We can then use the Hausdorff metric h (see [4]) induced by d to define a distance between Herbrand interpretations. This distance can be used for measuring the difference between two programs (more precisely: between their least Herbrand models). We will see for example that if $S = \{P(a), P(f^2(a)), P(f^4(a)), \ldots\}$,

$T_1 = S \cup \{P(f^9(a))\}$ and $T_2 = S \cup \{P(f(a))\}$, then $h(S, T_1) < h(S, T_2)$.

This article is organized as follows. We begin with some preliminaries concerning metric spaces and logic. Then we define our distance d on the set $\mathcal{E}$ of expressions. We prove that d is indeed a metric on $\mathcal{E}$, and every subset of $\mathcal{E}$ is closed. Although this metric generates the *discrete topology*, it is still interesting for our purposes. This metric will induce a Hausdorff metric h on the set of all subsets of $\mathcal{E}$, which includes the set of all Herbrand interpretations. This can be used to measure the closeness of a program (more precisely, of its least Herbrand model) to a target interpretation. Although the Hausdorff metric may look unfamilar to some readers, its application in our situation of Herbrand interpretations is actually fairly simple and concrete. By considering elements in the symmetric difference between two Herbrand interpretations S and T, we can find some necessary and some sufficient conditions for upper bounds on the distance $h(S, T)$. In real application, we usually want to find a program which is correct w.r.t. some true examples E^+ and false examples E^-. In this situation we use $h(M_H \cap (E^+ \cup E^-), E^+)$. Notice that if $E^+ \cup E^- = \mathcal{B}$, then E^+ is the related Herbrand interpretation. Here we have the original model inference problem again.

1.1 Discussion and related work

In machine learning, using distances to compare two concepts is not new. For example, distance plays an important role in instance-based learning, case-based reasoning (see [1, 5, 6]) and neural networks (see [2]), which use concepts like similarity, nearest neighbors, etc. In related fields such as data mining, metrics is also used to group data [9]. However, defining distances based on tree structures in two levels (d and h) as given here is a novel approach. (In the field of semantics, the difference between two streams of values (input or output streams) is sometimes defined by considering only the first place where the streams differ. The way we compare trees here, may be considered as a generalization of this idea. Moreover, the Hausdorff metric has been used in [3]. It measures the difference between processes in concurrent programming. Its definition depends on metrics on some functional spaces.)

Some people may think that the tree structures of atoms are not important for application, because the applications of ILP often restrict attention to function-free languages. There are two reasons for this argument. Usually a database has the attribute-value format, and if we want to do data mining in this situation, a direct way to express a rule is as a function-free clause. Even if we choose to express some concept by means of function symbols, we will not get a deep tree structure because attributes are typed. For example, the salary of some person cannot be applied twice, so a structure such as $salary(salary(x))$ does not make sense. However, the theoretical developement of ILP should not be stopped by the fact that more complex applications are not readily apparent. In fact, finding mathematical concepts as target concepts is also a kind of application of ILP. Shapiro [18] has shown how to find a program which characterizes multiplication and addition by using examples and the successor function in the natural numbers. His paper is one of the most important papers in ILP. Moreover, the modeling of complicated scientific experiments in physics and chemistry, involving mathematical concepts like groups or matrix operations, will probably require use of function symbols. In fact, chemical reactions can be considered as functions over the set of chemicals. If we want to use ILP for data mining in these fields rather than in simpler commercial databases, we may need more than just function-free languages.

One might also think that flattening [17] will solve the problem of additional complexity brought about by functions, by transforming clauses with functions to function-free form. However, a side effect of flattening is that the number of literals in a clause will increase in proportion to the number of eliminated function symbols. Thus the complexity is not removed, but appears in another form. If we choose to keep the function symbols instead of applying flattening, then a direct measure of the difference between tree structures is necessary in order to be able to measure the degree of approximation.

One might also argue that the difference between atoms is not important; that it is the difference between clauses that we should measure. However, our aim in ILP is usually to find a program, a set of clauses rather than a single clause. The various clauses in a program usually "interact" and depend on each other to produce the right results. Since our aim is to find sets of clauses rather than individual clauses, we should look for a way to measure the distance between sets rather than individual clauses. One way to compare sets of clauses is to measure the distance between their least Herbrand models; the difference between individual clauses will not be very helpful here.

In the literature there are also distances defined for objects with complex structures. For example, in [6] a similarity measure is given for structured representation that is based on graph edit operations (the number and the cost of operations needed to transform one graph to another are used to define the distance). This is quite different from the distances given here. In the first place we have here distances defined on two levels: one for ground expressions, the other for sets of ground expressions. Furthermore, we do not use graph operations to compare two graphs. In a graph, an edge can go from any node to any other one. We, on the contrary, compare two static trees in the direction from top to bottom.

2 Preliminaries

2.1 Metric space and Hausdorff metric

Definition 1. Let $\mathcal{E}$ be a set and $\Re$ be the set of real numbers. A mapping $d : \mathcal{E} \times \mathcal{E} \to \Re$ is called a *metric* or *distance* on $\mathcal{E}$ if it has the following properties:

1. $d(x, y) \geq 0 \ \forall x, y \in E$ and $d(x, y) = 0$ iff $x = y$.
2. $d(x, y) = d(y, x) \ \forall x, y \in \mathcal{E}$.
3. $d(x, y) + d(y, z) \geq d(x, z) \ \forall x, y, z \in \mathcal{E}$ (*triangle inequality*).

The pair $(\mathcal{E}, d)$ is called a *metric space*. Given $\epsilon > 0$ and $x \in \mathcal{E}$, the *open ϵ-ball* $B(x, \epsilon)$ *centered at* x is the set $\{y \mid d(x, y) < \epsilon\}$. A set $T \subseteq \mathcal{E}$ is called *open* if for every $x \in T$, there is an open ball centered at x in T. A set $T \subseteq \mathcal{E}$ is *closed* if $\mathcal{E} \backslash T$ is open. The sets $\mathcal{E}$ and $\emptyset$ are both open and closed. A metric space is *bounded* if the metric is bounded, i.e. there is an m such that $d(x, y) \leq m, \forall x, y \in \mathcal{E}$.

It is well known that the union of an arbitrary collection of open sets and the intersection of a finite collection of open sets are open themselves. Given a real function f defined on a set U and $\emptyset \neq S \subseteq U$, we let $inf_{x \in S} f(x)$ denote the greatest lower bound (infimum) of $\{f(x) \mid x \in S\}$ if it exists. We use *sup* (supremum) for the dual concept. For example, let $d(x, y) = |x - y|$ be the usual metric defined on $\mathfrak{R}$. Consider the closed intervals $S = [0, 1]$ and $T = [2, 5/2]$. Then $inf_{x \in S} d(x, 5/2) = 3/2$ and $inf_{y \in T} d(0, y) = 2$.

Definition 2. Let $(\mathcal{E}, d)$ be a bounded metric space and $\mathcal{C}(\mathcal{E})$ be the set of all closed subsets of $\mathcal{E}$. For non-empty $T \in \mathcal{C}(\mathcal{E})$ and $x \in \mathcal{E}$, let $d(x, T) = inf_{y \in T} d(x, y)$. For non-empty $S, T \in \mathcal{C}(\mathcal{E})$, let $\rho(S, T) = sup_{x \in S} d(x, T)$, and let $h(S, T) = sup(\rho(S, T), \rho(T, S))$. Furthermore, define $h(\emptyset, \emptyset) = 0$ and $h(\emptyset, T) = 1$ if $T \neq \emptyset$. It can be shown that h is a metric on $\mathcal{C}(\mathcal{E})$ (see exercise 3 of 3.16 in [4]). This is called the *Hausdorff metric induced by d*.

We can also artificially define: $\rho(\emptyset, \emptyset) = 0$; if $T \neq \emptyset$, then $\rho(\emptyset, T) = 0$ and $\rho(T, \emptyset) = 1$. With this definition we also have $h(\emptyset, T) = sup(\rho(\emptyset, T), \rho(T, \emptyset)) = 1$, as above.

Example 1. Let us consider $\mathfrak{R}$ with $d(x, y) = |x - y|$ defined as above. Let $S = [0, 1]$ and $T = [2, 5/2]$. Then $\rho(S, T) = 2$ and $\rho(T, S) = 3/2$. Thus $h(S, T) = 2$.

Example 2. Let $\emptyset \neq S \subseteq T$ and $S \neq T$. Then $\rho(S, T) = sup_{x \in S} d(x, T) = 0$ and $\rho(T, S) = sup_{x \in T} d(x, S) = sup_{x \in T \backslash S} d(x, S)$. Now let $S = [0, 1]$, $T = [0, 2]$ in $\mathfrak{R}$. Then $h(S, T) = 1$.

Remarks

1. If $S \subseteq T$, then $\rho(S, T) = 0$. According to Definition 2, $\rho(S \backslash T, T) = \rho(\emptyset, T) = 0$ also. If $S \not\subseteq T$, then $S \backslash T \neq \emptyset$ and $\rho(S, T) = \rho(S \backslash T, T)$. Thus in general, $\rho(S, T) = \rho(S \backslash T, T)$.
2. Since $\emptyset$ does not contain any elements, we cannot use the definition of *inf* and *sup*. All the results in this article that also apply to $\emptyset$ are true, but we will often omit the trivial cases of proofs w.r.t. $\emptyset$, focusing only on the nonempty sets.
3. If $h(S, T) < \epsilon$, then each point in S is within an ϵ distance of a point in T and vice versa. If $h(S, T) > \epsilon$, then there is an $x \in S$ such that $d(x, y) > \epsilon \; \forall y \in T$ or there is an $y \in T$ such that $d(x, y) > \epsilon \; \forall x \in S$.

2.2 Definite programs and least Herbrand models

In the sequel we will consider some fixed first-order language with a finite number of function symbols (including constants) and a finite number of predicate symbols. For most definitions from logic, we refer to [12, 14]. Let us just recall the following:

- *Terms* are defined inductively as follows: constants and variables are terms, and if $t_1, \ldots, t_n$ are terms and f is a function symbol of *arity* n, then $f(t_1, \ldots, t_n)$ is a term.
- An *atom* has the form $P(t_1, \ldots, t_n)$ where P is an n-ary predicate symbol and each t_i is a term.
- A *definite program clause* (often abbreviated to *clause* in this paper) is an implication of the following form: $A \leftarrow B_1, \ldots, B_n$, where A and B_i are atoms. It should be read as "B_1 and ... and B_n together imply A." A is called the *head* of the clause, $B_1, \ldots, B_n$ is the *body*. Each variable in a clause is universally quantified, but we will not write out the quantifiers explicitly. A term or clause is *ground* if it does not contain any variables.
- A *definite program* (or just *program*) is a finite set of clauses.
- An *Herbrand interpretation* T assigns to each ground atom in the language a truth-value (*true* or *false*). T may be identified with the set of ground atoms to which it assigns *true*. A ground clause is true under T if its head is true and/or at least one of the atoms in its body is false under T. A non-ground clause is true under T if all its ground instances are true under T. An Herbrand interpretation T is called an *Herbrand model* of a definite program H, if all clauses in H are true under T.
- It can be shown that the intersection of all Herbrand models of a definite program H is itself an Herbrand model of H. This is called the *least Herbrand model* of H, denoted by M_H. It equals the set of all ground atoms that are logically implied by H.

2.3 Positions of symbols in an expression

Definition 3. An *expression* is a ground term or a ground atom. (In this article, we use p, q, etc. in general to denote arbitrary function or predicate symbols occuring in an expression.) An expression e has a tree structure. We can express this structure by coding the *positions* of symbols in e in the following way.

1. The leftmost symbol in e has $\langle 1 \rangle$ as its position.
2. If $\langle a_1, a_2, \ldots, a_n \rangle$ is the position of a predicate or function symbol p occurring in e, and p has $k > 0$ arguments, then the leftmost symbol of the i-th argument has $\langle a_1, \ldots, a_n, i \rangle$ as its position in e.

For an expression e and position *pos*, we use $e(pos)$ to denote the symbol at position *pos* in e.

The *depth* of a symbol occurrence is the length of its position. The *depth* of an expression e, denoted by $depth(e)$, is the depth of the symbol in e with the greatest depth.

Given expressions e and e', we say they are *the same to* (at least) *depth* n if for every $k \leq n$, $\langle a_1, a_2, \ldots, a_k \rangle$ is a position of a symbol in e iff it is also a position of the same symbol in e'.

Example 3. Consider $e = P(g(b), f(a, g(b)))$ and $e' = P(g(b), f(a, b))$. Then $e(\langle 1 \rangle) = P$, $e(\langle 1, 1, 1 \rangle) = b$ and $e(\langle 1, 2, 2, 1 \rangle) = b$. The depth of e is 4 and the depth of e' is 3. Expressions e and e' are the same to depth 2. They are not the same to depth 3, because e has g at position $\langle 1, 2, 2 \rangle$, while e' has b at that position. Consider also $e = P(a, g^2(a))$ and $e' = P(a, g^3(a))$. Then e and e' are the same to depth 3.

Notice that if $e = e'$, then e and e' are the same to any depth. If $depth(e) = n$ and $e \neq e'$, then e and e' may be the same to depth $n - 1$, but not more.

3 A metric on expressions

From now on we use $\mathcal{E}$ to denote the set of all expressions in a first-order language. We would like to define a metric d, bounded by 1, on $\mathcal{E}$ such that $d(s, t)$ can be used to measure the difference between s and t.

Definition 4. We define $d : \mathcal{E} \times \mathcal{E} \to \Re$ as follows.

1. $d(e, e) = 0, \forall e \in \mathcal{E}$
2. If $p \neq q$, then $d(p(s_1, \ldots, s_n), q(t_1, \ldots, t_m)) = 1$
3. $d(p(s_1, \ldots, s_n), p(t_1, \ldots, t_n)) = \frac{1}{2n} \sum_{i=1}^{n} d(s_i, t_i)$

Example 4. The following examples illustrate how d works.
$d(f(a), P(a, b)) = 1$,
$d(f(a), f(b)) = \frac{1}{2} d(a, b) = \frac{1}{2}$,
$d(g(f(a), g(a, b)), g(f(b), b)) = \frac{1}{2 \cdot 2}(d(f(a), f(b)) + d(g(a, b), b))$
$= \frac{1}{4}(\frac{1}{2} + 1) = \frac{3}{8}$.
Let $T = \{P(f(a)), P(f^3(a)), P(f^5(a)), \ldots\}$. Suppose d is a metric (as we will prove below). Since $d(P(f^2(a)), P(f^3(a)) = \frac{1}{8}$, we have $d(P(f^2(a)), T) = \frac{1}{8}$.

Notice that differences between terms that occur at low depth are given more "weight" than differences at higher depth.

Theorem 5. $(\mathcal{E}, d)$ is a metric space with d bounded by 1.

Proof:
d bounded by 1: It is clear that $d(e, e') \leq 1$ if it is defined by item 1 or 2 above. Now suppose item 3 of the definition is used: $d(e, e') = d(p(s_1, \ldots, s_n), p(t_1, \ldots, t_n)) = \frac{1}{2n} \sum_{i=1}^{n} d(s_i, t_i)$ and suppose $d(s_i, t_i) \leq 1, \forall i$ (induction hypothesis). Then $d(e, e') \leq \frac{1}{2n}(1 + \ldots + 1) = \frac{n}{2n} = \frac{1}{2}$.
d is a metric: We prove only $d(r, s) + d(s, t) \geq d(r, t)$, by induction on the depth of these expressions. Suppose $depth(r) = depth(s) = depth(t) = 1$, so r, s, and t are function or predicate symbols of arity 0. If $r = s = t$, then $d(r, s) = d(s, t) = d(r, t) = 0$. Otherwise, $r \neq s$ and/or $s \neq t$, then $d(r, s) + d(s, t) \geq 1 \geq d(r, t)$.
Suppose this inequality is true if the depth of r, s, t is at most k, and assume the expression among r, s, t that has greatest depth, has depth $k + 1$.

- $r(\langle 1 \rangle) \neq t(\langle 1 \rangle)$: In this situation $d(r,t) = 1$. However, if $r(\langle 1 \rangle) = s(\langle 1 \rangle)$, then $d(s,t) = 1$. Thus the inequality holds.
- $r(\langle 1 \rangle) = t(\langle 1 \rangle) \neq s(\langle 1 \rangle)$: In this situation $d(r,s) + d(s,t) = 2 \geq d(r,t)$.
- $r(\langle 1 \rangle) = t(\langle 1 \rangle) = s(\langle 1 \rangle)$:

$$d(p(r_1,\ldots,r_n),p(s_1,\ldots,s_n)) +$$
$$d(p(s_1,\ldots,s_n),p(t_1,\ldots,t_n))$$
$$= \frac{1}{2n}\sum_{i=1}^{n} d(r_i,s_i) + \frac{1}{2n}\sum_{i=1}^{n} d(s_i,t_i)$$
$$= \frac{1}{2n}\sum_{i=1}^{n}(d(r_i,s_i) + d(s_i,t_i))$$
$$\geq \frac{1}{2n}\sum_{i=1}^{n} d(r_i,t_i) = d(r,t).$$

Example 5. Let $e = P(a,b)$, $e' = P(a,c)$, $e'' = P(c,d)$. Then $d(e,e') = \frac{1}{4}$, and $d(e,e'') = \frac{1}{2}$.

In general, if $e \neq e'$, then there is $n \geq 0$ such that they are the same to depth n but not the same to depth $n + 1$. Given e and e', the upper and lower bounds of $d(e,e')$ are given by the following two lemmas.

Lemma 6. If e and e' are the same to at least depth n, then $d(e,e') \leq \frac{1}{2^n}$.

Proof: $n = 0$: This means $d(e,e') \leq 1$.
$n = k + 1$: Let $e = p(s_1,\ldots,s_m)$ and $e' = p(t_1,\ldots t_m)$. Then $d(e,e') = \frac{1}{2m}\sum_{i=1}^{m} d(s_i,t_i) \leq \frac{1}{2m} \cdot \frac{m}{2^k} = \frac{1}{2^{k+1}}$.

Lemma 7. Let M be an integer which is greater than the maximal arity of all function and predicate symbols in the logic language. Then if e and e' are not the same to depth n, we have $d(e,e') > \frac{1}{(2M)^n}$.

Proof: $n = 1$: Then $d(e,e') = 1 > \frac{1}{2M}$.
$n = k + 1$: Let $e = p(s_1,\ldots,s_m)$ and $e' = p(t_1,\ldots t_m)$. There is an i such that s_i and t_i are not the same to depth k. That means $d(s_i,t_i) > \frac{1}{(2M)^k}$. Now $d(e,e') = \frac{1}{2m}\sum_{j=1}^{m} d(s_j,t_j) \geq \frac{1}{2m}d(s_i,t_i) > \frac{1}{2M}d(s_i,t_i) > \frac{1}{(2M)^{k+1}}$.

Lemma 8. Every element $e \in \mathcal{E}$ is an open set.

Proof: Let M be defined as in Lemma 7. Given e with $depth(e) = n$, we will prove that the open ball $B = \{t \in E \mid d(t,e) < \frac{1}{(2M)^n}\}$ contains only e. Consider an arbitrary $e' \neq e$ with $depth(e') = m$.

- If $n \geq m$, then e and e' can be the same only to some $k < m$ (see remark after Example 3). Thus $d(e,e') > \frac{1}{(2M)^n}$ according to lemma 7.
- If $n < m$, then e and e' can only be the same to depth $k < n$. Then $d(e,e') > \frac{1}{(2M)^n}$ according to lemma 7.

Thus $d(e,e') > \frac{1}{(2M)^n}$ for all $e' \neq e$. Since every open ball is open and the open ball B contains only one point e, we have that $\{e\}$ is open.

Since the union of open sets is open, every subset of $\mathcal{E}$ is open and hence every subset of $\mathcal{E}$ is closed as well. Thus we have the following theorem:

Theorem 9. Every subset of $\mathcal{E}$ is both open and closed.

Remark A metric space is a special kind of topological space. A topological space in which every single point constitutes an open set is called a *discrete topological space*.

4 Hausdorff metric on $\mathcal{C}(\mathcal{E})$

Since every subset of $\mathcal{E}$ is closed, we have that $\mathcal{C}(\mathcal{E})$ equals the set of all subsets of $\mathcal{E}$. We can now define the distance between two subsets of $\mathcal{E}$ by means of the Hausdorff metric h on $\mathcal{C}(\mathcal{E})$.

Example 6. Let $S = \{P(a), P(f^2(a)), P(f^4(a)), \ldots\}$ and $T = \{P(f(a)), P(f^3(a)), \ldots\}$. Then $\rho(S, T) = sup_{x \in S} d(x, T) = sup\{1/2, 1/8, 1/32, \ldots\} = 1/2$ and $\rho(T, S) = sup_{x \in T} d(x, S) = sup\{1/4, 1/16, 1/64, \ldots\} = 1/4$. Thus $h(S, T) = 1/2$.

Example 7. Let $S = \{P(a), P(f^2(a)), P(f^4(a)), \ldots\}$ and $T = S \cup \{P(f^3(a))\}$. Then $\rho(S, T) = 0$ and $\rho(T, S) = sup_{x \in T \setminus S} d(x, S) = d(P(f^3(a)), S) = 1/16$. Thus $h(S, T) = 1/16$.

Theorem 10. Consider $S, T \subseteq E$. Suppose their symmetric difference $S \bigtriangleup T = (S \setminus T) \cup (T \setminus S)$ has the following property: for every $e \in S \setminus T$, there is an e' in T such that e and e' are the same to depth n. For every $e \in T \setminus S$, there is $e' \in S$ with the same property. Then $h(S, T) \le \frac{1}{2^n}$.

Proof: We know $S = (S \cap T) \cup (S \setminus T)$. If $e \in S \cap T$, then $d(e, T) = 0$. If $e \in S \setminus T$, there is an $e' \in T$ such that e and e' are the same to depth n. By lemma 6 we have $d(e, e') \le \frac{1}{2^n}$. Thus $d(e, T) \le \frac{1}{2^n}$. Hence we have $\rho(S, T) \le \frac{1}{2^n}$. Similarly, we have $\rho(T, S) \le \frac{1}{2^n}$.

Theorem 11. Let M be defined as in Lemma 7. If $h(S, T) \le \frac{1}{(2M)^n}$, then

- For every $e \in S \setminus T$, there is an $e' \in T$ such that e and e' are the same to at least depth $n - 1$.
- For every $e \in T \setminus S$, there is an $e' \in S$ such that e and e' are the same to at least depth $n - 1$.

Proof: We prove this by contradiction. Suppose for some $e \in S \setminus T$ we have for every $e' \in T$ that e and e' are not the same to depth $n - 1$. By lemma 7, we have $d(e, e') > \frac{1}{(2M)^{n-1}}$. That means $d(e, T) \ge \frac{1}{(2M)^{n-1}}$, so $\rho(S, T) \ge \frac{1}{(2M)^{n-1}}$. Thus $h(S, T) = sup(\rho(S, T), \rho(T, S)) \ge \rho(S, T) \ge \frac{1}{(2M)^{n-1}} > \frac{1}{(2M)^n}$. This is a contradiction. Similarly for the analogous situation of $\rho(T, S)$.

In the following examples, $\mathcal{B}(\subseteq \mathcal{E})$ is the set of all ground atoms (Herbrand base).

Example 8. Let $\mathcal{B} = \{P(a), P(f(a)), P(f^2(a)), P(f^3(a)),\ldots\}$. Let $S = \{P(a), P(f^2(a)), P(f^4(a)),\ldots\}$ and $T = (S \cup \{P(f^{99}(a))\}) \setminus \{P(f^{100}(a))\}$. Consider $e = P(f^{99}(a)) \in T \setminus S$. Then $d(e, S) = \frac{1}{2^{100}}$. Now let $e = P(f^{100}(a)) \in S \setminus T$. We have $d(P(f^{100}(a)), T) = \frac{1}{2^{101}}$. Thus $h(S, T) = \frac{1}{2^{100}}$. Now consider a program H, with the following clauses:

$P(a)$

$P(f^2(x)) \leftarrow P(x)$

Then $M_H = S$. Suppose the target interpretation is T. Then the model inference problem is approximately solved using H, where the "quality" of the approximation can be measured by $h(M_H, T) \leq \frac{1}{2^{100}}$.

Example 9. Let $\mathcal{B} = \{Q(a), P(a), P(f(a)), P(f^2(a)), \ldots\}$, $S = \{P(a), P(f^2(a)), P(f^4(a)),\ldots\}$ and $T = S \cup \{Q(a), P(f^{99}(a))\}$. Then $h(S, T) = 1$. This means that S and T are far from each other, according to our metric.

Now suppose that the target is T. Consider the same program H as in the above example. Then H does not give a good approximation to the target concept. However, suppose we have another program H'

$P(a)$

$Q(a)$

$P(f^2(x)) \leftarrow P(x)$

Then $M_{H'} = S \cup \{Q(a)\}$ and $h(M_{H'}, T) \leq \frac{1}{2^{100}}$.

Remark From the examples above we may get the impression that if two interpretations S and T differ only in ground atoms with large depth, then they are close to each other in h. This is not completely correct, as we can see from the following example. Let $S = \{P(a)\}$ and $T = \{P(a), P(f^{100}(a))\}$. Then $\{e \in S \mid depth(e) \leq 100\} = \{e \in T \mid depth(e) \leq 100\}$, but $h(S, T) = \frac{1}{2}$. In fact, $h(S, T)$ is small if for every element e in S we can find an e' in T which has the same structure as e to a large depth and vice versa. Now $P(f^{100}(a))$ is already different from any element in S from depth 2. If we consider $S' = S \cup \{P(f^{99}(a))\}$, then $h(S', T) = \frac{1}{2^{100}}$, which is rather small.

5 Metric on examples

The model inference problem concerns an interpretation T, which can be expressed as a subset of the set of all ground atoms $\mathcal{B}$ (namely the subset of *true* ground atoms). In this case, the distance between a target and the found program H is given by $h(M_H, T)$, which will be 0 iff M_H is correct w.r.t. T.

In applications, however, we are not given the complete T, but only a sample from T: a set of ground atoms $E = E^+ \cup E^-$, where E^+ is called the set of *positive examples* and E^- the set of *negative examples*. We would like to find a program H which implies all the positive examples and none of the negative ones. In this situation we may also only find a program which is not completely correct w.r.t. E, and we would like to use our distance to measure the degree of approximation. Unfortunately, we cannot straightforwardly use $h(M_H, E^+)$ instead of $h(M_H, T)$. For example, let $E^+ = \{P(0), P(f^2(0))\}$ and $E^- = \{P(f(0)), P(f^3(0))\}$. Then

$H = \{P(0), (P(f^2(x)) \leftarrow P(x))\}$ is a correct program w.r.t. to these examples. Since H implies much more than just the atoms in E^+, we have for instance $d(P(f^4(0)), P(f^2(0))) = \frac{1}{2^4}$. Thus we have $h(M_H, E^+) \geq \frac{1}{2^4}$, which gives the impression that a correct program may not even be a good approximation. To solve this problem, we restrict attention from the set of all ground atoms B to the set of given example E, because this is all we know about T. (If $E = B$, we have the original situation given in the last sections.) Given a program H, we consider $S = M_H \cap E$ and $h(S, E^+)$. Notice that $S \setminus E^+$ contains negative examples which are implied by H and $E^+ \setminus S$ contains positive examples which are not impled by H. Thus both negative and positive examples play a role for the distance $h(S, E^+)$. If H is correct w.r.t. E, then $h(S, E^+) = 0$.

6 Summary and future work

This article has been motivated by the problem in ILP of measuring differences between the least Herbrand models of a definite program and a target interpretation. Our aim was to define a distance between Herbrand interpretations in a natural way. We started with a definition of a metric d on the set of expressions $\mathcal{E}$, which allowed us to define the Hausdorff metric h on $\mathcal{C}(\mathcal{E})$, the set of all closed subsets of $\mathcal{E}$. Since every subset of $\mathcal{E}$ is closed, every Herbrand interpretation is such a closed subset. Thus h can be used to measure the distance between two Herbrand interpretations S and T. Moreover, $h(S, T)$ can be characterized by elements in the symmetric difference $S \triangle T$. This implies that we have a concrete idea of an 'approximation' to a target interpretation (or to E^+ in practical applications where T is unknown), which may turn out to be very useful in ILP.

It should be noted that it is in general undecidable whether some ground atom is a member of M_H. In order to deal with this, we may use the idea of h-easyness, which is also used in [18]. This amounts to bounding the maximal number of resolution steps that can be taken when trying to deduce an atom from H.

There are the following possible lines for future work.

First of all, there should be more applications of the Hausdorff metric in Inductive Logic Programming, especially on topics related to mathematics, chemistry and physics. I think one can show by applications that function-free languages are not satisfactory for these fields.

Secondly, given examples $E = E^+ \cup E^-$ and abbreviating $S = M_H \cap E$, we can use $h(S, E^+)$ as a heuristic in the search for an H that is correct w.r.t. given E^+ and E^-. Initially we start with an empty (or otherwise inadequate) H, so $h(S, E^+)$ will be high. Then we stepwisely adjust H in such a way that $h(S, E^+)$ decreases. Eventually we hope to end up with an H for which $h(S, E^+)$ is small (even 0, in case the final H is fully correct w.r.t. E^+ and E^-).

Thirdly, one motivation of this article is to find a good hypothesis even when there is noise in data. Suppose E is a set of examples which contains noise. Suppose H is a program which is correct with respect to examples if the examples are correctly given. Let $S = M_H \cap E$. If a given wrong positive example

e is close to some $e' \in S$, i.e. $d(e, e')$ is small, then $inf_{x \in S} d(e, x)$ is also small and $h(S, T)$ will not become large because of e, and we may well be able to find a good approximation in this case. If the wrong e is distant from all elements in S, then S will not be a good approximation of E^+. More research about different types of noise and their influences on h should be done in the future.

Four, we may systematically analyze distance measures between clauses, even though this seems not very useful at first sight (see subsection 1.1). That means we first have to generalize d to general clauses (the distances in the literature usually only apply to function-free clauses). Suppose we have two programs with clauses containing functions, then we may compare three kinds of distances between the programs. One is the h of this article. One is a generalization of d to clauses (if we can find a satisfactory one). The third approach is to flatten clauses and apply some other distance defined for function-free clauses.

Fifth, we can compare h with the difference measure of PAC-learning, that uses a probability distribution on the set of possible examples. For instance, the more complex examples may be assigned a lower probability, in analogy with the *universal* probability distribution [11].

Finally, since all results in this paper could be proved by considering only the tree structure of expressions, and do not depend on the details of first-order logic, metrics like the ones defined here may be applicable in fields of computer science other than ILP.

Acknowledgements My thanks go to Ronald de Wolf and Jan Willem Nienhuys for their help.

References

1. D. W. Aha, D. Kibler, and M. K. Albert. Instance-based learning algorithms. *Machine Learning*, 6:37–66, 1991.
2. R. Beale and T. Jackson *Neural Computing, an Introduction* Adam Hilger.
3. J. W. de Bakker and J. I. Zucker. Processes and the denotational semantics of concurrency. *Information and Control*, 1/2, 1984.
4. J. Dieudonné. *Foundations of Modern Analysis.* Academic Press, 1969.
5. W. Emde and D. Wettschereck. Relational instance-based learning. In: L. Saitta, editor, *Proceedings of the 13th International Conference on Machine Learning (ICML-96)*, pages 122–130. Morgan Kaufmann, 1996.
6. H. Bunke and B.T. Messmer. Similarity measure for strutured representations In: S. Wess, K.D. Althoff and M. Richter, editors, *Topics in Case-Based Reasoning, First European workshop, EWCBR-93*, pages 106-118, 1993. Springer-Verlag.
7. E. M. Gold. Language identification in the limit. *Information and Control*, 10:447–474, 1967.
8. A. Hutchinson. Metrics on Terms and Clauses. In: M. Someren, G. Widmer, editors. Proceedings of the 9th European Conference on Machine Learning (ECML-97), pages 138-145, 1997. Springer-Verlag.
9. D. T. Kao, R. D. Bergeron, M. J. Cullinane, and T. M. Sparr. Semantics and mathematics of science datasampling. Technical Report 95-14, Department of Computer Science, University of New Hampshire, 1995.

10. M. J. Kearns and U. V. Vazirani. *An Introduction to Computational Learning Theory*. MIT Press, Cambridge (MA), 1994.
11. M. Li and P. Vitányi. *An Introduction to Kolmogorov Complexity and Its Applications*. Springer-Verlag, Berlin, second edition, 1997.
12. J. W. Lloyd. *Foundations of Logic Programming*. Springer-Verlag, Berlin, second edition, 1987.
13. S. H. Nienhuys-Cheng and R. de Wolf. A complete method for program specialization based on unfolding. In: W. Wahlster, editor, *Proceedings of the 12th European Conference on Artificial Intelligence (ECAI-96)*, pages 438–442. Wiley, 1996.
14. S. H. Nienhuys-Cheng and R. de Wolf. *Foundations of Inductive Logic Programming*, LNAI Tutorial 1228, Springer-Verlag, May 1997.
15. G.D. Plotkin. A Note on Inductive Generalization. *Machine Intelligence*, 5:153–163, 1970.
16. J.C. Reynolds. Transformational Systems and the Algebraic Structure of Atomic Formulas. *Machine Intelligence*, 5:135–153, 1970.
17. C. Rouveirol. Flattening and saturation: Two representation changes for generalization. *Machine Learning*, 14:219–232, 1994.
18. E. Y. Shapiro. Inductive inference of theories from facts. Research Report 192, Yale University, 1981.
19. D. Wettschereck. *A Study of Distance-Based Machine Learning Algorithms*. PhD thesis, Oregon State University, 1994.

Appendix

A recently published article [8] defines a size function as a certain type of real valued function on the set of substitutions. A size function S can induce a pseudo-metric d_S on the set of terms and literals. This pseudo-metric induces a Hausdorff pseudo-metric on clauses. For this a clause should be interpreted as a set of literals. Some differences between the approach of [8] and the method outlined above are:

1. [8] uses pesudo-metrics rather than metrics, i.e. different elements may have 0 distance. The Hausdrff metric induced by a metric is defined on closed sets otherwise it would be a pseudo-metric. In [8] not even all finite subsets of terms are closed whereas in our metric space of expressions every subset is closed.
2. In [8] a concrete size function S is given. With this S and the weights W assigned to function symbols in the manner of [8] one obtains for any n, if $k > 0$
$$d_S(P(f^n(a)), P(f^{n+k}(a))) = W(a) + W(f).$$
Using our definition of d, we have
$$d(P(f^n(a)), P(f^{n+k}(a))) = \frac{1}{2^{n+1}}.$$
3. Since on the one hand $d_S(P(x,x), P(x,y)) = 0$ and on the other hand two alphabetical variants can have a positive distance, [8] tries to adapt the distance definition. In the new definition variants would have distance 0. However, two clauses may be equivalent even they are not variants. For example, let $C = P(a) \leftarrow Q(f(a))$ and $D = P(a) \leftarrow Q(f(a)), Q(x)$. Then C and D are subsume equivalent and hence logically equivalent. Since $d_S(Q(x), Q(f(a))) = $

$W(f) + W(a) > 0$, the proposed new definition will induce a positive distance between C and D. In our method the difference between programs is indicated by the distance h between their least Herbrand models, and two logically equivalent programs have zero distance.

Realizing Progol by Forward Reasoning

Tomonobu OZAKI, Koichi FURUKAWA,
Tomoko MURAKAMI and Ken UENO

Graduate School of Media and Governance, Keio University
5322 Endo, Fujisawa, Kanagawa 252, JAPAN

Abstract. Current implementation of coverage check for evaluating the candidate hypothesis in A^*-like search in Progol is based on backward reasoning of Prolog. But it contains some kinds of redundancy. In this paper, we propose an alternative algorithm based on forward reasoning of extended MGTP (Model Generation Theorem Prover). Since this alternative can remove the redundant computations, we can expect to realize a more efficient search process.

1 Introduction

Recently many ILP systems, such as Progol[6], FOIL[8] and Golem[5], have been developed and used for many nontrivial applications with significant results.

ILP system explores the hypothesis space to induce hypotheses. Several ways of achieving this objective have been proposed; an enumeration method by using refinement operator[9], calculation of Relative Least General Generalization[5], best first search based on information gain[8] and so on.

Progol is one of the typical ILP systems using refinement operator. Progol first constructs the most specific hypothesis(MSH) for one given example to induce the best hypothesis. Because of MSH, the hypotheses space of Progol become drastically smaller than that constructed without MSH. However, in dealing with a great number of data such as KDD(Knowledge Discovery in Databases) applications, large amount of the executing time are still required. The increasing computational cost is caused by (1) a large number of enumerated candidate hypotheses and (2) a time-consuming process of the coverage check for those candidates. Therefore the approaches from these two aspects would be considered to improve the performance of the system. From the first aspect, the improved enumeration algorithm in Progol from a viewpoint of the Input/Output relation in the literals forming the MSH are proposed elsewhere[7].

In this paper, to improve the system, we concentrate on the second aspect, *i. e.* the coverage check for evaluating enumerated hypotheses. Progol adopts backward reasoning of Prolog technology for this coverage check. On the other hand, we introduce an alternative coverage check by using forward reasoning of MGTP (Model Generation Theorem Prover)[3] technology. Furthermore, we show that some redundancies in A^*-like algorithm can be easily removed by extended MGTP technology.

2 Overview of MGTP

MGTP is a model-generation based theorem prover for first-order logic. An MGTP input clause called MG-clause is represented with an implicational form:

$$A_1, \cdots, A_n \rightarrow B_1; \cdots; B_m. \quad (1)$$

where A_i, B_j are literals, '$\rightarrow$' denotes *implication*, ',' denotes *and*, ';' denotes *or*. Some MG-clauses are represented with '$A \rightarrow B, C$.', which is logically equivalent to the following two MG-clauses '$A \rightarrow B$.' and '$A \rightarrow C$.' The MG-clause (1) means that if all antecedents A_i are *true* in the current model M, then M is splitted into m models $M \cup \{B_1\}, \cdots, M \cup \{B_m\}$. At that time no copy of the current model for each splitted model is generated, but the current model is held in common.

MGTP begins with empty model(ϕ), and then extends and splits the model by applying MG-clauses. If there is no model to be extended, MGTP terminates(see Fig.1).

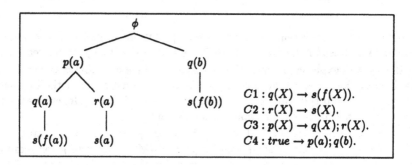

Fig. 1. Proof Tree of MGTP

An MG-clause is said to be range-restricted if and only if every variable in its consequent is found also in its antecedent. Every MG-clause must be satisfied with this condition. For an MG-clause which violates this condition, a *dom* predicate should be added to its antecedent to remedy the situation. This transformation does not change the satisfiability status of the original set of MG-clauses. For instance, the MG-clause for *append* should be written as:

$$dom(X) \rightarrow append([], X, X).$$
$$append(X, Y, Z), dom(W) \rightarrow append([W|X], Y, [W|Z]).$$

where *dom* represents all possible constants in a problem domain *i. e.* Herbrand Universe.

3 Overview of A^*-like Algorithm

Progol obtains the best hypothesis among candidates lying on the subsumption lattice. To achieve this objective, Progol searches from general to specific through the lattice according to A^*-like algorithm. A^*-like algorithm is a kind of exhaustive search with pruning capability based on A^* search strategy using some heuristic function.

In this search algorithm, the subsumption lattice can be represented as a concept tree. New candidate hypotheses are created by expanding a leaf of this concept tree according to some heuristics. a newly created candidates has one more literal added in its antecedent than its parent. For instance, a candidate hypothesis '$H \leftarrow B_1, B_2$' must be created from '$H \leftarrow B_1$'. That means a newly created candidate is more restricted and specific than its parent. Every newly created candidate hypothesis should be evaluated by its size and the number of examples covered by it together with given background knowledge.

Because of the evaluation algorithm, each time a new candidate hypothesis is created, Progol needs to compute a set of covered examples. Most of the execution time in performing the entire task will be spent at this coverage check. Therefore the efficient implementation for this computation can directly improve the entire system.

4 Coverage Check by MGTP

Progol realizes coverage check based on Prolog technology. In this computation, Progol sets each example as a Prolog goal and executes it. Then the successful goals are counted as the number of covered examples. However backward reasoning such as Prolog may explore the same node in several times by backtrack. This duplicate computation by backtrack is one of the main factors of the heavy computation in Prolog[2].

On the other hand, avoidance of backtrack can be done by forward reasoning. This is one of the reasons why we propose an alternative coverage check by MGTP. Coverage check by MGTP is performed based on forward reasoning. In other words, MGTP can naturally avoid backtrack, and in opposition to original Progol's one by one coverage check, it computes a set of covered examples at a time. In the following subsections, we show the concrete coverage check methods by MGTP.

4.1 Basic Coverage Check Method

First we show the basic idea to realize coverage check by MGTP. It can be achieved by adding a candidate hypothesis into background knowledge, then executing MGTP and finally counting elements in the intersection of the set of examples and the set of atoms derived by MGTP (see Fig.2).

This basic method may contain some drawbacks. The first one is due to forward reasoning. A naive forward inference often generates a large amount of

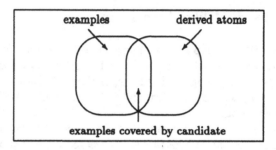

Fig. 2. Basic Coverage Check by MGTP

atoms which are irrelevant to the goals. These atoms are obstacles for achieving high efficiency.

The second drawback is caused by MGTP itself. As we described in section 2, some MG-clauses need *dom* predicates to satisfy with the range-restricted condition. The *dom*-defining clauses are essentially to create the whole Herbrand universe for the clause set. The most of the atoms derived by *dom*-defining clauses are meaningless to our aim. It would be very difficult to obtain a meaningful result by MGTP without an appropriate control for suppressing the generation of irrelevant atoms.

4.2 Applying Magic-set to Coverage Check

The problem of generating atoms which are irrelevant to objective goals is deeply concerned with the query evaluation of deductive database. To recover the drawback, we employ the powerful magic-set method[1].

Magic-set method simulates backward reasoning in forward reasoning by clause transformation. *Magic* predicates are first computed to generate inference demands, and then the inference is performed based on forward reasoning triggered by the demands. In other words, this method is intuitively bottom-up inference on demand.

In general it is necessary to analyse the modes of predicates to apply the magic-set method. In the case of Progol, the costs of the mode analysis and clause transformation can be decreased by using mode declarations. Normal clause transformation is done based on the mode of target predicate.

However, in general, since each antecedent in created candidate hypothesis has different mode, whenever a newly candidate is created, we need to analyse modes and transformation against all clauses including given background knowledge for every newly created candidate.

To reduce the cost of this analysis and transformation, we employ magic-set method based on not actual modes but mode declarations. The modes are decided independent from the created candidate hypotheses by utilizing mode declarations. Hence the given background knowledge can be transformed only once as a pre-process for coverage check.

MG-clauses with magic-set for a candidate hypothesis '$reverse([A|B], C) \leftarrow append(B, [A], C).$' and a background knowledge '$append([], A, A).$' are shown in Fig.3.

$\leftarrow modeh(1, reverse([+int| + list], -list))?$
$\leftarrow modeb(1, append(+list, [+int], -list))?$

$\%reverse([A|B], C) : -append(B, [A], C).$
$magic\_reverse([X|Y]), append(Y, [X], Z) \rightarrow reverse([X|Y], Z).$

$\%append([], A, A).$
$magic\_append([], X) \rightarrow append([], X, X).$

Fig. 3. Examples of Magic transformation

4.3 Recovering Range-restricted Condition

In many cases the range-restricted condition of an MG-clause can be recovered by magic-set method. However it is not the case for the candidate hypotheses. In general, if the I/O relation of a clause is incomplete, then the magic-set transformation cannot recover the range-restricted condition.

That is *dom* predicates are required to deal with the I/O incomplete candidates, and therefore the serious problem of *dom*-explosion comes up to the surface again.

We show the improved method for non-recursive and recursive candidate hypotheses respectively to avoid this problem.

Non-recursive Hypothesis For each non-recursive candidate hypothesis, a literal '*exam*' which denotes an example is simply added to its antecedent. Also an atom '$exam(E_i)$' corresponding to each example E_i is stored in the initial model. That is, instead of empty model ϕ, MGTP begins with $exam(E_i)$ as the initial model, Let us show a simple example in Fig.4.

$\leftarrow modeh(1, p(+int, -int))?$ $\%magic\ transformation\ +\ exam$
$example : p(A, B).$ $exam(p(A, B)), magic\_p(A), f(A, C)$
$candidate : p(A, B) : -f(A, C). \Rightarrow$ $\rightarrow p(A, B).$

Fig. 4. An example of transformation of non-recursive hypothesis

The added literal '$exam(p(A, B))$' not only recovers the candidate's range-restricted condition, but also plays the role of a filter. Therefore the intersection of E and the set of atoms derived by MGTP can be obtained directly in the inference process.

Recursive Hypothesis The improved method for recursive candidate hypothesis first selects some literals in MSH, and then adds these to the antecedent of candidate to make it an I/O complete hypothesis. In [4] we introduced the idea of 'path-set', which is a set of literals needed for a given hypothesis to satisfy the I/O complete condition in order to estimate Progol's heuristic function. Our improved method uses the path-set, not to estimate the heuristic function, but to select literals for I/O completion. Let us explain this with the example in Fig.5.

$$MSH : p(A^+, B^-) : -f(A^+, C^-, D^-), g(C^+, D^-), p(D^+, E^-),$$
$$i(E^+, E^+, F^-), j(D^+, E^+, B^-).$$
$$Candidate : p(A^+, B^-) : -f(A^+, C^-, D^-), p(D^+, E^-).$$
$$New\ Candidate : p(A^+, B^-) : -f(A^+, C^-, D^-), h(D^+, E^-), j(D^+, E^+, B^-).$$

Fig. 5. An example of transformation of recursive hypothesis

Since this candidate needs at least one literal j to become I/O complete, a new candidate is obtained from the original by adding the literal j. Then we apply magic-transformation to the new candidate.

By applying this method to the search process, only I/O complete candidates will be selectively created and evaluated. Since the correct hypothesis must be I/O complete, this method preserves the search completeness.

5 Redundant Computation in Progol's A^*-like Algorithm

As a whole, Progol may have some kinds of redundant computations in coverage check for hypotheses evaluation. These kinds of redundancy can be divided into two categories: (1)Duplicate Computation and (2)Irrelevant Computation.

5.1 Duplicate Computation

Consider the following case where a newly candidate hypothesis
$$f(A) \leftarrow h(A), i(A). \quad (\mathcal{H}_0)$$
is created and to be evaluated. Progol sets each example as a Prolog goal and executes it for the evaluation. Let "? $- f(e)$." be such a Prolog goal. Then $\mathcal{H}_0$ is called and the goal is replaced by a new goal "? $- h(e), i(e)$.", for further evaluation.

On the other hand, as described previously, another candidate hypothesis
$$f(A) \leftarrow h(A), i(A), j(A). \quad (\mathcal{H}_1)$$
is created by adding one literal to the antecedent of $\mathcal{H}_0$. When $\mathcal{H}_1$ is called, the given goal is replaced by "? $- h(e), i(e), j(e)$.". Consider the evaluation of the new goal. Since the first two predicate calls are exactly the same as the previous goal, the Progol's A^*-like search algorithm duplicates the same computation on this part.

As showed above, the coverage check in A^*-like algorithm contains a large amount of duplicate computations in all.

5.2 Irrelevant Computation

Furthermore the coverage check in Progol contains another kind of redundancy. Let us explain it with the above case. $\mathcal{H}_1$ is more restricted and specific than $\mathcal{H}_0$ because $\mathcal{H}_1$ must be created from $\mathcal{H}_0$. Therefore the examples which have not been covered by $\mathcal{H}_0$ can not be covered by $\mathcal{H}_1$. Despite of this important feature, whenever a new candidate is created, Progol checks whether each given example is covered by it. This drawback makes worse the efficiency in the case of dealing with a large number of examples.

6 Removing Redundancy by extended MGTP

As described in section2, MGTP keeps the result of inference $i.$ $e.$ the results of coverage check in the models. By making the most effective use of this feature, the redundant computation can be naturally and easily removed.

6.1 Removing Duplicate Computation

First, a new algorithm for removing duplicate computation is considered. In the coverage check of a newly created candidate hypothesis, the inference results of its parent hypothesis can be utilized to avoid duplication.

For example, in the case of executing MGTP for evaluation of $\mathcal{H}_1$, the result of $\mathcal{H}_0$ is utilized as an initial model. The result of $\mathcal{H}_0$ contains $h(e),i(e)$ corresponding to covered example, therefore the only inference of $j(e)$ is required. For $h(e)$ and $i(e)$, not inference but matching is required.

Several candidate hypotheses may be created from one parent hypothesis. In that case the initial model can be shared. This model sharing is realized by regarding MGTP's model splitting for the disjunctive consequent as the splitting for the newly created candidates.

This extended MGTP technology, $i.$ $e.$ utilizing the inference result and its sharing, is more effective when a candidate hypothesis has several literals in its antecedents and when intensional background knowledge is used.

6.2 Removing Irrelevant Computation

The second redundant computation of Progol is due to irrelevant coverage check. The function of keeping the result of coverage check for each example is required to avoid this redundancy.

MGTP can provide this function naturally and efficiently. Since MGTP contains only the derived atoms in its model, the covered examples must be in the model, and therefore we can extract the covered examples from the model. That is to say the result of coverage check is held in the model as the covered examples themselves. Note that the covered examples by the parent candidate, *i.e* the derived atoms from the parent candidate, should be the objects of the next coverage check.

7 Conclusion and Future Work

In this paper, we presented an alternative algorithm of coverage check by MGTP. It computes a set of covered examples by candidate hypothesis together with background knowledge at a time in opposition to Progol's one by one coverage check. This method makes use of magic-set like MSH construction[4]. Furthermore we described some improved methods of this computation.

A^*-like algorithm by using MGTP was also described. We pointed out the redundant computations in this process, and introduced an extended MGTP technique which can suppress these redundancies. Since most of the time in executing the entire task will be spent at the search process, we can expect a high degree of efficiency of the system by this method.

References

1. Beeri, C. and Ramakrishnan, R.: On the Power of Magic, *J.* of Logic Programming, Vol. 10, pp.255-299 (1991).
2. Ishizuka, M.: Computational Cost of Hypothetical Reasoning and Its Fast Inference Mechanism, *J.* of Japanese Society for Artificial Intelligence, Vol. 9, No. 3, pp.342-349 (1994).
3. Fujita, H. and Hasegawa, R.: A Model Generation Theorem Prover in KL1 Using a Ramified-Stack Algorithm, *Proc.* of the 8th International Conference of Logic Programming, pp.535-548 (1991).
4. H.Fujita, N.Yagi, T.Ozaki, K.Furukawa. A New Design and Implementation of Progol by Bottom-up Computation. *Proc. of the 6th International Workshop on Inductive Logic Programming*, 1996.
5. Muggleton, S. and Feng, C.: Efficient Induction of Logic Programs. *Proc.* First Conference on Algorithmic Learning Theory, pp.368-381, Ohmsha, Tokyo (1990).
6. Muggleton, S.: Inverse entailment and Progol, *New Generation Computing*, 13, pp.245-286 (1995).
7. Ozaki, T., Furukawa, K., Murakami, T. and Ueno, K.: Improving A^*-like search in Progol by the Input/Output Relation of Variables, SIG-FAI-9701, pp.30-35 (1997).
8. Quinlan, J. R. and Cameron-jones, R. M.: Induction of Logic Programs: FOIL and Related Systems. *New Generation Computing,* 13, pp.287-312 (1995).
9. Shapiro, E.: Inductive Inference of Theories from Facts, *Research Report 192*, Department of Computer Science, Yale University (1981).

Probabilistic First-Order Classification

Uroš Pompe and Igor Kononenko

University of Ljubljana, Faculty of Computer and Information Science,
Tržaška 25, SI-1001 Ljubljana, Slovenia
tel: +386-61-1768 386 fax: +386-61-1768 386
e-mail: {uros.pompe, igor.kononenko}@fri.uni-lj.si

Abstract. We discuss the problem of classification using the first order hypotheses. This paper proposes an enhancement of classification based on the naive Bayesian scheme that is able to overcome the conditional independence assumption. Several experiments, involving some artificial and real-world, both propositional and relational domains, were conducted. The results indicate that the classification performance of propositional learners is reached when the richer first-order knowledge representation is not mandatory. This holds also in the domains where such representation is more convenient. Our framework can also benefit from the use of the hypotheses describing negative information. In such case, the classification becomes more noise resistant.

1 Introduction

One of the reasons that propositional learners sometimes achieve better classification results than their relational siblings, coming from the field of *Inductive Logic Programming* (ILP) (Muggleton 1992), is probably that the former often employ probabilistic reasoning techniques to obtain additional information from the hypotheses and use it to classify new examples.

The probabilistic aspects of the hypothesis were considered before within ILP (Muggleton 1996; Pompe and Kononenko 1995b; Ali and Pazzani 1993). The HYDRA system (Ali and Pazzani 1993) uses probabilistic evaluation of clauses to determine the reliability of the clause and returns the class of the most reliable clause that covers the test example. In (Pompe and Kononenko 1995b), we developed the first-order naive Bayesian classifier that is, in contrast to HYDRA, able to take into account the redundant information when available. The present paper extends this work by introducing a mechanism of extracting additional information from the hypothesis and by handling the dependencies between the classification rules.

Section 2 contains a quick overview of the previous work. The main contribution of the paper is described in Sect. 3. In Sect. 4, we evaluate the performance of our probabilistic scheme on a series of artificial and one real world domain. The final section contains the summary of our findings.

2 Probabilistic Classification

The common way of using the first-order hypothesis is to interpret it procedurally. More formally (Lloyd 1987), given the hypothesis $\mathcal{H}$, which is in our case a *normal program* without *function symbols* (except constants), the background knowledge B, and an unclassified example e_t, we are looking for the *first computed answer* θ_c obtained with SLDNF-resolution of the goal $\leftarrow e_t$. The class can be encoded with either a sign of the example, or with *ground substitution* $\theta = \{v_1/F_1, \ldots, v_n/F_n\}$ where it holds $domain(\theta) \subseteq vars(e_t)$. The variables in the set $domain(\theta)$ are called the *class variables*. To alleviate the problem of insufficient instantiation a *default rule* is used in our procedural classifier. If the instantiation of the class variables fails, this rule returns the majority class.

Hypothesis $\mathcal{H}$ can be viewed alternatively as a set of *classification rules* $\mathcal{H} = \{C_1, \ldots C_n\}$. Given the probability distribution P_F over the set of possible classes $F = \{F_1, \ldots, F_r\}$, and the conditional probability distributions $P(F_i|C_j)$ over the set of learning examples E, we can compute the probability of the class of the new instance e_t by the formula

$$\tilde{P}(F_i|\mathcal{H}_\lambda) = P(F_i) \prod_{C_j \in \mathcal{H}_\lambda} \frac{P(F_i|C_j)}{P(F_i)} \; , \tag{1}$$

where $\mathcal{H}_\lambda$ is the set of classification rules covering e_t. The formula assumes that the classification rules are *conditionally independent*. Recently, Domingos and Pazzani (1996) showed that this was not such a strong assumption as it had been thought before. The probabilities $P(F_i)$ are computed using the *Laplace's law of succession* while the conditional probabilities $P(F_i|C_j)$ are assessed using the *m-estimate* (Cestnik 1990) over the set of covered learning examples.

Similarly to the procedural case, the hypothesis $\mathcal{H}$ is augmented with the *closed world assumption* classification rule (CWA rule). This is an implicit rule covering the examples $E - Cov(\mathcal{H}, E)$, where $Cov(T, S)$ denotes the set of examples $\{e : \leftarrow e$ is refutable in $T \cup B\}$. . For the binary classification, another enhancement can be applied when the hypothesis $\mathcal{H}$ is non-recursive. We can reverse the sign of examples in the training set and the system can learn learn the *negative* hypothesis $\mathcal{H}^-$ which describes the negative class from the original training examples. The two hypotheses $(\mathcal{H}, \mathcal{H}^-)$ are then merged and the resulting hypothesis is given to our Bayesian classifier. We will show later empirically, this technique improves the predictive power of the classifier.

3 Extracting Additional Information

3.1 Splitting and Merging Clauses

The basic element of the inference scheme described above is a normal clause that covers a given instance. To extract more information from the hypothesis $\mathcal{H}$ we need to consider also clauses that "partially" cover the instance. For that purpose, we shall for each clause $C \in \mathcal{H}$ generate a set of clauses as follows: In a greedy manner we try to split the clause C_{jk} into two clauses C_j and C_k with syntactic limitations as described below. Then we test whether the two new clauses satisfy the independence condition ((4) in Sect. 3.2). If the condition is satisfied then the original clause C_{jk} is retained and the process is terminated. Otherwise, the process of splitting the clauses is recursively repeated on both C_j and C_k. We call this process "the inner clause splitting." If we look at the hypothesis $\mathcal{H}$ from the logical point of view, the inference rule having the weakest precondition (and based on the hypothesis $\mathcal{H}$) is a clause of the form:

$$Head(C) \leftarrow L. \qquad , L \in Body(C) \wedge C \in \mathcal{H}. \qquad (2)$$

We can easily see that many such rules do not make much sense.

Example 1. Given the clause:

```
mesh(A,N) :- long(A), neighbour(A,C),
             opposite(A,D), not(fixed(C)),
             equal(D,E), not_loaded(E).
```

and according to Formula 2 we obtain the set of rules

$$\{ \ mesh(A, N) \leftarrow long(A). \ , mesh(A, N) \leftarrow neighbour(A, C). \ ,$$
$$mesh(A, N) \leftarrow opposite(A, D). \ , mesh(A, N) \leftarrow not(fixed(C)). \ ,$$
$$mesh(A, N) \leftarrow equal(D, E). \ , mesh(A, N) \leftarrow not\_loaded(E).\} \ .$$

The fourth rule clearly violates the restrictions of the SLDNF-resolution as the non-ground negative literals should never be reached. The last two clauses are not interesting either since they represent nothing but the most trivial test for the provability of literals in their bodies. ■

We demand that the bodies of the generated rules are linked. Accordingly, the rules from (2) are merged in such a way that we obtain only linked clauses. After performing this step, it could happen that some rules subsume some other rules. We retain only the most specific rule in such a subsumption chain.

Example 2. After merging the rules from Example 1 we obtain:

1. $mesh(A, N) \leftarrow long(A).$
2. $mesh(A, N) \leftarrow neighbour(A, C), not(fixed(C)).$
3. $mesh(A, N) \leftarrow opposite(A, D), equal(D, E).$
4. $mesh(A, N) \leftarrow opposite(A, D), equal(D, E), not\_loaded(E).$

The third rule subsumes the fourth, so only the latter is retained. ■

In order to generate the final set of rules an additional preprocessing is needed to insure that the resulting rules satisfy our independence assumption from Sect. 2. Namely, the above generalization step can yield rules to become conditionally dependent. We therefore in a greedy manner search for dependent pairs of clauses and recursively join their bodies. We call this process "the inter clause merging." The next subsection defines when the two clauses are considered dependent.

3.2 Testing the Independence of Classification Rules

The question still remains how the dependence of rules is verified. If we look again at (1) we can see that the influence of two rules C'_j and C'_k is given by

$$\frac{P(F_i|C'_j)}{P(F_i)} \times P(F_i|C'_k) \quad . \tag{3}$$

We want to check whether this influence significantly differs from the influence of the joint rule C'_{jk}. Let θ be the *most general unifier* of atoms $Head(C'_j)$ and $Head(C'_k)$. Then C'_{jk} is a clause $(C'_j \cup C'_k)\theta$ and its influence on the class F_i is given by $P(F_i|C'_{jk})$. The approach we have taken is similar to the one described in (Kononenko 1991). We treat the rules C'_l as binary attributes. Let A be an atom from the set of atoms $\mathcal{U}$. C'_l is *true* over A if $A \in Cov(C'_l, \mathcal{U})$ and *false* otherwise. The coverage of C'_l is computed as described in Sect. 2 with a noticeable exception that the body of C'_l is proved in terms of the original hypothesis $\mathcal{H}$. That way, the meaning of the recursive predicate calls is preserved. Now we can use the theorem of Chebyshev for the estimation of the reliability of the probability approximation (see (Kononenko 1991) for details). The Chebyshev test was preferred over the chi-square because of its greater reliability when dealing with small number of training examples. The rules C'_j and C'_k are joint if the following inequality is satisfied:

$$1 - \frac{1}{4\epsilon^2 |Cov(C'_{jk}, E)|} \geq D_t \quad , \tag{4}$$

where D_t is the *dependency threshold*. ϵ is the average difference between (3) and $P(F_i|C'_{jk})$ over all classes. Both ϵ and $|Cov(C'_{jk}, E)|$ are non-negative, therefore the left hand side of (4) is always strictly smaller than 1.

Through the two step transformation of the original hypothesis $\mathcal{H}$, we actually use two different values of D_t. One for the inner clause splitting (D_{tc}) and one for the inter clause merging (D_{th}). If we set these parameters appropriately ($D_{tc} = -\infty, D_{th} = 1$), the classifier behaves identically to the naive Bayesian classifier from Sect. 2.

4 Evaluation

In order to evaluate our classification methodology we conducted a series of experiments involving artificial and real-world data sets. We used data from several propositional domains and two relational domains. The starting hypotheses were generated using ILP-R (Pompe and Kononenko 1995a). All propositional problems were transformed into equivalent relational ones as in (Pompe and Kononenko 1995b). When learning in such domains the use of recursion was not allowed. The value of parameter m (from *m-estimate*) was set to 2.0 in all experiments.

Where not specified otherwise, we performed 10-fold cross validation. When comparing results of different classification methodologies we used the two-tailed t-test with the confidence level of 99%.

4.1 Propositional Domains

BAYS: An artificial domain with 5 relevant attributes with decreasing relevance and with 5 random attributes. The relevant attributes are conditionally independent. The classification accuracy of the propositional naive Bayesian classifier is 80%, while the decision trees achieve around 70%.

P3,P4: The parity problem of order 3 and with 10 additional random attributes and 5% class noise.

BOOL: A Boolean function defined on 6 attributes with 10% of class noise (optimal recognition rate is 90%).

LED: A LED-digits problem with 10% of noise in attribute values. The optimal recognition rate is estimated to be 74%.

MESH15ATT: Contains, besides the 3 original attributes, 12 attributes derived from the relational background knowledge.

4.2 Relational Domains

MESH5R: This is the original finite element mesh design problem (Dolšak and Muggleton 1992). The testing procedure is a special case of leave-one-out. The results for classification accuracy reported by Džeroski (1991) are 22 % of for mFOIL and 29 % for GOLEM. Quinlan (1996) reports 21% for FOIL and 44% for FFOIL.

MESH5RS10: The same data as above but this time the testing was done by 10-fold cross validation.

KRK: The problem of legality of the King-Rook-King chess endgame. We collected the data from the original 5 random set of 100 examples each (Džeroski 1991). The resulting set was used for 10-fold cross validation except that we used the whole data set (5000 examples) for testing.

4.3 Results and Discussion

The ILP-R system can use two search heuristics (information gain and *Relief* based). We will show only the results with *Relief*. For comparison, Table 1 (taken from (Kononenko, Šimec, and Robnik 1996)) shows the classification accuracy of the state-of-the-art propositional learners on some of the domains. The results were obtained by averaging over 30 random splits, 70% for learning, 30% for testing.

Table 1. Classification accuracy of different propositional learning systems.

domain	LFC	Assistant-I	Assistant-R	naive Bayes	k-NN
BOOL	89.0 ± 1.6	89.0 ± 1.6	89.0 ± 1.6	66.6 ± 2.5	89.8 ± 1.6
P3	84.1 ± 10.1	65.6 ± 11.0	95.7 ± 2.1	55.5 ± 5.2	60.4 ± 6.7
P4	69.4 ± 13.8	59.3 ± 11.0	94.8 ± 1.6	55.1 ± 3.4	61.9 ± 3.8
LED	70.8 ± 2.3	71.1 ± 2.4	71.7 ± 2.2	73.9 ± 2.1	73.9 ± 2.1
MESH15	39.2	41.0	42.4	34.5	35.3

Table 2 shows results when interpreting the hypothesis naively. The second column represents experiments where only the original clauses were naively combined. The third column shows the classification accuracy when the clauses were split. Naive bayes performs identically as procedural classification on the two-class domains (BAYS, BOOL, P3, P4) as expected. It performs significantly better on the LED domain. The LED and the BAYS domains have an additional property of background knowledge being conditionally independent. The performance of totally naive interpretation is the highest for these two domains. However, the approach of splitting the clause is not well suited for in cases where there are strong dependencies between the literals (BOOL, P3, P4). The trouble with the MESH domains is the lack of generality of the hypotheses.

Table 2. Procedural, naive Bayes ($D_{tc} = -\infty, D_{th} = 1$), and totally naive ($D_{tc} = 1, D_{th} = 1$) interpretation. CWA rule in each case.

domain	Proc.	naive Bayes	naive
BAYS	71.5 ± 7.8	71.5 ± 7.8	76.5 ± 9.5
BOOL	88.6 ± 4.4	88.6 ± 4.4	53.1 ± 7.5
P3	95.0 ± 4.5	95.0 ± 4.5	53.5 ± 11.2
P4	94.0 ± 4.8	94.0 ± 4.8	55.0 ± 12.0
LED	33.6 ± 3.5	68.3 ± 4.1	73.1 ± 3.1
MESH5RS10	74.1 ± 7.6	77.3 ± 8.2	59.7 ± 6.5
MESH15ATT	34.5	37.4	37.8
MESH5R	34.5	33.5	31.3

We also compared the performance of our probabilistic classifier on the two-class domains, when we added negative rules to the hypothesis, with the classification accuracy using default CWA reasoning. In Table 3 the classification accuracy is almost alway increased with the addition of negative rules. The exceptions are the results for the naive interpretation for P3 and P4. These are due to the inappropriate classification technique.

Table 3. CWA rule vs. combined hypothesis ($\mathcal{H}+\mathcal{H}^-$); naive Bayes ($D_{tc} = -\infty, D_{th} = 1$), and totally naive interpretation ($D_{tc} = 1, D_{th} = 1$)

	$D_{tc} = -\infty, D_{th} = 1$		$D_{tc} = 1, D_{th} = 1$	
domain	$\mathcal{H}$	$\mathcal{H} + \mathcal{H}^-$	$\mathcal{H}$	$\mathcal{H} + \mathcal{H}^-$
BAYS	71.5 ± 7.8	72.0 ± 11.9	76.5 ± 9.5	80.0 ± 8.4
BOOL	88.6 ± 4.4	90.0 ± 3.8	53.1 ± 7.5	83.3 ± 5.9
P3	95.0 ± 4.5	96.0 ± 3.7	53.5 ± 11.2	51.5 ± 11.4
P4	94.0 ± 4.8	95.5 ± 3.5	55.0 ± 12.0	53.0 ± 9.5

We tested our classifier for the noise resistance. Table 4 compares the performance of the procedural classifier with the naive Bayes on the KRK domain. The hypotheses are augmented with the negative rules. The Bayesian interpretation performs worse when no noise is present. As expected, it achieves higher classification accuracy when noise is introduced.

Table 4. Greater noise resistance on KRK domain (proc. vs. naive Bayes)

Noise %	Proc.	naiveBayes
0	99.8 ± 0.0	98.7 ± 0.0
5	92.7 ± 0.8	97.2 ± 0.6
10	85.8 ± 0.7	88.8 ± 1.3
15	81.3 ± 1.9	82.8 ± 2.2
20	75.4 ± 2.6	77.9 ± 1.7
30	68.1 ± 1.4	70.8 ± 2.0
50	59.7 ± 1.6	62.1 ± 2.2
80	52.5 ± 1.3	54.3 ± 0.9

Finally, we also performed experiments where the Bayesian classifier was dependency-aware ($D_{tc} = 0.5, D_{th} = 0.5$). This semi-naive version behaved somewhere in between the naive Bayes and the totally naive interpretation. It was able to detect dependencies in P3 and P4 domains but it had trouble with the clauses covering noisy examples. While it was able to retain the relevant relationships within the clause, the noisy clauses were usually split (over-generalization) since the noise is by definition independent of the class.

5 Conclusions

Our approach to classification with the first-order theories introduced additional parameterization. If we have information about the properties of the background knowledge and hypothesis, whether or not the clauses and the background predicates are conditionally independent of each other, the experimentation may not be necessary. If this information is not available it can be quickly retrieved by performing few experiments with carefully selected values for D_{tc} and D_{th}.

The presented Bayesian classification scheme can benefit from the redundant information. As a special case, in the two-class domains, the positive and the negative hypothesis can be merged to give higher classification results and better noise resistance.

Particularly in multi-class domains, we can achieve much better classification accuracy than with the common procedural interpretation. The latter only returns the first computed answer which may not always be what we want. The Bayesian classification is able to take into account also the computed answers that are reached later during the resolution.

And finally, further work should be concentrated on automating the selection of appropriate parameter values D_{tc} and D_{th}.

References

[Ali and Pazzani 1993] Ali, K. M. and M. J. Pazzani (1993). Hydra: A noise-tolerant relational concept learning algorithm. In *Proceedings of the 13th IJCAI*, Chambery, France, pp. 1064–1070.

[Cestnik 1990] Cestnik, B. (1990). Estimating probabilities: A crucial task in machine learning. In *Proceedings of European Conference on Artificial Intelligence*, Stockholm, pp. 147–149.

[Dolšak and Muggleton 1992] Dolšak, B. and S. Muggleton (1992). The application of inductive logic programming to finite elements mesh design. In S. Muggleton (Ed.), *Inductive Logic Programming*. Academic Press.

[Domingos and Pazzani 1996] Domingos, P. and M. J. Pazzani (1996). Beyond independence: Conditions for the optimality of the simple Bayesian classifier. In L. Saitta (Ed.), *Proceedings of the Thirteenth International Conference on Machine Learning*, Bari, Italy, pp. 105–112. Morgan Kaufman.

[Džeroski 1991] Džeroski, S. (1991). Handling noise in inductive logic programming. Master's thesis, University of Ljubljana, Faculty of electrical engineering and computer science, Ljubljana, Slovenia.

[Kononenko 1991] Kononenko, I. (1991). Semi-naive Bayesian classifier. In Y. Kodratoff (Ed.), *Proceedings of European Working Session on Learning*, Porto, pp. 206–219. Springer Verlag.

[Kononenko, Šimec, and Robnik 1996] Kononenko, I., E. Šimec, and M. Robnik (1996). Overcoming the myopia of inductive learning algorithms with ReliefF. Journal of Applied Intelligence.

[Lloyd 1987] Lloyd, J. W. (1987). *Foundations of Logic Programming* (Second ed.). Berlin, Germany: Springer Verlag.

[Muggleton 1992] Muggleton, S. (1992). *Inductive Logic Programming*. London, England: Academic Press.

[Muggleton 1996] Muggleton, S. (1996). Stochastic logic programs. In L. De Raedt (Ed.), *Advances in Inductive Logic Programming*, pp. 254–264. Amsterdam, Netherlands: IOS Press.

[Pompe and Kononenko 1995a] Pompe, U. and I. Kononenko (1995a). Linear space induction in first order logic with Relief. In R. Kruse, R. Viertl, and G. Della Riccia (Eds.), *CISM Lecture notes*. Udine, Italy: Springer Verlag.

[Pompe and Kononenko 1995b] Pompe, U. and I. Kononenko (1995b). Naive bayesian classifier within ILP-R. In L. De Raedt (Ed.), *Proceedings of the 5th International Workshop on ILP*, Leuven, Belgium, pp. 417–436. Katholieke Universiteit Leuven.

[Quinlan 1996] Quinlan, J. R. (1996). Learning first-order definitions of functions. *Journal of Artificial Intelligence Research 5*, 139–161.

Learning Horn Definitions with Equivalence and Membership Queries

Chandra Reddy & Prasad Tadepalli

Dearborn 303, Department of Computer Science
Oregon State University, Corvallis, OR-97331. USA
Phone: +1 541 753 2770; Fax: +1 541 737 3014
{reddyc,tadepalli}@cs.orst.edu

Abstract. A Horn definition is a set of Horn clauses with the same head literal. In this paper, we consider learning non-recursive, function-free first-order Horn definitions. We show that this class is exactly learnable from equivalence and membership queries. It follows then that this class is PAC learnable using examples and membership queries. Our results have been shown to be applicable to learning efficient goal-decomposition rules in planning domains.

1 Introduction

In this paper, we consider learning Horn definitions — multiple Horn clauses with a single head — in the exact learning model [Angluin, 1988]. Learning Horn definitions is a fundamental problem both in the Inductive Logic Programming (ILP) literature as well as the Computational Learning Theory literature. Since it is NP-hard to test membership in this concept class, it immediately follows that even non-recursive function-free Horn definitions are hard to learn from examples alone [Schapire, 1990]. Using only equivalence queries, single non-recursive Prolog clauses are learnable [Cohen, 1995a, Džeroski, Muggleton, & Russell, 1992] with restrictions such as determinacy and bounded arity. Restricted versions of single recursive clauses are also shown to be learnable [Cohen, 1995b]. However, learning multiple clauses or even slightly more general versions of either recursive or non-recursive clauses is shown to be hard without further help [Cohen, 1995c]. Page [1993] has shown that non-recursive Horn defintions with predicates having fixed arity and with the restriction that only the variables that occur in the head literal of a clause appear in the body of the clause are learnable using equivalence and subset queries. In this paper, we examine the learnability of a more general class.

In particular, we show that first-order non-recursive function-free Horn definitions are exactly learnable from membership and equivalence queries with no other restrictions. Our approach is similar to Angluin's algorithm for learning Propositional Monotone DNF [Angluin, 1988]. The algorithm exploits the fact that there is at most one positive literal in a Horn clause, which makes it possible to show that any clause which is implied by the target must be subsumed by one of the clauses in the target. Our membership queries, in effect, check whether a hypothesis clause is subsumed by a target clause. Since it is NP-complete to decide subsumption, for the teacher to answer the membership queries efficiently, in practice, the hypothesis language should be restricted so that deciding subsumption is efficient. Kietz and Lübbe [1994] show that the restrictions to determinate clauses or to constant-locailty clauses make deciding subsumption a polynomial-time problem.

Our research is motivated by a practical application that involves learning goal-decomposition rules (d-rules) in planning. We show that this problem can be reduced to one of learning Horn definitions, which enabled us to apply our learning algorithm for Horn definitions to efficiently learn d-rules.

The rest of the paper is organized as follows: Section 2 presents some formal preliminaries about Horn definitions. Section 3 describes the learning problem, proves some properties of Horn definitions, describes the learning algorithm and proves its correctness. Section 4 employs this result to show that goal-decomposition rules are learnable. Section 5 concludes the paper by mentioning some implications of this result.

2 Preliminaries

In this section, we define and describe the terms we use in the rest of the paper, omitting some of the standard terminology and notation of logic (as given in standard books such as [Lloyd, 1987]).

Definition 1. A **Horn clause** is a finite (multi)set of literals that contains at most one positive literal. It is treated as a disjunction of the literals in the set with universal quantification over all the variables. The positive literal, if it exists, is called the *head* of the clause. A Horn clause is **function-free** if it does not contain any function symbols of arity 1 or more.[1] A Horn clause is **non-recursive** if the head of the Horn clause occurs only as a positive literal.

Definition 2. A **function-free Horn definition** is a set of function-free Horn clauses with all clauses having the same head literal. It is **non-recursive** if the head literal does not occur as a negative literal in any clause in the definition.

Definition 3. A clause D **subsumes** a clause E if there exists a substitution θ such that $D\theta \subseteq E$.[2] We denote this as $D \succeq E$, and read it as D subsumes E or as D is more general than E.

Definition 4. If D and E are clauses such that $D \succeq E$, then a literal l in a clause E is relevant (irrelevant) w.r.t the clause D, if $D \not\succeq E - \{l\}$ ($D \succeq E - \{l\}$, respectively).

---

[1] Note that this definition of a function-free Horn clause allows constants—functions with arity-0.

[2] Note that when we say $D \subseteq E$, we mean that all the *literals* in D are also in E—but not that the extension of D is in the extension of E. Also, $|D|$ is the number of literals in D, and not the size of the extension.

Definition 5. If C and D are two clauses such that $D \succeq E$, then a **condensation** of E w.r.t. D is a clause E' such that $E' \subseteq E$, $D \succeq E'$, and for any $l \in E'$, $D \not\succeq E' - \{l\}$.

For example, if $D = \{\neg l_1(x), l_2(y)\}$ and $E = \{\neg l_1(a), l_2(b), l_2(c), l_3(c)\}$, then both $\{\neg l_1(a), l_2(b)\}$ and $\{\neg l_1(a), l_2(c)\}$ are condensations of E w.r.t. D.

Definition 6. Least general generalization of a set of clauses S over $\succeq$ is a clause D such that (1) for every E in S, $D \succeq E$, and (2) if there exists a clause F such that for every E in S, $F \succeq E$, then $F \succeq D$.

The definitions 3 and 6 are due to Plotkin[1970]. For a proof of existence of least general generalization see [Plotkin, 1970] and [Nienhuys-Cheng & de Wolf, 1996].

We follow the description in [Muggleton & Feng, 1990] of Plotkin's algorithm to find the least general generalizations (lgg) of a set of clauses. The lgg of two clauses C_1 and C_2 is $\bigcup_{p_1 \in C_1, p_2 \in C_2} lgg(p_1, p_2)$. The lgg of two predicates $p(a_1, a_2 \ldots a_n)$ and $p(b_1, b_2 \ldots b_n)$ is $\{p(lgg(a_1, b_1), lgg(a_2, b_2) \ldots lgg(a_n, b_n))\}$; if the predicate symbols are not equal, their sign differs or their arity differs, then their lgg is $\{\}$, the empty set. The lgg of two terms a and b is itself, if they are the same; else, it is a variable v, where v stands for $lgg(a, b)$ throughout the computation of the lgg of the pair of clauses.

For example, let $C_1 = \{\neg l_1(a, b), \neg l_2(a, c), l_3(b)\}$ and $C_2 = \{\neg l_1(c, d), \neg l_1(b, a), \neg l_2(c, c), l_3(a)\}$. Then $lgg(C_1, C_2) = \{\neg l_1(x, y), \neg l_1(z, u), \neg l_2(x, c), l_3(u)\}$, where the variables x, y, z and u stand for the pairs $lgg(a, c)$, $lgg(b, d)$, $lgg(a, b)$ and $lgg(b, a)$, respectively.

Note that $|lgg(C_1, C_2)|$ can be equal to $|C_1| \times |C_2|$.

Lemma 7. Let C_1, H_1 and H_2 be Horn clauses. Then $C_1 \succeq H_1$ and $C_1 \succeq H_2$ if and only if $C_1 \succeq lgg(H_1, H_2)$.

Proof. The only-if part follows from the property (2) of the definition of least-general generalization. The if part follows from the transitive property of $\succeq$. □

We state the following fact explicitly, although it is straightforward, for it is useful later.

Proposition 8. If $C_1 \succeq H_1$ then $C_1 \succeq H_2$ for any H_2 such that $H_1 \subseteq H_2$.

3 Learning Horn Definitions

In this section, we first specify our learning problem. Next we describe the learning algorithm and then give the learnability result.

3.1 Learning Problem

Our learning problem is motivated by learning control knowledge for planning in structural domains. The following definitions reflect that motivation.

A *scene* is a conjunction of positive ground literals describing a set of objects.[3] We call the predicates that occur in scenes *base predicates*. We differentiate the base predicates from a special predicate called the *goal predicate*. An *instance* is a 2-tuple comprising a scene *scene* and a ground goal literal g, meaning that g is true in *scene*. We alternately write an instance as a clause *scene* $\rightarrow$ g.

We consider the hypothesis space of Horn definitions for the goal predicate. An instance $\langle scene, g \rangle$ is in a hypothesis H iff the minimal model of H with respect to the literals in *scene* satisfies g. In other words, $\langle scene, g \rangle$ is an instance of H iff $H \models (scene \rightarrow g)$. Such an instance is a *positive example* of H. All other instances are *negative examples*.

Henceforth, Σ denotes the target concept in the hypothesis space.

Example 1. The following illustrates the above definitions in a toy version of an air-traffic control domain.
$\Sigma = \{$
```
((plane-at ?p ?loc) (level L1 ?loc) (free-runway ?r)
(short-runway ?r) (can-land-short ?p)) → (land-plane ?p),
((plane-at ?p ?loc) (level L1 ?loc) (free-runway ?r)
(long-runway ?r)) → (land-plane ?p)
```
$\}$
The first clause in Σ gives the conditions under which a plane can land on short runways. The second clause is for long-runway landing. The following is a positive example of Σ (for the second clause):
```
((plane-at P737 10) (lelvel L1 10) (free-runway R1) (long-runway R1)
(short-runway R2) (wind-speed high) (wind-dir south) (free-runway R2))
→ (land-plane P737).                                                  □
```

Before stating the learning problem, we define the queries we will need [Angluin, 1988]. A *membership query* takes as input an instance x, and outputs *yes* if x is in Σ, and *no* otherwise. An *equivalence query* takes as input a set H of hypotheses, and outputs *yes* if the set of instances in H is the same as the set of instances in Σ; otherwise, returns a *counterexample* from $H \oplus \Sigma$ —i.e., an instance that is in one but not in the other.

The learning problem in the exact learning framework [Angluin, 1988] is the following. An algorithm *exactly learns* a concept in function-free non-recursive Horn definition representation in polynomial time using equivalence queries if and only if it runs in time polynomial in the size of Σ and in the size of the largest counterexample, and outputs a function-free non-recursive Horn definition that is extensionally equivalent to Σ.

3.2 Strong Compactness of Non-recursive Horn Definitions

In this section we describe a property of non-recursive Horn definitions, which is called *strong compactness* by Lassez, et al. [1988] and Page [1993], and relate this property to membership queries.

---
[3] We employ closed-world assumption and assume that all other literals are negative.

Strong compactness says that for non-recursive Horn definitions if we know that a clause is logically implied by a set of clauses Σ, then we can conclude that that clause is subsumed by a clause in Σ. The following lemma, in addition, says that the converse is true. This is useful to show later that each hypothesis in our algorithm is always a specialization of some target clause.

Lemma 9. *Let $\Sigma = \{C_1, C_2, \ldots, C_n\}$ be a set of horn clauses, where each C_i is $\{\neg c_{i1}, \ldots, \neg c_{ik_i}, p\}$, and $c_{i1}, \ldots, c_{ik_i}$ and p are first-order positive literals. Further let $H_1 = \{\neg h_1, \ldots, \neg h_m, q\}$ be a horn clause, where q and $h_1, \ldots, h_m$ are first-order positive literals. Also, suppose that the predicate symbols of p and q are distinct from those of c_{ij} and h_i. Then, $\Sigma \models H_1$ if and only if there exists a t, $1 \leq t \leq n$, such that $C_t \succeq H_1$. We call C_t the* **target clause** *of H_1, and H_1 the* **hypothesis clause** *of C_t.*

Proof. This is a direct consequence of the Subsumption theorem [Kowalski, 1970]. $\square$

If a clause H_1 has variables, to determine $\Sigma \models H_1$ is to determine whether all instances in H_1 are also in Σ—which is the same as a subset query [Angluin, 1988]. However, by substituting each variable in H_1 by a unique constant, we can form an instance of H_1. We call this procedure Instantiate. Now, determining whether $\Sigma \models H_1$ is equivalent to asking whether $\Sigma \models$ Instantiate(H_1). Asking whether $\Sigma \models$ Instantiate(H_1) is the same as a membership query. In effect, this membership query simulates a subset query.

3.3 Learnability of Function-free Non-recursive Horn Definitions

Horn-learn is an algorithm to learn non-recursive function-free Horn definitions using equivalence and membership queries (Figure 1). Horn-learn makes use of Generalize algorithm. Generalize takes as input a Horn clause and generalizes it by eliminating literals from that Horn clause. It removes a literal from the Horn clause and checks whether the resultant Horn clause is overgeneral. It can do this by substituting each variable in the hypothesis clause with a unique constant and asking a membership query. If it is overgeneral the literal is not eliminated; otherwise, it is eliminated to form a new, more general Horn clause.

Horn-learn starts with hypothesis H that is initially empty. As long as H is not equivalent to the target concept C, the equivalence query returns an example e that is not included in H, and the algorithm modifies H to cover e. To include e in H, Horn-learn checks each Horn clause H_i of H whether generalizing H_i to cover e would not make the hypothesis overgeneral—i.e., a check whether $lgg(H_i, e)$ is in the concept. If so, concluding that it has found the right Horn clause H_i to include e in, Horn-learn further generalizes $h = lgg(H_i, e)$, by removing irrelevant literals using membership oracle (using Generalize), and replaces H_i in H by the new generalized h. If there is no such H_i, Horn-learn generalizes e and makes it a new Horn clause of H.

The generalization process of Generalize serves a critical purpose. Recall that the size of lgg grows as a product of the sizes of the hypotheses being generalized.

Unless the hypothesis size is limited, it can grow exponentially in the number of examples used to create the hypothesis. Lemma 10 and Lemma 11 together show that Generalize guarantees that the sizes of the hypothesis clauses are at most the sizes of their corresponding target clauses. Lemma 10 shows that Generalize does not overgeneralize in the process.

Horn-learn
1. Let Σ be the target concept.
2. $H := \{\}$ /* empty hypothesis, initially */
3. $m := 0$ /* number of clauses in the hypothesis */
4. while equivalence(H, Σ) is not true and e is a counterexample do
/* fix the clause in H for the example e */
5.   if $(m > 0)$ then, Let $Hbe\{H_1, H_2, \ldots, H_m\}$
6.   found := false; $i := 1$
7.   while $(i \leq m)$ and found is false do
8. $h := lgg(e, H_i)$
9.   if $\Sigma \models h$ then found := true;
                                    /* Member?(Instantiate(h)) implements $\Sigma \models h$*/
10.   else $i := i + 1$
11.   endwhile /* $i \leq m$ */
12.   if found = false then $h := e$; $m := m + 1$;
/* further generalize h */
13. $H_i :=$ Generalize(h)
14. endwhile
15. return H

Generalize(h)
1. $h' := h$
2. for each literal l in h do
3.   if $\Sigma \models h' - \{l\}$ then $h' := h' - \{l\}$
                                    /* Implemented by Member?(Instantiate$(h' - \{l\})$) */
4. Return h'.

Fig. 1. Horn-learn: An algorithm to learn Horn definitions

Lemma 10. *If the argument h of Generalize is not overgeneral, then, at the end of Generalize, h' has a target Horn clause C_j—i.e., $C_j \succeq h'$. Moreover, h' in line 4 of Generalize is a condensation of h w.r.t. C_j.*

Proof. In the beginning of Generalize, h', which is the same as the argument h, is not overgeneral. h' is modified only when the modification still leaves the result inside Σ. That is, $\Sigma \models h'$. By Lemma 9, there exists a target Horn clause for h', say C_j, and $C_j \succeq h'$.

To show that h' in line 4 of Generalize is a condensation of h w.r.t. C_j, we need only to show that for any literal $l \in h'$, $C_j \not\succeq (h' - \{l\})$. Suppose that for some

$l \in h'$, $C_j \succeq (h' - \{l\})$. Let h'' be the value of h' when l is considered for removal in the loop of lines 2—3. Since $h' \subseteq h''$, by Proposition 8, $C_j \succeq (h'' - \{l\})$. From Lemma 9, $\Sigma \models (h'' - \{l\})$. In that case, l would have been removed by line 3 of Generalize. But, $l \in h'$, a contradiction. Therefore, for any literal $l \in h'$, $C_j \not\succeq (h' - \{l\})$. $\qquad\qquad\qquad\qquad\qquad\qquad\qquad\qquad\qquad\qquad\qquad\qquad\square$

Lemma 11. *If h' is a condensation of h w.r.t. C_j, then $C_j\theta = h'$ for some substitution θ. Moreover, $|h'| \leq |C_j|$.*

Proof. Suppose h' is a condensation of h w.r.t. C_j. Then there exists a θ such that $C_j\theta \subseteq h'$. Suppose $C_j\theta \subset h'$. Then, for some $l \in h' - C_j\theta$, $C_j\theta \subseteq h' - \{l\}$. Hence, $C_j \succeq (h' - \{l\})$. This is a contradiction, since h' is a condensation w.r.t. C_j. Therefore, $C_j\theta = h'$. This implies that $|h'| = |C_j\theta| \leq |C_j|$. $\qquad\quad\square$

The following definition relates an example to a hypothesis clause and to a target clause.

Definition 12. *If $C_1, C_2, \ldots, C_n$ are the Horn clauses in the target concept Σ, and $H_1, H_2, \ldots, H_m$ are the Horn clauses in the hypothesis H, then a correct hypothesis Horn clause in H for an example e is a Horn clause H_i such that for some $1 \leq j \leq n$, $C_j \succeq e$ and $C_j \succeq H_i$.*

Lemma 13. *In Horn-learn, suppose that e is a counterexample returned by the equivalence query such that e is covered by Σ, but not by H. Then Horn-learn includes e in a correct hypothesis Horn clause in H for e if and only if one exists.*

Proof. First the only-if part. Horn-learn includes e in H_i of H if $\Sigma \models lgg(e, H_i)$. If $\Sigma \models lgg(e, H_i)$, then, by Lemma 9, $C_j \succeq lgg(e, H_i)$ for some C_j of C. Then, by Lemma 7, $C_j \succeq e$ and $C_j \succeq H_i$. Therefore, if Horn-learn includes e in H_i of H, then H_i is a correct hypothesis Horn clause for e.

Now, the if part of the claim. Let H_i be a correct hypothesis Horn clause for e in H such that no H_k such that $k < i$ is one. Then there exists a C_j of C such that $C_j \succeq e$ and $C_j \succeq H_i$. This implies, by Lemma 7, that $C_j \succeq lgg(e, H_i)$. By Lemma 9, $\Sigma \models lgg(e, H_i)$. Also, for $k < i$, $C_j \not\succeq H_k$, which implies $\Sigma \not\models lgg(e, H_k)$. Therefore, H_i is the first clause in the hypothesis H for which $\Sigma \models lgg(e, H_i)$. Then, by lines 7–13 in Fig. 1, e is included in H_i by assigning $lgg(e, H_i)$ to H_i (after further generalizing it using Generalize). $\quad\square$

Lemma 14. *Suppose that e is a counterexample such that e is covered by Σ, but not by H. Then Horn-learn adds a new Horn clause to H that includes e if and only if H does not already have a correct hypothesis Horn clause for e.*

Proof. By lines 11 and 12, and Lemma 13. $\qquad\qquad\qquad\qquad\qquad\qquad\qquad\square$

Lemma 15. *The following are invariant conditions of Horn-learn:*
1. Every Horn clause H_i in the hypothesis H has a target clause;
2. Every Horn clause C_j in the target concept Σ has at most one hypothesis clause.

Proof.

Proof of (1). For every Horn clause H_i in H, $\Sigma \models H_i$ (by lines 8–13 of Horn-learn, and Lemma 10). Therefore, by Lemma 9, H_i has a target Horn clause.

Proof of (2). First, we show that any new hypothesis clause added to H has a target clause distinct from the target clauses of the other hypothesis clauses in H. Next, we show that if two hypothesis clauses have distinct target clauses at the beginning of an iteration of the loop of lines 4–14, then they still have distinct target clauses at the end of the iteration.

Let H_i be the first hypothesis Horn clause in H for C_j. That is, there is no H_k such that $k < i$ and H_k is a hypothesis Horn clause in H for C_j. Another hypothesis clause $H_{i'}$ with the target clause C_j would have been added to H such that $i' > i$, only if there was a counterexample e belonging to C_j for which H_i is not the correct hypothesis Horn clause (by Lemma 14). That means $C_j \succeq e$ and $C_j \not\succeq lgg(H_i, e)$. This implies, by Lemma 7, $C_j \not\succeq H_i$. That is a contradiction, because H_i is a hypothesis Horn clause for C_j. Therefore, such a $H_{i'}$ cannot exist in H. That is, $H_{i'}$ could have been added only if it had a distinct target clause.

Let C_j and $C_{j'}$ be two distinct target clauses for the clauses H_i and $H_{i'}$ in H, respectively, at the beginning of an iteration of the loop of lines 4–14. That means, $C_j \succeq H_i$ and $C_j \not\succeq H_{i'}$. Also, $C_{j'} \succeq H_{i'}$ and $C_{j'} \not\succeq H_i$.

At most one of H_i and $H_{i'}$ can change in an iteration of the loop. If neither changes, we are done with the proof. Suppose that H_i changes without loss of generality. H_i can change in the lines 8 and 13. We need to show that both these changes maintain that $C_{j'} \not\succeq H_i$. Since $C_{j'} \not\succeq H_i$, $C_{j'} \not\succeq lgg(H_i, e)$ (by Lemma 7). Therefore, line 8 maintains the property. In line 13, Generalize returns a superset of its argument. By Proposition 8, $C_{j'} \not\succeq \mathsf{Generalize}(lgg(H_i, e))$, thus maintaining the property. Therefore, H_i and $H_{i'}$ have different target clauses at the end of the iteration. □

Now to the main theorem on the exact learnability.

Theorem 16. *Function-free non-recursive Horn definitions are exactly learnable using equivalence and membership queries.*

Proof. We prove this theorem by showing that Horn-learn exactly learns function-free non-recursive Horn definitions.

Part 2 of Lemma 15 implies that for every H_i of H, there is a C_j such that $C_j \succeq H_i$. That means, H covers no example that is not covered by the target concept C. In other words, H is never over-general in Horn-learn. Therefore, every counterexample is an example that is covered by Σ, but not by H.

Equivalence query guarantees that whenever Horn-learn gets a new example, it is not already covered by the hypothesis H. At the end of each iteration, before asking an equivalence query, by Lemma 13 and Lemma 14, Horn-learn guarantees that all the previous examples are covered by H. Each example, either modifies an existing hypothesis Horn clause (its correct hypothesis Horn clause) or adds a new Horn clause. The minimum change in H that is required to cover a new example is a change of a variable in its correct hypothesis Horn clause if one exists. That is, each new example, except the ones that add new Horn clauses, contributes at least one variable. Let n be the number of Horn clauses in a concept, l be the maximum number of literals in a clause in the concept, v be the maximum number of variables in a clause in the concept, and k be the number of literals in the largest counterexample. Because **Generalize** guarantees that each Horn clause in the hypothesis has at most as many literals as there are in its target Horn clause (by Lemma 10 and Lemma 11), the number of variables in each Horn clause is at most v. Part 1 of Lemma 15 guarantees that H has at most n Horn clauses. Therefore, the total number of variables is at most nv. **Horn-learn** requires n examples to add each of the n Horn clauses in H. It requires at most nv examples to variablize all the Horn clauses in H. Therefore, **Horn-learn** requires $n(v+1)$ examples, and, hence, $n(v+1)$ equivalence queries.

Let m be the number of hypothesis clauses in the hypothesis H at any time. Then, for each of the base examples that form new Horn clause in H, **Horn-learn** asks at most m membership queries for deciding that there is no correct hypothesis Horn clause in H, and at most k membership queries to simplify and generalize using **Generalize** (because there are at most k literals in an example). Each new Horn clause has at most l literals (by Lemma 10). For each of the other examples, at most m membership queries are needed to determine a correct hypothesis Horn clause, and kl (which is the size of lgg) number of membership queries to generalize using **Generalize**. Therefore, the total number of queries is at most $mn + kn + nv(m + kl)$, which is at most $n^2 + kn + nv(n + kl)$. This is also the upper limit on the running time of the algorithm. □

By the above theorem and the transformation result from the exact learning model to the PAC model [Angluin, 1988], we have the following.

Corollary 17. *Function-free non-recursive Horn definitions are PAC-learnable using membership queries.*

4 Learnability of Goal-Decomposition Rules

In AI planning, domain-specific control knowledge is necessary to make planning task computationally feasible. Goal-decomposition rules (d-rules) is a natural method for representing control knowledge [Reddy, Tadepalli, & Roncagliolo, 1996]. They are similar to hierarchical transition networks [Erol, Hendler, & Nau, 1994].

A d-rule is a 3-tuple $\langle g, c, sg \rangle$ that decomposes a goal g into a sequence of subgoals sg, provided condition c holds in the initial state. Goal g is a positive first-order literal, condition c is a conjunction of positive first-order literals. Subgoals sg are first-order positive literals.

The following is an example of a simple d-rule from Blocks-world (BW) domain:

```
goal: (on ?x ?y)
subgoals: ((clear ?x) (clear ?y) (put-on ?x ?z ?y))
conditions: ((block ?x) (block ?y) (table ?z))
```

A goal may have multiple d-rules—i.e., multiple condition-and-subgoals pairs. For example, there could be some other rules for the goal (on ?x ?y) with different condition-and-subgoals pairs. We call these disjunctive d-rules. If a goal does not appear anywhere in the conditions or subgoals, then we refer to them as non-recursive d-rules. The above example is a non-recursive d-rule.

In this section, we show that non-recursive disjunctive d-rules are learnable by converting them into a set of function-free non-recursive Horn clauses. The examples for this purpose are positive examples, each of which has a goal, and a sequence of successive states starting from an initial state and leading to a goal state. This can be viewed as specifying the initial condition and a sequence of subgoals, with both including several irrelevant literals. Each component is ground—i.e., it does not contain any variables. The subgoals component, in addition to having irrelevant literals, may have some sequence information missing. In the above example, if block ?x is already clear in the initial state, then the related example comes with no information on the relative order of the subgoals (clear ?x) and (clear ?y).

The conversion of d-rules to Horn-clauses is straightforward, except for the sequences in subgoals components. To represent the sequential order of subgoal literals, we annotate all literals using situation-calculus like notation. Each literal is added the name of the situation it is true in as an additional parameter, and the relative order of situations is specified with new predicates. Since literals for a condition are true in an initial state, they are assigned the first situation. For instance, in our BW example, a training example would be the following.

```
((block a S0) (block b S0) (block c S0) (table Tab S0) (clear a S0)
(clear c S0) (clear a S1) (clear b S1) (put-on a Tab b S2) (notAfter
S0 S0)
(notAfter S0 S1) (notAfter S1 S1) (notAfter S1 S2) (notAfter S2 S2))
→ (on a b S2)
```

From the theorem in the previous section it follows that d-rules along with the relative order of the subgoal literals can be learned from examples and membership queries.

We have implemented an efficient version of this scheme, and demonstrated in [Reddy, Tadepalli, & Roncagliolo, 1996, Reddy & Tadepalli, 1997b] that it can successfully learn d-rules for efficient planning in two other domains: a variation of STRIPS world [Fikes, Hart, & Nilsson, 1972], and Kanfer-Ackerman air-traffic control domain [Ackerman & Kanfer, 1993].

5 Discussion

In this work, we have shown that first-order function-free non-recursive Horn definitions are learnable utilizing reasonable resources and queries. From this, it is a straightforward extension that first-order monotone DNFs are PAC-learnable using membership queries. This is a more general result than the learnability of propositional monotone DNFs [Angluin, 1988]. Another related concept class to Horn definitions is Horn sentences; Horn sentences allow different head literals in a set of Horn clauses, as opposed to single head literal for all Horn clauses in

Horn definitions. It is shown that propositional Horn sentences are exactly learnable from equivalence and membership queries [Angluin, Frazier, & Pitt, 1992, Frazier & Pitt, 1993]. The entailment queries in [Frazier & Pitt, 1993] are similar to our queries, but differ in one crucial aspect. The queries in [Frazier & Pitt, 1993] ask about intermediate predicates in a hierarchy of predicates, whereas our queries concern single-level clauses. Learnability of first-order function-free Horn sentences from entailment and membership queries is an important open question, which we are investigating at present. As mentioned in the introduction, Page [1993] shows that non-recursive and "simple"—that is, only the terms in the head of a clause can appear in the body of the clause— Horn definitions with predicates of fixed arity are PAC-learnable using equivalence and subset queries. This class considered by Page handles functions, whereas the class we considered is function-free.

There is a difference between what an example means in ILP, and what it means in our case along with the cases of [Haussler, 1989] and [Angluin, Frazier, & Pitt, 1992]. An example in ILP comprises a ground head literal and an indication whether it is a positive or a negative example. In our case, it is a conjunction of ground relations (literals) describing a set of objects such that it satisfies a head predicate. Since our motivation is planning in a structural domain, this notion for an example is natural. However, the extended instances in the ILP work in [Cohen, 1995b] are similar to our notion of examples.

The algorithm in Figure 1 is similar in spirit to an ILP system called CLINT [De Raedt & Bruynooghe, 1992] in the sense that they both are incremental and interactive. Like in our algorithm, CLINT uses queries to eliminate irrelevant literals. CLINT raises the generality of hypotheses by proposing more complex hypothesis clauses, whereas our algorithm uses lgg.

Several pieces of research have used the lgg idea in different ways for the purpose of generalization. Haussler [1989] considers learning multiple conjunctive concepts. In the hypothesis language considered by him where the number of objects per scene is fixed, lgg of two hypotheses has at most the size of one of the hypotheses, but is not unique. Haussler uses queries to select an lgg which is in the target. On the other hand, in our case, lgg is unique, but its size grows exponentially in the number of hypotheses of which it is lgg. We use queries to reduce the size of the hypothesis generated by the lgg (see Generalize procedure in Fig. 1). Frazier and Pitt [1996] also use a pruning procedure similar to our Generalize procedure to limit the size of lgg in Classic learning. GOLEM [Muggleton & Feng, 1990] is another system that uses lgg to generalize hypotheses. GOLEM mitigates the problem of combinatorial explosion due to lgg in two ways: (1) by restricting the hypothesis language to ij-determinate Horn clauses which guarantee polynomial-sized lgg; and (2) by using negative examples to eliminate literals from the hypotheses. In the case of [Page, 1993], the simplicity and the fixed arity restrictions make the size of lgg polynomial in the sizes of the hypotheses being generalized.

For concept learning problems, answering membership queries can be unreasonably demanding. However, as mentioned in the introduction, the work in this paper is motivated by the practical application of learning goal-decomposition rules (d-rules) for planning. Note that the membership queries are d-rules hypothesized by the learner. In our application, the d-rule learner can automatically answer these queries by generating random planning problems that must use the hypthesized d-rules, and then trying out these d-rules in solving the planning problems [Reddy & Tadepalli, 1997a, Reddy & Tadepalli, 1997b]. Similar to our application of the learning algorithm to speedup learning in planning, Page [1993] has proposed a way to apply his algorithm to learning LEX's [Mitchell, Utgoff, & Banerji, 1983] control rules.

It is possible that in some cases the membership queries asked by the learner must respect a background domain theory. Consider a case where such queries are answered automatically by a theorem prover or by running a simulator. It is natural to want to restrict the queries so that they are not irrational or inconsistent with the domain theory. One open question is what kinds of restrictions are needed to be placed on the domain theory so that it is possible to learn with only consistent membership queries.

Acknowledgments. We gratefully acknowledge the support of ONR under grant # N00014-95-1-0557 and NSF under grant # IRI-9520243. We thank Roni Khardon and the anonymous reviewers for their insightful comments.

References

[Ackerman & Kanfer, 1993] Ackerman, P., and Kanfer, R. 1993. *Kanfer-Ackerman Air Traffic Control Task© CD-ROM Database, Data-Collection Program, and Playback Program.* Dept. of Psychology, Univ. of Minn., Minneapolis, MN.

[Angluin, Frazier, & Pitt, 1992] Angluin, D.; Frazier, M.; and Pitt, L. 1992. Learning conjunctions of horn clauses. *Machine Learning* 9:147–164.

[Angluin, 1988] Angluin, D. 1988. Queries and concept learning. *Machine Learning* 2:319–342.

[Cohen, 1995a] Cohen, W. 1995a. Pac-learning non-recursive prolog clauses. *Artificial Intelligence* 79(1):1–38.

[Cohen, 1995b] Cohen, W. 1995b. Pac-learning recursive logic programs: efficient algorithms. *Jl. of AI Research* 2:500–539.

[Cohen, 1995c] Cohen, W. 1995c. Pac-learning recursive logic programs: negative results. *Jl. of AI Research* 2:541–573.

[De Raedt & Bruynooghe, 1992] De Raedt, L., and Bruynooghe, M. 1992. Interactive concept learning and constructive induction by analogy. *Machine Learning* 8(2):107–150.

[Džeroski, Muggleton, & Russell, 1992] Džeroski, S.; Muggleton, S.; and Russell, S. 1992. Pac-learnability of determinate logic programs. In *Proceedings of the Fifth Annual ACM Workshop on Computational Learning Theory*, 128–135.

[Erol, Hendler, & Nau, 1994] Erol, K.; Hendler, J.; and Nau, D. 1994. HTN planning: complexity and expressivity. In *Proceedings of the Twelfth National Conference on Artificial Intelligence (AAAI-94)*. AAAI Press.

[Fikes, Hart, & Nilsson, 1972] Fikes, R.; Hart, P.; and Nilsson, N. 1972. Learning and executing generalized robot plans. *Artificial Intelligence* 3:251–288.

[Frazier & Pitt, 1993] Frazier, M., and Pitt, L. 1993. Learning from entailment: An application to propositional Horn sentences. In *Proceedings of the Tenth International Conference on Machine Learning*, 120–127.

[Frazier & Pitt, 1996] Frazier, M., and Pitt, L. 1996. CLASSIC learning. *Machine Learning* 26:151–194.

[Haussler, 1989] Haussler, D. 1989. Learning conjunctive concepts in structural domains. *Machine Learning* 4:7–40.

[Kietz & Lübbe, 1994] Kietz, J.-U., and Lübbe, M. 1994. An efficient subsumption algorithm for inductive logic programming. In *Proceedings of the Eleventh International Conference on Machine Learning*, 130–138.

[Kowalski, 1970] Kowalski, R. 1970. The case for using equality axioms in automatic demonstration. In *Lecture Notes in Mathematics*, volume 125. Springer-Verlag.

[Lassez, Maher, & Marriott, 1988] Lassez, J.-L.; Maher, M.; and Marriott, K. 1988. Unification revisited. In Minker, J., ed., *Foundations of Deductive Databases and Logic Programming*. Morgan Kaufmann.

[Lloyd, 1987] Lloyd, J. 1987. *Foundations of Logic Programming* (2nd ed.). Berlin: Springer-Verlag.

[Mitchell, Utgoff, & Banerji, 1983] Mitchell, T.; Utgoff, P.; and Banerji, R. 1983. Learning by experimentation: Acquiring and refining problem-solving heuristics. In Michalski, R., and et al., eds., *Machine learning: An artificial intelligence approach*, volume 1. Morgan Kaufmann.

[Muggleton & Feng, 1990] Muggleton, S., and Feng, C. 1990. Efficient induction of logic programs. In *Proceedings of the First Conference on Algorithmic Learning Theory*, 368–381. Ohmsha/Springer-Verlag.

[Nienhuys-Cheng & de Wolf, 1996] Nienhuys-Cheng, S.-H., and de Wolf, R. 1996. Least generalizations and greatest specializations of sets of clauses. *Jl. of AI Research* 4:341–363.

[Page, 1993] Page, C. 1993. *Anti-Unification in Constraint Logics: Foundations and Applications to Learnability in First-Order Logic, to Speed-up Learning, and to Deduction*. Ph.D. Dissertation, University of Illinois, Urbana, IL.

[Plotkin, 1970] Plotkin, G. 1970. A note on inductive generalization. In Meltzer, B., and Michie, D., eds., *Machine Intelligence*, volume 5. New York: Elsevier North-Holland. 153–163.

[Reddy & Tadepalli, 1997a] Reddy, C., and Tadepalli, P. 1997a. Inductive logic programming for speedup learning. To appear in IJCAI-97 workshop on Frontiers of ILP.

[Reddy & Tadepalli, 1997b] Reddy, C., and Tadepalli, P. 1997b. Learning goal-decomposition rules using exercises. In *Proceedings of the 14th International Conference on Machine Learning*. Morgan Kaufmann.

[Reddy, Tadepalli, & Roncagliolo, 1996] Reddy, C.; Tadepalli, P.; and Roncagliolo, S. 1996. Theory-guided empirical speedup learning of goal-decomposition rules. In *Proceedings of the 13th International Conference on Machine Learning*, 409–417. Morgan Kaufmann.

[Schapire, 1990] Schapire, R. 1990. The strength of weak learnability. *Machine Learning* 5:197–227.

Using Abstraction Schemata in Inductive Logic Programming

Ken SADOHARA[1] and Makoto HARAGUCHI[2]

[1] Electrotechnical Laboratory
1 - 1 - 4 Umezono, Tsukuba, 305 Japan
E-mail:sadohara@etl.go.jp
[2] Division of Electronics and Information Engineering
Hokkaido University N13-W8, Kita-ku, Sapporo, 060 Japan
E-mail:makoto@db.huee.hokudai.ac.jp

Abstract. We consider inductive logic programming guided by a language bias called abstraction schemata which enables us to specify a partial structure for a target program. Specifically, to improve the efficiency of such learning, we discuss a class of programs for which it is possible to devise a learning algorithm capable of identifying and pruning unpromising uses of the schemata. This identification process includes the bias shift problem: how to decide whether a hypothesis space contains no correct program with respect to a given example specification. For solving this problem, a required property of hypothesis spaces is discovered. This result yields a class of programs that are beyond the representational capabilities of previous approaches — most notably, non-trivial programs with local variables.

1 Introduction

In this paper, we are concerned with the inductive learning of logic programs using a kind of language bias, called *abstraction schemata* [9, 7]. Specifically, we show that for a class of *linearly-moded programs* [6], it is possible to devise a learning algorithm capable of identifying and pruning unpromising uses of the schemata.

Our abstraction schemata define a partial structure for a target program, for example what type of recursion is used and how variables are shared among literals in a clause. By making the specification of the schemata open to the user of a learning system, the user can direct the synthesis of a program so that it has a specified structure. For instance, the learning system presented in this paper produces different programs for sorting lists (quick-sort or insertion-sort) from the same background knowledge and the same example specification, depending on the type of divide-and-conquer strategy given as abstraction schemata. This usage of abstraction schemata is well-suited for learning problems of the design-from-specification type because the assumption that users — designers in this case — know a partial structure of a target program beforehand seems to be natural.

Within Inductive Logic Programming (ILP), usage of schemata as a language bias has been studied by many researchers. In the literature [5, 2], a target program is obtained from second-order schemata by substituting second-order predicate variables with predicate symbols. However, this imposes the very strong bias of defining the entire structure of a target program, which typically cannot be guessed beforehand.

To relax this strong restriction, [2] exploits the generality structure of schemata and [1] integrates predicate sets with schemata. However neither of these approaches are flexible enough to allow users to define the structure of a target program partially. The notion of abstraction schemata was introduced by [9] to realize a language bias capable of such partial specification. Such usage of abstraction in learning was formalized more generally in [8, 7], using a method of abstracting logic programs similar to that used by [4]. This formalization, which is discussed in detail in the main body of this paper, can be rendered informally as follows:

Given abstraction schemata P, a logic program B and sets T, F of ground atoms, Find a logic program Q such that $Q \cup B$ covers all examples in T but none of the examples in F and $Q \cup B$ is *similar to* P, where *similar to* is a technical term meaning that an abstracted version of $Q \cup B$ is subsumed by P.

As well as specifying a partial structure of the target program at an abstract level, abstraction schemata differs from ordinary schemata in being represented in the same formalism as the target logic programs. Therefore, they are called *source programs*. In this respect, the above framework can be likened to analogical reasoning with logic programs, as exemplified in [13]. This is why the framework is referred to as Analogical Logic Program Synthesis from examples (ALPS, for short).

Although [8] presents an ALPS algorithm whose learnability is ensured, it is extremely inefficient. One of the reasons for this inefficiency is that it can not prune away useless similarities in synthesizing a target program. The algorithm searches not only for a target program but also for a similarity which justifies that the program is similar to a given source program. Every similarity induces a subspace of the hypothesis space consisting of programs similar to the source program. By searching the subspace of each similarity for a program correct with respect to given examples, the ALPS algorithm guarantees the synthesis of a target program that is correct and similar to the source program. However, among similarities, there may exist inappropriate similarities such that subspaces induced by the similarities contain no correct programs. The algorithm searches even such useless subspaces, and this is what makes it inefficient. We therefore need a mechanism for identifying inappropriate similarities and skipping the search of useless subspaces.

This essentially involves the same problem as the bias shift problem [12]: how to decide whether a single hypothesis space contains no correct programs. Since the literature [12] has shown that the bias shift problem is unsolvable in general, we should consider how the hypothesis space employed in a learning algorithm can be restricted. In the literature [3, 8], it is shown that the bias shift problem is solvable for a nontrivial class of programs called *linear programs*, where a class is said to be trivial if it is finite. However, this class is very restricted: for example, it does not allow local variables, where local variables are variables occurring only in the body of a clause. Since most practical programs have local variables, this is a severe shortcoming. To remedy this situation, this paper considers a class of *linearly-moded programs* — a nontrivial class of programs with local variables — for which the bias shift problem is solvable. This solvability result follows from a property of hypothesis spaces that ensures the solvability of the bias shift problem. Based on the result, we present an ALPS algorithm that can refute inappropriate similarities for the class.

2 The Problem Specification of ALPS

In this section, the framework of ALPS formalized in [8, 7] is presented. In the framework, the notion of similarity between logic programs plays an important role.

We first define mappings between expressions, which are later used for describing similarities between two programs. A *vocabulary* is the pair of a finite set of function symbols and a finite set of predicate symbols. For a vocabulary V, the set of terms (resp., atoms) constructed from V is denoted by $\text{Term}(V)$ (resp., $\text{Atom}(V)$).

Definition 1. Let V_1 and V_2 be vocabularies. A mapping $\phi : \text{Term}(V_1) \cup \text{Atom}(V_1) \to \text{Term}(V_2) \cup \text{Atom}(V_2) \cup \{\bot\}$ is *substitution-preserving mapping* (SPM, for short) from V_1 to V_2 if ϕ satisfies the following conditions.

1. For any variable V, $\phi(V) = V$.
2. For any term $t \in \text{Term}(V_1)$, $\phi(t) \in \text{Term}(V_2)$.
3. For any atom $A \in \text{Atom}(V_1)$, $\phi(A) \in \text{Atom}(V_2) \cup \{\bot\}$.
4. For any $e \in \text{Term}(V_1) \cup \text{Atom}(V_1)$, $\phi(e\theta) = \phi(e)\phi(\theta)$, where
   $\phi(\theta) = \{X_1/\phi(t_1), \ldots, X_n/\phi(t_n)\}$ for any substitution $\theta = \{X_1/t_1, \ldots, X_n/t_n\}$.

In the above definition, the symbol '$\bot$' does not appear in any vocabulary and $\phi(e) = \bot$ means that ϕ is not defined for e.

For a definite clause $C = H \leftarrow B_1, \ldots, B_n$, $head(C)$ denotes H, $body(C)$ denotes the set $\{B_1, \ldots, B_n\}$ and n is the *body-length* of C. Throughout this paper, a *logic program* is a finite set of definite clauses. We extend ϕ for any set S of atoms, any definite clause C and any logic program Q as follows.

$$\phi(S) = \{\phi(A) \mid A \in S \text{ and } \phi(A) \neq \bot\} \quad \phi(Q) = \{\phi(C) \mid C \in Q \text{ and } \phi(C) \neq \bot\}$$

$$\phi(C) = \begin{cases} \phi(head(C)) \leftarrow \phi(body(C)) & \text{if } \phi(head(C)) \neq \bot \\ \bot & \text{otherwise} \end{cases}$$

Furthermore, we need the following subsumption relation. For definite clauses C and D, $C \preceq D$ iff there exists a substitution θ such that $C\theta \subseteq D$. For logic programs P and Q, $P \preceq Q$ iff for any $C \in Q$, there exists a clause $D \in P$ such that $D \preceq C$.

Armed with these definitions, a notion of similarity is defined as follows.

Definition 2. Let P and Q be logic programs, and let ϕ be a SPM from $V(Q)$ to $V(P)$, where $V(P)$ is the vocabulary of P. Q is *similar to* P *w.r.t.* ϕ iff $P \preceq \phi(Q)$.

Intuitively speaking, if Q is similar to P w.r.t. ϕ then for any ground atom A, whenever there exists a proof PT of A in Q, there exists a proof of $\phi(A)$ in P that is an abstracted version of PT. That is, P simulates Q at an abstract level by ϕ.

Using the notion of the similarity, the problem specification of ALPS is stated as follows. Let L_o be the set of ground atoms over a vocabulary V. For $M \subseteq L_o$ and $\alpha \in L_o$, if $\alpha \in M$ (resp., $\alpha \in M^c$) then $\langle \alpha, \text{true} \rangle$ (resp., $\langle \alpha, \text{false} \rangle$) is called a *fact from* M, where S^c denotes the complementary set of S. A *presentation of* M is a sequence of facts from M such that $\{\alpha_i \mid \langle \alpha_i, \text{true} \rangle\} = M$ and $\{\alpha_i \mid \langle \alpha_i, \text{false} \rangle\} = M^c$. A logic program Q is said to be *correct w.r.t.* M if $\mathcal{M}(Q) = M$. For finite sets $T \subseteq L_o$ and $F \subseteq L_o$, a logic program Q is said to be *consistent with* $\langle T, F \rangle$ if $T \subseteq \mathcal{M}(Q)$ and $F \subseteq \mathcal{M}(Q)^c$ hold, where $\mathcal{M}(Q)$ denotes the least Herbrand model of Q. For a class $\mathcal{C}$ of logic programs over V, an *ALPS problem for* $\mathcal{C}$ is defined as follows [3].

---

[3] In the specification, we assume every program in $\mathcal{C}$ includes a common background theory.

Given a program P, a class Φ of SPMs from V to $V(P)$ and a presentation of M, Find $Q \in C$ and $\phi \in \Phi$ such that Q is correct w.r.t. M, and is similar to P w.r.t. ϕ.

M and $\langle Q, \phi \rangle$ are called an *intended model* and a *solution*, respectively. *ALPS algorithms for C* are effective procedures that solve ALPS problems for C. An ALPS algorithm A is said to *identify a solution in the limit* if A eventually produces the solution and never produces a different output. We refer to the ordinary inductive learning problems, i.e. ALPS problems without source program, as *LPS problems*.

If $\mathcal{M}(Q)$ is recursive for any $Q \in C$, there exists an ALPS algorithm for C that identifies a solution in the limit [8, 7]. This algorithm searches subspaces $C[P, \phi]$ of C (defined as follows) for a correct program.

Definition 3. Let $\mathcal{P}$ be an ALPS problem for C in which P, Φ and M are given. For a SPM $\phi \in \Phi$, $C[P, \phi]$ denotes the set of programs in C that is similar to P w.r.t. ϕ. ϕ is said to be *inappropriate* in $\mathcal{P}$ if $C[P, \phi]$ contains no program correct w.r.t. M.

For any inappropriate similarity ϕ, it is useless to search the subspace $C[P, \phi]$ for a correct program. The algorithm searches even such useless subspace, and this makes it inefficient. Therefore, for obtaining a more efficient ALPS algorithm, we need a mechanism for identifying inappropriate similarities and skipping the search of useless subspaces. This essentially involves the same problem as the *bias shift problem* [12]: how to decide whether a single hypothesis space contains no correct program. More precisely, this problem is deciding that an LPS problem has no solution, which is also discussed in [3] as the refutability of the hypothesis space.

Definition 4 (Mukouchi and Arikawa [3]). An LPS algorithm A for C is said to *refutably infer C* if A satisfies the following condition: for any presentation of any intended model M, if there exists a program in C correct w.r.t. M, A identifies a correct program in the limit, otherwise A outputs 'refuted' and terminates. C is said to be *refutably inferable* if there exists an LPS algorithm that refutably infers C.

Since the literature [12] has shown that the bias shift problem is unsolvable in general, next section is devoted to restricting the hypothesis space employed in a learning algorithm so that the bias shift problem is solvable.

3 Refuting Inappropriate Similarities

This section concerns how the class of programs employed in an ALPS algorithm can be restricted so that the algorithm can refute inappropriate similarities. To this end, we consider a property of hypothesis spaces to solve the bias problem.

The following defines the key concept.

Definition 5. A logic program P is *reduced with respect to* a finite set X of ground atoms if $X \subseteq \mathcal{M}(P)$ but $X \not\subseteq \mathcal{M}(P')$ for any $P' \subset P$. For a class C of logic programs, $C^n(X) \stackrel{\text{def}}{=} \{P \in C \mid P \text{ is reduced with respect to } X, \sharp P = n\}$, $C^{\leq n}(X) \stackrel{\text{def}}{=} \bigcup_{i=0}^{n} C^i(X)$, where $\sharp S$ denotes the cardinality of S.

Definition 6 (Shinohara [11]). A class C of logic program has *bounded finite thickness* if $C^{\leq n}(X)$ is finite for any finite set X of ground atoms and any $n \geq 0$.

Using the property, we can obtain the following sufficient condition to solve the bias shift problem. Roughly speaking, bounded finite thickness ensures that it is sufficient to test the finite set $C^{\leq n}(X)$ instead of the possibly infinite set $C^{\leq n}$ in order to show nonexistence of correct programs.

Lemma 7. *If a class C of logic programs satisfies the following conditions, $C^{\leq n} \stackrel{\text{def}}{=} \{P \in C \mid \sharp P \leq n\}$ is refutably inferable for any $n \geq 0$.*

1. *C has bounded finite thickness and $C^i(X)$ is uniformly and recursively generable [4].*
2. *C is closed under the subset operation, i.e. for any P and Q, $P \subseteq Q \in C \Rightarrow P \in C$.*
3. *For any $P \in C$, $\mathcal{M}(P)$ is recursive.*

Proof sketch. By generalizing the proof of Theorem 27 in [3], we can show the following algorithm refutably infers $C^{\leq n}$, where the procedure read-store reads a fact $\langle \alpha, v \rangle$ and stores α in S_v.

Procedure $\mathcal{RINF}(n, C)$
begin
  $S_{true} := \emptyset$; $S_{false} := \emptyset$; read-store(S_{true}, S_{false})
  while $S_{true} = \emptyset$ **do begin**   output $\{\}$; read-store(S_{true}, S_{false}) **end**
  $\mathcal{RINF}(S_{true}, S_{false}, n, C)$; output 'refuted'
end.
Procedure $\mathcal{RIS}(\text{var } S_{true}, \text{var } S_{false}, n, C)$
begin
  $T_0 := S_{true}$; $F_0 := S_{false}$
  for $k = 1$ **to** n **do begin**
    recursively generate $C^k(T_{k-1})$
    for each $P \in C^k(T_{k-1})$ **do**
      while P is consistent with $\langle S_{true}, S_{false} \rangle$ **do begin**
        output P; read-store(S_{true}, S_{false})
      end
    $T_k := S_{true}$; $F_k := S_{false}$
  end
end.

For the class of linear programs with at most $n \geq 0$ clauses, it is known that the bias shift problem is solvable [3, 8]. This is also proved from the above lemma since the class is proved to have bounded finite thickness [11]. In the next section, we discuss another class which allows programs with local variables whereas the class of linear programs does not allow.

Concerning the bounded finite thickness, the following proposition holds.

Proposition 8. *If a class C of logic programs has bounded finite thickness then any subclass $C' \subseteq C$ has bounded finite thickness.*

Theorem 9. *If a class C of logic programs over a vocabulary V satisfies the conditions in Lemma 7 then the following ALPS algorithm for $C^{\leq n}$ $(n \geq 0)$ identifies a solution in the limit.*

---

[4] There exists an effective procedure that enumerates all elements in $C^i(X)$ and stops for any X and any i.

Input a source program P, a recursively enumerable set $\Phi = \{\phi_j\}_{j \in N}$ of SPMs
   from V to $V(P)$ and a presentation of an intended model
Output a logic program or the sign 'refuted'
Procedure $\mathcal{ALPS}(n, C, P, \Phi)$
begin
   $S_{true} := \emptyset$; $S_{false} := \emptyset$; $i := 1$; read-store(S_{true}, S_{false})
   while $S_{true} = \emptyset$ do begin   output $\{\}$; read-store(S_{true}, S_{false}) end
   repeat
      $\mathcal{RIS}(S_{true}, S_{false}, n, C[P, \phi_i])$; $i := i + 1$
   forever
end.

Proof. From the proposition 8, $C[P, \phi_i]$ has bounded finite thickness for any $i \geq 1$.
Since $C[P, \phi_i]$ is recursive subclass of C for any $i \geq 1$, $C[P, \phi_i]^k(X)$ is uniformly and
recursively generable for any finite set X of ground atoms and any $k \geq 0$. Moreover,
$C[P, \phi_i]$ is closed under the subset operation since C is closed and any $Q' \subseteq Q$
is similar to P w.r.t. ϕ_i for any $Q \in C[P, \phi_i]$. Finally, we easily see that $\mathcal{M}(Q)$
is recursive for any $Q \in C[P, \phi_i]$. Therefore, from the lemma 7, $\mathcal{RIS}(n, C[P, \phi_i])$
refutably infers $C[P, \phi_i]$, and thus $\mathcal{ALPS}$ identifies a solution in the limit.   □

4   Linearly-moded Programs

In this section, we show that for a class of *linearly-moded programs*, the bias shift
problem is solvable, and thus there exists an ALPS algorithm that can refute inappropriate similarities.

The class of linearly-moded programs is identified in [6] with respect to the
learnability from positive examples. A linearly-moded program consists of linearly-
moded clauses, and for any predicate symbol appearing in linearly-moded clauses,
an input/output mode is annotated. $p(s; t)$ denotes an atom with input arguments
s and output arguments t. For example, the following programs are linearly-moded,
and also isort $\cup$ BK and qsort $\cup$ BK are linearly-moded.

$$
BK = \begin{cases}
\texttt{decons([X|Xs]; [X], Xs)} \leftarrow \\
\texttt{insert([], [H]; [H])} \leftarrow \\
\texttt{insert([X|Xs], [H]; [H, X|Xs])} \leftarrow H \leq X \\
\texttt{insert([X|Xs], [H]; [X|Ys])} \leftarrow H > X, \texttt{insert(Xs, H; Ys)} \\
\texttt{partition([X|Xs]; [X], Ls, Bs)} \leftarrow \texttt{p(Xs, X; Ls, Bs)} \\
\texttt{p([Y|Ys], X; [Y|Ls], Bs)} \leftarrow Y \leq X, \texttt{p(Ys, X; Ls, Bs)} \\
\texttt{p([Y|Ys], X; Ls, [Y|Bs])} \leftarrow Y > X, \texttt{p(Ys, X; Ls, Bs)} \\
\texttt{p([], X; [], [])} \leftarrow \\
\texttt{append([], X; X)} \leftarrow \\
\texttt{append([X|Xs], Ys; [X|Zs])} \leftarrow \texttt{append(Xs, Ys; Zs)}
\end{cases}
$$

$$
\text{isort} = \begin{cases}
\texttt{sort([]; [])} \leftarrow \\
\texttt{sort(Xs; Ys)} \leftarrow \texttt{decons(Xs; H,Zs), sort(Zs; Ws), insert(Ws,H; Ys)}
\end{cases}
$$

$$
\text{qsort} = \begin{cases}
\texttt{sort([]; [])} \leftarrow \\
\texttt{sort(Xs; Ys)} \leftarrow \texttt{partition(Xs; H,Ls,Bs), sort(Ls; L), sort(Bs; B)} \\
\qquad\qquad\qquad \texttt{append(H, B; V), append(L, V; Ys)}
\end{cases}
$$

An important property of linearly-moded programs is that for any ground goal
$\leftarrow p(s; t)$, if there exists an LD-refutation G with answer substitution σ then $\|t\| \leq$

$\|s\|$ and $\|v\sigma\| \leq \|u\sigma\| \leq \|s\|$ hold for each atom $r(u;v)$ in G, where $\|x\|$ denotes the size of terms x and an LD-refutation is a SLD-refutation under Prolog's selection rule. This property yields a result on completeness of depth-bounded resolution for linearly-moded programs, and thus the least Herbrand model of every linearly-moded program is recursive [6, Theorem 4]. Moreover, for any finite set T of ground atoms and any linearly-moded program P reduced w.r.t. T, the size of any atom in any clause in P is at most ℓ, where $\ell = 2 \times \max\{\|s\| \mid p(s;t) \in T\}$. Let $\mathcal{LM}_m$ be the set of linearly-moded programs consisting of clauses of body-length at most $m \geq 1$ and

$$\mathcal{LM}_m^{\leq n}(\ell) = \{P \in \mathcal{LM}_m \mid \sharp P \leq n, \text{the size of any atom in any clause in } P \text{ is at most } \ell\}.$$

Then, $\mathcal{LM}_m^{\leq n}(\ell)$ is finite (except for the renaming of variables) and contains all programs reduced w.r.t. T. Therefore, the class $\mathcal{LM}_m$ has bounded finite thickness [6, Theorem 5]. Furthermore, we see that $\mathcal{LM}_m^{\leq n}$ is closed under the subset operation, and $\mathcal{LM}_m^k(\ell)$ is uniformly and recursively generable. From these observations and the Lemma 7, $\mathcal{LM}_m^{\leq n}$ is refutably inferable, and thus there exists an ALPS algorithm for $\mathcal{LM}_m^{\leq n}$ that can refute inappropriate similarities.

5 An ALPS System

Based on the results in previous sections, we implemented an ALPS algorithm for a subclass of $\mathcal{LM}_m^{\leq n}$. Unlike the algorithm $\mathcal{ALPS}$, the algorithm employed in the implemented system, which is similar to an algorithm in [8], adopts techniques used in Shapiro's Model Inference System (MIS) [10]. More precisely, the hypothesis space $\mathcal{LM}_m^{\leq n}$ is divided into subspaces

$$\mathcal{LM}_m^{\leq n}[P, \phi_1], \ \mathcal{LM}_m^{\leq n}[P, \phi_2], \ \mathcal{LM}_m^{\leq n}[P, \phi_3], \ \ldots$$

and then each $\mathcal{LM}_m^{\leq n}[P, \phi_i]$ is searched with a MIS-like procedure.

Our MIS-like procedure differs from MIS in the start point of the refinement. Let $\mathcal{L}$ be the set $\{C \in \mathcal{LM}_m \mid \phi(C) = \bot \text{ or } \exists D \in P \ D \preceq \phi(C)\}$. Then, the set of programs with at most $n \geq 0$ clauses in $\mathcal{L}$ is $\mathcal{LM}_m^{\leq n}[P, \phi]$. Whereas MIS starts the refinement from the empty clause, our procedure starts the refinement from $\min(\mathcal{L})$, where $\min(\mathcal{L})$ denotes the set of clauses in $\mathcal{L}$ minimal with respect to the ordering $\preceq$. By virtue of a property of SPMs: $C_1 \preceq C_2$ implies $\phi(C_1) \preceq \phi(C_2)$, we see that this search is 'sound'. That is, if a clause C_2 is subsumed by a clause $C_1 \in \min(\mathcal{L})$, then $C_2 \in \mathcal{L}$ because there exists a clause $D \in P$ such that $D \preceq \phi(C_1) \preceq \phi(C_2)$. Therefore, if a refinement operator ρ is complete, i.e. for any clause C_2 and any $C_1 \in \min(\mathcal{L})$, $C_1 \preceq C_2$ implies $C_2 \in \rho^*(C_1)$, then this search is 'complete' and 'sound'. In this way, a target program is obtained from $\min(\mathcal{L})$ by the refinement provided there exists the target program in $\mathcal{LM}_m^{\leq n}[P, \phi]$. That is, the basic operation of our system is that each similarity induces $\min(\mathcal{L})$ and the model inference fills the gap between $\min(\mathcal{L})$ and the target program.

Unfortunately the refinement operator employed in our system is not complete and thus our system works only for a proper subclass of $\mathcal{LM}_m^{\leq n}$. At present, the following result of execution was obtained. Under the following condition: $n = 2$ (the number of clauses), $m = 5$ (the length of clauses), BK as a background knowledge, $(\{\Box, [\,|\,]\}, \{\texttt{sort}, \texttt{decons}, \texttt{insert}, \texttt{partition}, \texttt{append}\})$ as a vocabulary,

$\{(\text{sort}([], []), \text{true}), (\text{sort}([1], [1]), \text{true}), (\text{sort}([2,3,1], [1,2,3]), \text{true})\}$ as a set of examples and DivConq1 as a source program, the system produced isort and ϕ_{is}. On the other hand, when DivConq2 was given as a source program, the system produced qsort and ϕ_{qs}. Here, DivConq1 and DivConq2 are following logic programs.

DivConq1 =
$\left\{\begin{array}{l} \text{s}([];) \leftarrow \\ \text{s}(\text{X};) \leftarrow \text{divide}(\text{X}; \text{ Y, Z}), \text{s}(\text{Z};) \\ \text{divide}([\text{X}|\text{Xs}]; [\text{X}], \text{Xs}) \leftarrow \end{array}\right.$

DivConq2 =
$\left\{\begin{array}{l} \text{s}([];) \leftarrow \\ \text{s}(\text{X};) \leftarrow \text{divide}(\text{X}; \text{ Y, Z, W}), \text{s}(\text{Z};), \text{s}(\text{W};) \\ \text{divide}([\text{X}|\text{Xs}]; [\text{X}], \text{Ys}, \text{Zs}) \leftarrow \end{array}\right.$

Furthermore, ϕ_{is} and ϕ_{qs} are the following SPMs.

$\phi_{is}(t) = t$
$\phi_{is}(\text{sort}(t_1; t_2)) = \text{s}(t_1;)$
$\phi_{is}(\text{decons}(x; y, z)) = \text{divide}(x; y, z)$
$\phi_{is}(A) = \perp$

$\phi_{qs}(t) = t$ (for any list t)
$\phi_{qs}(\text{sort}(t_1; t_2)) = \text{s}(t_1;)$
$\phi_{qs}(\text{partition}(s; t, u, v)) = \text{divide}(s; t, u, v)$
$\phi_{qs}(A) = \perp$ (for the other atoms A)

We see that isort $\cup$ BK is similar to DivConq1 w.r.t. ϕ_{is}, and qsort $\cup$ BK is similar to DivConq2 w.r.t. ϕ_{qs}. This result shows that our system allows user to direct the synthesis of a program so that it has a specified structure.

References

1. H. Adé. Declarative bias for specific-to-general ilp systems. *Machine Learning*, 20:119–154, 1995.
2. J-U.Kietz and S. Wrobel. Controlling the complexity of learning in logic through syntactic and task-oriented models. *Inductive Logic Programming*, pages 335–359. ACADEMIC PRESS, 1992.
3. Y. Mukouchi and S. Arikawa. Towards a mathematical theory of machine discovery from facts. *Theoretical Computer Science*, 137:53–84, 1995.
4. D.A. Plaisted. Theorem proving with abstraction. *Artificial Intelligence*, 16:47–108, 1981.
5. L.D. Raedt and M. Bruynooghe. Interactive concept-learning and constructive induction by analogy. *Machine Learning*, 8:107–150, 1992.
6. M.R.K. Krishna Rao. A class of prolog programs inferable from positive data. LNAI 1160, pages 272–284. Springer-Verlag, 1996.
7. K. Sadohara. *A study on analogical logic program synthesis from examples*. PhD thesis, Tokyo Institute of Technology, 1996.
8. K. Sadohara and M. Haraguchi. Analogical logic program synthesis algorithm that can refute inappropriate similarities. LNAI 997, pages 266–281. Springer-Verlag, 1995.
9. S. Sakurai and M. Haraguchi. Towards learning by abstraction. *Proc. 2nd Workshop on Algorithmic Learning Theory*, pages 288–298, 1991.
10. E.Y. Shapiro. Inductive inference of theories from facts. Technical Report 192, Yale University Computer Science Dept., 1981.
11. T. Shinohara. Inductive inference of monotonic formal systems from positive data. *New Generation Computing*, 8:371–384, 1991.
12. I. Stahl. The appropriateness of predicate invention as bias shift operation in ilp. *Machine Learning*, 20:95–117, 1995.
13. B. Tausend and S. Bell. Analogical reasoning for logic programming. *Inductive Logic Programming*, pages 397–408. ACADEMIC PRESS, 1992.

Distance Induction in First Order Logic

Michèle Sebag

LMS – CNRS ura 317   LRI – CNRS ura 410
Ecole Polytechnique, 91128 Palaiseau   Université Paris-Sud, 91405 Orsay
Michele.Sebag@polytechnique.fr

Abstract. A distance on the problem domain allows one to tackle some typical goals of machine learning, e.g. classification or conceptual clustering, via robust data analysis algorithms (e.g. k-nearest neighbors or k-means).

A method for building a distance on first-order logic domains is presented in this paper. The distance is constructed from examples expressed as definite or constrained clauses, via a two-step process: a set of d hypotheses is first learnt from the training examples. These hypotheses serve as new descriptors of the problem domain $\mathcal{L}_h$: they induce a mapping π from $\mathcal{L}_h$ onto the space of integers $\mathbf{N}^d$. The distance between any two examples E and F is finally defined as the Euclidean distance between $\pi(E)$ and $\pi(F)$. The granularity of this hypothesis-driven distance (HDD) is controlled via the user-supplied parameter d.

The relevance of a HDD is evaluated from the predictive accuracy of the k-NN classifier based on this distance. Preliminary experiments demonstrate the potentialities of distance induction, in terms of predictive accuracy, computational cost, and tolerance to noise.

1 Introduction

The expert indeed knows to which extent any two examples or hypotheses on a problem domain, are similar: a relevant distance indeed represents a powerful, even if implicit, background knowledge. Distances can support many machine learning tasks:

• A distance or similarity function is needed to cluster the examples, which is the core of unsupervised learning [9, 4]. Clustering also constitutes a main stage of knowledge discovery in databases (KDD) [8]: one must somehow divide the enormous amount of available data, in order for knowledge to be conquered. Inductive logic programming (ILP) [15] can benefit from clustering, too: e.g. *KBG* uses a similarity function specifically designed for first-order languages, and gradually constructs hypotheses by generalizing the most similar examples and/or hypotheses [2].

• A distance allows the retrieval of the examples or hypotheses most similar to the instance at hand. In case-based reasoning (CBR), the retrieval stage commands the success of the whole process; hence much attention has been paid in CBR to developing flexible distances or similarity functions on structured domains [1]. Retrieving the nearest neighbors of the instance at hand also constitutes the core of instance-based learning. The ILP system *RIBL* [7] consists of a k-NN classifier relying on an extended version of the first-order distance of *KBG*.

A fruitful combination of inductive learning and k-NN classifier in attribute-value domains is described in [5]: *RISE* uses as default rule the majority vote of the k rules whose hypotheses are the closest to the instance at hand [5].

• In the field of analogy, one looks for "optimal" mappings from the source onto the target context; the optimality criterion most often refers to a relational or structural distance [10, 3].

In this paper, we first compare the respective advantages and weaknesses of rules and distances in regard to supervised learning. We then discuss previous work devoted to constructing distances on first-order languages [2, 7]. Section 3 presents an alternative to distances based on syntax and weights, namely *hypothesis-driven distances* (HDD). We show that a set of d hypotheses induces a mapping π from the problem domain $\mathcal{L}_h$ onto the space of vectors of integers $\mathbf{N}^d$. A distance on $\mathcal{L}_h$ then follows, by defining the distance between two any examples or further hypotheses E and F as the Euclidean distance between $\pi(E)$ and $\pi(F)$. The properties and biases of HDDs are studied.

DISTILL (for *Distance Induction with* STILL) uses the ILP system *STILL* [18] to construct rather blindly d hypotheses, where d is supplied by the user. These hypotheses only serve here as system of coordinates: further examples or hypotheses are given a numerical description within this system. *DISTILL* finally computes the distance between any two examples with same polynomial complexity as in *STILL* (section 4).

This approach is validated on the mutagenesis problem: the 1-NN classifier based on the distance constructed by *DISTILL*, demonstrates to be quite competitive with respect to prominent ILP learners such as *FOIL* [16] and *PROGOL* [14] on this problem. *DISTILL* also improves on *STILL* [18]: it involves one less parameter and shows little sensitivity with respect to parameter d for $d \geq 30$.

We last conclude with some perspectives for further research.

2   State of the art

This section first presents our motivation for constructing distances on first-order logic space, and briefly recalls some previous work devoted to this aim.

2.1   Rules *versus* Distances

The main advantages of instance-based (e.g. k-NN) classifiers versus standard rule learning are extensively discussed in [7]: simply put, k-NN classifiers accurately deal with both symbolic and numerical data, on one hand, and with noisy data, on the other hand. Further, the predictive accuracy obtained by a k-NN classifier (in leave-one-out evaluation mode) gives hints into the quality of the data, and derives lower bounds on the optimal predictive accuracy [6].

Practically, a k-NN classifier allows for a flexible modeling of the target concept, more easily than rules or even oblique decision trees [11]. This can be exemplified as follows: in the bidimensional space $\mathbb{R}^2$, a set of n rules characterizes the target concept as the union of n rectangles; an oblique decision tree with n leaves characterizes it as the union of n polygons. And a set of N examples, plus a distance, induces a fine grained partition of the problem domain into N cells (the Voronoï cells); the target concept is characterized as the union of those cells that are centered on a positive example.

Compared to rules, instance-based classifiers suffer from their low intelligibility: the classification of an instance is justified by exhibiting the most similar example(s), rather than a high-level hypothesis.

2.2 Related work

Most distances on attribute-value languages are computed as the weighted sum of the elementary distances d_i defined on the attribute domains:

given $E = \wedge_i[att_i = V_i]$ and $F = \wedge_i[att_i = W_i]$, $d(E, F) = \sum_i w_i d_i(V_i, W_i)$

The distance accuracy (evaluated as the predictive accuracy of the corresponding k-NN classifier) critically depends on weights w_i, usually adjusted by trial and error. These can also be determined by an optimization algorithm [12].

Weight-based distances have been first extended to first-order logic languages in [2] and later refined in [7]. In both cases, the distance between any two conjunctive formulae is basically computed from that of their literals; the distance between two literals (built on the same symbol of predicate) is computed from the distance between their arguments, the weight of the predicate, and the weights of the predicate arguments. A global perspective on the examples, accounting for the semantics of the domain, is offered by computing the distance between two terms from the distance between the literals where they both appear. (Combinatorial explosion is prevented via syntactic restrictions on the literals examined). In KBG [2], the distances between terms are computed via a fixed point method, whereas $RIBL$ [7] uses an iterative resolution.

The resulting similarity map critically depends on both the syntax and the weights. This limitation is partly addressed by $RIBL$, which iteratively refines the weights proposed by the expert.

To sum up, these distances combine built-in knowledge (the elementary distances on the domains of attributes or predicate arguments), with weights, i.e. non-declarative biases either manually or automatically adjusted.

3 Hypothesis-driven distances

This section investigates how a set of hypotheses can be used to map a problem domain onto a metric space. The properties and limitations of the distance constructed from this mapping, or hypothesis-driven distance (HDD), are studied.

3.1 Principle

Let $\mathcal{L}_h$ denote the language of hypotheses (including the language of instances via the single representation trick). Let $\mathcal{H} = \{h_1, \dots h_d\}$ denote a set of d hypotheses. One notices [19] that $\mathcal{H}$ induces a mapping π from $\mathcal{L}_h$ onto the boolean space of dimension d, by associating to any example or hypothesis E the vector of booleans coding whether E is subsumed by h_i, noted $E \prec h_i$:

$$\pi : \mathcal{L}_h \to \{0,1\}^d$$
$$E \to \pi(E) = (\pi_1(E), \dots, \pi_d(E)), \quad \text{where } \pi_i(E) = 1 \text{ iff } E \prec h_i$$

Note that this projection onto $\{0,1\}^d$ does not make any assumption on $\mathcal{L}_h$: besides $\mathcal{H}$, it only invokes the covering test (checking whether $E \prec h_i$).

And $\{0,1\}^d$ is a metric space; a distance on $\mathcal{L}_h$ thus naturally follows, by setting:

$$\forall E, F \in \mathcal{L}_h, \; dist(E,F) = \sum_{i=1}^{d} |\pi_i(E) - \pi_i(F)|$$

By construction, $dist$ is symmetrical and satisfies the triangular inequality:

$$\forall E, F, G, \; dist(E,F) \leq dist(E,G) + dist(G,F)$$

Still, it does not satisfy the identity relation[1]: $(dist(E,F) = 0) \not\Rightarrow (E = F)$.

3.2 Local behavior of HDD

Hypotheses-based distances locally depend upon the context. Consider examples E and F, together with the single hypothesis h (Table 1). As E is covered by h ($\pi(E) = 1$), and F is not ($\pi(F) = 0$), one has $dist(E,F) = 1$.

Table 1: Mapping based on hypothesis h = [Atom = carbon] $\wedge$ [Type > 20]

	Initial description				Mapping
	Atom	Size	Type	El. charge	π
E	carbon	small	22	3.45	1
F	carbon	large	17	5.22	0

Consider examples E' and F' constructed from E and F via replacing a common feature ($Atom = carbon$) by another feature (say $Atom = oxygen$). Any weight-based distance $dist_w$ would give $dist_w(E,F) = dist_w(E',F')$. More generally, weight-based distances are invariant by translation (consistently modifying a feature shared by any two examples does not modify their distance).

This is not necessary the case for hypotheses-based distances, due to the fact that $\pi(E)$ globally depends on E (since $\pi(E') = \pi(F') = 0$, $dist(E',F') = 0$). A modification of any given feature of E may, or not, have an effect on $\pi(E)$ depending on the other features.

A hypothesis-driven distance thereby encodes local discontinuities of the problem domain, corresponding to the frontiers of hypotheses h_i.

---

[1] Properly speaking, $dist$ is hence a semi-distance, rather than a distance. The distinction is omitted in what follows for the sake of simplicity.

The property of *non invariance by translation* is desirable as it enables to emulate the "versatile similarities" of experts. An expert may consider two devices manufactured by a given firm, as very similar; what s/he really means is that same failures are likely observed on these devices. But (rather unexpectedly for the naive knowledge engineer) the same devices manufactured by another firm, happen to be judged quite dissimilar...

3.3 Limitations of HDDs

HDDs do not present any interest whenever they are based on a concise set of hypotheses $\mathcal{H}$: e.g. *dist* gets rather coarse if any example is covered by a single hypothesis, such as happens if $\mathcal{H}$ is a decision tree (either E and F are covered by the same hypothesis, and $dist(E, F) = 0$, or $dist(E, F) = 2$).

The granularity of a HDD increases with the redundancy of $\mathcal{H}$ (i.e. the average number of h_i covering any example) and more precisely with the number and diversity of hypotheses h_i. Still, a HDD does not involve in any way the conclusions associated to hypotheses h_i; this suggests that the relevance of a HDD is potentially independent from the relevance of $\mathcal{H}$ (see section 4.3).

Still, the structure of the boolean space does not reflect the structure of the problem domain. A hypothesis h_i usually covers less than half the problem space: $\pi_i(E) = 1$ is thus less frequent than $\pi_i(E) = 0$, whilst 1 and 0 play equivalent roles in the boolean space.

3.4 Projection onto $\mathbf{N}^d$

We therefore consider more complex hypotheses. Let h_i now be a disjunction of formulae in $\mathcal{L}_h$, with $h_i = s_{i,1} \vee \ldots \vee s_{i,n_i}$, and let $\pi_i(E)$ (section 3.1) be now defined as the number of formulae $s_{i,j}$ covering E. This allows π to map the problem domain $\mathcal{L}_h$ onto a richer metric space, that of integer vectors $\mathbf{N}^d$. The corresponding HDD is naturally defined as:

$$dist(E, F) = \sqrt{\sum_i (\pi_i(E) - \pi_i(F))^2}$$

The ordered structure of $\mathbf{N}$ reflects a logical structure on the problem domain. Let h_i^M denote the $M - of - N$ hypothesis constructed from the disjunctive h_i, defined as: $E \prec h_i^M$ iff E is covered by at least M formulae $s_{i,j}$. One easily shows that h_i^{M+1} is covered by h_i^M. The set of hypotheses $\{h_i^M$, for $M = 1..n_i\}$, is a sequence of nested hypotheses which can be viewed as neighborhoods, or balls, of increasing specificity; π_i thereby corresponds to a "dimension" of the problem domain, and the coordinate $\pi_i(E)$ of E on this dimension precisely gives the rank of the most specific ball E belongs to.

4 Distance Induction based on Disjunctive Version Space

This section is devoted to learning a HDD from examples expressed as definite or constrained clauses.

4.1 Principle

The presented mechanism relies on the disjunctive version space (DiVS) approach; more details on *DiVS* in attribute-value and first-order logic languages are respectively found in [17] and [18]. The elementary step in *DiVS* consists of characterizing the most general hypothesis $D(E, F)$ covering example E and discriminating example F, where E and F satisfy distinct target concepts.

In attribute-value languages, $D(E, F)$ simply is the disjunction of the maximally general selectors[2] covering E and rejecting F:

Table 2: Hypothesis $D(E, F)$ and corresponding mapping

	\multicolumn{4}{c}{Initial description}	Mapping
	Atom	Size	Type	El. charge	π
E	carbon	small	22	3.45	3
F	carbon	large	17	5.22	0
I	oxygen	small	18	7.11	2

$$D(E,F) = [Size = small] \lor [Type > 17] \lor [El.\ charge < 5.22]$$

Given the user-supplied number d of dimensions, $\mathcal{H}$ is iteratively constructed by setting $h_i = D(E_i, F_i)$, where E_i and F_i are randomly selected in the training set such that they satisfy distinct target concepts.

Construction of $\mathcal{H} = \{h_1, \ldots, h_d\}$
    For $i = 1$ to d,
        Randomly select E_i **and** F_i **in the training set**
            with $Class(E_i) \neq Class(F_i)$
        Construct h_i **discriminating** E_i **from** F_i.

For any further example I, the coordinate $\pi_i(I)$ on dimension $D(E_i, F_i)$ is computed as the number of selectors in $D(E_i, F_i)$, satisfied by I. E_i and F_i respectively get the highest and lowest coordinates on this dimension.

4.2 DISTILL

DiVS has been extended and adapted to first order logic via the *STILL* algorithm [18]. Due to space limitations, *STILL* will only be illustrated on a short example. Let E and F be definite clauses; let C be constructed from E by turning any occurence of a term t_i in E into a distinct variable X_j, and let substitution θ be defined as $\theta = \{X_j/t_i\}$.

$$E : tc(e) \quad : -atom(e, a, oxy, 18), atom(e, b, carbon, 22), cc(a, b)$$
$$F : {}^-tc(f) : -atom(f, c, carbon, 24), atom(f, d, hydr, 3)$$
$$C : tc(X) \quad : -atom(X', Y, Z, T), atom(X'', U, V, W), cc(R, S)$$

---

[2] We restrict ourselves to selectors $[att = V]$, where V denote a discrete value or a numerical interval. Selector $[att = (a, +\infty)]$ is written $[att > a]$ for the sake of convenience.

A constrained clause $G\gamma$ in the chosen language belongs to the set $D(E, F)$, iff either G or γ discriminate F. G is discriminant iff it includes a discriminant predicate (e.g. cc). Otherwise, G subsumes F and the set of substitutions mapping G onto F is denoted Σ; then, γ is discriminant iff it is incompatible with all substitutions in Σ, or equivalently belongs to all $D(\theta, \sigma)$ within an equivalent attribute-value representation:

Table 3: Attribute-value reformulation and (part of) a discriminant constraint

	X	X'	Y	Z	T	X''	U	V	W	$T-W$
θ	e	e	a	oxy	18	e	b	$carbon$	22	-4
σ_1	f	f	c	$carbon$	24	f	c	$carbon$	24	0
σ_2	f	f	d	$hydr$	3	f	d	$hydr$	3	0
σ_3	f	f	c	$carbon$	24	f	d	$hydr$	3	21
σ_4	f	f	d	$hydr$	3	f	c	$carbon$	24	-21

$$D(\theta, \sigma_1) = [Z = oxygen] \vee [T < 24] \vee [W < 24] \vee [T - W < 0]$$

The disjunctive hypothesis $D(E, F)$ discriminating E from F is therefore completely described by the set of discriminant predicates, and the disjunctive constraints $D(\theta, \sigma)$ for σ ranging in Σ. This characterization gets intractable on really relational domains (e.g. $|\Sigma|$ goes up to 40^{40} in the mutagenesis problem). *STILL* therefore constructs a polynomial approximation of $D(E, F)$, noted $D_\eta(E, F)$, by only considering η substitutions $\sigma_1, ..\sigma_\eta$ randomly sampled in Σ. The construction of $D_\eta(E, F)$ is in $\mathcal{O}(\eta \times V^2)$, where V denotes the maximal number of arguments in an example.

Deciding whether $D_\eta(E, F)$ covers a further instance I is similarly intractable, as it requires to explore the set Σ' of substitutions mapping C onto I. A polynomial approximation of the covering test is similarly provided by considering only K substitutions randomly selected in Σ'.

The coordinate of I on dimension $D_\eta(E, F)$ is the number of discriminant predicates involved in I, augmented with the maximal value of $C\tau \star D_\eta(E, F)$, taken over K substitutions τ randomly selected in Σ'. And $C\tau \star D_\eta(E, F)$ is the minimum number of selectors in $D(\theta, \sigma_j)$ satisfied by τ, for $j = 1 \ldots \eta$. Finally, the distance between any two examples has complexity $\mathcal{O}(d \times K \times \eta \times V^2)$.

4.3 Experimentation

This approach is evaluated on the well-studied mutagenesis problem [13, 21]. Table 4.(a) reports the best results obtained by *FOIL*, *PROGOL* and *STILL* [20, 18]. *FOIL* and *PROGOL* have been evaluated via 10-fold crossvalidation; *STILL* was evaluated in a similar way, only including 25 runs (with different random seeds) instead of 10, as recommended for evaluating stochastic processes. Run times (in seconds) are measured on HP-735 workstations.

DISTILL is evaluated from the average predictive accuracy of the 1-NN classifier based on *dist*, via the same protocol as *STILL*. The experiments focus on the influence of the number d of constructed hypotheses, varied in 10..100. The two other parameters of *DISTILL*, inherited from *STILL*, are set to their default value ($\eta = 300$ and $K = 3$).

Another experimentation goal is to study what happens if the provided examples are not classified at all, by removing the test $Class(E) \neq Class(F)$ in the construction of $\mathcal{H}$ (section 4.1). The corresponding algorithm is termed *UNDISTILL*, for *Unsupervised Distance Induction*.

Tables 4.b and 4.c respectively give the results obtained by *DISTILL* and *UNDISTILL* (with run times in seconds on a HP-710).

Table 4: Predictive accuracy on the 188-compound problem

(a) Reference results

System	Accuracy	Time
FOIL	86 ± 3	.5
PROGOL	88 ± 2	40 950
STILL	93.6 ± 4	< 120

(b) DISTILL

D	Accuracy	Time
10	88.6 ± 4.8	7
30	93.6 ± 5	19
50	94.7 ± 3.7	31
70	$\mathbf{96.7 \pm 4.3}$	43
90	95.3 ± 2.4	56

(c) UNDISTILL

D	Accuracy	Time
10	86.7 ± 6.9	6
30	94.2 ± 3.8	19
50	93.3 ± 3.8	31
70	93.3 ± 5.3	44
90	$\mathbf{94.7 \pm 2.6}$	56

It was conjectured that the relevance of $\mathcal{H}$ was not a necessary condition to derive a relevant HDD (section 3.3); one is nevertheless surprised that *DISTILL* and *UNDISTILL* obtain comparable results. In retrospect, it appears that hypotheses are used to make distinctions on the problem domain: the soundness of these distinctions does not matter provided they allow for a sufficiently precise scattering of the problem domain.

Practically, the good performances of UNDISTILL suggest that distance induction does not depend on the noise of the data, and can be employed for supervised learning.

5 Conclusion

Rather than syntactically comparing two examples, we propose to compare the way these respectively behave with respect to a set of hypotheses. Hypothesis-driven distances strongly depend on the selection of the hypotheses: HDDs typically bring no further information if these hypotheses are concise and intelligible (section 3.3). We therefore used a disjunctive version space approach: a set of d hypotheses is constructed as the maximally general hypotheses discriminating d pairs of examples (E_i, F_i). E_i and F_i are randomly selected in *UNDISTILL*, and they are further required to satisfy distinct target concepts in *DISTILL*.

Experimental validation shows that both *DISTILL* and *UNDISTILL* supersede other ILP learners on the mutagenesis dataset, for $d \geq 30$. Incidentally, this confirms that a stochastic bias (meant as the selection of E_i and F_i) can be a sound alternative to knowledge-demanding biases.

Further work will consider how the set of hypotheses can be pruned or augmented. Other perspectives are offered by coupling this distance with standard data analysis algorithms (e.g. k-means or factorial analysis) to achieve conceptual clustering or graphical representation of the data.

This approach will also be experimented on other and larger datasets, facing with the multiple challenges of knowledge discovery in data bases.

References

1. A. Aamodt and E.Plaza. Case-based reasoning : Foundational issues, methodological variations, and system approaches. *AICOM*, 7(1), 1994.
2. G. Bisson. Learning in FOL with a similarity measure. In *Proceedings of 10th AAAI*, 1992.
3. A. Cornuejols. Analogy as minimization of description length. In G. Nakhaeizadeh and C. Taylor, eds, *Machine Learning and Statistics : The interface*. Wiley, 1996.
4. C. DeCaestecker. Incremental concept formation with attribute selection. In K. Morik, editor, *Proc. of EWSL 1989*, pages 49–58. Pitman, London, 1989.
5. P. Domingos. Rule induction and instance-based learning: A unified approach. In *Proceedings of IJCAI-95*, pages 1226–1232. 1995.
6. R.O. Duda and P.E. Hart. *Pattern Classification and scene analysis*. John Wiley and sons, Menlo Park, CA, 1973.
7. W. Emde and D. Wettscherek. Relational instance based learning. In L. Saitta, editor, *Proceedings of ICML-96*, pages 122–130, 1996.
8. U.M. Fayyad, G. Piatetsky-Shapiro, and P. Smyth. From data mining to knowledge discovery: An overview. In *Advances in Knowledge Discovery and Data Mining*, pages 1–34. MIT Press, 1996.
9. D. Fisher. Iterative optimization and simplification of hierarchical clusterings. Technical report, Vanderbilt University, TR CS-95-01, 1995.
10. D. Gentner. Structure mapping : A theoretical framework for analogy. *Cognitive Science*, 7:155–170, 1983.
11. D. Heath, S. Kasif, and S. Salzberg. Induction of oblique decision trees. In *Proceedings of IJCAI-93*, pages 1002–1007. Morgan Kaufmann, 1993.
12. J. D. Kelly and L. Davis. A hybrid genetic algorithm for classification. In *Proceedings of IJCAI-91*, pages 645–650. Morgan Kaufmann, 1991.
13. R.D. King, A. Srinivasan, and M.J.E. Sternberg. Relating chemical activity to structure: an examination of ILP successes. *New Gen. Comput.*, 13, 1995.
14. S. Muggleton. Inverse entailment and PROGOL. *New Gen. Comput.*, 13:245–286, 1995.
15. S. Muggleton and L. De Raedt. Inductive logic programming: Theory and methods. *Journal of Logic Programming*, 19:629–679, 1994.
16. J.R. Quinlan. Learning logical definition from relations. *Machine Learning*, 5:239–266, 1990.
17. M. Sebag. Delaying the choice of bias: A disjunctive version space approach. In L. Saitta, editor, *Proceedings of ICML-96*, pages 444–452. 1996.
18. M. Sebag and C. Rouveirol. Tractable induction and classification in FOL. In *Proceedings of IJCAI-97*, to appear.
19. M. Sebag and M. Schoenauer. A rule-based similarity measure. In S. Wess, K.-D. Althoff, and M. M. Richter, eds, *Topics in Case-Based Reasonning*, volume 837 of *LNCS*, pages 119–130. Springer Verlag, 1994.
20. A. Srinivasan and S. Muggleton. Comparing the use of background knowledge by two ILP systems. In L. de Raedt, editor, *Proceedings of ILP-95*. Katholieke Universiteit Leuven, 1995.
21. *ESPRIT Project LTR 20237 ILP²*. PPR-1, 1997.

Carcinogenesis Predictions Using ILP*

A. Srinivasan[1], R.D. King[2], S.H. Muggleton[1], M.J.E. Sternberg[3]

[1] Oxford University Comp. Lab., Wolfson Bldg., Parks Rd, Oxford, UK
[2] Dept. of Comp. Sc., University of Wales Aberystwyth, Ceredigion, UK
[3] Biomolecular Modelling Lab., ICRF, 44 Lincoln's Inn Fields, London, UK

Abstract. Obtaining accurate structural alerts for the causes of chemical cancers is a problem of great scientific and humanitarian value. This paper follows up on earlier research that demonstrated the use of Inductive Logic Programming (ILP) for predictions for the related problem of mutagenic activity amongst nitroaromatic molecules. Here we are concerned with predicting carcinogenic activity in rodent bioassays using data from the U.S. National Toxicology Program conducted by the National Institute of Environmental Health Sciences. The 330 chemicals used here are significantly more diverse than the previous study, and form the basis for obtaining Structure-Activity Relationships (SARs) relating molecular structure to cancerous activity in rodents. We describe the use of the ILP system Progol to obtain SARs from this data. The rules obtained from Progol are comparable in accuracy to those from expert chemists, and more accurate than most state-of-the-art toxicity prediction methods. The rules can also be interpreted to give clues about the biological and chemical mechanisms of carcinogenesis, and make use of those learnt by Progol for mutagenesis. Finally, we present details of, and predictions for, an ongoing international blind trial aimed specifically at comparing prediction methods. This trial provides ILP algorithms an opportunity to participate at the leading-edge of scientific discovery.

1 Introduction

The task of obtaining the molecular mechanisms for biological toxicity has been a prominent area of application for Inductive Logic Programming (ILP) systems. Recently, this has seen the use of an ILP program to the task of predicting the mutagenic activity of a restricted class of molecules [12, 21]. The results reported, while interesting, were preliminary for the following reasons. Firstly, the data pertain to a relatively homogeneous class of compounds –although, in themselves, they were more diverse than those analysed previously by ILP (see [13]). Secondly, while some comparative studies were performed ([22]), they were not against state-of-the-art methods designed specifically for toxicity prediction. Finally, a single success is clearly not sufficient grounds for claiming general applicability of a technique. In this paper we remedy each of these shortcomings.

---

* Large sections of this paper also appear, with consent, in *Intelligent Data Analysis in Medicine and Pharmacology*, N. Lavrač, E. Keravnou, B. Zupan Eds.,Kluwer Academic Publishers

In the course of doing so, we present an important new problem where any scientific discoveries made by ILP programs will be measured against international competition in true blind trials.

This paper is organised as follows. Section 2 describes the problem of carcinogenesis prediction of rodent bioassays. These assays are conducted as part of the National Toxicology Program (NTP) by the U.S. National Institute for Environmental Health Sciences (NIEHS). A prominent feature associated with the NTP is the NIEHS Predictive Toxicology Evaluation – or PTE – project ([6]). The PTE project identifies a "test" set of chemicals from those currently undergoing tests for carcinogenicity within the NTP. Predictions on this test set were invited and then compared against the true activity observed in rodents, once such data are available. The description of these blind trials, including details of a trial scheduled for completion in 1998, is described in Section 3. Section 4 describes the use of the ILP program Progol ([17]) to extract molecular descriptions for cancerous activity. These are used to compare against state-of-the-art predictions on an earlier trial in the PTE project (Section 4.4). Predictions of the activity of chemicals in the ongoing PTE trial are also in Section 4.4. Section 5 presents details of an Internet site designed to encourage predictions from other ILP programs. Section 6 concludes this paper.

2 The Carcinogenesis problem and the NTP data base

Prevention of environmentally-induced cancers is a health issue of unquestionable importance. Almost every sphere of human activity in an industrialised society faces potential chemical hazards of some form. In [9], it is estimated that nearly 100,000 chemicals are in use in large amounts every day. A further 500–1000 are added every year. Only a small fraction of these chemicals have been evaluated for toxic effects like carcinogenicity. The U.S. National Toxicology Program (NTP) contributes to this enterprise by conducting standardised chemical bioassays – exposure of rodents to a range of chemicals – to help identify substances that may have carcinogenic effects on humans. However, obtaining empirical evidence from such bioassays is expensive and usually too slow to cope with the number of chemicals that can result in adverse effects on human exposure. This has resulted in an urgent need for models that propose molecular mechanisms for carcinogenesis. It is envisaged that such models would (a) generate reliable toxicity predictions for all kinds of chemicals; (b) enable low cost identification of hazardous chemicals; and (c) refine and reduce the reliance on the use of large number of laboratory animals [6]. Pattern-recognition methods can "...help identify, characterise, and understand the various mechanisms or modes of action that determine the type and level of response observed when biological systems are exposed to chemicals" [6].

Tests conducted by the NTP have so far resulted in a data base of more than 300 compounds that have been shown to be carcinogenic or otherwise in rodents. Amongst other criteria, the chemicals have been selected on the basis of their carcinogenic potential – for example, positive mutagenicity tests – and on evidence of substantial human exposure ([9]). Using rat and mouse strains (of both genders) as predictive surrogates for humans, levels of evidence of carcinogenicity are obtained from the incidence of tumours on long-term (two years) exposure to the chemicals. The NTP assigns the following levels of evidence: CE, clear evidence; SE, some evidence; E, equivocal evidence; and NE, no evidence. Precise definitions for determining these levels can be found in [9], and a complete listing of all chemicals tested is available at the NTP Home Page: *http://ntpserver.niehs.nih.gov/*.

The diversity of these compounds present a general problem to many conventional SAR techniques. Most of these, such as the regression-based techniques under the broad category called Hansch Analysis ([15]), can only be applied to model compounds that have similar mechanisms of action. This "congeneric" assumption does not hold for the chemicals in the NTP data base, thus limiting the applicability of such methods. The Predictive Toxicology Evaluation project undertaken by the NIEHS aims to obtain an unbiased comparison of prediction methods by specifying compounds for blind trials. One such trial, PTE-1, is now complete. Complete results of NTP tests for compounds in the second trial, PTE-2, will be available by mid 1998.

3   The blind trials PTE-1 and PTE-2

The PTE project ([6]) is concerned with predictions of overall cancerous activity of a pre-specified set of compounds. This overall activity is either "POS" if the level of activity is CE or SE, or "NEG". The PTE project identifies a set of compounds either scheduled for, or currently undergoing, NTP tests. Information concerning the bioassays is disseminated with the view of encouraging the use of state-of-the-art toxicity prediction schemes. Once the true results of biological activity are available, the project collects a set of leading predictors and publishes their results. The first of these trials, termed PTE-1 is now complete, and results for 39 chemicals are available in [3]. [4]

A second round of toxicology evaluation – PTE-2 – consisting of 30 compounds (of which 5 are inorganic) is currently in progress. True biological activity for 13 of these have been determined at the time of writing of this paper. A complete description of chemicals in PTE-2, along with a schedule of dates is available in [6]. The remaining activity levels should be determined by 1998. In this paper, we intend to use Progol to obtain structural alerts from chemicals in the NTP data base. In the first instance, predictions from these alerts will be compared against other predictions available for PTE-1. This will be followed by predictions for compounds in PTE-2.

---

[4] A preliminary effort by the ILP system Progol in presented in [14]. The results in this paper subsume these early results as a number of toxicology indicators were unavailable to us at that time. Further details are in Section 4.

4 Carcinogenesis predictions using Progol

4.1 Aims

The experiment described here has the following aims.

1. Use the ILP system Progol to obtain rules for carcinogenicity from data that does not include compounds in PTE-1 and PTE-2.
2. Predict carcinogenic activity of compounds in PTE-1, and compare against other state-of-the-art toxicity prediction methods.
3. Predict carcinogenic activity of compounds in PTE-2.

4.2 Materials

Data Figure 1 shows the distribution of compounds in the NTP data base having an overall activity of $POS(+)$ or $NEG(-)$.

Compounds	+	−	Total
PTE-1	20	19	39
PTE-2	≥ 7	≥ 6	30
Rest	162	136	298

Fig. 1. Class distribution of compounds. Complete details of PTE-2 will be available by 1998.

Background knowledge The following background knowledge is available for each category of compounds listed in Fig.1. Complete Prolog descriptions of each of the following are available via anonymous ftp to *ftp.comlab.ox.ac.uk*, in the directory *pub/Packages/ILP/Datasets*.

Atom-bond description. These are ground facts representing the atom and bond structures of the compounds. The representation first introduced in [21] is retained. These are Prolog translations of the output of the molecular modelling package QUANTA. Bond information consist of facts of the form *bond(compound,atom1,atom2,bondtype)* stating that *compound* has a bond of *bondtype* between the atoms *atom1* and *atom2*. Atomic structure consists of facts of the form *atm(compound,atom,element,atomtype,charge)*, stating that in *compound*, *atom* has element *element* of *atomtype* and partial charge *charge*.

Generic structural groups. This represents generic structural groups (methyl groups, benzene rings etc.) that can be defined directly using the atom and bond description of the compounds. Here we use definitions for 29 different structural groups, which expands on the 12 definitions used in [22]. We pre-compute these structural groups for efficiency. An example fact that results is in the form *methyl(compound,atom_list)*, which states that the list of atoms *atom_list* in *compound* form a methyl group. Connectivity amongst groups is defined using these lists of atoms.

Genotoxicity. These are results of short-term assays used to detect and characterise chemicals that may pose genetic risks. These assays include the *Salmonella* assay, in-vivo tests for the induction of micro-nuclei in rat and mouse bone marrow etc. A full report available at the NTP Home Page lists the results from such tests in one of 12 types. Results are usually + or − indicating positive or negative response. These results are encoded into Prolog facts of the form *has_property(compound,type,result)*, which states that the *compound* in genetic toxicology *type* returned *result*. Here *result* is one of p (positive) or n (negative). In cases where more than 1 set of results are available for a given type, we have adopted the position of returning the majority result. When positive and negative results are returned in equal numbers, then no result is recorded for that test.

Mutagenicity. Progol rules from the earlier experiments on obtaining structural rules for mutagenesis are included ([12, 20]). Mutagenic chemicals have often been found to be carcinogenic ([7]), and we use all the rules found with Progol (see [20] for a complete listing).

Structural indicators. We have been able to encode some of the structural alerts used in [1]. At the time of writing this paper, the NTP proposes to make available nearly 80 additional structural attributes for the chemicals. Unfortunately, this is not yet in place for reuse in experiments here.

Prediction methods The ILP system used here is P-Progol (Version 2.3). This a Prolog implementation of the Progol algorithm ([17]), and we will refer to this simply as Progol in the rest of this paper. P-Progol is available via anonymous ftp to *ftp.comlab.ox.ac.uk*, in the directory *pub/Packages/ILP*. The other toxicity prediction methods compared against Progol's PTE-1 predictions are: Ashby [23], RASH [10], TIPT [2], Benigni [5], DEREK [19], Bakale [4], TOPKAT [8], CASE [18], and COMPACT [16]. We take the PTE-1 predictions of each these algorithms as reported in [3].

4.3 Method

The task is to obtain a theory for carcinogenesis using the 298 chemicals under the "Rest" category in Fig.1. This theory is then to be used to predict the classes of compounds in PTE-1 and PTE-2. Progol constructs theories within the language and statistical constraints provided by the user. In domains such as the one considered here, it is difficult to know beforehand any reasonable set of constraints to provide. Further, it is not evident that the theory returned by default settings within the program is the best possible. Consequently, we adopt the following three-stage procedure.

Stage 1: Parameter identification. Identify 1 or more critical parameters for Progol. Changing these should result in significant changes in the theory returned by Progol.

Stage 2: Model selection. This proceeds as follows.

1. Randomly select a small subset of the 298 chemicals to act as a "validation" set. The remaining chemicals form the "training" set for Progol.

2. Systematically vary the critical parameters. For each setting obtain a theory from the training set, and record its accuracy on the validation set.

3. Return the theory with the highest accuracy on the validation set.

Stage 3: Model evaluation. The predictions for PTE-1 and PTE-2 by the theory returned from Stage 2 are recorded. For other toxicity prediction methods, the probability that Progol classifies PTE-1 compounds in the same proportion as that method is obtained using McNemar's Test (see below).

For a given set of background predicate definitions, theories returned by Progol are usually affected by the following parameters: (1) c, bounding the number of literals in any hypothesised clause; (2) *noise*, bounding the minimum acceptable training set accuracy for a clause; and (3) *nodes*, bounding the number of clauses searched. Initial experimentation (Stage 1) suggested that the most sensitive parameter for Progol was *noise*. The experiments here consider theories arising from 4 settings corresponding *noise* values 0.35, 0.30, 0.25, and 0.20. For the data here, the size of the validation set is taken to be 30% of the 298 chemicals – that is, 89 compounds. Of these 49 are labelled + and the remaining 40 are labelled −. This leaves 209 compounds for training. Of these 113 are + and the remaining 96 are −.

We also note one other detail concerning the procedure for obtaining a final theory. The Prolog implementation used here can obtain clauses using two different search strategies. The first is as in [17], and results in redundant examples being removed after an acceptable clause is found. A second strategy retains these examples, which gives correct estimates for the accuracy of the clause found. Clauses obtained in this fashion can have significant overlap in the examples they make redundant. The preferred final theory is then the subset of these clauses that has maximal compression (within acceptable resource limits).[5]

McNemar's Test McNemar's test for changes is used to compare algorithms For a pair of algorithms, this is done by a cross-comparison of the compounds correctly and incorrectly classified as shown in Fig.2.

---

[5] This subset is currently obtained by a companion program to P-Progol called T-Reduce (Version 1.0). Compression of a set of clauses is defined analogous to the measure in [17], namely, $P - N - L$ where P is the positive examples covered by the theory, N is the negative examples covered by the theory, and L is the number of clauses in the theory. T-Reduce is available on request from the first author.

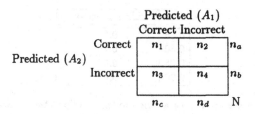

Fig. 2. Cross-comparison of the predictions of a pair of algorithms $A_{1,2}$ n_1 is the number of compounds whose class is correctly predicted by both algorithms. Similarly for the entries $n_{2,3,4}$.

The null hypothesis is that the proportion of examples correctly classified by both algorithms is the same. If there is no significant difference in the performance of the two algorithms, half of the $n_2 + n_3$ cases whose classifications disagree should be classified correctly by A_1 and A_2 respectively. Because of small numbers, we directly estimate the probability of a chance classification using the binomial distribution, with probability of success at 0.5. In effect, this is likened to probability of obtaining at least n_2 (or n_3, if greater) heads in a sequence of $n_2 + n_3$ tosses of a fair coin.

It is evident that repeated cross-comparisons will yield occasions when Progol's performance will apparently seem better than its adversary. For repeated comparisons of a given pair of algorithms on different random samples of data, it is possible to apply a correction (known as the Bonferroni adjustment) for this problem. The situation of repeated comparisons of different pairs of algorithms on a given set of data (as is here) does not, on the surface, appear to be amenable to the same correction. However, adopting the spirit of the correction, we advocate caution in quantitative interpretations of the binomial probabilities obtained.

4.4 Results and discussion

Figure 3 tabulates the accuracies on the validation set for each of the parameter settings explored. These results lead to the choice of 0.30 as the preferred setting for minimum noise for acceptable clauses.

Figure 4 shows an English translation of the theory with highest validation accuracy in Fig.3. The actual rules obtained by Progol in terms of the background predicates is in Appendix A. Each disjunct in Fig.4 represents a rule followed by Progol. Rules 1-3 are based on biological tests. Additional comments on the rules follow.

Rule 1. The result of the Ames biological test for mutagenicity. The effectiveness of the Ames test is widely recognised, but it is gratifying that Progol identifies it as the most important.

Noise	Validation accuracy
0.35	0.63
0.30	0.70
0.25	0.63
0.20	0.65

Fig. 3. Validation set accuracies at the model selection stage. "Noise" values provide a lower bound on the training set accuracy for a clause hypothesised by Progol. "Validation accuracy" is the corresponding accuracy on the validation set of the theory obtained from Progol at that noise level.

Rule 2. This rule is a test based on using whole (not cell culture) Drosopha. Like the Ames test it tests for mutagenicity.

Rule 3. This rule is puzzling as it would be expected that a positive test for chromosome aberration would be a test for carcinogenesis, not a negative test. More specialised variants of this rule were obtained in other theories obtained in Stage 1 of the experimental methodology, suggesting absence of chromosal aberrations does have some role to play, reasons for which requires investigation.

Rule 4. Aromatic compounds are often carcinogens and the low partial charge indicates relative reactivity. The use of a precise number for partial charge is an artifact of using the information from QUANTA, resulting from a particular molecular substructure around the aromatic carbon.

Rule 5. Amine groups are recognised by Ashby ([23]) as indicators of carcinogenesis. This rule is a more accurate specification of this rule.

Rule 6. Aromatic hydrogen with a very high partial charge (often chlorinated aromatics). Such aromatics are relatively unreactive (perhaps giving time to diffuse to DNA).

Rule 7. The high partial charge on the hydroxyl oxygen suggests that the group is relatively unreactive. The significance of the aromatic (or resonant) hydrogen is unclear.

Rule 8. Compounds with bromine have been widely recognised as carcinogens ([23]).

Rule 9. A tetrahedral carbon with low partial charge. The Progol rules for mutagenicity are shown to have utility outside of their original application domain. This is interesting as it displays perhaps the first reuse of ILP-constructed knowledge between different scientific problems.

Predicting PTE-1 Figure 5 tabulates the accuracies of the different toxicity prediction methods on the compounds in PTE-1. This shows Progol to be comparable to the top 3 state-of-the-art toxicity predictors.

This result should be seen in the following perspective. The only method apparently more accurate than Progol is that of Ashby, which involves the par-

Compound A is carcinogenic if:

(1) it tests positive in the Salmonella assay; or
(2) it tests positive for sex-linked recessive lethal mutation in Drosphila;
(3) it tests negative for chromosome aberration (an in-vivo cytogenetic assay); or
(4) it has a carbon in a six-membered aromatic ring with a partial charge of -0.13; or
(5) it has a primary amine group and no secondary or tertiary amines; or
(6) it has an aromatic (or resonant) hydrogen with partial charge $\geq$ 0.168; or
(7) it has an hydroxy oxygen with a partial charge $\geq$ -0.616 and an aromatic (or resonant) hydrogen; or
(8) it has a bromine; or
(9) it has a tetrahedral carbon with a partial charge $\leq$ -0.144 and tests positive on Progol's mutagenicity rules.

Fig. 4. Progol's theory for carcinogenesis.

Method	Type	Accuracy	P
Ashby†	Chemist	0.77	0.29
Progol	ILP	0.72	1.00
RASH†	Biological potency analysis	0.72	0.39
TIPT†	Propositional ML	0.67	0.11
Bakale	Chemical reactivity analysis	0.63	0.09
Benigni	Expert-guided regression	0.62	0.02
DEREK	Expert system	0.57	0.02
TOPKAT	Statistical discrimination	0.54	0.03
CASE	Statistical correlation analysis	0.54	< 0.01
COMPACT	Molecular modelling	0.54	0.01
Default	Majority class	0.51	0.01

Fig. 5. Comparative accuracies on PTE-1. Here P represents the binomial probability that Progol and the corresponding toxicity prediction method classify the same proportion of examples correctly. The "Default" method predicts all compounds to be carcinogenic. Methods marked with a † have access to short-term in-vivo rodent tests that were unavailable to other methods. Ashby and RASH also involve some subjective evaluation to decide on structural alerts.

ticipation of human experts and a large degree of subjective evaluation. All the methods with accuracy close to Progol (Ashby, RASH, and TIPT) have access to biological data that was not available to Progol (information form short-term - 13 week - rodent tests). It should also be noted that all the methods compared with Progol were specifically developed for chemical structure activity and toxicity prediction. Some recent information available to us suggest that results are also results are comparable to those obtained by a mixture of ILP and regression with additional biological information. [6]

---

[6] Personal communication from S. Kramer to the second author.

Predicting PTE-2 Figure 6 tabulates the predictions made by the theory in Fig.4 for compounds in PTE-2. The results to date show that Progol has currently predicted $8/13 \approx 62\%$ of the compounds correctly. Progol is currently ranked equal first for accuracy. The accuracy of Progol is again comparable to Ashby (7/13) and RASH (8/13) (no predictions are available as for TIPT). The lower accuracy of Progol (and the other participating methods) in PTE-2 compared with PTE-1 probably reflects the different distribution of compounds in PTE-2 compared to PTE-1 and training data. For example: the percentage of compounds with positive a Ames test in PTE-2 is only 16% compared to an average 42% for PTE-1 and the training data. The changing distribution has been previously noted in [23] and probably reflects a different testing strategy by the NIEHS.

5 The PTE Challenge: a Forum for Evaluating Carcinogenicity Predictions

We have developed an Internet site that maintains theories predicting activity values for PTE-1 and PTE-2. The site can be found at:

http://www.comlab.ox.ac.uk/oucl/groups/machlearn/PTE.

An important concern in developing this site was to provide a forum for the useful comparative study of ILP algorithms on an important scientific problem. In the absence of good theoretical arguments for the choice of any one algorithm, empirical studies remain invaluable. To this extent, we believe that submissions of the best theories obtained by ILP algorithms could provide a good indication of their applicability to the task of carcinogenesis prediction. Each submission takes the form of a prediction of activity values for compounds in the two "test" sets, and is to be accompanied by a description page conforming to template shown in Fig.7. It is our intention to obtain an evaluation of the theories from an expert in carcinogenicity prediction.

6 Conclusions

The carcinogenesis prediction trials conducted by the NIEHS offer ILP systems a unique opportunity to participate in true scientific discovery. The prediction of chemical carcinogenesis is both an important medical problem and a fascinating research area. This paper provides initial performance benchmarks that we hope will act as an incentive for participation by other ILP systems in the field. Progol has achieved accuracy as good or better that current state-of-the-art methods

Compound Id.	Name	Actual	Progol
6533-68-2	Scopolamine hydrobroamide	-	-
76-57-3	Codeine	-	-
147-47-7	1,2-Dihydro-2,2,4-trimethyquinoline	+	-
75-52-8	Nitromethane	-	-
109-99-9	Tetrahydrofuran	+	+
1948-33-0	t-Butylhydroquinone	-	+
100-41-4	Ethylbenzene	+	-
126-99-8	Chloroprene	+	+
8003-22-3	D&C Yellow No. 11	+	-
78-84-2	Isobutyraldehyde	-	-
127-00-4	1-Chloro-2-Propanol	T.B.A.	+
11-42-2	Diethanolamine	T.B.A.	-
77-09-8	Phenolphthalein	+	-
110-86-1	Pyridine	T.B.A.	+
1300-72-7	Xylenesulfonic acid, Na	-	-
98-00-0	Furfuryl alcohol	T.B.A.	+
125-33-7	Primaclone	+	+
111-76-2	Ethylene glycol monobutyl ether	T.B.A.	-
115-11-7	Isobutene	T.B.A.	-
93-15-2	Methyleugenol	T.B.A.	-
434-07-1	Oxymetholone	T.B.A.	-
84-65-1	Anthraquinone	T.B.A.	+
518-82-1	Emodin	T.B.A.	+
5392-40-5	Citral	T.B.A.	-
104-55-2	Cinnamaldehyde	T.B.A.	-
10026-24-1 †	Cobalt sulfate heptahydrate	T.B.A.	+
1313-27-5 †	Molybdenum trioxide	T.B.A.	-
1303-00-0 †	Gallium arsenide	T.B.A.	-
7632-00-0 †	Sodium nitrite	T.B.A.	+
1314-62-1 †	Vanadium pentozide	T.B.A.	-

Fig. 6. Progol predictions for PTE-2. The first column are the compound identifiers in the NTP database. The column headed "Actual" are tentative classifications from the NTP. Here the entry T.B.A. means "to be announced" – confirmed classifications will be available by July, 1998. The 5 compounds marked with a † are inorganic compounds.

of toxicity prediction. Results from other studies ([20]) suggest that addition of further relevant background knowledge should improve the Progol's prediction accuracy even further. In addition, Progol has produced nine rules that can be biologically and chemically interpreted and may help to provide a better understanding of the mechanisms of carcinogenesis.

The results for the prediction of carcinogenesis, taken together with the previous applications of predicting mutagenicity in nitroaromatic compounds, and the inhibition of angiogenesis by suramin analogues [11], show that ILP can play an important role in understanding cancer related compounds.

Consortium

Default

Name

A. Srinivasan

Address

Oxford University Computing Laboratory Wolfson Building, Parks Road Oxford OX1 3QD, UK

Materials

Data

The data is partitioned into 3 groups: (A) compounds in PTE-1; (B) compounds in PTE-2; and (C) compounds in the rest. As of 14/04/97, these had the following distribution:

Category	Carcinogenic	Non-carcinogenic
A	20	19
B	at least 7	at least 6
C	162	136

Program

Given a training set, the algorithm **MajClass** calculates the most frequently occuring class. The theory constructed by this algorithm classifies all compounds as this most frequently occuring class. **MajClass** uses the Prolog data representation followed in experiments with Progol

Method

1. Compounds in Category C are provided as the training set to **MajClass**
2. The resulting theory is used to classify compounds in Categories A, and B.

Results

Based on the distribution of compounds in Category C, the theory constructed by **MajClass** classifies all compounds as being carcinogenic. This gives it no explanatory power.

Comments

References

Fig. 7. Example of a description page in an entry to the PTE Challenge. Here the description is for a Majority Class algorithm. A template for this page is available at the Internet site for the challenge.

Acknowledgements

This research was supported partly by the Esprit Basic Research Action Project ILP II, the SERC project project 'Experimental Application and Development of ILP' and an SERC Advanced Research Fellowship held by Stephen Muggleton. Stephen Muggleton is a Research Fellow of Wolfson College Oxford. R.D. King was at Imperial Cancer Research Fund during the course of much of the early work on this problem. We would also like to thank Professor Donald Michie and

David Page for interesting and useful discussions concerning the use of ILP for predicting biological activity.

References

1. J. Ashby and R.W. Tennant. Definitive relationships among chemical structure, carcinogenicity and mutagenicity for 301 chemicals tested by the U.S. NTP. *Mutation Research*, 257:229–306, 1991.

2. D. Bahler and D. Bristol. The induction of rules for predicting chemical carcinogenesis. In *Proceedings of the 26th Hawaii International Conference on System Sciences*, Los Alamitos, 1993. IEEE Computer Society Press.

3. D. Bahler and D. Bristol. The induction of rules for predicting chemical carcinogenesis in rodents. In L. Hunter, D. Searls, and J. Shavlick, editors, *Intelligent Systems for Molecular Biology-93*, pages 29–37. MA:AAI/MIT, Cambridge, MA, 1993.

4. G. Bakale and R.D. McCreary. Prospective ke screening of potential carcinogens being tested in rodent bioassays by the US National Toxicology Program. *Mutagenesis*, 7:91–94, 1992.

5. R. Benigni. Predicting chemical carcinogenesis in rodents: the state of the art in the light of a comparative exercise. *Mutation Research*, 334:103–113, 1995.

6. D.W. Bristol, J.T. Wachsman, and A. Greenwell. The NIEHS Predictive-Toxicology Evaluation Project. *Environmental Health Perspectives*, pages 1001–1010, 1996. Supplement 3.

7. A.K. Debnath, R.L Lopez de Compadre, G. Debnath, A.J. Schusterman, and C. Hansch. Structure-Activity Relationship of Mutagenic Aromatic and Heteroaromatic Nitro compounds. Correlation with molecular orbital energies and hydrophobicity. *Journal of Medicinal Chemistry*, 34(2):786 – 797, 1991.

8. K. Enslein, B.W. Blake, and H.H. Borgstedt. Prediction of probability of carcinogenecity for a set of ntp bioassays. *Mutagenesis*, 5:305–306, 1990.

9. J.E. Huff, J.K. Haseman, and D.P. Rall. Scientific concepts, value and significance of chemical carcinogenesis studies. *Ann Rev Pharmacol Toxicol*, 31:621–652, 1991.

10. T.D. Jones and C.E. Easterly. On the rodent bioassays currently being conducted on 44 chemicals: a RASH analysis to predict test results from the National Toxicology Program. *Mutagenesis*, 6:507–514, 1991.

11. R.D. King, S. Muggleton, A.Srinivasan, C. Feng, R.A. Lewis, and M.J.E. Sternberg. Drug design using inductive logic programming. In *Proceedings of the 26th Hawaii International Conference on System Sciences*, Los Alamitos, 1993. IEEE Computer Society Press.

12. R.D. King, S.H. Muggleton, A. Srinivasan, and M.J.E. Sternberg. Structure-activity relationships derived by machine learning: The use of atoms and their bond connectivities to predict mutagenicity by inductive logic programming. *Proc. of the National Academy of Sciences*, 93:438–442, 1996.

13. R.D. King, S.H. Muggleton, and M.J.E. Sternberg. Drug design by machine learning: The use of inductive logic programming to model the structure-activity relationships of trimethoprim analogues binding to dihydrofolate reductase. *Proc. of the National Academy of Sciences*, 89(23):11322–11326, 1992.

14. R.D. King and A. Srinivasan. Prediction of rodent carcinogenicity bioassays from molecular structure using inductive logic programming. *Environmental Health Perspectives*, 104(5):1031–1040, 1996.

15. H. Kubini. *QSAR: Hansch Analysis and Related Approaches.* VCH, New York, 1993.

16. D.F.V. Lewis, C. Ionnides, and D.V. Parke. A prospective toxicity evaluation (COMPACT) on 40 chemicals currently being tested by the National Toxicology Program. *Mutagenesis*, 5:433–436, 1990.

17. S. Muggleton. Inverse Entailment and Progol. *New Gen. Comput.*, 13:245–286, 1995.

18. H.S. Rosenkranz and G. Klopman. Predicition of the carcinogenecity in rodents of chemicals currently being tested by the US National Toxicology Program. *Mutagenesis*, 5:425–432, 1990.

19. D.M. Sanderson and C.G. Earnshaw. Computer prediction of possible toxic action from chemical structure. *Human Exp Toxicol*, 10:261–273, 1991.

20. A. Srinivasan, Ross D. King, and Stephen Muggleton. The role of background knowledge: using a problem from chemistry to examine the performance of an ILP program. *Under review (available from the first author)*, 1996.

21. A. Srinivasan, S.H. Muggleton, R.D. King, and M.J.E. Sternberg. Mutagenesis: ILP experiments in a non-determinate biological domain. In S. Wrobel, editor, *Proceedings of the Fourth International Inductive Logic Programming Workshop.* Gesellschaft fur Mathematik und Datenverarbeitung MBH, 1994. GMD-Studien Nr 237.

22. A. Srinivasan, S.H. Muggleton, R.D. King, and M.J.E. Sternberg. Theories for mutagenicity: a study of first-order and feature based induction. *Artificial Intelligence*, 85:277–299, 1996.

23. R.W. Tennant, J. Spalding, S. Stasiewicz, and J. Ashby. Prediction of the outcome of rodent carcinogenicity bioassays currently being conducted on 44 chemicals by the National Toxicology Program. *Mutagenesis*, 5:3–14, 1990.

A Rules obtained by Progol

The rules obtained by Progol are given below. The number of positive and negative examples explained by each rule refer to the validation set. The order of rules is as in Figure 4.

```
% 56 positive examples, 24 negative examples
active(A) :-
    has_property(A,salmonella,p).

% 16 positive examples, 0 negative examples
active(A) :-
    has_property(A,drosophila_slrl,p).

% 19 positive examples, 8 negative examples
active(A) :-
    has_property(A,chromaberr,n).

% 5 positive examples, 1 negative example
active(A) :-
    atm(A,B,c,22,-0.13).
```

```
% 30 positive examples, 11 negative examples
active(A) :-
    ind(A,di10,B), ind(A,amino,B).

% 16 positive examples, 5 negative examples
active(A) :-
    atm(A,B,h,3,C), gteq(C,0.168).

% 5 positive examples, 2 negative examples
active(A) :-
    atm(A,B,o,45,C), gteq(C,-0.616), atm(A,D,h,3,E).

% 6 positive examples, 1 negative example
active(A) :-
    atm(A,B,br,94,C).

% 10 positive examples, 3 negative examples
active(A) :-
    mutagenic(A), atm(A,B,c,10,C), lteq(C,-0.144).
```

Discovery of First-Order Regularities in a Relational Database Using Offline Candidate Determination

Irene Weber

Institut für Informatik, Universität Stuttgart,
Breitwiesenstr. 20–22, 70565 Stuttgart, Germany
email: Irene.Weber@informatik.uni-stuttgart.de

Abstract. In this paper, we present an algorithm for the discovery of first order clauses holding in an relational database in the framework of the nonmonotonic ILP setting [1]. The algorithm adopts the principle of *offline candidate determination* algorithm used for mining association rules in large transaction databases [4]. Analoguous to the measures used in mining association rules, we define a support and a confidence measure as acceptance criteria for discovered hypothesis clauses.

The algorithm has been implemented in C with an interface to the relational database management system INGRES. We present and discuss the results of an experiment in the KRK domain and conclude.

1 Introduction

As the interest in knowledge discovery in databases (KDD) is generally increasing [2], some recent work on Inductive Logic Programming (ILP) concentrates on the application and adaption of ILP approaches to discovery tasks, e.g., [1, 3].Because of the related formalism, the first order approaches of ILP seem especially interesting for knowledge discovery in relational databases. For instance, unlike propositional learning algorithms, these approaches do not require that the relevant data be composed into one single relation, but rather can take into account data which are organized in several database relations with various connections existing among them.

In this paper, we present a data mining algorithm which discovers regularities in extensional or relational databases, i.e., in databases consisting of sets of ground facts. The regularities take the form of first order horn clauses. Formally, the approach belongs into the framework of the nonmonotonic semantics of ILP as defined in [1], that is, the approach addresses the task of finding all out of a predefined set of regularities which hold in the given database. This task has some similarity with the well-known KDD task of mining association rules in large item sets [4]. Therefore, it is possible to adopt the key idea of *off-line candidate determination* developed in this latter field [4] in order to minimize the number of database accesses in the ILP framework.

2 The Discovery Task in ILP

2.1 The Nonmonotonic Setting of ILP

The approach presented here as well as the ILP systems Claudien [1] and Mobal/RDT [3] belong into the framework of the nonmonotonic ILP setting [1]. The task in this framework is to find regularities holding in a given database where the database as well as the discovered regularities consist of sets of logical formulae, i.e., logical theories.

A formal specification of the nonmonotonic ILP setting can be given as follows. The database is denoted by $\mathcal{D}$ and the model of the database by $\mathcal{M}(\mathcal{D})$. The set of discovered regularities, i.e., the learning hypothesis, is denoted $\mathcal{H}$. $\mathcal{L}_D$ and $\mathcal{L}_H$ are logical languages for representing the database and the discovered regularities respectively. $\mathcal{M}(\mathcal{D}) \models h$ means that formula h is *logically entailed* or *satisfied* by $\mathcal{M}(\mathcal{D})$.

Given: a theory or database $\mathcal{D} \in \mathcal{L}_D$
      a hypothesis language $\mathcal{L}_H$
Find: a hypothesis $\mathcal{H} \subseteq \mathcal{L}_H$ such that

$$\forall h \in \mathcal{H} : \quad \mathcal{M}(\mathcal{D}) \models h \qquad \qquad \textit{(validity)}$$
$$\forall h \in \mathcal{L}_H : \mathcal{M}(\mathcal{D}) \models h \; \Rightarrow \; \mathcal{H} \models h \qquad \textit{(completeness)}$$
$$\not\exists c \in \mathcal{H} : \quad \mathcal{H} \setminus \{c\} \models c \qquad \qquad \textit{(nonredundancy)}$$

2.2 Definitions of Support and Confidence

In the nonmonotonic ILP setting as specified above, all formulae which are true in the chosen model of the theory are accepted as hypothesis clauses. When dealing with large and noisy real-world databases in practical data mining, this acceptance criterion is not always appropriate. On the one hand, it may be too weak, since it can accept regularities describing noise or single incidental events which are not representative for the database and therefore uninteresting for practical purposes. On the other hand, the criterion can be overly strong because it rules out regularities which describe large parts of the database while being contradicted by just some single cases or noise. What is needed here, is an alternative criterion which takes into account the coverage and the accuracy of a regularity in the database. The coverage and accuracy of a regularity are among the most fundamental criteria for judging the relevance of findings in KDD. Such criteria are used, for instance, in the approaches for mining for association rules in large transaction databases [4], and in the ILP systems Claudien [1] and Mobal/RDT [3].

In this section, we define two measures for the coverage and accuracy of regularities represented as range-restricted definite clauses in a first order framework. (A clause is called range-restricted if all its head variables occur also in its body.) In analogy to [4], these measures are termed support and confidence respectively. Since the measures realise quantitative evaluations of the coverage and accuracy of clauses, the selected model of the database is required to be finite. This is always the case when the mining takes place in a (finite) relational database since then the database and the model are identical.

The definitions of the two measures use the terms *extension* and *projection*. For the sake of completeness, we recall their definitions here. In the following, $var(c)$ denotes the ordered set of variables of a logical formula c, and θ denotes a ground substitution for the variables of c.

Definition 1. The **extension** $ext(c)$ of a clause c in a given database $\mathcal{D}$ is the set of all (distinct) ground instances of the variables in c such that $\mathcal{D}$ satisfies $c\theta$, i.e., $ext(c) = \{vars(c)\theta \mid \mathcal{D} \models c\theta\}$. The cardinality of the set $ext(c)$ is abbreviated $\|c\|$.

Definition 2. For an ordered set of variables $Vars$ and a definite clause c with $Vars \subseteq vars(c)$, the **projection** of $ext(c)$ on $Vars$, written $ext(c)|_{Vars}$, is the set of all distinct restrictions of $ext(c)$ on $Vars$, i.e., $ext(c)|_{Vars} = \{Vars\theta \mid \mathcal{D} \models c\theta\}$. $\|ext(c)|_{Vars}\|$ is abbreviated $\|c\|_{Vars}$.

A definite clause c with head $head(c)$ describes regularities in the database concerning the instances of $head(c)$. Ideally, the clause represents a typical and frequent regularity in the database. This means that the clause should apply to many of the instances $head(c)$ which are derivable from the database. Accordingly, we define the support of a clause c in a database as the fraction of the ground instances of its head $head(c)$ for which the clause body $body(c)$ is true to all ground instances of $head(c)$ which are true in the database. Thus, a clause has maximum support if it applies to all instances of $head(c)$ which are derivable from the database.

Definition 3. The **support** $sup(c)$ of a clause c in a database $\mathcal{D}$ is

$$sup(c) = \begin{cases} 0 & \text{if } \|head(c)\| = 0 \\ \dfrac{\|c\|_{vars(head(c))}}{\|head(c)\|} & \text{else} \end{cases}$$

The body of a clause c which is accepted as a hypothesis clause should reflect a regularity concerning the instances of $head(c)$ in the database as exactly as possible, i.e, should cover only few instantiations of the clause head which are not contained in the database and thus considered false due to the Closed World assumption. Accordingly, the confidence measure is defined as the ratio of those instantiations of the clause head which are described by the clause body and which are contained in the database (i.e., which are "'true instances"') to all instances of the clause head which the clause body can describe. Part of these head instances are not contained in the database, i.e, these are the "'false instances"' covered by the clause body.

Definition 4. For a database $\mathcal{D}$ and a range-restricted clause c, the **confidence** $conf(c)$ in $\mathcal{D}$ is

$$conf(c) = \begin{cases} 0 & \text{if } \|body(c)\|_{vars(head(c))} = 0 \\ \dfrac{\|c\|_{vars(head(c))}}{\|body(c)\|_{vars(head(c))}} & \text{else} \end{cases}$$

Since duplicates are removed when determining the sizes of the extensions, the counter of the fraction is always less than or equal to the denominator in the definitions of *sup* and *conf*, so that both measures range between 0 and 1.

3 Adapting Offline Candidate Determination for Clause Discovery

In this section we present an algorithm which adapts the key idea of *offline candidate determination*[1] used in the OCD algorithm for discovering association rules in large transaction databases [4] to an algorithm for clause discovery in the problem setting defined above. Crucial for the applicability of the idea is the observation that the support decreases monotonically when specialising a clause by adding literals to the clause body. This monotonicity property of the support measure shows that the measure is sensible within the generalization model of θ-subsumption which is in common use in ILP. Since the property is quite easy to see, we omit the proof here.

A top-down clause discovery algorithm can exploit this monotonicity property for pruning the search space. When a clause falls below the required minimum support, all specialisations of this clause are below the threshold as well, and therefore can be excluded safely from the search space. The clause discovery algorithm presented here assumes that the hypothesis space of discovery is predefined in the following way. All potential hypothesis clauses have a common head literal *head*. The body of each potential hypothesis clause consists of literals taken from a fixed set of possible body literals B. Consequently, if the set B contains n literals, the hypothesis space which is searched by the algorithm contains $2^n - 1$ clauses. Additionally, a support threshold σ and a confidence threshold γ are specified. The task is to find all hypothesis clauses in the hypothesis space which are satisfied with at least support σ and confidence γ in the given database.

The algorithm organizes the search for hypothesis clauses as follows. The hypothesis space is searched top-down, i.e., the more general clauses are considered first. In the s-th step of the search process, clauses with s body literals are tested against the database. This means that their support value, and in case that the clause is range-restricted, their confidence value are computed. If a clause reaches the required support as well as the required confidence threshold, it is accepted as a hypothesis clause. It must not be specialised further since a specialisation by adding more body literals yields redundant clauses. Because of the monotonicity of the support measure, neither must such clauses be specialised which do not reach the required support threshold. Thus, after the s-th step of the search, the algorithm has produced a set $\mathcal{H}$ of hypothesis clauses found so far as well as a set L_s of clauses with s body literals which have enough support but which are not range-restricted or do not reach the confidence threshold, and thus must must be specialised further by adding more body literals.

The core idea of offline candidate determination (OCD) carried over to clause discovery is the following observation. As adding a body literal to a clause can never lead to an increase of support it holds that if a clause $c = head \leftarrow l_1, \ldots, l_s$ reaches the specified support threshold, all clauses the body of which consists of a subset of the body literals of c, $\{l_1, \ldots, l_s\}$, must also reach the specified support threshold.

---

[1] The term *offline candidate determination* is "historically motivated" as the algorithm is an improvement of an approach for mining association rules which generated candidates during the database pass.

Consequently, it is possible to determine a set C_{s+1} of candidate clauses with $s+1$ body literals which must be tested against the database in the next step of the discovery process such that C_{s+1} is minimal but does contain all possible hypothesis clauses with $s + 1$ body literals. This minimal candidate set C_{s+1} must meet the following condition.

Condition 1 C_{s+1} *contains all clauses with $s + 1$ body literals $l_{i_1}, \ldots, l_{i_{s+1}}$ such that L_s contains $s + 1$ clauses the bodies of which are subsets of $\{l_{i_1}, \ldots, l_{i_{s+1}}\}$.*

The candidate set C_{s+1} is computed as follows.

First compute a collection C'_{s+1} by forming pairwise unions of bodies of those clauses in L_s that have all but one body literal in common, i.e., $C'_{s+1} := \{head \leftarrow B \cup B' \mid head \leftarrow B$ and $head \leftarrow B' \in L_s$ and $|B \cap B'| = s - 1\}$. Then compute C_{s+1} from C'_{s+1} by checking all members of C'_{s+1} on Condition 1.

In sum, this yields the following clause discovery algorithm.

(1) *initialization:* $C_1 := \{c = h \leftarrow l \mid l \in \mathcal{B}\}$; $\mathcal{H} := \emptyset$; $s := 1$;
(2) **while** $C_s \neq \emptyset$ **do**
(3)   *database pass:* $\mathcal{H} := \mathcal{H} \cup \{c \in C_s : sup(c) \geq \sigma$ and $conf(c) \geq \gamma\}$
(4) $L := \{c \in C_s \setminus \mathcal{H} : sup(c) \geq \sigma\}$;
(5)   *candidate determination:* compute C_{s+1} from L;
(6) $s := s + 1$;

The hypothesis set $\mathcal{H}$ output by the algorithm is minimal wrt. the subst relation, that is, it does not contain clauses the literals of which are a subset of other clauses in $\mathcal{H}$. However, it does not explicitly check nonredundancy wrt. to θ-subsumption.

Example 1. The following simple family database is given:

parent(adam, alf).	parent(alf, bob).	male(adam).	has_son(adam).
parent(anna, alf).	parent(cleo,bob).	male(alf).	has_son(anna).
parent(adam, arthur).	parent(arthur, bea).	male(arthur).	has_son(alf).
parent(anna, arthur).	parent(cassy, bea).	male(bob).	has_son(cleo).

The parameters of the discovery task are $\sigma = 0.50$ and $\gamma = 0.75$. The head literal is has_son(X) and the set of body literals is $\mathcal{B} = \{$ parent(X,Y), parent(Z,X), male(Y), male(Z) $\}$. At the beginning, the hypothesis is empty, i.e., $\mathcal{H} = \emptyset$. The following table shows the candidate sets C_1 and C_2. Evaluation of these candidate clauses in the database passes yields the support and confidence values in the respective columns of the table.

Candidate set	Candidate clause	Support	Confidence
C_1	(1) has_son(X):- parent(X,Y)	$\frac{4}{4} = 1$	$\frac{4}{6} = 0.67$
	(2) has_son(X):- parent(Z,X)	$\frac{1}{4} = 0.25$	$\frac{1}{4} = 0.25$
	(3) has_son(X):- male(Y)	1	-
	(4) has_son(X):- male(Z)	1	-
C_2	(5) has_son(X):- parent(X,Y), male(Y)	$\frac{4}{4} = 1$	$\frac{4}{4} = 1$
	(6) has_son(X):- parent(X,Y), male(Z)	$\frac{4}{4} = 1$	$\frac{4}{6} = 0.67$
	(7) has_son(X):- male(Y), male(Z)	1	-

In the first database pass, clause (2) does not reach the required support threshold and is discarded. Clauses (1), (3), and (4) have sufficient support, but their confidence is too low or undefined. So, the hypothesis $\mathcal{H}$ remains empty and $L_1 = \{$ has_son(X):- parent(X,Y); has_son(X):- male(Y); has_son(X):- male(Z)$\}$. Clauses (5), (6), and (7) result from the candidate determination of the second loop. Clause (5) reaches the support as well as the confidence threshold and thus can be added to the hypothesis, thus $\mathcal{H} = \{$ has_son(X):- parent(X,Y), male(Y) $\}$. Clauses (6) and (7) still have a too low confidence value, so $L_2 = \{$ has_son(X):- parent(X,Y), male(Y); has_son(X):- male(Y), male(Z)$\}$. This set L_2 does not allow the generation of new candidates because of Condition 1. Thus, C_3 is empty and the algorithm stops with output $\mathcal{H} = \{$ has_son(X):- parent(X,Y), male(Y) $\}$.

4 Example Application

4.1 Implementation of the Algorithm

The algorithm has been implemented in C with an interface to the relational database management system INGRES. Support and confidence of clauses are computed with SQL queries. The discovery algorithm and the RDBMS run on different machines and communicate via TCP/IP. The implemented algorithm differs in two details from the basic algorithm sketched above. First, clauses containing literals which are not linked to the clause head[2] are not tested on the database. This is reasonable as a clause c with unlinked literals $\{l_{n-j}, \ldots, l_n\}$ has identical support and confidence as the clause resulting when the unlinked literals are removed. Thus, testing a clause with unlinked literals yields no information, as the linked subclause of such a clause was tested in a former pass. Second, clauses containing singleton variables are not tested, because for the given database and hypothesis language (see below) existential questions were known to be useless. E.g., for literals like $p(X, Y)$ where the variable X is a head variable or linked to the head, the database is known to contain at least one fact for each possible value of X.

4.2 The KRK Database

For our experiment, we used the KRK dataset provided by the Oxford university computing laboratory [3]. Usually, this dataset serves as a testbed for classification tasks. The database consists of a 8-ary relation ILLEGAL storing 10000 example chess boards, 3240 representing illegal KRK endgame positions, the rest describing legal endgame positions. The attributes of the relation ILLEGAL are ID (unique example no.), CLASS (indicating whether the board represents a legal or illegal chess position), WKING_COL, WKING_ROW, WROOK_COL, WROOK_ROW, BKING_COL, BKING_ROW (the row and column of the white king, white rook, and black king, each taking values from 0 to 7). As background knowledge, 2-ary relations EQUAL, NOT_EQUAL and ADJACENT are provided.

---

[2] A literal in a clause is linked to the clause head iff it shares variables with the clause head or with a literal that is linked to the clause head.

[3] http://www.comlab.ox.ac.uk/oucl/groups/machlearn/chess.html

4.3 Interfacing the Algorithm to an RDBMS

The algorithm has to access the database in order to compute the support and confidence of hypothesis clauses. These computations are performed by standard SQL queries to an RDBMS where the database is stored. The literals defined in the set B are mapped onto the relations in the database by defining a database view for each literal. This mapping is done manually by the user, thus selecting the data items to be included in the search process. The SQL queries computing support and confidence of a clause are generated from the view definitions and the clause as needed by the system. For example, the view defining the head literal for test run, ILLEGAL(ID) is defined `illegal_pos(Id)="create view illegal_pos as select id from illegal where class = 'p';"`.

The size of the hypothesis space of the algorithm is determined by the size of the set B containing the literals from which hypothesis clauses are built, and the parameters specifying the minimum support and confidence of hypothesis clauses.

For a literal set B containing b literals, $2^b - 1$ clauses can be built. In the i-th pass of the algorithm, clauses with i literals are generated and evaluated. Their number equals $\binom{b}{i}$ and, thus, grows exponentially with length of the clause. Therefore, the maximum number of body literals in a hypothesis clause should be bounded by a user-settable parameter. In the application reported here, the hypothesis language is restricted to linked clauses without singleton variables. Usually, their number is much smalle, but difficult to estimate in the general case. Only these clauses are evaluated by database queries. In the KRK experiment, the literal set consisted of 24 literals. Six literals defined the column and row of three pieces on the board. For instance, WKING_COL(ID,WKC) defined the column of the white king on an example board. 18 literals defined the relations among either the rows or the columns of each pair of the pieces, on the board. E.g., the literal EQUAL(WKR,BKR) states that the white king and the black king are placed in the same row.

4.4 Results

In our test run, the support threshold was set to 0.0001, the confidence threshold was 1.0. This parameter setting simulates a classification task, and thus allows a rather objective evaluation of the "usefulness" of discovered regularities. This parameter setting enforces a nearly worst case, since the support treshold excludes only those clauses which cover no instance of the head literal, and the confidence threshold forces clauses to be maximally specialised. The maximum pass number was restricted to 6. The test run took about 20,5 hours[4]. 7 hours were used for offline candidate determination. Summed over all passes, 841 clauses were tested on the database. The algorithm accepted 22 clauses, 8 of them having 5 body literals, and 14 having 6 body literals, for example,

```
illegal_pos(Id) <- wrook_row(Id,Wrr), bking_row(Id,Bkr), wking_row(Id,Wkr),
    eq(Bkr,Wrr), noteq(Wkr,Wrr).           Sup: 0.328/Conf: 1.000
illegal_pos(Id) <- bking_col(Id,Bkc) , bking_row(Id,Bkr), wking_col(Id,Wkc),
    wking_row(Id,Wkr), eq(Bkc,Wkc), adjac(Bkr,Wkr).   Sup: 0.083/Conf: 1.000
```

---

[4] The algorithm was running on a Sun Ultra I with 192 MB, the RDBMS was running on a SUN 10/512 with 112 MB. Both machines were used by other users as well.

When tested for classification accuracy on the 10.000 test examples provided in the KRK dataset, the coverage of these clauses (interpreted as a prolog program) was 0.9830 and their accuracy was 0.9943. [3] report comparable results for similar experiments on a different KRK data set, e.g., for Foil up to 0.981 cov./0.994 acc. This shows that our approach is able to find useful and sensible clauses, but the discovery process took very long. Similar run times result for more favorable parameter settings.

5 Discussion and Conclusion

In this paper, we presented an algorithm for discovering first order definite and range-restricted clauses holding in a relational database. This algorithm employs offline candidate determination in order to minimize the number of required database accesses.

Work related to our approach includes Mobal/RDT [3] as well as clausal discovery engine Claudien [1]. Both Mobal/RDT and Claudien use elaborate mechanisms for declaring their hypothesis space (rule schemata and the DLAB declarative bias, respectively) and organizing the search. In contrast to these approaches, the hypothesis space of our system is less restricted, and the mechanism for ordering the search space is kept very simple (namely the OCD algorithm). The idea is that such a simple mechanism (compared to, e.g., θ-subsumption tests) is useful when searching large and unrestricted hypothesis spaces. The OCD part of the algorithm consumed about one third of the total runtime of the algorithm. It is hard to say whether this overhead for search organization compared to the time spent with clause evaluation and database access is acceptable since we do not have any know any comparable figures for other systems such as Claudien and Mobal/RDT. A problem of the approach is that the OCD component of the current implementation carries along and processes many unlinked clauses which do not belong to the hypothesis space and which are not excluded by more restrictive parameter settings. A speed-up of this time is achievable by a smarter implementation of the subset test, (e.g., hash-tables as in the Apriori algorithm [4]). The current implementation stores clauses in an ordered list.

An interesting topic for further research is to find improved mappings between the logical and relational formalism and mechanisms for declaring the hypothesis space which are better suited for the use with RDBMSs and exploit the characteristics of normalized relational databases.

References

1. L. De Raedt and M. Bruynooghe. A theory of clausal discovery. In *Proc. of IJCAI-93, Chambéry*, 1993.
2. U. Fayyad, G. Piatetsky-Shapiro, P. Smyth, and R. Uthurusamy. *Advances in Knowledge Discovery and Data Mining*. MIT Press, Cambridge, MA, 1995.
3. G. Lindner and K. Morik. Coupling a relational learning algorithm with a database system. In Y. Kodratoff, G. Nakhaeizadeh, and C. Taylor, editors, *Workshop Notes of the ECML-95 Workshop Statistics, Machine Learning and Knowledge Discovery in Databases*, 1995.
4. H. Mannila, H. Toivonen, and I. Verkamo. Efficient algorithms for discovering association rules. In *AAAI-94 Workshop on Knowledge Discovery in Databases*, 1994.

Which Hypotheses Can Be Found with Inverse Entailment?

Akihiro YAMAMOTO*.

Meme Media Laboratory
Hokkaido University
Email : yamamoto@meme.hokudai.ac.jp

Abstract. In this paper we give a completeness theorem of an inductive inference rule *inverse entailment* proposed by Muggleton. Our main result is that a hypothesis clause H can be derived from an example E under a background theory B with inverse entailment iff H subsumes E relative to B in Plotkin's sense. The theory B can be any clausal theory, and the example E can be any clause which is neither a tautology nor implied by B. The derived hypothesis H is a clause which is not always definite. In order to prove the result we give a declarative semantics for arbitrary consistent clausal theories, and show that SB-resolution, which was originally introduced by Plotkin, is a complete procedural semantics. The completeness is shown as an extension of the completeness theorem of SLD-resolution. We also show that every hypothesis H derived with saturant generalization, proposed by Rouveirol, must subsume E w.r.t. B in Buntine's sense. Moreover we show that saturant generalization can be obtained from inverse entailment by giving some restriction to it.

1 Introduction

In this paper we identify the class of hypotheses which can be generated with inverse entailment. *Inverse entailment* is an inductive inference rule proposed by Muggleton [9]. It is used to learn a clause H from a positive example E under a background theory B. Any consistent clausal theory (conjunctions of clauses) is allowed to be the theory B, and any clause which is neither a tautology nor logically implied by B can be given as the example E. The hypothesis H generated with the rule is not always definite. Because the conditions on B, E, and H are weaker than those for most other inference rules for ILP, we expect inverse entailment should be applied to areas to which ILP techniques have not been applied yet. However, inverse entailment is not given its logical foundations enough. In this paper we construct the logical foundations of inverse entailment.

We say a hypothesis H is *correct* if $B \wedge H \models E$ and $B \wedge H$ is consistent. Muggleton [9] proposed that every hypothesis derived with inverse entailment is correct and that every correct hypothesis H can be derived. In the terminology

---

* This work was accomplished while the author was visiting Fachgebiet Intellektik, Fachbereich Informatik, Technische Hochschule Darmstadt, Germany

in Rouveirol [12] he said inverse entailment is *complete* as an inductive inference rule. We showed in [14] that his proposition does not hold in general, by giving a case in which some correct hypotheses cannot be derived with inverse entailment. We also show that every correct hypothesis H can be derived if B is a ground reduced definite program and E is a ground unit clause. Furukawa et. al. [5] gave another condition for B under the same assumptions on E and H. These conditions are not sufficient when we apply inverse entailment to areas the knowledge of which is not represented as definite programs. In order to find more relaxed conditions, we clarify in this paper which hypotheses can be derived with inverse entailment in general. If the class of derivable hypotheses is identified, we could make inverse entailment complete by giving some conditions on hypothesis space so that it is subsumed by the identified class.

Our main result is that a hypothesis H is derived with inverse entailment iff H subsumes E relative to B whenever E is not a tautology and $B \not\models E$. The relative subsumption was defined by Plotkin [11]. If H subsumes E relative to B, it holds that $B \wedge H \models E$. This means that the definition of completeness in [12] is too restricted to represent the ability of inverse entailment. In this paper we revise the definition so that we can represent the ability in the form of a completeness theorem.

Every hypothesis H derived with inverse entailment subsumes a ground clause K which is a disjunction of literals in a set

$$\text{Bot}(E, B) = \{\neg L \mid L \text{ is a ground literal and } B \wedge \overline{E} \models L\}.$$

The formula $\overline{E}$ is obtained from $\neg E$ by replacing each variable in it with a Skolem constant symbol. The set $\text{Bot}(E, B)$ is called the *bottom set* of E under B[1]. In our theory we use the set

$$LC(B \wedge \overline{E}) = \{L \mid B \wedge \overline{E} \models L\}$$

instead of $\text{Bot}(E, B)$, because $LC(B \wedge \overline{E})$ can be regarded as a *declarative semantics* of $B \wedge \overline{E}$. As a procedural semantics we adopt SB-resolution, which was introduced by Plotkin [11] with the name C-derivation. We prove a theorem between the two semantics by extending the completeness theorem of SLD-resolution, with Kowalski's subsumption theorem [7] and a property on relative subsumption given in [11].

Inverse entailment is not the first inference rule based on the strategy that every hypothesis is generated by generalizing highly specified clauses. Rouveirol [13] gave another inference rule based on the strategy which we call the *saturant generalization* rule. She assumed that the background theory B is a definite program and the positive examples E are definite clauses. Every hypothesis H generated with the rule is a definite clause. Saturant generalization derives hypotheses by generalizing clauses called saturants. We show that saturant generalization can be obtained from inverse entailment by giving some restrictions

---

[1] In [9] a disjunction of all literals in $\text{Bot}(E, B)$ is used and called *the bottom clause*, but we do not use it because it may consists of infinitely many literals.

to its usage. For this purpose we represent inverse entailment with SOLDR-resolution [15]. SOLDR-resolution is an extension of SLD-resolution and is also a restricted version of SOL-derivation proposed by Inoue [6]. We also prove the completeness of saturant generalization w.r.t. the generalized subsumption relation proposed by Buntine [2].

This paper is organized as follows: In the next section we provide formal definitions of inverse entailment, and saturation. We give a new definition of completeness of inductive rules in Section 3. In Section 4 we introduce SB-derivation and give its properties, give a relation between inverse entailment and relative subsumption, and prove the completeness of inverse entailment. In Section 5 we compare saturant generalization with inverse entailment. We also show the completeness of saturant generalization. In Section 6 we give some concluding remarks.

2 Preliminaries

2.1 Terminology in Logic

We assume that readers are familiar with the concepts of first-order logic and logic programming. We fix a first-order language $\mathcal{L}$. $HB(\mathcal{L})$ and $GL(\mathcal{L})$ denote the set of all ground atoms of $\mathcal{L}$ and the set of all ground literals, respectively.

A *clausal theory* is a finite conjunction of clauses. In this paper we define a *clause* as a formula of the form

$$F = \forall x_1 \ldots x_k (A_1 \vee A_2 \vee \ldots \vee A_n \vee \neg B_1 \vee \ldots \vee \neg B_m)$$

where $n \geq 0$, $m \geq 0$, A_i's and B_j's are all atoms, and $x_1, \ldots, x_k$ are all variables occurring in the atoms. We represent the clause F in the form of implication:

$$A_1, A_2, \ldots, A_n \leftarrow B_1, \ldots, B_m.$$

For the clause F, we define clauses F^+ and F^- as follows:

$$F^+ = A_1, A_2, \ldots, A_n \leftarrow,$$
$$F^- = \leftarrow B_1, B_2, \ldots, B_m.$$

The *complement* of F is a clausal theory

$$\overline{F} = (\neg A_1 \wedge \neg A_2 \wedge \ldots \wedge \neg A_m \wedge B_1 \wedge \ldots \wedge B_m)\sigma_F$$

where σ_F is a substitution which replaces each variable in F with a Skolem constant symbol.

A *definite clause* is a clause of the form

$$A_0 \leftarrow A_1, \ldots, A_n$$

and a *goal clause* is a clause of the form

$$\leftarrow A_1, \ldots, A_n.$$

A clausal theory consisting of definite clauses is called a *definite program*.

Definition. Let A be a ground atom and I be an Herbrand interpretation. A definite clause $A_0 \leftarrow A_1, \ldots, A_m$ *covers* A in I if there is a substitution θ such that $A_0\theta = A$ and $A_i\theta$ is true in I for every $i = 1, \ldots, n$.

The covering relation is used in defining the T_P operator [8].

Definition. For a definite program P and an Herbrand interpretation I, we define $T_P(I)$ as

$$T_P(I) = \{A \in HB(\mathcal{L}) \mid A \text{ is covered by some clause in } P\}.$$

We will often use the subsumption relation between two clauses.

Definition. A clause D *subsumes* a clause C if there is a substitution θ such that every literal in $D\theta$ occurs in C.

Two well-known extensions of the subsumption relation have been proposed: the relative subsumption relation defined by Plotkin [11], and the generalized subsumption relation defined by Buntine [2].

Definition [11]. Let H and E be two clauses. H *subsumes* E *relative to* B, written as $H \succeq_P E$ (B), if there is a clause F such that

$$B \models \forall y_1 \ldots y_n(E' \leftrightarrow F')$$

and H subsumes F, where E' and F' are obtained by removing universal quantifiers from E and F respectively, and $y_1 \ldots y_n$ are all variables occuring in E' and F'.

Definition [2]. Let H and E be two definite clauses. H *subsumes* E *w.r.t.* B, written as $H \succeq_B E$ (B), if $T_H(M) \supseteq T_E(M)$ for every Herbrand model M of B.

2.2 Inverse entailment and saturation

We give a formal definition of the inverse entailment rule in [9].

Definition. Let B be a clausal theory and E be a clause. The *bottom set* of E under B is a set of literals

$$\mathrm{Bot}(E, B) = \{L \in GL(\mathcal{L}) \mid B \wedge \overline{E} \models \neg L\}.$$

Definition. A clause H is *derived by the inverse entailment rule* from E under B if H subsumes some ground clause K which is a disjunction of literals in $\mathrm{Bot}(E, B)$.

Example 1 [9]. Let us define B_1 and E_1 as follows:

$$B_1 = (\mathrm{pet}(x) \leftarrow \mathrm{cat}(x)) \wedge (\mathrm{cuddly\text{-}pet}(x) \leftarrow \mathrm{small}(x), \mathrm{fluffy}(x), \mathrm{pet}(x)),$$
$$E_1 = \mathrm{cuddly\text{-}pet}(x) \leftarrow \mathrm{fluffy}(x), \mathrm{cat}(x).$$

The complement of E_1 is

$$\overline{E_1} = (\text{fluffy}(c_x) \leftarrow) \wedge (\text{cat}(c_x) \leftarrow) \wedge (\leftarrow \text{cuddly-pet}(c_x))$$

where c_x is a Skolem constant symbol for the variable x. The bottom set of E_1 under B_1 is

$$\text{Bot}(E_1, B_1) = \{\text{cuddly-pet}(c_x), \text{small}(c_x), \neg\text{fluffy}(c_x), \neg\text{cat}(c_x), \neg\text{pet}(c_x)\}.$$

A clause

$$H_1 = \text{small}(x) \leftarrow \text{fluffy}(x), \text{cat}(x)$$

is derived with inverse entailment because H_1 subsumes a clause

$$K_1 = \text{small}(c_x) \leftarrow \text{fluffy}(c_x), \text{cat}(c_x).$$

No procedure with which we can generate all elements of the bottom set is given in [9], but we showed in [15] they can be generated with SOLDR-resolution when B is a definite program and E is a definite clause.

For the saturant generalization rule proposed in [13] it is assumed that every background theory B is a definite program and that every example E is a definite clause. The rule consists of two sub-rules: saturation and generalization. Every hypothesis generated by the rule is a definite clause.

Definition. Let E be a definite clauses, and B a definite program. A definite clause K is a *saturant* of E under B if

1. $K^+ = E^+$, and
2. K^- is a disjunction of literals in a set

$$\text{Bot}^-(E, B) = \{\neg A \mid A \in HB(\mathcal{L}) \text{ and } B \wedge \overline{E^-} \models A\}.$$

Note that, for a definite clause E, $\overline{E^-}$ is a definite program.

Definition. Let B be a definite program and E be a definite clause. A hypothesis H is *derived by the saturant generalization rule* from E under B if H subsumes some saturant K of E.

Our definition is different from the original one in two points: In the original definition it is assumed that B and E are flattened before saturation, while we do not assume it. The set $\text{Bot}^-(E, B)$ is defined with the operator $T_{B \wedge \overline{E^-}}$ in the orignal definition, while we define it with logical consequence. We need not mind the first difference because flattening is used to make the implementation of generalization easier and have no theoretical effect. The second change is justified by the well known fact that, for any $A \in HB(\mathcal{L})$, $B \wedge \overline{E^-} \models A$ iff there is $m \geq 0$ such that $A \in T_{B \wedge \overline{E^-}}{}^m(\emptyset)$ [8].

3 Completeness of Inductive Inference Rules

Generally speaking an inductive inference rule is a rule with which hypotheses are derived from a given example E under a background theory B. Each hypothesis H must be correct, that is, it explains E with the support of B. We define the correctness in logical terminology.

Definition. Let B be a background theory and E an example. A hypothesis H is a *correct* for E under B if $B \wedge H$ is consistent and $B \wedge H \models E$. An inductive inference rule $\mathcal{R}$ is *correct* if every hypothesis derived from E under B with $\mathcal{R}$ is correct for E under B.

In order to define the completeness of an inductive inference rule, we introduce generalization relations.

Definition. Let $\mathcal{B}$ and $\mathcal{H}$ be sets of formulas. A triary relation $\succeq \in \mathcal{B} \times \mathcal{H} \times \mathcal{H}$ is a *generalization relation* on $\mathcal{H}$ parameterized with $\mathcal{B}$ if $\succeq (B, H, E)$ implies $B \wedge H \models E$. In the followings we write $H \succeq E \ (B)$ instead of $\succeq (B, H, E)$.

Directly from the definition, the *implication relation* $\succeq_I$ defined as

$$H \succeq_I E \ (B) \iff B \wedge H \models E$$

is a generalization relation.

Definition. An inductive inference rule $\mathcal{R}$ is *complete* w.r.t. a generalization relation $\succeq$ if $\mathcal{R}$ is correct and every hypothesis H such that $H \succeq E \ (B)$ can be derived from E under B with $\mathcal{R}$.

The completeness defined in [12] can be regarded as the completeness w.r.t. the implication relation $\succeq_I$ in our definition. We can show, with an example used in [14], that neither inverse entailment nor saturant generalization is complete w.r.t. the implication relation.

Example 2. Let us consider the following B_2 and E_2:

$$B_2 = (even(0) \leftarrow) \wedge (even(s(x)) \leftarrow odd(x)),$$
$$E_2 = odd(s(s(s(0)))) \leftarrow .$$

We can show that the bottom set is

$$Bot(B_2, E_2) = \{odd(s(s(s(0)))), \neg even(0)\}.$$

A correct hypothesis

$$H_2 = odd(s(y)) \leftarrow even(y)$$

cannot be derived with inverse entailment because H_2 subsumes none of the following clauses:

$$K_2^1 = odd(s(s(s(0)))) \leftarrow even(0),$$
$$K_2^2 = odd(s(s(s(0)))) \leftarrow,$$
$$K_2^3 = \leftarrow even(0),$$
$$K_2^4 = \square.$$

Since K_2^1 and K_2^2 are all the saturants of E_2 under B_2, H_2 cannot be derived by saturant generalization.

4   Completeness of Inverse Entailment

In this section we show that the inverse entailment rule is complete w.r.t. Plotkin's relative subsumption.

At first we introduce SB-resolution and give a useful theorem on it proved by Plotkin.

Definition. Let S be a clausal theory and C a clause. An *SB-derivation* of a clause D from (T, C) is a sequence of clauses $C_0 = C, C_1, \ldots, C_n = D$ such that

1. each C_i $(i \geq 1)$ is a clause in S or a binary resolvent of $C_{\pi(i,1)}$ and $C_{\pi(i,2)}$ such that $\pi(i, j) < i$ for $j = 1, 2$, and
2. for every $i = 0, 1, \ldots, n - 1$ there is exactly one pair (h, k) which satisfies $\pi(h, k) = i$.

An SB-derivation of an empty clause $\square$ from (T, C) is called an *SB-refutation* of (T, C).

Theorem 1 [11]. *Let H and E be clauses and B a clausal theory. Then $H \succeq_P E\ (B)$ iff one of the following three holds:*

1. *E is a tautology.*
2. *$B \models E$.*
3. *There is an SB-refutation of $(B \wedge \overline{E}, H)$.*

Corollary. *The relation $\succeq_P$ is a generalization relation.*

We can show that SLD-resolution, which is famous in logic programming theory, is a special type of the SB-resolution. Let P be a definite clause and G be a goal clause. Then an SLD-derivation, as formalized in [8], can be transformed into a sequence of clauses

$$G = G_0, C_1, G_1, C_2, G_2, \ldots, C_n, G_n$$

where every C_i is a variant of a clause in P and every G_i is a resolvent of G_{i-1} and C_i. It is easy to check that the sequence is an SB-derivation of G_n from (P, G).

Now we give a *declarative semantics* of an arbitrary clausal theory w.r.t. which SB-resolution is complete, by referring the completeness theorem of SLD-resolution.

Theorem 2 [8]. *For a definite program P and a goal clause $G = \leftarrow A_1, \ldots, A_n$, the following three are equivalent:*

1. *There is an SLD-refutation of $P \wedge G$.*

2. *There is a substitution θ such that $\{A_1\theta, A_2\theta, \ldots, A_n\theta\} \subseteq M(P)$ where $M(P)$ is the least Herbrand model of P.*

3. *$P \wedge G$ is unsatisfiable.*

Since the least Herbrand model $M(P)$ coincides with the set

$$LC(P) = \{A \in HB(\mathcal{L}) \mid P \models A\},$$

the condition 2 in Theorem 2 is equivalent to the following condition 2':

2' There is a substitution θ such that $\{A_1\theta, A_2\theta, \ldots, A_n\theta\} \subseteq LC(P)$.

We extend the definition of $LC(S)$ so that it may be defined for any clausal theory S.

Definition. For a clausal theory S we define

$$LC(S) = \{L \in GL(\mathcal{L}) \mid T \models L\}.$$

For a definite program P, the two definitions of $LC(P)$ are identical because no negative ground literal is a logical consequence of P. If a clausal theory S is unsatisfiable, $LC(S) = GL(\mathcal{L})$. Otherwise, no pair of literals in $LC(S)$ is complementary. Since no ground literal is a tautology, $LC(S) = \emptyset$ if S is a tautology. When S is a consistent and C is an arbitrary clause, we get a theorem which is an extension of the equivalence of 1 and 2' in Theorem 2.

Theorem 3. *Let S be a consistent clausal theory and C a clause*

$$A_1, A_2, \ldots, A_n \leftarrow B_1, \ldots, B_m.$$

There is an SB-refutation of (T, C) iff there is substitution θ such that

$$\{\neg A_1\theta, \neg A_2\theta, \ldots, \neg A_n\theta, B_1\theta, B_2\theta, \ldots, B_m\theta\} \subseteq LC(S).$$

Proof. (if part) Since no single literal is a tautology, the conclusion is directly derived from Kowalski's subsumption theorem [7, 10].
(only-if part) Let $R : C_0 = C, C_1, \ldots, C_n = \square$ be an SB-refutation of (T, C). Without loss of generality, we can assume that no pairs of variants of clauses S occurring in R share variables. Let μ be the composition of all mgu's used to construct the refutation R and $C_{i_1}, \ldots, C_{i_k}$ are all clauses which are variants of clauses in S. Then for any substitution σ, the sequence

$$C_0\mu\sigma = C\mu\sigma, C_1\mu\sigma, \ldots, C_n\mu\sigma = \square$$

is an SB-refutation of $(T', C\mu\sigma)$ where

$$T' = C_{i_1}\mu\sigma \wedge \ldots \wedge C_{i_k}\mu\sigma.$$

In the case $C\mu\sigma$ is ground, we get $T' \models \neg C\mu\sigma$, that is,

$$\{\neg A_1\mu\sigma, \ldots, \neg A_n\mu\sigma, B_1\mu\sigma, \ldots, B_m\mu\sigma\} \subseteq LC(T').$$

Since $T \models T'$, $LC(T') \subseteq LC(T)$ and the proof is completed. $\qquad\square$

Now we show that the relation between inverse entailment and Plotkin's relative subsumption.

Lemma 1. *Let H and E be clauses and B be a clausal theory. Assume that E is not a tautology and that $B \not\models E$. Then H is derived from E under B with inverse entailment iff $H \succeq_P E\ (B)$.*

Proof. Since the bottom set $\mathrm{Bot}(E, B)$ can be represented as

$$\mathrm{Bot}(E, B) = \{L \mid \neg L \in LC(B \wedge \overline{E})\},$$

the lemma is directly proved with Theorem 1 and Theorem 3. □

By the corollary of Theorem 1 and Lemma 1, we get the completeness of inverse entailment.

Theorem 4. *Inverse entailment is complete w.r.t. Plotkin's relative subsumption if E is not a tautology and that $B \not\models E$.*

From the soundness of resolution principle, it holds that $T \wedge C$ is unsatisfiable if there is an SB-refutation of (T, C). However, the converse does not hold in general, that is, we cannot extend the implication $3 \Rightarrow 1$ of Theorem 2. This is the reason why the inverse entailment rule is not complete w.r.t. $\succeq_I$.

Example 3. Let us consider Example 2 again. For $S_2 = B_2 \wedge \overline{E_2}$, we get

$$LC(S_2) = \{\neg odd(s(s(s(0)))), even(0)\}.$$

Though $S_2 \wedge H_2$ is unsatisfiable, there is no SB-refutation of (S_2, H_2) because H_2 subsumes none of K_2^i for $i = 1, 2, 3, 4$.

5 Comparing Saturant Generalization with Inverse Entailment

In order to compare saturant generalization with inverse entailment, we analyze the structure of $LC(P \wedge G)$ for a definite clause P and a goal G.

At first we define $LC^+(C)$ and $LC^-(S)$ for any clausal theory S as follows:

$$LC^+(S) = LC(S) \cap HB(\mathcal{L}),$$
$$LC^-(S) = LC(S) - LC^+(S).$$

The following lemma can be proved easily.

Lemma 2. *Let P be a definite program and G a goal. If $P \wedge G$ is consistent, $LC^+(P \wedge G) = LC(P) = M(P)$.*

Theorem 5. *Let B be a definite program and E be a definite clause. Assume that E is not a tautology and that $B \not\models E$. Then it holds that*

$$\mathrm{Bot}^-(E, B) = \{\neg A \mid A \in LC^+(B \wedge \overline{E})\}$$

where $\mathrm{Bot}^-(E, B)$ is the set used in the definition of saturants.

Proof. From the condition for B and E, $\overline{E^-}$ is a definite program, $\overline{E^+}$ is a goal clause, and $B \wedge \overline{E}$ is consistent. Then the equation is obtained from Lemma 2.

$\square$

Since $\overline{E^+}$ belongs to the set $LC^-(B \wedge \overline{E})$, it is clear that every hypothesis generated with saturant generalization can be generated with inverse entailment.

We give a more precise relation between the two rules from a procedural viewpoint. We use SOLDR-resolution, which was introduced in [15] to generate the elements of $LC^-(P \wedge G)$.

SOLDR-resolution is formalized as an extension of the formalization of SLD-resolution in [8]. An SOLDR-derivation is defined with *computation rule*, assuming an order of literals in every goal clause. We also assume variables in each variant of a clause in P are *standardized apart* from variables in the others[8].

Definition [15]. Let P be a definite program, G be a goal, R be a computation rule. An *SOLDR-derivation* of (P, G) is a finite sequence of quadlaplets $\langle G_i, F_i, \theta_i, C_i \rangle$ $(i = 0, 1, 2, \dots, n)$ which satisfies the following conditions:

1. G_i and F_i are goal clauses, θ_i is a substitution, and C_i is a variant of a clausal formula in P the variables of which are standardized apart by renaming.
2. $G_0 = G$ and $F_0 = \square$.
3. $G_n = \square$.
4. F_i consists of at most one literal.
5. If $G_i =\leftarrow A_1, \dots, A_k$, $C_i = B_0 \leftarrow B_1, \dots, B_k$, A_m is the atom selected from G by R, then one of the following three holds:
   (a) (Skip) $F_i = \square$ and θ_i is an empty substitution. C_i can be any clause. G_{i+1} and F_{i+1} are, respectively,

   $$G_{i+1} = \leftarrow A_1, \dots, A_{m-1}, A_{m+1}, \dots, A_k,$$
   $$F_{i+1} = \leftarrow A_m.$$

   (b) (Reduce) $F_i =\leftarrow A$ and θ_i is an mgu of A and A_m. C_i can be any clause. $G_{i+1} = G_i \theta_i$, and $F_{i+1} = F_i \theta_i$.
   (c) (Resolve) B_0 and A_m are unifiable, and θ_i is an mgu of the two. G_{i+1} and F_{i+1} are, respectively,

   $$G_{i+1} = \leftarrow (A_1, \dots, A_{m-1}, B_1, \dots B_k, A_{m+1}, \dots, A_k)\theta_i,$$
   $$F_{i+1} = F_i \theta_i.$$

F_n is called the *consequence* of the SOLDR-derivation.

Theorem 6 [15]. *Let P be a definite program and G a goal such that $P \wedge G$ is consistent. Then a ground literal L is in $LC^-(P \wedge G)$ iff L is a ground instance of some consequence of SOLDR-derivation of (P, G).*

This theorem shows that every positive literals in $Bot(E, B)$ can be generated by using SOLDR-resolution.

Let us consider an SOLDR-derivation of $(B \wedge \overline{E^-}, \overline{E^+})$. The literal $\overline{E^+}$ can be obtained if the skip operation at the first step of the SOLDR-derivation. If we represent a procedure of inverse entailment with SOLDR-resolution, a procedure of saturant generalization can be obtained by restricting the usage of the skip operation in SOLDR-resolution.

The difference of the two rules can also be represented by the completeness theorem of saturant generalization. The following theorem proved by Buntine[2] is helpful.

Theorem 7 [2]. *Let H and E be definite clauses, and B be a definite program. Then $H \succeq_B E$ (B) iff, for some substitution θ, $H^+\theta = E\sigma_E$ and $B \wedge \overline{E^-} \models \neg(H^-\theta)$.*

Corollary. *The relation $\succeq_B$ is a generalization relation.*

From the discussion above and logic programming theory, $B \wedge \overline{E^-} \models \neg(H^-\theta)$ iff H^- subsumes some disjunction of literals in $\mathrm{Bot}^-(E, B)$. This is followed by the completeness of saturant generalization.

Lemma 3. *Let H and E be definite clauses and B be a definite program. Then a definite clause H is derived with saturant generalization from E under B iff $H \succeq_B E$ (B).*

Theorem 8. *Saturant generalization is complete w.r.t. Buntine's generalized subsumption.*

6 Concluding Remarks

In this paper we showed that inverse entailment is complete w.r.t. Plotkin's relative subsumption and saturant generalization is complete w.r.t. Buntine's generalized subsumption. We also showed that saturant generalization can be obtained from inverse entailment. In order to get the results, we used the set $LC(S)$ as declarative semantics of a consistent clausal theory S, and showed that SB-resolution, which is an extension of SLD-resolution, can be a complete procedural semantics for S.

Cohen [3, 4] showed the learnability of definite programs by using the same strategy that inverse entailment is founded on. He gave a class of definite clauses which is learnable in polynomial time. For every hypothesis H in the class, the predicate symbol of H^+ does not occur in H^-. Because this condition implies that H subsumes an example E relative to B, we are now interested in extending his result so that we can treat non-definite clauses as hypotheses. He also showed that it is difficult to learn any class of definite clauses if the predicate symbol of H^+ is allowed to occur in H^-. One of the approaches to overcoming the difficulty is using the framework *learning with queries*. Recently Arimura [1] has given a learnable class of definite programs according to this approach. It is also a quite interesting subject whether or not his learning method can be extended so that non-definite clauses may be derived as hypotheses.

From the new proof of the subsumption theorem in [10], the set $LC(S)$ can be represent with the same operator as T_P. Let us define GR^n as follows:

$$GR^0(S) = \left\{ C \mid C \text{ is a ground instance of a clause in } S \right\},$$

$$GR^n(S) = GR^{n-1}(S) \cup \left\{ C \left| \begin{array}{l} C \text{ is a resolvent of } C_1 \text{ and } C_2 \\ \text{both of which are in } GR^{n-1}(S) \end{array} \right. \right\},$$

$$GR^\omega(S) = \cup_{n \geq 0} GR^n(S).$$

Then it holds that $LC(S) = GR^\omega(S) \cap GL(\mathcal{L})$. For a definite program P, $GR^\omega(P) \cap GL(\mathcal{L}) = T_P{}^\omega(\emptyset)$ since $T_P{}^\omega(\emptyset) = LC(P)$. We conjecture that a covering operator for any non-definite clause S could be defined with the set $GR^n(S)$.

Acknowledgements

The author wishes to thank Prof.Dr. Wolfgang Bibel and the members of his group for many discussions and suggestions on this issue. He also thanks the anonymous referees for their valuable comments.

References

1. H. Arimura. Learning Acyclic First-order Horn Sentences From Implication. To appear in the Proceedings of the 8th International Workshop on Algorithmic Learning Theory, 1997.
2. W. Buntine. Generalized Subsumption and Its Applications to Induction and Redundancy. *Artificial Intelligence*, 36:149–176, 1988.
3. W. W. Cohen. Pac-learning Recursive Logic Programs: Efficient Algorithms. *J. of Artificial Intelligence Research*, 2:501–539, 1995.
4. W. W. Cohen. Pac-learning Recursive Logic Programs: Negative Results. *J. of Artificial Intelligence Research*, 2:541–573, 1995.
5. K. Furukawa, T. Murakami, K. Ueno, T. Ozaki, and K. Shimazu. On a Sufficient Condition for the Exisitence of Most Specific Hypothesis in Progol. SIG-FAI-9603, 56–61, Resarch Reprot of JSAI, 1997.
6. K. Inoue. Linear Resolution for Consequence Finding. *Artificial Intelligence*, 56:301–353, 1992.
7. R. A. Kowalski. The Case for Using Equality Axioms in Automatic Demonstration. In *Proceedings of the Symposium on Automatic Demonstaration (Lecture Notes in Mathematics 125)*, pages 112–127. Springer-Verlag, 1970.
8. J. W. Lloyd. *Foundations of Logic Programming : Second, Extended Edition*. Springer - Verlag, 1987.
9. S. Muggleton. Inverse Entailment and Progol. *New Generation Computing*, 13:245–286, 1995.
10. S.-H. Nienhuys-Cheng and Ronald de Wolf. The Subsumption Theorem in Inductive Logic Programming: Facts and Fallacies. In L. de Raedt, editor, *Proceedings of the 5th International Workshop on Inductive Logic Programming*, pages 147–160, 1994.

11. G. D. Plotkin. *Automatic Methods of Inductive Inference*. PhD thesis, Edinburgh University, 1971.

12. C. Rouveirol. Completeness for Inductive Procedures. In *Proceedings of the 8th International Workshop on Machine Learning*, pages 452–456. Morgan Kaufmann, 1991.

13. C. Rouveirol. Extentions of Inversion of Resolution Applied to Theory Completion. In S. Muggleton, editor, *Inductive Logic Programming*, pages 63–92. Academic Press, 1992.

14. A. Yamamoto. Improving Theories for Inductive Logic Programming Systems with Ground Reduced Programs. Submitted to New Generation Computing, 1996.

15. A. Yamamoto. Representing Inductive Inference with SOLD-Resolution. To appear in the Proceedings of the IJCAI'97 Workshop on Abduction and Induction in AI, 1997.

Author Index

Lecture Notes in Computer Science

Lecture Notes in Artificial Intelligence (LNAI)